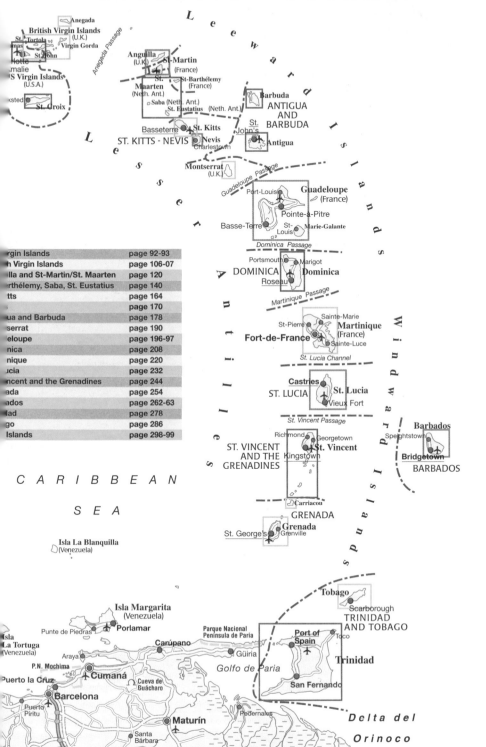

ATLANTIC OCEAN

S0-ATY-502

0 miles

Anegada

British Virgin Islands (U.K.)

St. Tortola
Virgin Gorda

mas
St. John

Charlotte
malie
US Virgin Islands (U.S.A.)

xsted
St. Croix

Leeward Islands

Anguilla (U.K.)
St-Martin (France)
St. Maarten (Neth. Ant.)
St-Barthélemy (France)
Saba (Neth. Ant.)
St. Eustatius (Neth. Ant.)

Barbuda

ANTIGUA AND BARBUDA

St. John's

Basseterre St. Kitts
ST. KITTS - NEVIS
Nevis
Charlestown

Antigua

Montserrat (U.K.)

Guadeloupe Passage

Port-Louis

Guadeloupe (France)

Pointe-à-Pitre

Basse-Terre
St-Louis
Marie-Galante

Dominica Passage

Portsmouth
Marigot

DOMINICA Dominica
Roseau

Martinique Passage

St-Pierre
Sainte-Marie

Martinique (France)

Fort-de-France
Sainte-Luce

St. Lucia Channel

Castries
St. Lucia
ST. LUCIA
Vieux Fort

St. Vincent Passage

Richmond
Georgetown

St. Vincent
ST. VINCENT AND THE GRENADINES
Kingstown

Speightstown

Barbados

Bridgetown
BARBADOS

Carriacou

GRENADA

St. George's
Grenada
Grenville

Windward Islands

Lesser Antilles

CARIBBEAN SEA

Isla La Blanquilla (Venezuela)

Tobago

Scarborough
TRINIDAD AND TOBAGO

Isla Margarita (Venezuela)

Punte de Piedras
Porlamar

Isla La Tortuga (Venezuela)

Carúpano

Araya
Güiria

Parque Nacional Península de Paria

Port of Spain
Toco

P.N. Mochima

Cumaná

Cueva de Guácharo

Golfo de Paria

Trinidad

Puerto la Cruz

Barcelona

San Fernando

Puerto Píritu

Pedernales

Delta del Orinoco

Maturín

Santa Bárbara

INSIGHT GUIDES

CARIBBEAN

APA PUBLICATIONS

Part of the Langenscheidt Publishing Group

INSIGHT GUIDE
CARIBBEAN

ABOUT THIS BOOK

Editorial
Managing Editor
Lesley Gordon
Project Editor
Siân Lezard
Series Manager
Rachel Fox

Distribution
North America
Langenscheidt Publishers, Inc.
36–36 33rd Street 4th Floor
Long Island City, NY 11106
orders@langenscheidt.com

UK & Ireland
GeoCenter International Ltd
Meridian House, Churchill Way West
Basingstoke, Hampshire RG21 6YR
sales@geocenter.co.uk

Australia
Universal Publishers
1 Waterloo Road
Macquarie Park, NSW 2113
sales@universalpublishers.com.au

New Zealand
Hema Maps New Zealand Ltd (HNZ)
Unit 2, 10 Cryers Road
East Tamaki, Auckland 2013
sales.hema@clear.net.nz

Worldwide
Apa Publications GmbH & Co.
Verlag KG (Singapore branch)
38 Joo Koon Road, Singapore 628990
apasin@signet.com.sg

Printing
Insight Print Services (Pte) Ltd
38 Joo Koon Road, Singapore 628990
Tel: (65) 6865 1600. Fax: (65) 6861 6438

©2008 Apa Publications GmbH & Co.
Verlag KG (Singapore branch)
All Rights Reserved
First Edition 1992
Fifth Edition 2005
Updated 2008
Reprinted 2009

CONTACTING THE EDITORS

We would appreciate it if readers
would alert us to errors or out-
dated information by writing to:
**Insight Guides, P.O. Box 7910,
London SE1 1WE, England.**
insight@apaguide.co.uk

www.insightguides.com

The first Insight Guide pioneered the use of creative full-color photography in travel guidebooks in 1970. Since then, we have expanded our range to cater for our readers' need not only for reliable information about their chosen destination but also for a real understanding of the culture and workings of that destination. Now, when the internet can supply inexhaustible (but not always reliable) facts, our books marry text and pictures to provide those much more elusive qualities: knowledge and discernment. To achieve this, they rely heavily on the authority of locally based writers and photographers.

How to use this book

Insight Guide: Caribbean is carefully structured to convey an understanding of the islands and their people as well as to guide readers through the sights and activities:

◆ The **Best of Caribbean** section at the front of the guide helps you to prioritize what you want to do.

◆ The **Features** section, indicated by a yellow bar at the top of each page, covers the natural and cultural history of the Caribbean in a series of informative essays.

◆ The main **Places** section, indicated by a blue bar, is a

complete guide to all the sights and areas worth visiting. Places of special interest are coordinated by number with full-color maps.

◆ The **Travel Tips** listings section, with an orange bar, provides full information on travel, hotels, shops, restaurants, and activities, and includes a handy A–Z section of essential practical information.

The contributors

The current edition was edited by **Caroline Radula-Scott** and builds on the original produced by **David Schwab**.

Polly Pattullo, whose books include *The Gardens of Dominica*, wrote the chapters on Dominica and Montserrat, and the feature on Tropical Plants. **James Ferguson**, whose books include the *Traveller's History of the Caribbean*, added to the history section originally written by the late historian **Gordon Lewis**, and wrote A Caribbean Blend, Passion and Poetry, and the chapter on Grenada. He also updated novelist **Maryse Condé**'s chapter on Guadeloupe and contributed to the music chapter originated by Barbadian writer **Michelle Springer**. Creole Cuisine was written by **Sally Miller**.

Caribbean specialist **Trudie Trox** contributed chapters on the BVI, Saba, and Statia, and wrote features on Architecture, Underwaterworld, Yachting and Sailing, and Carnival. **Christine Rettenmeier** wrote Trinidad, Tobago, and the ABC Islands, and **Robert Möginger** Antigua and St Lucia.

Contributors to previous editions include **Larry Breiner**, **Sarah Cameron**, **Louisa Campbell**, **Pamela Harris**, **Dawn King-Steele**, **Simon Lee**, **Jeanne Morgan**, **Charles Seibert**, **Bob Shacochis**, **Rachel Wilder**, and **David Yeadon**.

This updated version was commissioned by **Lesley Gordon** and edited by **Siân Lezard**. It was updated by a team of Caribbean specialists, including **Rob Coates**, **Maria Crawford**, **Skye Hernandez**, **Evette Peterson**, and **Caroline Popovic**. The book was proofread by **Sylvia Suddes**.

Photography for this edition was provided by **Bob Krist** and **David Sanger**, their contributions were added to the originals taken by **Mitch Epstein** and others.

Map Legend

— · — · ·	International Boundary
— — — —	Parish Boundary
— · — · —	National Park/Reserve
— — — —	Ferry Route
✈ ✈	Airport: International/Regional
🚌	Bus Station
P	Parking
ⓘ	Tourist Information
✉	Post Office
⛪ † ⚚	Church/Ruins
†	Monastery
☪	Mosque
✡	Synagogue
🏰	Castle/Ruins
∴	Archeological Site
∩	Cave
⚔	Statue/Monument
★	Place of Interest

The main places of interest in the Places section are coordinated by a number with a full-color map (e.g. ❶), and a symbol at the top of every right-hand page tells you where to find the map.

INSIGHT GUIDE
CARIBBEAN

CONTENTS

Dutch-
inspired
architecture
on the ABC
Islands

THE BEST OF THE CARIBBEAN

Unique attractions, festivals and carnivals, best beaches, diving and snorkeling, food and drink, shopping... here at a glance are our recommendations, plus some essential tips for travelers

TOP ATTRACTIONS

From breathtaking scenery, marine parks, and turtle-watching to dramatic forts and dockyards.

● **Pitons, St Lucia** The ultimate Caribbean landmark is spectacular from every angle. *See page 231.*

● **Night-time turtle watching** Many beaches attract giant leatherbacks in the egg-laying season, especially in Trinidad. *See page 280.*

● **Brimstone Hill Fortress, St Kitts & Nevis**. This 17th-century British fort is the best preserved in the region, with stupendous views. *See page 168.*

● **Nelson's Dockyard, Antigua** The last surviving Georgian dockyard in the world is full of character. *See page 182.*

● **Kura Hulanda Museum, Curaçao** The region's best museum, this private collection includes a moving permanent exhibition on the slave trade. *See page 298.*

● **Montserrat Volcano Observatory** Allows you a first-hand glimpse of nature's devastating power. *See page 190.*

● **Coral World Marine Park, St Thomas** A truly imaginative under-sea experience, with "sea trekking". *See page 95.*

BEST BEACHES

Some of the finest beaches in the world are to be found in the Caribbean.

● **Englishman's Bay, Tobago** Undeveloped, with an offshore reef, this half-moon beach is stunning and peaceful. *See page 289.*

● **Palm Beach, Barbuda** Seemingly endless white sands separate the ocean from the lobster-breeding area of Codrington lagoon. *See page 185.*

● **Grand Anse, Grenada** Over a mile (2 km) of white sands are accompanied by fine views, shady palms, and plentiful watersports on offer. *See page 257.*

● **Magen's Bay, US Virgin islands** Always voted in the world's top ten, this mile-long sweep on St Thomas is ideal for swimming, sheltered as it is by two peninsulas. *See page 96.*

● **Deadman's Bay, British Virgin Islands** Turquoise waters, palm-fringed sands, and a glorious view of island-outcrops mark this romantic spot on Peter Island off Tortola. *See page 112.*

● **Maracas Bay, Trinidad** Surrounded by forest-covered mountains, this fine spot draws a local crowd keen to party, while Atlantic surf ensures an invigorating swim. *See page 280.*

LEFT: the Pitons, St Lucia. **ABOVE:** Grand Anse, Grenada.

BEST OUTDOOR ADVENTURES

● **Hike to the Boiling Lake, Dominica** The six-hour round trip won't disappoint; deep rainforest, thick tree ferns and waterfalls are all to be found en route. *See page 211.*

● **Sailing tours in the Grenadines** Chains of tiny volcanic islands make this the most idyllic spot for sailing; the rugged and spectacular scenery was the backdrop for *Pirates of the Caribbean. See page 243.*

● **Wind- and kite-surfing** Many islands have great conditions, but Bonaire, Aruba, Nevis, Tortola and St Lucia are particularly good. *See page 358.*

● **Hiking Trinidad's northern coastline** One of the few remaining undeveloped coastlines, a long trail traverses cliffs, rainforest, stunning beaches, and lagoons. *See page 280.*

● **Harrison's Cave, Barbados** A tram guides you through huge limestone caverns with thousands of dripping stalactites and plentiful streams and waterfalls. *See page 272.*

BEST CARNIVALS

The setting and the sunshine provide the perfect backdrop to the ultimate in parties.

● **Port-of-Spain, Trinidad** Jan–Feb/ Mar. Arguably the best of the Caribbean celebrations is a fully participatory affair with a rich history, 100,000 costumed revellers, unremitting soca and steelpan music, and a season-long lead-up of events for every taste and age group. *See page 352.*

● **Willemstad, Curaçao** Jan–Feb/Mar. With a month-long festival culminating in the main event, this is a friendly and often wild party featuring the region's best tumba and tambu music performers. *See pages 295 and 350.*

● **Fort-de-France, Martinique** Jan–Feb/ Mar. Puppets, red devils, drag queens, and stringed instruments characterise the largest celebration in the French Antilles, continuing through Ash Wednesday and accompanied by zouk, salsa, soca, and reggae. *See page 222.*

● **Crop Over, Barbados** Aug. Traditionally celebrating the final sugar harvest, this festival is one of the region's most exuberant, with soca music, elaborate street parades, and dancing. *See page 351.*

● **St Kitts and Nevis** Dec–Jan. A smaller but still exciting carnival, engulfing both islands in calypso performances, partying, and a fantastic "*j'ouvert*" event on Boxing Day. *See page 163.*

ABOVE: cocktails taste great in the Caribbean sun.
RIGHT: a local girl displays an Anegada lobster, British Virgin Islands.
BELOW: goat-racing, Buccoo village, Tobago.

UNIQUE EVENTS AND FESTIVALS

- **Goat and crab races, Tobago** These Easter-time events are taken very seriously indeed, with large bets placed on favoured animals – and "jockeys". *See page 352.*
- **Shakespeare Mas, Carriacou, Grenada** Recitations of this most famous of bards' works take on Carnivalesque proportions, with elaborate masks and costumes, and prizes. *See page 351.*
- **Mango festival, Antigua** July–Aug. A celebration of the region's favourite fruit, with competitions for biggest produce and best "magic mango menu". *See page 351.*
- **Flower festivals, St Lucia** "La Rose" in August and "La Marguerite" in October reach their climax in the town of Micoud, with masquerades, dancing, and feasting. *See page 352.*

BEST FOOD AND DRINK

The freshest fruits of land and sea; food tastes best when it hasn't had to travel...

- **Seafood** From St Lucia's fish "fries" each Friday or Saturday night to fresh lobster from Anguilla to Tobago, or conch stews and curries, the region's favourite food is easily its most delicious. *See page 71.*
- **Rotis, Trinidad** Where India meets the Caribbean, this staple of Trinidadian cuisine is a variety of vegetable, meat or seafood curries wrapped in a large layered "skin". Try a shrimp roti with curried potato, channa dahl, and green mango. *See page 74.*
- **Bouillon, French Antilles /region-wide** A soupy stew served across the French-influenced islands, often made with fresh fish such as dorado, with lime, tomato and spices, or, as in St Lucia, with chicken or other meats, and lentils, red beans, dumplings and plantain. *See page 338.*
- **Oil down, Grenada** A delicious stew made with chicken, goat or saltfish, cooked down with breadfruit, and other vegetables, in coconut milk. For other specialties, *see page 338.*
- **Dutch-world specialties** The ABC Islands offer numerous Dutch- and Indonesian-influenced dishes, such as thick *pinda saus* (peanut sauce) served with meats or even fries; keshi yena, Edam or Gouda cheese stuffed with local meats and vegetables; and *sopi iguana* (iguana soup). *See page 71.*
- **Ti-punch** Drunk on around half the islands but perhaps best enjoyed on Martinique, this is both sweet and sour, made with either white or dark rum, freshly-squeezed lime and sugar or cane syrup. *See page 343.*
- **Fresh fruit juices** From passion fruit or mango to the delicious Christmastime red sorrel, and from creamy soursop to sweet citrus, the selection of fruits is second to none. *See page 338.*

BEST DIVING AND SNORKELING

- **Tobago** Known for its drift dives, brain corals, and large numbers of manta rays, the sites around Speyside are exquisite. *See page 356.*
- **Bequia and Tobago Cays, the Grenadines** Two marine parks, superb for diving and snorkeling with a range of sites including coral reefs and walls. *See page 356.*
- **Reserve Cousteau, Guadeloupe** Remarkable for its warm waters, these colourful reefs are popular with both divers and snorkelers. *See page 355.*

- **Bonaire Marine Park** Protected walls of coral stretching the entire length of the island's west coast, with 80-plus named sights, make this the king of Caribbean shore dives. *See pages 310 and 354.*
- **Saba Marine Park** Pristine reefs in crystal-clear waters lie a short boat ride off-shore; highlights are pinnacles, and a labyrinth created by lava flows. *See page 355.*

- **Antigua & Barbuda** Surrounded by shallow reefs and sunken wrecks, these twin islands are perfect for beginners' dives and snorkeling among vast schools of reef fish. *See page 354.*

LEFT: snorkeling in Tobago Cays, the Grenadines.
ABOVE: market stall, Pointe-à-Pitre, Guadeloupe.
BELOW: Eagle Beach, Aruba.

BEST SHOPPING

- **Redcliffe and Heritage Quays, Antigua** The former is a network of waterfront warehouses, containing restaurants and boutiques, while the latter has duty-free goods. *See page 179.*
- **St Martin/Sint Maarten** On the French side Marigot offers chic boutiques, and a lively souvenir market, while Philipsburg has bargains on jewellery, and electronics. *See page 127.*

- **Pointe-à-Pitre, Guadeloupe** Caribbean charm with old wooden houses and lively spice and flower markets accompanies a modern European mall. *See page 198.*
- **Port-of-Spain, Trinidad** For West Indians downtown is the place for bargains in fabric and dressmaking, while two out-of-town malls hold something for everyone. *See page 279.*

MONEY-SAVING TIPS

Travel off-season The climate between April and June is almost as good as January and February on most islands, with accommodation and other prices reduced by around 30%. *See page 316.*

Use local transport Car rental can be prohibitively expensive, and public transport surprisingly useable on many islands. If you don't mind unpredictable (though frequent) schedules and cosy journeys, public buses can be a great way to meet local people. *See page 317.*

Fly with a charter company If you're traveling trans-Atlantic and independently, extra seats on chartered planes can go at half the price of scheduled services if you book at the right time. *See page 316.*

Book an apartment Most islands have a variety of self-catering options, and if traveling with three or more people they can save you money. *See page 324.*

Talk to the locals Local restaurants usually offer bargains in comparison with hotels – and often serve equally good food. And you are putting money back into the local community – ask around for the top spots. *See page 338.*

WELCOME

Stay a while in the sunny Caribbean and you will discover
a rainbow of cultures and a rich and exciting history

The Lesser Antilles, from St Thomas in the north to Aruba, off the Venezuelan coast in the south, comprise some of the most magnificently beautiful landscapes on the face of the earth. Within this chain of more than 20 major islands and countless uninhabited cays and islets – known also as the Eastern Caribbean and the West Indies – there seems to be every conceivable shade of blue in the water, every variation of flower, every species of brightly colored bird. The air is balmy and perfumed, the nights are consistently clear, the days are bathed in warm sunshine. Even when it is wet, the rain is warm, refreshing and usually comes in short bursts. Indeed, it seems as if everything, the climate, the waters, the land, is unimaginably perfect.

But in some ways such beauty has been a bit of a curse. The world tends to forget that the Lesser Antilles is not one great holiday resort but a collection of small nations and territories struggling to forge economic and political identities; that it possesses both a remarkable and often tragic history, fought over for centuries by warring European countries, and that it has an astonishingly diverse culture – each island proud of its own.

There is a story told by an English historian about discovering a British school in which there were German nuns teaching local children out of an English textbook which they had to explain in Spanish. A wonderful analogy for a history and culture produced by startling combinations. Begin with two remarkable primitive indigenous societies, add the influence of the 16th-century gold-seeking Spaniards and their European rivals: the French, English, Dutch, Danes and even the Knights Templars of Malta; add pirates, religious and political refugees, and a huge African slave culture, then stir in Hindus, Jews and Rastafarians and you have the dizzying recipe that makes up these islands.

As these hospitable Caribbean isles become more and more accessible, with tourism now the mainstay of their economy, there is a danger that their soul will be submerged in the onslaught of leisure developers. But if you tread carefully you can help preserve the spirit of the Caribbean and all it entails, and because the people are, in general, so open, you can easily explore all its realms; political, religious and cultural. Read on... ❑

PRECEDING PAGES: messing about in Meads Bay, Anguilla; fun in the sea.
LEFT: a welcoming smile.

ISLANDS IN THE SUN

The rich diversity of these tropical islands is plain to see – from their mountain rainforests to the ocean deep

The islands of the Lesser Antilles form a delicate necklace of coral, basalt, and limestone stretching from the Virgin Islands in the north through a 1,500-mile (2,400-km) arc to the Dutch islands of Aruba, Bonaire, and Curaçao off the coast of Venezuela in the south.

Each small landmass is often within sight of another. So when Amerindians, the earliest people to colonize the Eastern Caribbean, started to move north from South America, they could stand at the northern tip of one island and see – if only as a blurry mauve outline across a truculent channel – the southern tip of the next island. It was an encouragement, perhaps, to move on, to see what new creatures, plants, landscapes, opportunities lay on the horizon.

Each island to its own

The islands of the Eastern Caribbean are physically (and culturally) places of great variety. The images of sparkling white sand, clear turquoise sea, and shimmering coconut palms of the travel advertisements do the region a disservice. It is a far richer region than that, with each island's topography reflecting the story of its creation and its history.

From the pristine rainforests of Dominica and St Lucia, where rain pounds the mountain tops with up to 300 inches (760 cm) of water annually and tree ferns shimmer in a silver light, to the dry, brittle scrublands of acacia and logwood of St Martin or Barbuda, there seems to be a vegetation for every mood. Even if you stay on only one island, there is often a remarkable range of ecology to be explored: from rainforest canopy to coastal swamp and coral reef.

The flatter islands are less varied and, in many cases, they have been more vulnerable to exploitation. Thus Antigua and Barbados lost their original forest covering to sugar-cane plantations, leaving a landscape largely of

LEFT: the wild Atlantic coastline of Barbados.
RIGHT: canefields spread across land deforested by the early colonists.

"bush", with residual areas given over to the cultivation of sugar cane and vegetables, or rearing livestock.

The ocean and the deep blue sea

Yet wherever you arrive in the Caribbean you are greeted by a sweetness of smell and the

breezes of the cooling trade winds. Its tropical climate delivers relatively constant hours of sunshine, and a temperature hovering around 86°F (30°C) in the eastern Caribbean.

The trade winds, which guided the first Europeans to the Caribbean at the end of the 15th century, blow in from the northeast, first over the typically wilder coasts of the wetter windward sides, which are buffeted by the tempestuous Atlantic Ocean, and then across in a more gentle fashion to the tranquil, leeward Caribbean Sea.

The contrast of the two coasts is often striking, with the wilder Atlantic side of most Eastern Caribbean islands having more in common with a Scottish seascape than the gentle white-sand beaches of the hotter and drier Caribbean coast usually only a few miles away.

Alive and kicking

With the exception of Barbados, which is perched out on its own, much of the island chain (from Saba to Grenada), was created by volcanic action when the two tectonic plates which sit beneath the "necklace" shifted. The eastward-moving American plate pushed under the westward-moving Caribbean plate and threw up what became this pattern of islands. However, Barbados, to the southeast, was

formed by a wedge of sediments pushed up slowly; it is encrusted with the remnants of ancient coral reefs which developed as the water became shallower over the sediments. To the south, Trinidad and Tobago were joined to Venezuela during the ice age when the sea levels were much lower, accounting for the similar fauna and flora on the islands.

Some islands are much older than others: those that have been worn down by erosion, subsided below sea level and then raised up again are the flatter, drier islands of Anguilla, St Martin, Barbuda, and Antigua, on the outside of the volcanic rim.

The geologically younger islands are physically more dramatic, with mountain ranges and steep-sided valleys. Some, such as Montserrat, Guadeloupe, St Vincent, and Martinique, have experienced volcanic activity in the 20th century – from the devastation of the town of St Pierre in Martinique in 1902, when some 30,000 people were suddenly wiped out, to the most recent activity, which started in 1995 in the Soufrière Hills in the south of Montserrat.

The Montserrat crisis resulted in the "closure" of two thirds of the island, the deaths of 19 people, and the evacuation of much of the population. In fact, *soufrière* (from the French word for sulfur) is the name given to volcanoes in the region. In St Lucia, for example, the "drive-in" volcano, with its moonscape of bubbling mud, mineral pools of boiling water, and sulfur springs, is the collapsed rim of a huge old volcano near the southern village of Soufrière.

This dramatic landscape continues underwater where there are mountains, including a submarine volcano just north of Grenada called Kick 'Em

---

RIP-ROARING HURRICANES

A hurricane blows up when the atmosphere's pressure plunges far lower than that of the surrounding air. Usually spawned in the Atlantic, continuous winds of up to 150 mph (240 kph) blow around the eye, a calm central zone of several miles across, where the sky is often blue.

Hurricanes can reach up to 500 miles (800 km) in width and travel at 10–30 mph (16–48 kph), speeding up across land before losing force and dying out. They leave a wake of massive destruction to towns, homes, and crops, but loss of life is minimal nowadays as islanders are warned of approaching storms and official hurricane shelters are allocated *(see Travel Tips)*.

Lists of hurricane names are drawn up six years in advance in alphabetical order by the National Hurricane Center in Miami. The tradition started during World War II when US servicemen named the storms after their girlfriends. In 1979, concern for equal rights included the use of male names.

Memorable hurricanes have been David (1979), which devastated Dominica; Hugo (1989), which flattened Montserrat; Luis (1995), which roared through the Leewards with Marilyn hot on his tail; Lenny (1999), which affected St Kitts; and Lili (2002) and Ivan (2004), which hit Grenada and St Vincent.

Jenny, caves, lava flows, overhangs, pinnacles, walls, reefs, and forests of elkhorn coral.

Volcanoes apart, the threat from hurricanes is a constant feature of life in parts of the Eastern Caribbean, especially in the belt that stretches north from St Lucia to the Virgin Islands. The hurricane season (June too soon, July stand by, August it must, September remember, October all over) interrupts the rainy season, from May to Christmas, often to devastating effect, endangering lives and destroying homes, businesses, and crops. The traditional dry season is from around Christmas to May, when water may be in short supply. It is then that the flowering trees and shrubs, like the red-bracted poinsettia, put on their most festive display.

DANGEROUS RESIDENTS

Trinidad is the only island that is home to four species of venomous snake – the bushmaster, two types of coral snake and the fer de lance.

the agouti, opossum, and the green monkey (found in Barbados, Grenada, and St Kitts and Nevis) were introduced by man. The mongoose, a creature that looks like a large weasel, was brought over to control rats and snakes, but as rats are nocturnal and mongooses aren't, they succeeded in becoming a pest too, plundering birds' nests and rummaging through garbage.

The islands in the middle of the necklace received fewer migrants of both bird and animal life. However, the relative isolation of some

Tropical wildlife

While the flora of the Lesser Antilles is of international importance, the region is less well-endowed with fauna. Many animals, such as

of them allowed for the evolution of endemic species: Dominica and Montserrat are the home of a large frog known as a mountain chicken, found nowhere else in the world; and Dominica, St Vincent, and St Lucia each have their own species of parrot.

While you may not always see a parrot, every day will bring a hummingbird winging its way in a million flutters "to a hibiscus near you". Indeed, birds are a constant presence, although you will have to go to Trinidad (for its 400 species) for the most exotic. Lizards and geckos are everywhere, iguanas are rare (and protected), while the poisonous fer de lance snake lives only on St Lucia, Martinique and Trinidad.

FAR LEFT: all that is left of an old sugar mill.
ABOVE LEFT: Grenada has recovered now, but Hurricane Ivan wreaked havoc in 2004.
RIGHT: the volcanic Pitons du Carbet in Martinique.

Linked to the land

These small islands – few have a population of more than a million (Trinidad) and some have under 20,000 (Anguilla, Nevis, Saba) – are essentially rural in character. Trinidad's Port-of-Spain is a modern cosmopolitan city and Bridgetown in Barbados is developing fast, but the capitals of most of the islands are like small market towns in Europe, often picturesque but usually parochial.

While the younger generation is growing up with television (usually American) and the internet, the sense of national identity remains linked to the land and its usages. This is true whether it

is the salt pans on the dry scrub of Anguilla (highest point 213 ft/65 meters above sea level) or an acre of hillside in Grenada burgeoning with root vegetables, citrus, and mango. And every cultivator will carry a cutlass in the way a city person carries a briefcase. "It's the pen of the farmer," as one islander described it.

The cliché of an earthly paradise is a tempting way to describe some of the still pristine corners of the region. Yet it is a distortion, for its history is of slavery and colonialism. Even now its people are forced by economic poverty to migrate from this "paradise" which cannot support them. This tension between the people and their history is captured in an almost unbearably beautiful way in the works of many Caribbean writers, particularly perhaps in the poetry of Derek Walcott of St Lucia.

A money spinner

In the last decades of the 20th century the economies began to shift away from agriculture to tourism. And it is now the region's greatest money spinner, bringing employment and dollars. Like the first colonizers, who dramatically altered the island hinterlands by clearing the forests – first for tobacco, then coffee and cocoa and then for sugar – the tourist industry has changed the coastlines for ever. The bays where fishermen once pulled in their nets, or where colonies of birds nested in mangrove stands, now provide for the very different needs of tourists.

The fragile environments of these small islands are, in some cases, in danger of sinking under the weight of visitors. Local environmental groups are vocal in contesting the destruction of important mangrove stands for hotel building; the damage done to coral reefs by careless tourists and the anchors of cruise ships; plus the cultural threat imposed on small societies by the hordes of holiday-makers.

Ecotourism is now the buzz word, and some islands, such as Dominica and Trinidad, which have not developed a "sand, sea, and sun" tourism have declared policies for developing a more sustainable tourism. And visitors, too, are discovering that there is more to the land- and seascapes of the Caribbean than the limited view from a sun lounger; between them, perhaps, the diversity of that island necklace will survive. ❑

TO TREAD LIGHTLY...

☞ choose a hotel that is locally owned, employs islanders, and uses island products.
☞ go on a whale-watching trip, making the whale an asset to tourism.
☞ leave coral for the fish, don't stand on it, and never drop anchor on a reef.
☞ ask permission before taking a person's photo.
☞ enjoy water sports that don't need a motor.
☞ keep to the trails in rainforests; use a guide.
☞ ensure offroad trips are on designated tracks.
☞ record or report any pollution you may see from the deck of your cruise ship.

LEFT: motmots from Trinidad and Tobago.
RIGHT: whale-watching is popular with ecotourists.

INSVLÆ AMERICANÆ
IN OCEANO SEPTENTRIONALI,
cum Terris adiacentibus.

FLO RIDA.

Gorfo De Mexico.

NOVÆ HISPANIÆ PARS.

YVCATAN

HONDVRAS.

NICARAGVA.

MAR DEL ZVR.

Ampl.mo Prud.mo Doct.mo Viro
D. ALBERTO CONRADI VANDER BVRCH,
I.C. Reip. Amsterdamensi Senatori, Collegij
Scabinorum Præsidi, Societatis Indicæ, quæ
ad Occidentem militat aßeßori, et nuper
ad Magnum Moscoviæ Ducem Legato,
Tabulam hanc inscribit Guiljelmus Blaeu.

Decisive Dates

AD **1000–1200** Carib tribes from South America travel north through the Lesser Antilles in dug-out canoes, displacing the resident Arawak-speaking people.
1493 and 1498 Christopher Columbus is the first European to discover the Eastern Caribbean islands.

COLONIZING THE ISLANDS: 16TH AND 17TH CENTURY
European settlers flock to the New World, bringing African slaves to work on their plantations and farms.
1535 Prince Rupert Bay in Dominica is used as a shelter for Spanish treasure ships.

1592 Spanish are first to settle the Eastern Caribbean in Trinidad, building the town of St Joseph. Three years later, Sir Walter Raleigh destroys it.
1623 The English establish their first colony on St Kitts, then Barbados (1627), Antigua (1632), Anguilla (1650), and the British Virgin Islands (1680).
1632 Irish Catholics settle on Montserrat, escaping Protestant persecution on St Kitts.
1635 The French colonize Guadeloupe and Martinique and in 1650 buy Grenada from the Caribs for some hatchets, glass beads, and two bottles of brandy.
1634–36 Dutch fleet takes ABC Islands; first Dutch colony on St Eustatius in 1636; Saba (1640).
1648 Treaty of Concordia officially divides St Martin between French (north) and Dutch (south).

SUGAR AND SLAVERY 1638–1797
Many of the islands had been planted with sugar cane and, by the end of the 17th century, King Sugar ruled.
1638–1779 Slave trade flourishes in Curaçao, where slaves are sold on to the sugar-growing islands.
1675 and 1695 Slave rebellions uncovered in Barbados and the ringleaders executed.
1690 St Kitts and Nevis hit by a severe earthquake and tidal wave wipes out Nevis's capital, Jamestown.
1704 Tobago is declared a neutral island by the European colonizers, and soon becomes a pirate base.
1725 Leprosy epidemic in Guadeloupe leads to the creation of a leper colony on La Désirade close by.
1754 St Thomas, St John, and St Croix become a royal colony of Denmark, named the Danish West Indies.
1765 St Vincent Botanical Gardens founded.
1775–83 American Revolution causes famine in British West Indies due to trade embargoes.
1779 Stock Exchange crash in Europe sends sugar industry further into decline.
1780s British introduce nutmeg to Grenada where it becomes a main crop, along with cocoa.
1784 France cedes St Barthélemy to Sweden in exchange for trading rights.
1793 Captain Bligh brings breadfruit plants from Tahiti to St Vincent on *The Bounty*.
1797 Over 5,000 Black Caribs deported from St Vincent after the British quell revolt. British invade Trinidad.

REFORM AND REBELLION 1802–1902
There were slave revolts across the Caribbean during the early 19th century, demanding liberty.
1802 Spanish Treaty of Amiens gives Trinidad to the British, and Tobago finally ceded to Britain by France. Louis Delgrès and 500 rebels blow themselves up at Matouba, Guadeloupe, when surrounded by the French.
1816 St Kitts, Nevis, Anguilla, and British Virgin Islands administered by British as a single colony.
1816 Easter Rebellion in Barbados of 5,000 slaves led by Bussa demanding freedom.
1828–45 Dutch West Indies governed from Suriname.
1834 Emancipation Act "frees" slaves in British West Indies. The French follow in 1848 and the Dutch in 1863. An "apprenticeship" system is introduced.
1845–1917 Thousands of East Indians arrive in Trinidad for an indentured period of five years; many remain.
1848 Slave rebellion in St Croix precipitates their emancipation in the Danish West Indies.
1878 St Barthélemy is given back to France by Sweden.
1888 Tobago amalgamates politically with Trinidad.
1902 Mont Pelée on Martinique erupts, destroying the capital St Pierre and killing 30,000 people. Two days before, La Soufrière on St Vincent erupted, killing 2,000.

GOING INDEPENDENT 1914–83

After the larger British islands became independent within the British Commonwealth, the smaller ones followed suit – although not all. The Dutch and French remain with their mother country.

1917 Danish West Indies sold to the US.

1917–24 Oil refineries built on Curaçao and Aruba.

1946 French islands change their status to *départements* of France, officially becoming regions in 1974.

1951 Universal suffrage granted to British colonies.

1954 Dutch islands granted full autonomy in domestic affairs as part of the Netherlands and in 1986 Aruba is given separate autonomy.

1958 Lord Glenconner buys Mustique in the Grenadines, giving Princess Margaret land as a wedding gift.

1958–62 Formation of the Federation of the British West Indies, which fails when Jamaica and Trinidad and Tobago decide to pursue independence.

1966 Barbados is granted independence.

1967 Britain's islands become states in voluntary association with Britain, with internal self-government.

1969 British invasion welcomed by Anguilla; officially becomes a British Dependent Territory in 1980.

1973 Foundation of CARICOM (Caribbean Community), an organization designed to liberalize movement of trade between member states.

1974 Grenada is first of the Associated States to be granted independence.

1976 Trinidad becomes a republic within the British Commonwealth.

1978 Dominica gains independence.

1979 St Vincent and the Grenadines gain independence. La Soufrière erupts. Grenada experiences a bloodless coup by Marxist-Leninists led by Maurice Bishop. St Lucia gains independence.

1981 Antigua and Barbuda granted independence as one nation, as are St Kitts and Nevis in 1983.

1983 US and Caribbean forces invade Grenada after the government is overthrown and Bishop murdered.

MODERN TIMES 1985–2005

Corruption and natural disasters create problems.

1985 Exxon closes oil refinery in Aruba with disastrous effects on the island's economy.

1987 Waters around Saba become a marine park.

1989 and 1995 Hurricane Hugo and then hurricanes Luis and Marilyn wreak havoc in the Caribbean.

1990 Arms smuggling scandal in Antigua involves Prime Minister's son Vere Bird Jr. Muslim fundamentalists attempt to overthrow government in Trinidad.

LEFT: enslaved Africans celebrate their freedom.
RIGHT: flag of the Republic of Trinidad and Tobago.

1992 St Lucian writer Derek Walcott wins Nobel Prize for Literature.

1993–95 Operation Dinero off Anguilla traps drug traffickers, money launderers, and arms dealers.

1994 Tropical Storm Debbie hits the Caribbean, dumping 26 inches (66 cm) of rain on St Lucia in just seven hours. In contrast, Guadeloupe is declared a disaster zone after the worst drought for 30 years.

1995 First prime minister of East Indian descent, Basdeo Panday, is elected in Trinidad.

1995–98 Volcanic activity on Montserrat results in three eruptions in 1997, causing death and destruction.

1999 EU quotas favoring Caribbean banana imports are ruled unfair by the World Trade Organisation.

2001 Trinidad-born Sir Vidia Naipaul is awarded the Nobel Prize for Literature.

2002 Haiti joins the Caribbean Community (CARICOM).

2004 Hurricane Ivan causes serious damage.

2005 Inauguration of the Caribbean Court of Justice (CCJ) in Port-of-Spain, Trinidad, to replace London's Privy Council as final appellate court.

2006 Trinidad and Tobago and Barbados sign up to the Caribbean Single Market and Economy (CSME).

2007 ICC Cricket World Cup takes place in islands across the Caribbean.

2008 Dominica signs up to Chavez of Venezuela's Bolivarian Alternative for the Americas (ALBA), a cooperation pact. The Dutch Antilles is disbanded; Curaçao and Sint Maarten gain independent status similar to Aruba's. ❏

THE COLONIAL PERIOD

When Christopher Columbus came upon the islands of the Caribbean, he threw names at many of them as he sailed past. The colonists arrived 100 years later

Accounts by Spanish historians and other European travelers tell of a vibrant Indian civilization which existed before the arrival of Columbus at the end of the 15th century. In fact, most of what is known about the Indians comes from these accounts and archeological excavations.

However, such observations have to be read with care because, with the single exception of the Dominican monk, Bartolomé de Las Casas (1474–1566), the defender of the Indians in the early 16th century, they were filled with the *hubris* of a European man who saw the native inhabitants as savage children hardly fit for missionary enterprise. Alternatively, some of the accounts presented the inhabitants of this new world in Utopian terms, in contrast to the decadence of European life. Beatriz Pastor, in *Discurso narrativo de la Conquista de América,* has shown how these psychologically conditioned responses oscillated between two opposite pictures: savage cannibalism or romantic primitivism. European visitors saw what they wanted to see.

Amerindian settlements

The Indians mainly comprised two completely different races, Tainos and Caribs, both from South America. The Arawak-speaking Tainos are believed to have settled on the islands around the time of Christ or earlier and lived in fishing and agricultural communities of a quite sophisticated character. Ruled by a chieftain or *cacique,* they possessed their own system of laws and government, based on patriarchical lineage. Their ceremonial grounds indicate complicated games and their boat-building technology was advanced, enabling them to travel great distances.

The more warlike Caribs *(see page 213)* ventured northward through the islands about 1,000 years later, killing the Taino men and taking their women. Word went round amongst the

conquering Europeans that the Caribs ate their captives, giving us the word cannibal.

Much of this Indian civilization disappeared under the pressures of European conquest and colonization. English and French soldiers and settlers undertook what were in effect genocidal wars against the native populations of the

islands during the 16th and 17th centuries. Today, only a handful of the descendant Caribs exist on a reservation in Dominica.

There were two general consequences of the Indian presence on the islands. The first was the growth of a European Utopian literature. European writers, using the travelers' accounts, invented the fiction of a natural, idyllic life situated in an imaginary island in the Antilles or the South Seas. Daniel Defoe's *Robinson Crusoe* (1719) is the best-known example. The second was the resistance of the Indians to becoming enslaved; few Caribs were prepared to play Man Friday to the white man's Crusoe. Thus the colonizers turned to Africa for labor.

LEFT: portrayal of early tribal life in the Caribbean. **RIGHT:** a Romantic interpretation of Christopher Columbus.

Colonial rivalry

The 16th, 17th and 18th centuries were the major formative period of the Lesser Antilles, marked, successively, by war and rivalry between European nations, the establishment of settlements and colonies and introduction of a sugar economy, the organization of the slave trade, the implantation of chattel slavery, the rise of white superiority and slave rebellions.

The early Spanish claim to the Caribbean islands was rapidly

BUCCANEERING SPIRIT

"If our number is small, our hearts are great; and the fewer persons we are, the more union, and the better shares we shall have in the spoil." Henry Morgan told his men after a pirate raid in 1668 yielded a booty of 250,000 "pieces of eight".

Dr Eric Williams, called it a condition of "in betweenity". The island of St Croix (now part of the US Virgin Islands), for example, changed sovereignty at least seven times in a period of less than 100 years, including a brief rule by the Knights Templars of Malta.

The European powers saw their new tropical possessions as an opportunity for enriching the emergent state systems of post-Reformation Europe, both Catholic and Protestant. And they wanted to weaken Spain's

challenged by its European rivals – England, France, Denmark and Holland. The Spanish hegemony was anchored mainly in the Greater Antilles – Cuba, Hispaniola and Puerto Rico – where there was real treasure, although there was a brief Spanish episode in Trinidad.

Because they were the first ports of arrival for the invading European fleets the Lesser Antilles bore the brunt of the inter-state rivalry. It was a period of almost uninterrupted insecurity for the region, when the political ownership of any island could suddenly change. The native populations could wake up on any morning to discover that they had a set of new masters. West Indian historian and politician,

influence in the New World. Through much of the 16th century Spain had dominated the high seas plying to and from the Caribbean with treasure. In an attempt to break their monopoly, Sir Francis Drake had become the first official pirate, reaping the rewards for Elizabeth I.

Pirates and buccaneers

European chancelleries and war ministries continued to use their pirates and buccaneers – fugitives from justice of all nationalities – to harass the Spaniards in the 17th century. Sir Henry Morgan (1635–88) started his infamous career as a British licensed privateer. Dutchman Esquemiling wrote *The Buccaneers and*

Marooners of America in 1674: "...from the very beginning of their conquests in America, both English, French, Dutch, Portuguese, Swedes, Danes, Courlanders, and all other nations that navigate the ocean, have frequented the West Indies, and filled them with their robberies and assaults."

The European governments eventually agreed to dispense with these motley forces because they were becoming too much of a nuisance to their own ships. Governor Woodes Rogers' suppression of the pirate stronghold in New Providence in the Bahamas in 1722 finally marked the end of piracy.

Stretched like a line of watchdogs across the route between Spain and her seaborne New World empire, the islands were perfectly positioned for the establishment of naval stations, like Nelson's Dockyard in Antigua. Indeed, if, as the saying goes, the Battle of Waterloo (1815) was won on the playing fields of Eton, then it is equally true to say that the Battle of Trafalgar (1805) was won in the naval stations of the Lesser Antilles.

Some of the most decisive battles were fought here, most notably when Admiral Rodney destroyed the French fleet in the Battle of the Saints off the Windwards in 1782. He then

Naval warfare

By 1700, the four great powers of Caribbean economic and military aggression – France, Holland, Spain, and Great Britain – had established flourishing island colonies when the Atlantic seaboard colonies of Massachusetts and Virginia were hardly beyond their first stages of settlement. The colonization of the islands and Spanish Main produced cities rivalling those of Europe in size and magnificence.

LEFT: battleships – a constant sight around the islands during the 1700s.
ABOVE: the colonial good life portrayed in an 18th-century cartoon.

destroyed the commercial port of St Eustatius, which had become a supply center of arms for the anti-English forces in the American Revolutionary War. Even today, Statians remember Rodney's sack of their island, known as the Golden Rock, just as Southerners remember Sherman's burning of Atlanta in the American Civil War.

The governments of both the mother country and local colony were forced, often at ruinous expense, to build defenses, such as the Brimstone Hill fortifications on St Kitts, against such calamities. For the small town populations of the time, life must have been marginal and precarious. St Croix alone, the island center of the

Danish West Indies, was occupied in the year of 1650 by three different European war parties.

Such warfare continued right into the period of the Napoleonic Wars, when the political map of the region was eventually settled by the 1815 Treaty of Vienna.

Profits of paradise

However, the history of the New World, called the Enterprise of the Indies, was not just war. War was simply the prelude to

A NEW LIFE

Welsh Royalist, Dutch Jew, Cromwell's transported prisoner, Puritan merchant, Catholic friar – all types of European travelled to a new life in the Antilles. Some sought adventure and others refuge but many were banished for a variety of crimes and misdemeanors.

Island patterns

From north to south these islands shared a common pattern of colonialism and slavery deriving prosperity from the sugar economy, either producing sugar or developing as commercial trade centers. For example, in the north, St Thomas, under Danish rule, developed as an important commercial trade center as it was too hilly for sugar, while St Croix, while ruled by the Danes, developed as a sugar

trade. Once the European powers had more or less settled their respective "spheres of influence" – Trinidad, for example, was finally ceded to Britain in the 1802 Treaty of Amiens that ended the Seven Year War – the Lesser Antilles settled down to its socio-economic-cultural development as peripheral economies of the European states.

That meant the development of sugar as a staple crop and the sugar plantation economy, supported by the slave trade, which lasted nearly 400 years, from 1500 to 1860, supplying a large and cheap labor force capable of doing heavy unremitting work under brutalizing tropical conditions.

plantation economy. Of course, there were differences between the individual islands. For instance, Barbados was English and Guadeloupe French. In the south, Trinidad emerged as a Franco-Hispanic Catholic society while Tobago became an English-speaking Protestant society of small farmers and fishing folk. Antigua became a sugar colony while mountainous Dominica had little to do but develop an infant lumber industry. In the French Antilles, Martinique early on developed a small creole middle class of professional elite, while Guadeloupe remained mainly peasant. This distinction survives even to the present day.

In the Dutch Antilles, Curaçao became another

commercial trade center as it was too arid for sugar, while Bonaire developed a small salt-pond industry and became a prison for rebellious slaves. Even the Lilliputian islands of Anguilla, Barbuda and the Grenadines, as dependent wards of large sugar islands, were affected by the sugar economy.

The slave trade

As a consequence of the Europeans' seemingly insatiable taste for sugar, the islands, with few exceptions, became arrival ports and slave markets. And the triangular trade, between the African trading posts, the European middle-

to survive unless he was also a planter-merchant.

The entire house of Antillean society was built over this slave basement. It became a strange melting pot of white colonists, black slaves, indentured servants, freed Indians, Catholics, Protestants, heretics, Jews, transported political prisoners, felons, "poor whites", all mingled in a fascinating exoticism under tropical skies. It was a *picaroon* world of all colors and creeds, slowly learning to co-exist with each other.

Naturally enough, it was a society of ranking status in three tiers, composed of upper-class whites, mulattos or freed persons of color – the

passage ports and the Antilles, laid the foundations of slavery as a domestic institution. Richard Ligon described in his book *A True and Exact History of the Island of Barbados* (1657) how the smallholdings of the early lower-class white immigrants were replaced with large-scale sugar plantations.

Later, the British dramatist and politician Richard Sheridan's study of the rise of the colonial gentry in 18th-century Antigua showed how no entrepreneur in that society could hope

LEFT: a working plantation showing the main house, mill, slave huts, slaves and owner.
ABOVE: Caribbean market in the 19th century.

consequence of the Antillean miscegenative habits – and slaves at the bottom of the pile.

White plantocracy

Each group had its own pride and prejudices. In turn, they saw the group of "free coloreds" as social upstarts, presumptuously claiming to be "white when in fact they were black." As a class, the white plantocracy was arrogant, racist, and socially gross. In fact, much of its own ancestry in the islands was suspect: the 18th-century, Jesuit traveler Père Labat noted in Martinique that his slave owner neighbors were originally engaged servants. These observations hardly made Labat popular in those old creole communities and explains why, after some 14 years, he was recalled by his superiors and never allowed to return.

The islands at this time were overcrowded not only with African slaves, but also with the white riffraff of Europe who hoped to become plantation owners and escape their lowly origins. Their skin color gave them a new status in the islands; and their sexual irresponsibility showed how they used it to unscrupulously advance their careers. In this sense, the social history of the islands during this period is in part the sexual exploitation of the black women by the white plantation males, whether overseers, accountants, indentured servants, or even masters. Better, after all, to be a *grand seigneur* in Martinique than a lowly serf in Provence.

> **ABSENTEE OWNERS**
>
> Plantation profits were sent to the absentee owners in England, who wasted them on a lifestyle of such prodigality that it disgusted even 18th-century observers.

the negrophobia of the time, listing some 128 grades of color, by which every person in the colony was awarded a status.

Few visitors failed to note the ostentatious display of wealth and the extravagant style of entertainment practised by the planters, one of the causes of their perennial indebtedness.

Absenteeism was endemic and plantation profits were sent to the owners in England, who wasted them on a lifestyle of prodigality that disgusted even 18th-century observers.

Most of the slave-owning class were vulgar to a degree and they lived in continuous fear of slave rebellion. Danish Virgin Islands Governor Gardelin's slave mandate of 1733 was typical in its severity of punishments for slaves guilty of bad behavior, not to mention slaves guilty of rebellious behavior. In the French Antilles the official Code Noir of 1785 reflected

Gens de couleur

A history of interracial breeding produced the second group in Antillean society, the "free coloreds" or *gens de couleur*. They were a highly significant group, in part because they occupied a marginal position between the whites and the slaves. Also, their numbers were growing rapidly while the numbers of whites tended to decline. After all, it was a rare white person who did not father colored children, except for the descendents of the Scottish-Irish "poor whites" of the 17th century, known today as "Redlegs" in Barbados.

The history, then, of the Antilles during much of this period was the story of this mulatto group's struggle for social status and for political and civil rights. The first breakthrough in political rights occurred in the late 18th century in Antigua, when free persons of mixed race possessing the necessary property qualifications were allowed to vote at elections.

Social respectability

This long drawn-out rise of the people of color was important for two reasons. In the first place, though hardly a revolutionary movement, it did revolutionize society. Like the whites, the mulattoes had important interests in slave holding. They resented their own sub-

edict of 1831 in the Danish Virgin Islands, permitting the legal registration of colored persons as white citizens on the basis of good conduct and social standing. The coloreds responded to those concessions by developing their own extravagant life style – wearing precious stones and silk stockings, holding masked balls, and adopting the use of ceremonial gunfire at funerals – which the government tried to curb.

Social snobbery thus supplanted common racial brotherhood, and the Antillean free coloreds, at least in this formative 18th century period, became known as a group given more to lavish social display than to mental activity

ordination, but did not resist the social structure of which it was a part. They needed the white group as a role model in their search for social respectability, and the whites needed them as allies against slave unrest and, even worse, slave rebellion. The coloreds also had to stay on good terms with the white governments, both local and abroad, in order to gain concessions for themselves.

A typical example was the remarkable royal

LEFT: a register listing slaves with age and race.
ABOVE LEFT: a British emancipation society's view of the horrors of slavery.
ABOVE RIGHT: mulattoes enjoying a dance.

and academia. Lafcadio Hearn wrote in his book on Martinique, although it applied to all the islands, "Travellers of the 18th century were confounded by the luxury of dress and jewelry displayed by swarthy beauties in St Pierre. It was a public scandal to European eyes."

The slave population

The slaves generally came from West Africa. Philip Curtin, in his definitive book, *The African Slave Trade*, estimated that from its beginnings in the early 16th century to its termination in the 19th century, some 12 million Africans were brought to the New World by means of the triangular trade. They arrived as unnamed chattel slaves, later to be renamed by their slave owners and masters, which accounts for the Europeanized names of their descendants.

The present-day reversion to African names is a phenomenon of the 20th century, since the Black Power movement began to influence black communities in the US, Europe and the Caribbean in the 1960s and 1970s. The loss of name was, in a psychological sense, important because it was a part of the total loss of liberty that deprived the African

> **RESISTANCE**
>
> As a form of rebellion, slaves retained a way of life – in dance, music, and religion – which endured alongside that of the white minority population.

of his right to be regarded as a human being, never mind an equal.

African traditions

Yet there was play as well as gruelling work. "Every people," wrote the political writer Edmund Burke (1729–97), "must have some compensation for its slavery." And so, from the very beginning, the slaves brought with them their traditions of song and dance. Music played a very large part in their lives; a music that emerged out of a blending and meeting of both the imported European musical forms and the various African song and dance formulations. These encounters gave rise to completely new,

exciting forms of dance and music which became uniquely Antillean.

A similar process of creolisation took place, during this early formative period, with language. In the New World setting – planter, overseer, slave, with all of their respective duties and obligations – had to learn to understand each other. The problem was solved, *ad hoc*, by the invention of creole *patois*, which differed between islands.

Slave rebellion

The habit of what was called in the French islands *petit marronage* – of running away from the estate for short periods of time to visit a woman friend, or attend a prohibited church meeting, or just simply to feel a taste of freedom – often escalated into rebellion.

Such rebellious attempts, all crushed with severe cruelty, occurred regularly, but most notably in St John in the Danish West Indies in 1733, Antigua in 1736, St Croix in 1759, Grenada in 1795, and Barbados in 1816.

Certainly they showed that slaves had a capacity for insurrectionary leadership. There were leaders like Tackey and Tomboy in Antigua, who planned to kill all the whites, and set up an Ashanti-type black kingdom on the island. Nanny Grigg, in Barbados, told her followers, according to the official record, that the only way to get freedom was to fight for it. Then there was Daaga, who led, although after Emancipation, a brief mutiny of the 1st West India Regiment in Trinidad in 1837. He told his interrogators, on the eve of his execution, that the seeds of the mutiny had been sown on the passage from Africa.

Two other forces helped destroy the slavery system in the 19th century. First, the economic factor: slave labor was more costly and less efficient than free wage labor, an over supply of sugar led to catastrophic drops in world prices, and the West Indian planters lost their privileged position in the British market as the world free-trade policies were established. Second, the influence of the British religious-humanitarian movement, led by William Wilberforce (1759–1833) and Thomas Clarkson (1760–1846), that finally convinced public opinion of the un-Christian character of the system. ❑

Chains of Slavery

For 300 years, slaves arrived in the West Indies in their thousands. They landed from ships in which they had been literally packed together like sardines in the hold for the months-long voyage from West Africa, each of them chained down to prevent rebellion or suicide.

Conditions in the ships were just sufficient to keep them alive, although many died on the journey known as the Middle Passage. Those that became ill with diseases that rampaged through the holds, such as smallpox and dysentery, were thrown overboard. That so many survived is due to the slave traders choosing only the strong, healthiest looking men, whom their African chiefs traded for metals, guns, ammunitions, trinkets and cloth.

Once off the ships in the Caribbean, in trading islands such as Curaçao and St Thomas, the slaves were sold to plantation owners. They became property – part chattel, part real estate – that could be sold or traded against debts.

On the plantations living conditions were abysmal. Slaves were housed in floorless huts, with barely enough food to keep them working for 12 hours a day, six days a week. Historian Karl Watson has written that slaves in Barbados started their day at half-past five, when the plantation bell summoned them to assemble in the main estate yard to receive instructions. After being given hot ginger tea, they were divided up into gangs of 20 to 60 and sent out to dig cane holes, to manure, or to cut and crop mature cane under a burning sun until dark.

The work discipline was relentless as John Luffman reported in the 1780s: "The negroes are under the inspection of white overseers...subordinate to these overseers are drivers, commonly called dog-drivers, who are mostly black or mulatto fellows of the worst dispositions; and these men are furnished with whips which, while on duty, they are obliged, on pain of severe punishment, to have with them, and are authorized to flog wherever they see the least relaxation from labor; nor is it a consideration with them, whether it proceeds from idleness or inability, paying, at the same time, little or no regard to age or sex."

The slaves were given their food weekly. A typical weekly ration consisted of 28 lbs (13 kg) of yams or potatoes, 10 pints (5 liters) of corn, 8 oz (225 g) of fish and 1¾ pints (1 liter) of molasses. The yearly ration of clothing would have been a jacket, shirt, pair of trousers and cap for a man and a jacket, gown, petticoat and cap for a woman.

The slaves that acquired skills fared better than the field workers, sometimes becoming overseers of other slaves – many rebellions were thwarted through slaves telling on each other – cattle keepers, carpenters, blacksmiths and tailors. Domestic slaves – maids, cooks and butlers – were also more trusted and better treated than field workers.

However, the white owners generally regarded their slaves as lazy, irresponsible, grossly sexualist, potentially rebellious, and rationally inferior.

And in many cases with good reason, because often the only way slaves could resist was through quiet, covert protest such as malingering, feigning illness, working slowly, sabotaging property, and even poisoning their masters.

Certain defense mechanisms evolved to make life tolerable. They disguised their feelings and adopted exaggerated attitudes of deference to the point of pretending to be the stupid black person in which the white mentality believed. They also preserved their African culture through music and religion, much to the annoyance of their owners.

Resistance showed that slavery could only be maintained by force, a proposition which Europeans found objectionable in the early 19th century. ❑

LEFT: runaway slave, or maroon, with musket.
RIGHT: slaves toiling on a sugar plantation.

ROADS TO INDEPENDENCE AND BEYOND

As the freed slaves struggled for survival, many of the colonies sought independence.
Now, with the decline of island agriculture, tourism is the major breadwinner

With slavery finally abolished – in the British islands in 1834, the French islands in 1848, and the Dutch islands in 1863 – the post-emancipation period began. This lasted until the vast social and political changes unleashed by World War II (1939– 45) started the ball rolling toward most of the islands being given independence.

The freed slaves, permitted for the first time to develop an independent economic life, and previously denied land of their own, started buying up parts of abandoned estates, fought for the use of Crown lands, and organized networks of staple crop production and sales outlets in the towns. They were joined by thousands of East Indian indentured contract workers brought to parts of the region from Asia between 1838 and 1917 to work on the labor-starved plantations.

New Caribbean farmers

Over the decades the emancipated slaves became the nutmeg farmers of Grenada, the fishermen-farmers of Antigua and Barbuda, the small banana growers in St Lucia, the small sugar producers of St Croix, the small cocoa farmers of Trinidad, and the market women, or "higglers," who became the mainstay of the developing town market economy.

Much of what they produced were cash crops, destined for sale in the local market or even for sale abroad. They were peasants in the sense that their lifestyle, with all of its old kinship patterns of family, was rural; but their economic values were capitalist. They operated, often with characteristic shrewdness, as sellers and buyers in a free-market island economy. As a class, however, they were stratified like all classes, for there were at once the rich farmers

PRECEDING PAGES: workers load the sugar-cane train in Guadeloupe in around 1900.
LEFT: a young indentured laborer from India who came to Trinidad in the 19th century.
RIGHT: breaking cocoa during harvest.

and the poor farmers, as is still the case today.

At the same time, an urban workforce evolved in the more thriving centers of trade and commerce, like St Thomas, Fort-de-France, Bridgetown, Port-of-Spain, and Willemstad. In

the 1900s another workforce developed around the oil refineries in Trinidad, Curaçao, and Aruba, and around the transatlantic banana companies like the Geest group in St Lucia.

With the oil companies came a full-scale process of industrial and financial capitalism resulting in technological dependency; the growing separation between the European and colonial economies, with an increasing imbalance of trade between the two; external ownership and control; the influx of foreign managerial personnel; and a system in which the West Indian colonies sold cheap and bought dear. In effect, they produced what they did not consume, and consumed what they did not produce.

Breakdown of colonial rule

Between the two world wars, the native workers served as a dependent, low-paid docile labor force for industry, commerce, and agriculture. Conditions that were bad enough in the 1920s were made worse by the onset of the Depression. The British colonies became known as the "slums of the empire" with a declining sugar industry supporting an estate labor force by means of an exploitative task-work system.

In St Kitts and St Vincent, the wage level had barely advanced beyond the daily shilling rate introduced after emancipation a century earlier. There was gross malnutrition and chronic sickness in the population; a housing situation characterized by decrepit, verminous, and unsanitary conditions; and a working class, when it had work, in a state of economic servitude to a well-organized employer class. The defense mechanisms of a strong trade-union movement were stultified by the existence of punitive legislation.

Such conditions led to the labor riots that swept through the English-speaking islands between 1935 and 1938 and to bloody encounters between workers and the police, especially in Barbados and Trinidad.

These riots, plus the findings of the British

PRIDE AND PREJUDICES

By the start of the 20th century, the economic power of the white population had weakened, but whiteness was still regarded as the ideal image. In contrast to the USA, which classified itself by a simple black-white caste system, in the Antilles the classification system was more a subtle "shade" prejudice.

Social status depended upon fine degrees of skin color with wealth and income a factor. Whereas in US society money talked, in Antillean society, money whitened. This led to evasive habits of identity, summed up by the Martinican phrase, *peau noire, masque blanc* (black skin, white mask). The whites retained their identity by marrying only within their own racial group.

Today, the prejudices relate more to ethnicity in as far as the "native" US Virgin Islanders look down on the immigrants from the Leeward Islands, Trinidadians regard Grenadian immigrants as "small islanders," and the East Indians and creole blacks retain stereotyped images of each other. The French and Dutch islands are experiencing a new white immigrant in big business or government, prone through ignorance to alienating the locals.

However, the Antilleans, with all their differences, still manage to lead a harmonious existence together.

Royal Commission of 1938, helped to further the formation of new worker movements, which led to the creation of new political parties seeking first, internal self-government and, second, independence.

Some of the new leaders, like Grantley Adams (1898–1971) in Barbados, were black middle-class lawyers. Most were grassroots leaders, such as Vere Bird in Antigua, Uriah Butler in Trinidad, Robert Bradshaw in St Kitts, and Eric Gairy in Grenada, among others. Since they were all greatly influenced by the politics of the British Labour Party, the parties they founded were also, in the main, called labour parties.

Trinidad and Tobago were immediately granted independence within the British Commonwealth (1962) and were soon followed by Barbados in November 1966. But the end of the Federation had left the smaller Leeward and Windward islands out in the cold. As a result, in 1967, the British Government took the opportunity to change their constitutional status to "associated states," a status that gave them the right to internal self-government but left the jurisdiction of foreign affairs and defense in the hands of London civil servants and politicians.

Through the creation of these states, some islands such as St Kitts, Nevis, and Anguilla

Winding road to independence

It was not a straightforward march toward independence. Initially a movement, led by Grantley Adams, favoring a federation between the islands, culminated in the short-lived West Indies Federation of 1958–62.

That experiment broke up mainly because Jamaica and Trinidad were not prepared to sacrifice any of their sovereignty to a central federal government. Nor did they want federal taxation.

LEFT: farm workers on strike in the 1940s.
ABOVE LEFT: historian Dr Eric Williams, the first Prime Minister of Trinidad and Tobago in 1962.
ABOVE RIGHT: Sir Grantley Adams, social reformer.

were lumped together as one. Anguilla took exception, breaking away in 1969 and demanding to be returned to British jurisidiction, and it remains so to this day.

One by one, the British islands gained independence within the British Commonwealth, but without any great enthusiasm to begin with. Grenada was the first in 1974, followed by Dominica in 1978, St Lucia and St Vincent and the Grenadines in 1979, Antigua and Barbuda in 1981, and St Kitts and Nevis in 1983. Nevis made an attempt at secession from St Kitts in August 1998, but failed when only 62 percent, instead of the two-thirds necessary, voted in favor in a referendum. However, Montserrat,

Turks and Caicos, Cayman Islands, and British Virgin Islands have clung to the Crown, and are known as Britain's Overseas Territories. To paraphrase Shakespeare: "Some states are born independent, some achieve independence, and some have independence thrust upon them."

Dutch and French loyalties

Political and constitutional developments were different in both the French and the Netherlands Antilles. After the abolition of slavery, these islands never questioned loyalty to the Dutch Crown or to the French Republic.

With the arrival of the oil companies, politi-

and Sint Maarten's reluctance to remain tied together with the other Dutch islands. The two islands opted for self-government much like Aruba's status, with all the islands remaining within the kingdom of the Netherlands.

The French Antilles have been marked by a close relationship with France. The *loi cadre* passed by the Paris National Assembly in 1946 established the islands as overseas departments, *départements d'outre-mer* (DOM) – with St Barthélemy and St Martin joining up with Guadeloupe to share equal status with Martinique. This gave the islanders all the rights of French citizens and equal representation in

cal and union leaders in the Netherlands Antilles became more involved in their relationships with them than with The Hague. There was, however, the same old inequity of power between the mother country and the colony, but it was an imbalance alleviated by the innovative Dutch Kingdom Statute of 1954, which gave the colonies direct representation in the Dutch cabinet and parliament as an autonomous state.

However, a strong separatist movement grew up in Aruba and the island finally broke away in 1986, forming its own parliamentary democracy with a status equal to the rest of the Netherland Antilles. In 2008, the Netherlands Antilles was formally disbanded, primarily due to Curaçao's

national politics with economic support from France, which has tempered the development of significant separatist movements. In 1974 their status improved when they became *régions* giving them more administrative power.

New nations

The new nation states saw the rise of a new and more modern government. Local trained civil servants replaced the colonial "expatriate" administrative staff. Also, there was the increasing involvement of the state in the economic sectors. Some industries were nationalized, and governments became majority shareholders in others. For example, in Trinidad, thanks to the oil boom of the 1970s, the government became involved in many different commercial enterprises. Such changes reflected and expressed wider socio-economic and cultural changes.

With the growth of industrialization and modernization – electronics in Barbados, oil refining in St Croix – came the expansion of the tourist industry. Many of the new states acquired their own national airlines – an insignia of national pride – like British West Indian Airways (BWIA) in Trinidad (now Caribbean Air-

PEDAL POWER

"The small Antillean countries have become bicycle economies with Cadillac tastes."

– W.H. BRAMBLE, CHIEF MINISTER OF MONTSERRAT (1961–1970)

influence has permeated the region, particularly the English-speaking islands, not only in obvious economic fashion but also in the more subtle and pervasive social and cultural fashion.

The modern US-style shopping malls and supermarkets that have appeared on the islands, usually next to the cruise ship docks, have helped Americanize practically every aspect of life in the Caribbean. US radio and television add to this saturation of American-style attitudes and behavior patterns.

lines) and the Leeward Islands Air Transport (LIAT). New education systems were founded, like the regional University of the West Indies (UWI) with main campuses in Jamaica, Trinidad, and Barbados. Privately owned condominiums, tracts of middle-class housing, and public-housing projects were also built. But modernity had its price as it caused a vast movement of rural depopulation with people flocking to the towns in search of a better standard of living.

Americanization has also been a major factor in the modernization of the Caribbean. The US

LEFT: Antigua and Barbuda celebrate independence.
ABOVE: one of LIAT's island-hopping planes.

Fresh challenges

Like their sister islands farther north, the Lesser Antilles are facing problems often linked with modern life. On some islands money and politics have mixed to encourage an element of government corruption: an ex-prime minister of Dominica was convicted of a plot (backed by South Africa), to overthrow the elected government of his successor; a top cabinet minister in Trinidad had to flee to Panama after being accused of making money on a race-course complex project; and a leading member of Antigua's former ruling family, the Birds, was embroiled in gun running and drug dealing.

The money involved in such scandals often

originates from international drug rings, arms merchants and organized crime syndicates. Thus, the small-island politician is entrapped in a world of high-stakes intrigue which he is ill-equipped to deal with.

Private lives, public secrets

Admittedly, there have been political leaders of high caliber, such as Grantley Adams and Errol Barrow in Barbados and Dr Eric Williams and A.N.R. Robinson in Trinidad and Tobago. But in the small islands, the politician can manipulate a system in which personal charisma is sometimes more important than ideology. Power can be obtained by a system in which votes are exchanged for favors and thus an elaborate network of family, friends and job-holders is held together by patronage. Since government is the main employer, the plums are jobs in the local civil service.

It is a kind of market-square politics that emphasizes crowd oratory. In this kind of political arena, private lives become public secrets. In Trinidad it is called *picong, mauvais langue,* robber talk. To listen to its most skilled practitioners at a Caribbean political meeting is to understand the Caribbean gift for talk, its spirit of ribald irreverence, its street defiance of the high and mighty, which is all pulled together in the famous Trinidadian calypso form.

The effects of big business

With economic development, an affluent middle class has emerged; and the basic standards of living, in housing, education and health, has improved immeasurably. But consumerist tastes have evolved through American movies, television and tourism, which can hardly be satisfied in these underdeveloped societies. It has generated expectations that cannot be realized.

Errol Barrow, the first prime minister of an independent Barbados, said that the high cost of living was not the problem but the cost of high living. Absolute standards of life have improved, but the gap between rich and poor still grows.

This is not helped by the tourist industry. From the Virgins to the ABC islands, the landscape is dotted with luxury resorts owned by overseas hotel chains offering all-inclusive vacations where everything can be paid for at home, meaning little revenue goes into the islands' pockets. At the same time, they drain local agriculture, because the average worker prefers to be a maid or a bartender in the hotels rather than remain on the land.

Worst of all, development by import capital has increased the structural dependency of the region's economy upon international capital from multinational companies. Some of them seek cheap labor, others – like the pharmaceutical companies – freedom from environmental legislation at home. Others – especially in high finance – set up offshore operations for worldwide business. These situations become hazardous when a small island becomes host to a single industry. In 1984, for example, major oil companies, such as Exxon, evacuated Aruba and Curaçao, devastating the islands' economies.

GREEN GOLD

Bananas are the perfect crop for the small Caribbean farmer. They take only six months to grow, are happy on steep hillsides and fruit all year round, providing a steady cash income. Even a hurricane is not a disaster, as bananas can be quickly replanted and harvested. So it is little wonder that they have been celebrated as the farmer's "green gold".

Nonetheless, with the decline of the industry as a result of the EU's termination of preferential trade deals and fierce competition from US producers, farmers have been known to turn to another green gold – marijuana.

The present situation

The years since the 1990s have not been kind to the region's beleagured small-island economies. Traditional export crops are increasingly threatened by competition from other parts of the world. The sugar industry, now confined to small parts of Barbados and Trinidad, is living on borrowed time, with subsidies all but disappeared as the EU reforms its Common Agricultural Policy. Also, changing dietary habits and the advent of sugar substitutes in the West has meant that "King Sugar" no longer rules.

SUGAR FREE

The advent of sugar substitutes in Europe and North America has meant that "King Sugar" no longer rules the Caribbean.

The region faces further competition from Latin American economies with the introduction of the Free Trade Area of the Americas in 2005, scrapping tariffs on goods exported into the US and vice versa. Free trade may also damage the region's precious manufacturing sector, making it vital to form their own common market in the future. Venezuela's programme, the Bolivarian Alternative for the Americas, has so far managed to entice only Dominica into its ranks, with a Petro-Caribe deal providing much needed finance.

Even more of a blow to small farmers is the crisis surrounding the region's banana industry. From the 1950s, smallholders in St Lucia, Dominica, St Vincent, and Grenada were guaranteed a market and stable prices thanks to preferential treatment by Britain and the EU. Complaints by the US and Latin American producers that the EU agreement was unfair led to a World Trade Organization (WTO) ruling, in 1997, that the EU system was illegal. Small growers cannot compete without protection against the big growers of Ecuador or Costa Rica.

LEFT: green gold of the Caribbean.
ABOVE: tourism is booming.

Most of the Caribbean is now firmly reliant on the tourist industry. Many islands are building on their few remaining tracts of undeveloped coastline in the search for foreign exchange – much to the consternation of the region's environmentalists – but alternative incomes are few and far between. The transhipment of South American cocaine remains an (albeit illegal) recourse for many of the region's urban gangs – with reach into business and political circles too – but with regional economic and legal integration through the Caribbean Community (CARICOM) more on the cards, cooperation in dealing with the region's major challenges and opportunities looks to provide solutions. ❑

A CARIBBEAN BLEND

The culture of the Lesser Antilles is bursting with vitality, all due to the
rich social mix of people living here that the French Antilleans call "créolité"

Almost everyone in the Caribbean islands is, in some sense, a stranger. Not just the tourists, of course, or the wealthy expatriate communities, European and North American, who have opted for a tropical idyll. But the "locals" who, although they and their ancestors may have been born in the Caribbean, are likely to have their roots in an entirely different continent.

The modern-day Caribbean is peopled by the descendants of African slaves, Indian and Chinese laborers, European colonists, and Middle Eastern traders. Even the indigenous Caribs originated from the great rivers and deltas of the South American mainland.

Many of today's people have ancestors who arrived in chains after being crammed into suffocating ships for weeks on end. The great majority came against their will, snatched from another life and brutally transplanted, like much of the flora and fauna of the West Indies, into a strange new world.

And yet their descendants have stayed and many have prospered. Slavery continues to cast a shadow over the region and is held responsible for all manner of economic and social problems, but the contemporary Caribbean wastes little time on nursing historic grudges. On the contrary, a strong and positive sense of identity, both national and regional, has grown out of past injustices, and most people look forward rather than back to a tortured history.

Creole mix

Caribbean societies are by their very nature a mix of different people and cultures. The word creole, originally referring to a European-descended settler born in the Americas, has come to signify this combination of cultural influences, blended into a distinctive whole. Languages, cooking, clothing, and architecture

PRECEDING PAGES: it's carnival time in St Lucia; whiling away the hours.
LEFT: making music.
RIGHT: Guadeloupe chic.

all carry the term, which, as in New Orleans, implies a highly spiced or highly colored fusion of ingredients.

The European factor

European influence has marked the Caribbean since the first Spanish expeditions, but in the

Eastern Caribbean the dominant nations were Britain, France and, to a lesser degree, Holland. Their imprint is still clearly to be seen in the cricket pitches of Barbados, the haute cuisine of Martinique, and in the gabled warehouses of Curaçao. But with the exception of a handful of left-over colonial outposts, the days of European rule are long gone, and it would be hard to see in any Caribbean territory a miniature imitation of the old metropolises.

Europeanness has merged into Africanness, the set of languages, customs, and beliefs that came to the Caribbean with the millions of slaves across the "middle passage". Surviving the culture shock of slavery and the imposition of colonial values, African influence is stubbornly omnipresent: in rural housing, agricultural techniques, food, music and dance, as well as belief systems such as the Yoruban Orisha or Shango faith, and the syncretic Spiritual Baptist (Shouter). In modern town centers, this heritage is not so obvious, but in fishing villages or farming communities it is unmistakable.

Asian influences

Add to this the sights, sounds and flavors of the Indian subcontinent, characterized by Hindu temples and prayer flags, and local variants on curry, and the creole mix begins to take shape.

Other ingredients are important too; more recent migrants from China, Madeira, and Africa have preserved elements of their respective culture, and few islands are without an influential group of Syrian or Lebanese-descended people. But perhaps most important is the constant contact with North America and its cultural exports.

In the French islands they have a word for it: *créolité*. It is what sets Caribbean people apart from other cultures, what makes island life distinctive and unique. It also implies that blending process, that ability to absorb influences and shape them into something different – it's a

dynamic process, one that never stops still, and one that perhaps accounts for the bursting vitality of the region's culture.

Creole tongue

Creole languages are widely spoken across the Caribbean and are a complex cocktail of linguistic elements. They all use West African grammatical structures and mostly European vocabulary. In Martinique and Guadeloupe (and to a lesser degree, St Lucia, Dominica, Grenada, and Trinidad), French

> **PAPIAMENTO**
>
> The common language of Aruba, Bonaire, and Curaçao, is papiamento – a combination of dialects with no fixed spelling – which is used for newspapers, books, and debates in parliament.

papiamento, spoken in some of the Dutch islands, but principally Curaçao. From there it spread more widely throughout the region via the men from many different islands who worked in the oil refineries. This language has had a magpie tendency to take words from wherever it could: Dutch, English, Spanish, Portuguese, and some African sources. The result can be baffling when heard but strangely familiar when seen in written form, especially if you know some Spanish. *Pan* means bread and *awa*

provides the basis for the local creole, with traces of English and Spanish. But don't expect to understand it even if your French is fluent.

Creole was spoken among slaves from widely differing backgrounds in Africa and so combines a multitude of different linguistic sources. Guadeloupean creole, for instance, contains the English-descended *kònbif* (corned beef) and *djòb* (job) as well as such African-inspired words as *koukou-djèdjè* (hide and seek) and *zanba* (devil).

Without doubt, the most eclectic creole is

LEFT: making friends in St John.
ABOVE: a model boat craftsman in St Lucia.

means water (*pan* and *agua* in Spanish), while *kaya* is not far from *calle* (street) or *aki* from *aqui* (here). The English speaker may recognize *motosaikel* (motorcycle).

A choice of worship

If linguistic ingenuity is a characteristic of Caribbean societies, then so too is religious feeling. Driving through small villages in Barbados or Antigua you would be excused for thinking that churches outnumbered potential parishioners. The profusion of church groups throughout the region is nothing short of spectacular, ranging from established Anglicans and Roman Catholics to the new generation of Pentecostals and other evangelical sects. Church-going on a Sunday morning is a serious business, as you'll soon notice from the sheer activity on country roads and village streets as people in their Sunday best head for their chosen service.

Religion, like language, is a living example of creole adaptability. The slave owners may have only half-heartedly imposed Christianity on their slaves, but they responded enthusiastically, soon creating an independent tradition of preaching and self-help. Many social institu-

it. Similar to Haitian voodoo practices, it can involve the use of magic spells and exotic potions either to cause harm to others or to seek cures for all sorts of problems. The obeahman or obeahwoman is still a figure who merits some considerable respect, not to say fear, in the community.

Back to Africa

Although originating in Jamaica, Rastafarianism has spread throughout the Lesser Antilles and is typical of the synthetic development of religious ideas.

tions – youth clubs, credit schemes, educational facilities – are intimately linked to the churches.

But Caribbean people have also given Christianity their own emphases and influences; in some cases religious practices from Africa were mixed in with the teachings of the testaments to produce local faiths. Trinidad's Shango, for instance, is a cult made up of African traditions blended with elements of Roman Catholic and Baptist Christianity.

In other cases, African belief systems have remained more or less unadulterated. Obeah, a form of sorcery originating in West African folklore, is still widely believed in throughout the islands, although few people will admit to

A mix of literal Old Testament reading and African mysticism, it seeks to right the wrongs suffered by black people across the world by reuniting them in the promised land of Ethiopia. Ras Tafari was the name of the late Emperor Haile Selassie (1892–1974) who is revered as a god by members of the movement. Not all of its adherents believe in a real return to Africa, but most are attracted by a lifestyle that is both rebellious toward authority and stringently devout to their cause.

The Indo-Caribbeans are also in evidence through their religion. In islands such as Trinidad and Guadeloupe, where indentured immigration was greatest after abolition, the landscape is dotted with Hindu temples, adorned with images of Krishna, Shiva, or Rama. Prayer flags flap limply outside village houses or amidst clumps of banana or bamboo, and Indian communities celebrate feast days, such as *Phagwa* and *Diwali*, with traditional music and dancing. Mosques add another dimension to the religious landscape.

LIFE IN THE SLOW LANE

Creole culture values freedom above all else – and freedom includes the right to live life at your own pace.

Living in harmony

It is a tribute to local tolerance that such a heady mix of religious faiths has rarely produced friction between differing practitioners. The established churches used to campaign against African religion, denigrating it as "superstition" or "black magic", but that is largely a thing of the past. The US-inspired evangelicals may be inclined to preach against obeah and its ilk, but their message is not widely followed.

This tolerance extends to many walks of life and may explain why the Eastern Caribbean islands, although poor and deprived by some definitions, have not witnessed the social strife that experts predicted in the transition toward independence. It is dangerous to generalize and stereotypes can be condescending, even when well-intentioned. Yet terms like "laid-back", known as "liming" on the islands, contain a grain of truth about local attitudes to life and personal relations, suggesting with some accuracy a general distaste for unnecessary stress and conflict. Some tourists have difficulty in adjusting to the slower pace of life in the Caribbean, detecting idleness in a measured approach to work in a tropical climate. The problem is largely theirs and their irritation is an unfortunate and mostly futile waste of energy. In the Caribbean, to be in a hurry is not necessarily considered a desirable attribute.

If the historically mixed peoples of the islands exhibit a common characteristic, it is probably this refusal to be hurried from a positive appreciation of life as it comes. Creole culture values freedom above all else – and freedom includes the right to live life at your own pace. Tolerance and respect for others are widely appreciated qualities, perhaps born from an innate understanding of how life once was without them. And they are readily extended to strangers, for here everybody knows what it is like to be a stranger. ❏

LEFT: school children in St Martin.
ABOVE: looking cool in St Vincent.

AND THE BEAT GOES ON

Caribbean music never stands still and the eastern islands, where fusion is a way of life, are among the most exciting musical regions in the world

Think of Caribbean music, and what do you come up with? Reggae would be an obvious first choice. Almost everybody can recognize the sound that took the world by storm in the 1970s with artists like Bob Marley and Peter Tosh and which is still a force to be reckoned with. And then what? Salsa became a phenomenon in the 1980s, with Cubans, Puerto Ricans, and mainland Latin Americans setting the pace. Then there's calypso and steel pan, the infectious good-time music that seems to evoke the region in its every note.

But these three totally different types of music are just the tip of an ever-growing musical iceberg. Leaving aside the bigger islands, such as Jamaica, Cuba, and Puerto Rico, even the smaller territories of the Lesser Antilles reveal an extraordinary diversity of styles and sounds that literally stretches from A to Z. In between Trinidad's aguinaldo and Martinique's zouk you'll find genres such as bélè (French islands), jing ping (Dominica), raggasoca (Barbados) and tambu (Dutch islands). And that's not to mention bouyon and parang.

Medley of influences

This baffling array of musical forms is testimony to the creativity and individuality of each Caribbean island. It also reminds us of the many different influences – linguistic as well as musical – which have left their mark on the region. European colonizers from Britain, France, and Spain brought their music and instruments with them, recalled today in dances such as the quadrille of Martinique and Guadeloupe. From Africa came the drum-based rhythms and tradition of collective participation that underlie almost all contemporary styles in the region. Indian migrants contributed distinctive instruments and harmonies, especially in multicultural Trinidad. More recently, American jazz, rock and roll, rap and hip hop

have been incorporated and adapted into local forms, together with everything else from Latin brass sections to Country & Western.

Caribbean music never stands still. Constantly borrowing and developing, it keeps pace with technological advances while remaining rooted in age-old traditions. In a region where

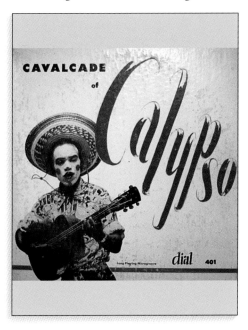

so many cultural influences, good and bad, have been absorbed, fusion is a way of life. No wonder that the Caribbean has a reputation for being one of the most exciting musical regions in the world.

Steel pan – a by-product of oil

You'll hear steel pan throughout the region, but Trinidad justifiably claims not just to have invented it, but to be world leader in playing it. There are still arguments over who it was who first realized the musical potential of a discarded oil drum in the 1930s. But there is no dispute that rhythm and percussion were already well established on the island. Predecessors included

---

PRECEDING PAGES: making parang music in Trinidad.
LEFT: in with the swing.
RIGHT: a calypso record sleeve from the 1950s.

the tamboo bamboo orchestras, which pounded bamboo tubes on the ground or beat them with sticks (used instead of drums banned by the British colonials as they thought it would encourage rioting) at folk dances, funeral wakes and, of course, Carnival. Other percussionists resorted to biscuit tins, dustbins, and kitchen pots until the versatility of the imported oil drum, a feature of Trinidad's booming petroleum industry, was discovered.

To begin with, steel pan and its players suffered a serious image problem. Associated with the slum areas of Port-of-Spain and tainted by regular violence, as gangs formed around competing bands to fight turf wars among themselves and against the police. It was only with the advent of corporate sponsorship and the commercialization of Carnival that the violence subsided. With the threat of companies withdrawing band sponsorship, a degree of peace broke out, and the previously violent rivalry subsumed into Panorama, the annual national steelband competition.

Calypso – voice of the people

The calypsonian was – and still is – the people's orator. In post-Emancipation times, as people flocked to the city in search of jobs and away

PARANG – A CHRISTMAS TRADITION

The build-up to Christmas in Trinidad wouldn't be the same without the Afro-Spanish tradition known as parang (from the Spanish *parar*, meaning "to stop at" or "put up at somebody's house"). The music is named after the roving performers who would move from house to house at the festive season with violins, cuatros, mandolins, guitars and maracas, along with the African-descended box drum and box bass.

Deeply traditional in form, the styles include Spanish names such as *aguinaldo, galerón*, or *paseo* and are largely descended from the carol singing of 18th- and 19th-century Spanish settlers.

from the plantation, the calypsonian took on the traditional role of the chantwell, the improvising vocalist who used to sing boasting and comic songs during rural stick-fighting sessions. His function involved the dissemination of gossip, the spreading of news, and the mocking of those in authority. By the early 20th century, his performances were taking place in special tents, in front of discerning audiences who judged the artist's topicality and originality.

Today, little has changed, although there are now female performers, and subjects such as feminism and domestic abuse provide up-to-date inspiration. The calypsonian's armory contains spontaneous improvisation, wit and picong (biting, literally piquant, observations). His (or her) songs may be narrative, oratorical, or extemporaneous, but it's likely they'll focus on sex, scandal, and what is known as "bacchanal".

Calypso is part of Trinidad's cultural lifeblood, which permeates through the whole of the Caribbean, and the climax comes each year at Carnival – or Crop Over in Barbados – which provides the background for fierce competition, lucrative prizes, and front-page head-

> ## A CALYPSONIAN IS...
>
> "...not only an articulator of the population, he is also a fount of public opinion. He expresses the mood of the people, the beliefs of the people."
>
> – MIGHTY CHALKDUST, Trinidadian teacher and Calypso Monarch

calypso into a more modern, danceable form which appealed to younger generations.

And the musical evolution continues to gain momentum with the creation of raggasoca, the fusion of Jamaican dancehall and local soca.

Ceremonial tuk

One thriving aspect of Barbados's annual Crop Over festival (historically held to mark the end of the cane-cutting season) is the tuk band. These percussive outfits are believed to date

lines. Trinidad's hall of fame includes legends such as Roaring Lion, Attila the Hun, and Lord Kitchener. The Mighty Sparrow is a Grenadian by birth, while Arrow, the singer of the 1980s' worldwide hit *Hot Hot Hot*, is from Montserrat.

That song, in fact, is actually more soca than calypso, a faster-paced, dance-oriented style that has evolved from the fusion of Afro and Indian influences within the Trinidadian music scene (the word "soca" was originally "so-kah" – letters of the Hindi alphabet). Soca turned

FAR LEFT: Barbadian calypsonian Red Plastic Bag.
LEFT: old oil drums are still used as steel pans.
ABOVE: brass is integral to soca, Carnival party music.

from as far back as the 17th century and later accompanied the island's local friendly societies, known as "landships", in ceremonies and outings. They are also thought to have modeled themselves on the marching bands of 18th-century British regiments.

Today's tuk band is made up of bass, snare and kettle drums, a penny whistle or flute, and usually a triangle. Despite what might seem at first to be a limited musical range, the bands' versatility is amazing and is often shown off in a wide repertoire of songs, covering the spectrum from European classical pieces to negro spirituals and current *Billboard* (Top Ten) hits.

But it is always the performance of original,

Caribbean-flavored material that brings out the best in the musicians, and thanks to the efforts of calypsonian Wayne "Poonka" Willcock and his group Ruk-a-Tuk International, tuk music has been staging something of a comeback in the mushrooming local festivals.

Begin the beguine...

The earliest authentic style to have come from Martinique and Guadeloupe is generally agreed to be the beguine, its bolero rhythm a firm favorite among dance orchestras from the 1930s to the 1950s. Over the following two decades, the French Antillean soundscape underwent significant changes due to migration and freshly imported influences. An important new ingredient was brought by Haitian immigrants in the form of kadans or "cadence", a subtle blend of musical accents, syncopation and instrumental color derived from the fast-paced merengue, the national dance music of the neighboring Dominican Republic.

From kadans evolved zouk in the 1980s, a genre which was less a fad than a true phenomenon, reaching beyond the confines of the Caribbean to touch the continents of Africa, America and Europe. Zouk trailblazers were the Guadeloupean band Kassav, whose founders,

ROUND-UP OF MUSIC FESTIVALS

Many islands stage music festivals in addition to annual Carnival celebrations *(see pages 282–83)*:

January Barbados Jazz Festival, St Croix Blues Festival; St Barths Music Festival (classic, folk, jazz)

February Mustique Blues Festival

March St Patrick's Day Festival, St Croix

April Holders Season, Barbados (opera); Maroon Music Festival, Carriacou; Plymouth Jazz Festival, Tobago

May St Lucia Jazz Festival; Big Drum Festival, Union Island; Gospel Fest, Barbados; Curaçao Jazz Festival; Curaçao Merengue Festival; Rapso Month, Trinidad; Spice Jazz Festival, Grenada; Aruba Soul Beach Music Festival

June St Kitts Music Festival; Aruba Jazz and Latin American Music Festival

July BVI Summer Festival (calypso); Gwoka Drum Festival, Guadeloupe

August Curaçao Salsa Festival; Pic-o-De-Crop Calypso Finals, Barbados

October St Croix Jazz and Caribbean Music Festival; Antigua Jazz Festival; World Creole Music Festival, Dominica;

November Curaçao Golden Artists Music Festival; Guadeloupe Creole Music Festival

December Carriacou Parang Festival; International Jazz Festival, Martinique; St Lucia Kalalu World Music Festival.

Pierre-Edouard Décimus and Jacob Devarieux, captured the festive mood and euphoria that marked the local *vidé* (spontaneous street carnival parade) and integrated old-style rhythmic dance elements into a modern good-time sound.

The success of Kassav and others marked the entry of French Caribbean music into the international marketplace. It also offered an original, rather than borrowed, model, including a long overdue emphasis on women's voices, that appeals not

A MUSICAL LEGACY

The late Trinidadian composer, Andre Tanker, was considered to be one of the great unsung musicians of the 20th century. His style influenced the island's modern rock groups such as Orange Sky and Jointpop.

serving popular Windward Caribbean Kulture (WCK) is a band specializing in bouyon, an eclectic mix of cadence-lypso and traditional jing ping, resulting in a compelling cocktail of pulsating drums *à la digital* and keyboards.

Jazz fusions

The Afro-American art form of jazz has also found a home in the Caribbean, to be mixed into the melting-pot of influences. Some 30 jazz festivals take place in the region each year, while

only to the Caribbean as a whole, but to aficionados of dance music from all over the world.

Sandwiched between French/Creole-speaking Martinique and Guadeloupe, the island of Dominica has long been influenced culturally and musically by the two French *départements*. But even if its rhythms are similar to those of its Gallic neighbors, there has still been room for innovation. Dominican cadence-lypso, commonly referred to as kadans, fuses Haitian konpa dance music with calypso, and the island's long-

LEFT: Monty Alexander is popular at jazz festivals.
ABOVE: Kassav, a Guadeloupean zouk band, has found international success.

local musicians have tirelessly experimented with a variety of fusions which embrace New Orleans rhythms and their own distinctively Caribbean flavors.

Notable jazz exponents from the Lesser Antilles who can be seen at many of the festivals include St Lucia's Luther François, a gifted saxophonist and one of the region's leading jazz composers; Barbadian saxophonist Arturo Tappin who merges jazz with reggae; "Professor" Ken Philmore (Trinidad) who plays steel pan jazz; Nicholas Brancker (Barbados) who plays funk/jazz bass and keyboard; and Trinidadian Clive Zanda who performs jazz inspired by calypso and folk music. ❑

PASSION AND POETRY

The Lesser Antilles has a rich literary tradition – albeit a relatively young one, because for centuries stories and poems were passed down by word of mouth

"Love for an island is the sternest passion: pulsing beyond the blood through roots and loam" – Phyllis Allfrey, Dominica

The islands of the Eastern Caribbean inspire passion and poetry in equal measure. And in impressive quantity. Few parts of the world can have produced so many top-class writers from so small a population. Although many of them today live in self-imposed exile, the landscapes, language and people of the islands fill their work with the unmistakable flavor of their home.

Yet literature is a relatively late arrival in the Caribbean. The great Barbadian novelist George Lamming was guilty of only slight exaggeration when he said in the 1960s that Caribbean writing was just 20 years old. However, there has, of course, always been plenty written about the region – from the 17th century, priests, merchants and other itinerant observers sent back their impressions of island life to be replaced in the 19th century by travel writers who invariably made their trip "down the islands" with a book in mind.

Early storytellers

But literature by local people was for a long time in short supply. Slavery, illiteracy and constant inter-colonial warfare were not ideal conditions for a thriving literary culture, while most slave owners or landlords were hardly bookish by inclination. Significantly, one of the earliest examples of Caribbean poetry is *Barbados* (1754) in which Nathaniel Weekes offers useful, if unromantic, advice to the island's planters: *"To urge the Glory of your Cane's success, Rich be your Soil, and well manur'd with Dung, Or, Planters! what will your Labours yield?"*

The culture of the slaves was oral rather than written, and their tales, riddles and proverbs were handed down by storytellers in spoken

form. Since slave-owning societies actively discouraged the formal education of the black majority, it was hardly surprising that few books were read, let alone written.

Even after emancipation, the Lesser Antilles lagged behind larger territories like Cuba or Haiti in literary output. The small islands

lacked publishers, bookshops, and libraries and, above all, a reading public. Amidst widespread poverty and lack of education, only occasional clerics or dilettantes put pen to paper, but their poetry tended to be little more than tropical adaptations of well-worn European conventions.

One remarkable exception to the rule was John Jacob Thomas, a self-educated black Trinidadian. In 1888, Thomas read *The English in the West Indies*, which was a study of British colonialism in the Caribbean by the eminent Oxford professor, James Anthony Froude. Incensed by Froude's patronizing and prejudiced view of black society, Thomas wrote a devastating riposte, *Froudacity: West Indian Fables*

LEFT: Nobel Prize-winner Derek Walcott.
RIGHT: George Lamming explored his Barbadian childhood in *In the Castle of my Skin*.

Explained (1889), in which he accused the pompous professor of "fatuity" and "skinpride".

On the literary map

Several factors coalesced in the 1940s and 1950s to put the region on the literary map. World War II and the immediate post-war years witnessed a massive increase in migration and mobility as islanders seized work opportunities in Europe and the US. Young men like Lamming and Trinidadians V.S. Naipaul (knighted in 1990 and Nobel Literature Laureate in 2001)

> **GUADELOUPE**
>
> "And yet it was a land of verdant hills and clear waters, beneath a sun every day more radiant."
> – SIMONE SCHWARZ-BART
> *(Between Two Worlds)*

and Samuel Selvon found themselves in London, exposed to a range of new influences. It may have been cold and hostile (as comically described in Selvon's masterpiece, *The Lonely Londoners*, 1956), but it had publishers and literary reviews eager for fresh material.

Other would-be writers from the English-speaking islands went to New York or Montreal, while those from Martinique and Guadeloupe reveled in the cultural ferment of post-war Paris. From these experiences of self-imposed exile emerged some of the enduring themes of Caribbean literature: identity, rootlessness, nostalgia, the bitter-sweet reality of returning home.

This period was also one of political and cultural revaluation as the islands moved toward independence or greater autonomy, creating a sense of nationalism, of regional identity, long suppressed by colonialism. Fast disappearing were the days when schoolchildren would have to write essays entitled *A Winter's Day*, and writers began to find a distinctive, Caribbean voice. Often this voice was satirical, mocking the colonial system and values which had dominated for centuries. The title of Barbadian Austin Clarke's memoir, *Growing Up Stupid Under the Union Jack* (1980) is typical of the anti-colonial genre.

Home-grown talent

As writers and intellectuals reassessed their mixed cultural heritage, the beginnings of a local literary establishment emerged. Most early authors were published in London or New York, but a handful of literary journals such as *Bim*, founded in Barbados in 1942, began to publish the work of home-grown talent. The 1950s was the decade in which Caribbean literature finally established itself overseas. Three novels created international reputations for their authors and set out some of the principal themes and attitudes which were to follow in much more fiction.

Lamming's *In the Castle of My Skin* (1953) explored the decline of British colonialism in Barbados and the awakening of new aspirations within a small rural community. Selvon's *The Lonely Londoners* (1956) followed a group of Trinidadian emigrants to Britain and the ensuing culture shock they endured. Naipaul's *The Mystic Masseur* (1957) painted a bitter-sweet picture of incompetence and pretentiousness in colonial Trinidad. Each novel, in its own way, dissected the legacy of British rule and the question of contemporary Caribbean identity.

The smaller English-speaking territories started producing top-rank literature in the 1970s and 1980s with work by Derek Walcott (St Lucia), Edward "Kamau" Brathwaite (Barbados), Jamaica Kincaid (Antigua), Earl Lovelace (Trinidad), and Caryl Phillips (St Kitts).

Official recognition came in the 1990s for two authors, whose work is rooted in the region. In 1992, Derek Walcott received the Nobel Prize for Literature, in tribute to his long and productive career as a poet and playwright. In 1990, his magnificent *Omeros*, a reworking of the Homeric legend amidst a fishing community in St Lucia, had confirmed his status as one of the world's leading poets. The previous year, the Martinican novelist Patrick Chamoiseau had won the Prix Goncourt for his complex novel *Texaco*, a sought-after sign of approval from the Parisian intellectual establishment.

Vibrant French literary scene

The literary productivity of two of the French overseas regions – Martinique and Guadeloupe – is as impressive as that of their Anglophone neighbors. The white Guadeloupean poet St-John Perse won the Nobel Prize for Literature in 1960 (although it is generally known he disliked his island of birth), while Martinique's Aimé Césaire wrote the trail-blazing surrealist epic, *Return to My Native Land* in 1939.

Nowadays, thanks to first-world levels of education and opportunity, the two islands enjoy a vibrant literary scene which is taken more and more seriously by the big Parisian publishers. Interestingly, many of the most prominent novelists from Martinique and Guadeloupe are women, who mix specifically female themes into the wider theme of French/Caribbean identity – Maryse Condé, Simone Schwarz-Bart, and Gisèle Pineau are three of the better known.

Influences from abroad

There are some common themes in the region's writing. Many Caribbean authors continue to examine the relationship, both positive and negative, between the islands and the old European powers. The reclamation of African identity has also been a pervasive theme, as shown in Earl Lovelace's novel, *Salt*, which won the Commonwealth Writers' Prize in 1997.

The influence of the US, from tourists to CNN, is another widespread motif as writers struggle to define what is culturally distinctive about their homelands. In this context, language itself is an important issue, and many authors are keen to highlight the richness of local Creole or patois. In the French islands, in particular, writers such as Chamoiseau and Raphaël Confiant have championed their expressive Creole against the dominance of "official" French.

US TV soaps feature prominently in *Tide*

Running, an unsettling study of sexploitation in Tobago by Grenadian-based Oonya Kempadoo.

The modern Caribbean writer is above all aware of the fragility of his or her island home in an age of mass tourism and rampant development. In accepting his Nobel Prize, Walcott spoke of a way of life threatened by such progress: "How quickly it could all disappear! And how it is beginning to drive us further into where we hope are inpenetrable places, green secrets at the end of bad roads, headlands where the next view is not of a hotel but of some long beach without a figure and the hanging question of some fisherman's smoke at its far end." ❏

THE BRIDGE OF BEYOND
Simone Schwarz-Bart

Two of a Kind

The small, mountainous island of Dominica is the birthplace of two celebrated novelists, both women from white families.

After a notoriously Bohemian career in 1930s Europe, Jean Rhys disappeared until her book *Wide Sargasso Sea* (1966) became a cult classic. Its eerie atmosphere of tropical menace and madness bears some resemblance to the decadent island world described in *The Orchid House* (1953) by Phyllis Allfrey. Although of the same generation, the two women never met (Rhys only returned to Dominica once) but they corresponded extensively.

LEFT: Trinidad's V.S. Naipaul wrote from London.
RIGHT: Simone Schwarz-Bart uses female themes.

CREOLE CUISINE

Between American fast-food joints and the international haute cuisine of the big hotels there is the delicious food of the Caribbean to be enjoyed

As the word creole generally means "born in the islands but originating from the outside world", it seems an appropriate collective name for the region's home cooking, given its history. However, despite the common thread uniting the creole cuisine of the islands, the miles of water that separate them, along with their diverse historic influences from the outside world, ensure that the food of each one is usually quite distinct and often unique.

The common thread is provided by the region's rich Amerindian and African heritage; the readily available fresh produce of the fertile land, with its year-round growing season; and the abundance of superb seafood from the surrounding Caribbean Sea and Atlantic Ocean. Meanwhile, the wonderful variation within the styles of cuisine has been created by the diversity of the European countries that colonized the islands, the introduction of indentured labour from the east, and the wide range of differing topography throughout the region.

Fresh from land and sea

When the European settlers started arriving, there was already some wild game on the islands, such as agouti, iguana, deer, hogs, land tortoises and guinea pigs, and they added chickens, cattle, sheep and pigs. Today, people in the country are still happy to run a small farm or raise their "stocks" on whatever pasture is available. On land the swamps and rivers can supply crabs and crayfish, but the best and most plentiful source of protein is the fish and other seafood which abounds in the ocean.

Caribbean seafood can be rated as some of the best in the world. As a result of the generally short distance from the sea to the table, it is served particularly fresh, contributing to its intense flavor. Grouper, barracuda, kingfish, swordfish, sea bream, jacks, parrotfish, snapper, tuna, albacor, bonito and dolphin are the

names of fish most heard of in these islands. Dolphin (also called dorado and mahi mahi) is an ugly, scaly fish not to be confused with the friendly mammal which is known as a porpoise, often referred to as a dolphin. Flying fish are only widely served in Barbados, where the intricate skill of deboning them has been perfected

and passed on down the generations.

The Caribbean waters also contain plenty of sea crab, spiny lobster, conch (sometimes called lambis) with their large beautiful shells, sea egg (sea urchin), octopus and, in the south, very large shrimp, also referred to as "giant prawns". The end result of this exciting array of fresh ingredients, prepared in a variety of tantalizing ways, is an exotic culinary extravaganza.

A culinary legacy

Foods that can be traced back to the Amerindians, are still found throughout the islands. Pepperpot stew, a mixture of meats, vegetables and hot peppers, cooked in black cassava juice

---

PRECEDING PAGES: flying fish for lunch.
LEFT: pick up a lobster in Grand Case, St Martin.
RIGHT: fresh island produce goes into the best meals.

(casareep), a natural preservative, was originally a means of preserving the hunter's bounty. Once brought to the boil daily, it will not go off. Even in this day and age, some establishments and households keep a pepperpot on the stove for months, in a traditional pottery *coneree*, adding in fresh ingredients as required. Pepperpot soup, freshly made with vegetables, such as okra, pumpkin and yam, has only been slightly modified since the Amerindian days with the introduction of imported salt meat.

Another favourite of the Amerindians, and still a popular snack, was roasted corn. The husk is removed and the corn is cooked over an open fire until it is completely black. It was in fact these highly self-sufficient people who gave the world the barbecue, derived from their word *barbacoa* meaning cooking over a fire.

The Amerindians also made delicious bread from cassava and corn. Fresh bread made with bran and wheat flour is the most common staple and can be smelled baking in the early morning in virtually every village and town.

An African inheritance

The African slaves were given by their masters rations of rice, imported salt cod, salt meat, and dried peas and beans on which to feed and

A FAIR EXCHANGE

In the early days of colonization and exploration, there was a tremendous exchange of horticulture and agriculture around the world. While the Caribbean gave the world the pineapple, pepper, cashew, avocado, runner bean, potato, sweet potato and tomato, to name some of the more famous produce indigenous to the region, the outside world returned the favor with many of the fruits, vegetables and herbs that are now frequently associated with this area – such as mango, lime, orange, banana, coffee, sugar cane, pigeon pea, yam, okra, nutmeg, cinnamon, clove, ginger, shallots, thyme, parsley and coconuts.

nourish themselves. They were also given small plots of land to grow produce to supplement their meagre fare. From this paltry larder came the basis of the delicious food served today. Every island has its own recipe for rice and peas, which is usually made with salt beef or pork and fresh herbs such as shallots and thyme. Fish cakes consisting of salt fish, flour, a variety of pepper and herbs, dipped in batter and deep fried, have an irresistible aroma.

To season their food, slaves grew thyme, marjoram, mint, sage, rosemary, shallots and peppers. Today, every island has its own "seasoning" made from finely chopped herbs, onions, garlic and pepper; and each one offers its own version of a fiercely hot pepper sauce, which should be sampled with caution.

Chicken, roasted, fried or stewed; roast pork, garlic pork, pickled pig's head, tail and trotters, pork stew, whole suckling pig roasted on a spit and ham has always been popular weekend and celebration fare – not a piece of the pig is spared. All the islands prepare variations of black pudding made from pigs intestine stuffed with the blood mixed with sweet potato and seasoning.

GRAPEFRUIT

Although most citrus came from the Pacific region, the grapefruit was conceived in Barbados in the 18th century. It is a cross between a sweet orange and a large, bitter citrus fruit called a shaddock, brought over from Polynesia by a Captain Shaddock.

starch such as rice or yam, to which is added any vegetables, seasonings, fish, meat or chicken that the cook can find to make a tasty and nutritious meal. As a result of the ingenius use of herbs and spices, stews in the Caribbean tend to be full of flavor.

An interesting observation about Caribbean cuisine is that the Amerindians, when first encountered by Europeans, were preparing many foods in exactly the same way as some West Africans thousands of

One pot cook ups

With most of the cooking being done over an open fire, usually with only one pot, many recipes developed for "one pot meals" which included a large variety of tasty soups such as split pea soup, callaloo soup made from eddoe leaves and crab, pumpkin soup, fish soup, peanut soup, and a "big soup" that you can stand the spoon up in, made with an assortment of root crops and fresh vegetables. Other one pot meals known as cook ups are based on a

LEFT: limes are an important ingredient in these dishes.
ABOVE: with a restaurant by the sea, a chef has no problem wondering what to cook.

miles across the Atlantic Ocean. For example, cou-cou or fungi – ground corn, boiled up with okras and mashed into a thick paste – is an indigenous dish of both the Caribbean and Africa. Still enjoyed today, it's usually served with a pungent salt fish, fresh fish or beef stew.

Caribbean sweet tooth

Since the 17th century when the European settlers set about planting sugar cane, the Caribbean people have developed a very "sweet tooth" blending the sought-after resulting product with island fruits to create such delicacies as tamarind balls, guava cheese, coconut sugar cakes, toolum, comforts and shaddock rind –

unique candies that have been prepared for generations of children. The preserves of lime and orange marmalade, guava jelly, nutmeg jelly, chutney and fruit jams are of a very high quality because the golden crystals of Caribbean sugar are bursting with tangy flavors.

Traditional desserts tend to come from a combination of British heritage and Caribbean style: bread 'n' butter pudding, rich fruit cake laced with rum, banana and coconut bread, jam

REFRESHING DRINKS

The abundance of fruit on the islands means that fresh fruit juices are served everywhere: guava, mango and soursop are some of the most exotic. Mauby is a bitter-sweet drink made from tree bark, and sorrel is a traditional Christmas drink created from the dried bright red blossom of a type of hibiscus.

corruption of the Scottish dish haggis, was introduced to Barbados by the Scots when they were exiled there after the Monmouth Rebellion of 1685.

The Spanish, left Trinidad a delicious legacy of their favorite dishes: *pastelles* (meat and grated corn steamed in a banana leaf), *escoviche* (pickled fish), *buljol* (salt fish, tomato, lime, pepper, garlic and avocado), to name just a few. In later years, Indian and Chinese food was introduced to Trinidad by large

puffs, chocolate pudding and coconut turnovers. And restaurants everywhere include their own versions of the delicious coconut pie on their dessert menu.

European flavors

The islands generally have a very separate and distinct cuisine from each other, depending on who they were colonized by. The French brought their *pâtisserie* (pastries), stuffed crab back, tomato and herb fish stews reminiscent of Provence, escargots in garlic, and frogs' legs (coyly called mountain chicken in Dominica), Jug Jug, a Christmas dish of pigeon peas, guinea corn flour, salt meat and herbs, and a

numbers of immigrants from Asia, and the roti – a thick curry wrapped in a chapati – is now sold throughout the region, keeping the American burger joints on their toes. Trinidadian Chinese cooking has also evolved into a new and delicious style, modified by the use of different ingredients.

The Dutch islands enjoy an Indonesian flavor to their dishes due to the Netherlands' connections with the Far East. So the food of the Caribbean is as diverse as the origins of its people – a multitude of exotic flavors, all drawn from the sun-blessed, fertile land, the bountiful seas and the creative genius of generations of multi-ethnic cooks and chefs. ❑

Yo ho ho

Rum has long been associated with pirates, smugglers and sailors and featured in many a classic "Boys' Own" adventure story as barrels of the liquid gold were rolled on to British shores by the light of the full moon – duty free.

It didn't take long to discover that a forceful fiery liquor could be produced from sugar cane and in Barbados in the 1640s, the first batches of locally distilled spirits were introduced, or rather experienced! Referred to as "kill-devil" by the English Royalist refugee Richard Ligon in *A True and Exact History of the Island of Barbados* in 1657, the drink was strong and barely fit to drink; those who imbibed it quickly felt its effects, as Ligon wrote, "It lays them to sleep on the ground."

Or, too much of it ended in a "rumbullion", an old English word for a noisy brawl – hence the name rum. Another early visitor to Barbados wrote that "the chiefe fudling they make on the Island is Rumbullion, alias Kill Divill, and this is made of sugarcanes distilled, a hot, hellish and terrible liquor."

Rum is actually made from molasses, the thick, black treacle left after the juice from the sugar cane has crystalized. Spring water – in Barbados it is filtered through coral rock – is then added and it is left to ferment. After distilling, more fresh water is added to what is now a colorless liquid of almost 95 percent alcohol and it is poured into oak barrels to slowly mature; the best rum is stored for at least seven years. The golden color develops from the secret ingredients added by the master blender, which may include vanilla, almond extract, caramel or older types of rum combined with the smoked interior of the barrel. It remains colorless when kept for a short time in stainless steel barrels.

Many of the islands have their own rum factories with their own brand that they are fiercely proud of, for example, Barbados, where it all began, has Mount Gay and Cockspur; Trinidad has Old Oak and Vat 19, and Martinique produces several including Trois Rivières and St Clément.

For sailors in the British Royal Navy, rum was an important ingredient in their daily rations – it helped keep them upright in stormy seas and raised morale. But they were mighty upset in 1731 when Admiral Vernon ordered that the spirit be diluted with water. This concoction was disparagingly called a "grog" after the admiral whose nickname had been Old Grog because he always wore a cloak of a coarse material called grogram.

Since then rum has been diluted with a wide variety of juices and mixers creating wonderful cocktails and punches that are sipped in beach bars, by swimming pools and on verandahs all over the Caribbean. The word punch originates from India, another of Britain's former colonies: the Indian word *panch* means five for the drink's five ingredients: "*One of sour* (lime juice)/*two of sweet* (sugar syrup)/*three of strong* (rum)/*four of weak* (water)/*five dashes of* (Angostura) *bitters and nutmeg spice/serve well chilled with lots of ice.*"

In the rum shops on islands such as Trinidad and Barbados (where you will find one in most villages) rum is drunk neat or "on the rocks". A rum shop is not merely a bar; it is a village store, a community center, an arena for fiercely competitive domino-playing, a place where tongues are loosened, politics discussed and rumors spread. "Man, leh we fire one on that!" is the exhortation prompted by a happy event.

It is still largely the province of men: "Men in de rum shop; women in de church," so the saying goes. And Lord Byron may have been thinking along the same lines when he wrote, "*There's nought no doubt so much the spirit calms/as rum and true religion.*" ❑

LEFT: sea eggs, or urchins are a Caribbean delicacy.
RIGHT: bottling the liquid gold.

GINGERBREAD AND BALLAST BRICK

Caribbean architecture reveals influences from Amerindians, Africa and the European colonizers, from simple Kunuku cottages to Great Houses

When Columbus hit upon the West Indies at the end of the 15th century, the dwellings he found there were nothing compared to what he was used to in Europe, and he wrote to a friend that the " [Indians] *live in rocks and mountains, without fixed settlements, and not like ourselves."* In fact Amerindians and Caribs slept in round or oval-shaped huts built of sticks and covered with a conical roof made of palms or grass from swamps.

The first Europeans left on islands to set up trading posts, and then the settlers, copied these Indian shelters, but soon introduced wall construction with wooden beams and shingles for the roofs. However, even after Emancipation the slaves rarely built with stone, and single-roomed thatched houses with walls of clay and straw were still in use in the 20th century.

A MEDLEY OF STYLES

When the sugar trade to Europe started, many ships brought huge amounts of red brick and stone in their hulls as ballast. And wealthy planters and merchants on islands like Barbados or Antigua built their Great Houses with it. In Statia's heyday ballast was used for the warehouses on the waterfront. Several styles developed, the Spanish adopting Moorish traditions, while the French introduced cast iron and, later, the American invention of mechanical saws gave rise to the intricate wooden lacework – gingerbread – on many façades.

▷ **MAGNIFICENCE**
Stollmeyer's Castle (1904) is one of the "Magnificent Seven" examples of architectural opulence in Port of Spain, and was inspired by Scottish and German castles.

▷ **THE GREAT HOUSE**
Planters modeled their homes on European styles adapting them to suit the climate, with thick walls, shutters and verandahs.

△ **ADMIRAL'S RETREAT**
The two-story verandah on this naval retreat (1855) in Nelson's Dockyard, Antigua, still provides shade and protection from heavy rain.

△ **COLONIAL STYLE**
Many hotels, such as Divi Little Bay in St Maarten, are being built with a colonial touch and traditional decor in an attempt to complement their tropical surroundings.

▷ **GINGERBREAD TRIM**
At the beginning of the 20th century, English, American and Dutch-influenced islands decorated façades with delicately sawn wooden lacework.

CHATTEL HOUSES: MOBILE HOMES

For the black population of Barbados, mobility was once essential to survival. After Emancipation the planters had to employ labor and, still wanting to control the freed slaves, allowed them to establish small settlements on their land. This made the workers dependent on their employer's good will and they were rapidly chased off the land if there were any problems. So the chattel house was developed: a small wooden "sleeping box" easy to dismantle and take along on a cart to another plantation.

Supported by big rocks or concrete blocks so that rainwater can pass underneath, the one-room house with an optional partition inside is made up of wooden planks fixed to a framework. Makeshift steps lead up to the only door opening on to the family's living space. Here parents and children, and often grandparents as well, used to sleep in one room. The cooking was done outside, as was any entertaining of neighbors and friends.

This nucleus of a family home – with one or two extensions – is still a common sight in Barbados, especially in the more remote country districts, and only a few years ago a whole village moved from a hilltop to a valley, where running water was available.

▽ **KUNUKU**
A few of these traditional one-room farmhouses with very thick walls of clay and cut grass can still be seen in Curaçao's hinterland.

▷ **SEA BREEZES**
The clever construction of houses on hills to harness the cooling trade winds through airy verandahs and Italian shutters makes modern air conditioning superfluous.

▽ **NOTHING BUT THE BEST**
Dining tables made of large pieces of mahogany were the pride of wealthy planters and often sat 30, laid with English silverware and bone china, for dinner.

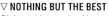

PLACES

A detailed guide to the entire Lesser Antilles, with principal sites clearly cross-referenced by number to the maps

At one time just getting to these tropical islands was an adventure; now the adventure can start on arrival. Whether you are cruising "down the islands" on an ocean liner, sailing between them on a yacht, or you have picked out one or two just to spend some time relaxing on, there is plenty to explore – under the sea, on the coasts, in the rainforests of the mountainous interiors, and around the streets of their tiny capitals.

Each island has a character of its own and conveys a different mood. With tourism the mainstay of their economies, their natural assets are available, sometimes controversially, for the benefit of the visitor. In the US Virgin Islands, St John is peaceful and dedicated to nature, whereas St Thomas only a few miles away is bustling and vigorous. Miniscule St-Barths is as chic as the Left Bank in Paris; Barbados still upholds the English tradition of afternoon tea. Tiny St Martin, ruled peacefully by two European nations, offers a frenetic nightlife on one side of the border in contrast to gourmet dining and quiet beaches on the other. Trinidad is host to one of the greatest street parties on earth, as is St Lucia to a major music festival and Barbados to a season of opera. Aruba extends a welcoming arm to gamblers.

The surrounding warm waters provide perfect conditions for sailing; all kinds of water sports, from windsurfing off the Atlantic shores to waterskiing in the calm Caribbean bays; and diving around the dramatic coral reefs and shipwrecks.

The terrain is equally diverse. One island has a salt lake, another a pitch lake and mountainous, rainforested Dominica has a boiling lake. What tiny and steeply vertical Saba lacks in beaches it makes up for in underwater scenery, whereas flat and arid Anguilla has an astonishing number of beaches.

Quite simply, you never know what to expect, not only from island to island, but past the next bend on their narrow roads. And that is one of the true pleasures of the Lesser Antilles. ❑

PRECEDING PAGES: farmers in Guadeloupe; Diamond Rock in Martinique offers a great view whilst relaxing; beach life in Barbados.
LEFT: the calm and charm of Cinnamon Bay, US Virgin Islands.

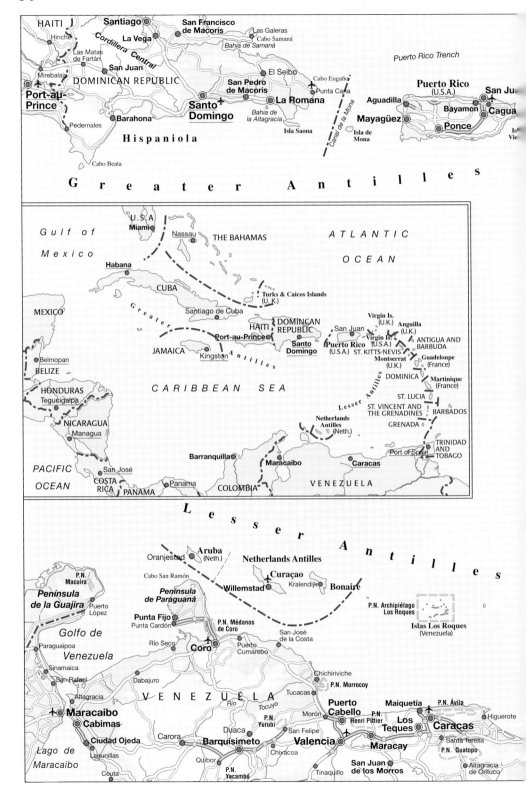

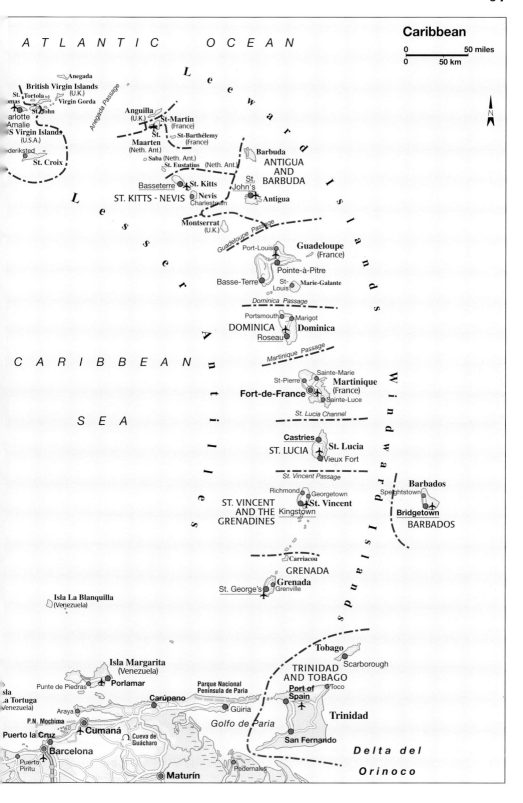

Caribbean

0   50 miles
0   50 km

A T L A N T I C   O C E A N

N

Anegada

British Virgin Islands (U.K.)

St. Tortola   Virgin Gorda

Anegada Passage

L e e w a r d   I s l a n d s

St. John

arlotte
Amalie
S Virgin Islands (U.S.A.)

eriksted

St. Croix

Anguilla (U.K.)

St-Martin (France)

St. Maarten (Neth. Ant.)

St-Barthélemy (France)

Saba (Neth. Ant.)

St. Eustatius (Neth. Ant.)

Barbuda

ANTIGUA AND BARBUDA

Basseterre   St. Kitts

ST. KITTS - NEVIS   Nevis
Charlestown

St. John's

Antigua

Montserrat (U.K.)

Guadeloupe Passage

L e s s e r

Port-Louis

Guadeloupe (France)

Pointe-à-Pitre

Basse-Terre   St-Louis   Marie-Galante

Dominica Passage

Portsmouth   Marigot

DOMINICA   Dominica
Roseau

Martinique Passage

C A R I B B E A N

A n t i l l e s

Sainte-Marie

St-Pierre   Martinique (France)
Fort-de-France   Sainte-Luce

S E A

St. Lucia Channel

Castries
ST. LUCIA   St. Lucia
Vieux Fort

W i n d w a r d   I s l a n d s

St. Vincent Passage

Barbados

Richmond   Georgetown   Speightstown
ST. VINCENT AND THE GRENADINES   St. Vincent
Kingstown   Bridgetown

BARBADOS

Carriacou

GRENADA

St. George's   Grenada
Grenville

Isla La Blanquilla (Venezuela)

Tobago
Scarborough

Isla Margarita (Venezuela)
Punte de Piedras   Porlamar

TRINIDAD AND TOBAGO

Parque Nacional Península de Paria

Port of Spain   Toco

Carúpano

Güiria

sla
La Tortuga (Venezuela)

Araya

P.N. Mochima

Puerto la Cruz

Cumaná

Cueva de Guácharo

Trinidad

Golfo de Paria

Barcelona

San Fernando

Puerto Píritu

Pedernales

Maturín

D e l t a   d e l

O r i n o c o

THE US VIRGIN ISLANDS

Cruising, sailing, diving, beautiful beaches, and a national park teeming with wildlife – the US Virgin Islands, or USVI, have them all, shared between St Thomas, St John and St Croix

Map on pages 92–3

G reen volcanic islands peer from the never-ending blues of the Caribbean for as far as the eye can see, their submerged feet concealing a vast underwater landscape. No one knows for certain how many islands there are but Christopher Columbus, on his second voyage of discovery in 1493, felt there were too many to count and named them after the 11,000 martyred virgins in the legend of St Ursula. However many there are, the United States of America has 68 of them, amounting to 136 sq. miles (352 sq. km) and Britain has around 50 (*see pages 105–113*).

Situated at the top of the Lesser Antilles chain, only three of the USVI are inhabited: St Thomas (pop. 55,000) is the most developed and can have up to eight cruise ships visiting on some days; neighboring St John (pop. 5,000) is the smallest and least developed, as it is mainly taken up by a national park; St Croix (pop. 50,000), 40 miles (64 km) to the southwest, is the largest of the three but is poorer and more tranquil than St Thomas. When sugar-cane production bowed out of the economy in the 1960s, the US started developing the islands' potential as a "holiday paradise" for Americans, and today more than two million visitors descend on them every year, the majority arriving by cruise ship or under sail – only just over a third fly in.

St Thomas, with USVI capital Charlotte Amalie, is the recipient of the largest proportion of vacationers and there is very little of the island left that hasn't been built on, which gives it rather a crowded feel: the airport runway juts out into the sea – there is no other place for it – a paved stretch of landfill which jumbo jets have to negotiate like aircraft carriers.

A thriving Danish colony

Columbus met with a hail of arrows on his visit to the Virgin Islands and as a result of such Carib ferocity, no European settlement was established until the 17th century when the Danes took St Thomas and St John.

St Croix, on the other hand, was settled first by the Dutch and English in around 1625, then by the Spanish in 1650, followed briefly by the Knights Templars of Malta under the sovereignty of France. Finally in 1733, St Croix was sold to Denmark, and the Danish West Indies officially became a colony in 1754.

The colony thrived with sugar growing on St Croix and a roaring slave trade in St Thomas, also an important stopping-off port for ships after crossing the Atlantic. However, by the beginning of the 20th century, as a result of the abolition of slavery, the drop in the price of sugar and the technological advances in shipping, so it was no longer necessary for ships to stop at St Thomas, the economy had gone into decline.

Meanwhile, the USA had been eyeing up the colony,

PRECEDING PAGES: sunset on Cruz Bay. **LEFT:** Magen's Bay, a popular beach. **BELOW:** view of Charlotte Amalie on St Thomas.

anxious to protect the Caribbean and the newly opened Panama Canal (1914) from the Germans, and bought the islands from Denmark for US$25 million in 1917. They were then ruled by the US Navy until 1931, when a civil government was established. The inhabitants were given US citizenship a year later but they still don't have the right to vote in presidential elections: the status of the USVI is as an unincorporated territory with a non-voting delegate in the House of Representatives. The government is structured like the US Federal Government with three branches – executive, legislative and judicial.

After World War II, the islands were neglected until American conflict with Cuba sent tourists looking for new white beaches, coral reefs and azure waters. The construction industry boomed, labor had to be imported from other Caribbean islands and at the same time new industrial centers opened up on St Croix. Now the USVI offers one of the highest standards of living in the Caribbean, although resentments have emerged between the islanders and immigrants providing cheap labor and US continentals going for the top jobs.

St Thomas – a popular island

The main island of St Thomas is often called "Rock City" because it is essentially one big mountain – its highest point being 1,550 ft (470 meters) – with one main town, Charlotte Amalie, the capital of the USVI, on its central south shore. The remainder of the island's coastline is a garland of beach resorts around a wooded interior of private homes – bright red, corrugated tin-roofed eyries set into the steep hillsides. In the end, it's a sense of confinement that compels you to move about and discover what a diversified place the 32-sq. mile (83-sq. km) island St Thomas really is.

Charlotte Amalie – a shoppers' paradise

Built by the Danes on the south coast of St Thomas and named after the Queen of Denmark in 1692, **Charlotte Amalie** (pronounced Ah-mahl-ya) ❶, the capital of all the USVI, is a bustling, congested town set round an equally bustling and congested harbor. Tax-free shopping is the name of the game here,

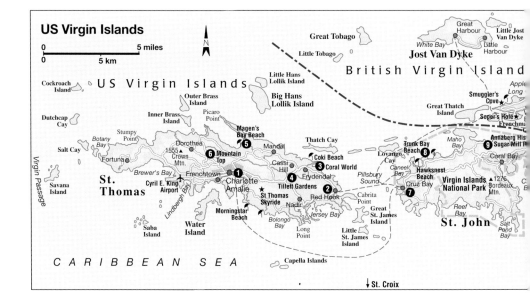

and you can wander along the narrow streets lined with old Danish shipping warehouses all converted into shops and restaurants. Brightly painted houses with filigree balconies give the downtown area the feel of a French quarter in the American Deep South. All the streets retain their Danish names displayed on corner buildings – Kongens Gade (King's Street), Dronningens Gade (Queen's Street), which is also called Main Street, and so on. These names are an example of the Danish traditions that the US has preserved.

Two blocks north of Main Street along Raadets Gade, you come to **Crystal Gade** and one of the oldest synagogues still in use in the western hemisphere. The present hurricane-proof building with an original sand floor dates from 1833 although its Hebrew congregation was formed by Sephardic Jews from Amsterdam and London in 1796. The adjacent **Weibel Museum** (open Mon–Fri; tel: 340-774 4312; www.onepaper.com/synagogue; donations welcome) charts the history of St Thomas Jews.

Wandering eastwards along the waterfront you can see the lines of docked boats, sleek yachts, and sailboats with names like *Windjammer* or *Kon Tiki* in the harbor. St Thomas hosts the Rolex Regatta (www.rolexcupregatta.com) around Easter time, a major yachting event attracting many competitors. The USVI competed in the Americas Cup for the first time in 2000. Sailing gets into your blood on these islands. The ferry that runs every two hours to St John waits here alongside the inter-island cargo ships: oafish, round-bellied boats with smoke stacks and circular windows; rusted hulls and lamp-lit, lived-in cabins furnished with little cooking stoves, clothes-strewn bunk beds and radios. Each has a backboard hanging off the side rail, listing their destinations: "Accepting cargo for St Martin, Dominica, St Lucia, and St Kitts."

Behind the wharf is the red-painted **Fort Christian** constructed in 1672 by Dutch settlers and one of the oldest American buildings. Among many uses, it served as a prison, with the last prisoner leaving in 1982. Now the dungeon houses the **Virgin Islands Museum** (open Mon–Fri; tel: 340-776 4566; donations welcome) displaying valuable Amerindian artefacts, local history, and colonial furniture. On Government Hill above the fort is the **Seven Arches**

Map on pages 92–3

An American paradise and a high crime rate often go hand in hand. Here it is unsafe to walk in Charlotte Amalie at night or go to remote beaches alone. Never leave any valuables unattended on the beach.

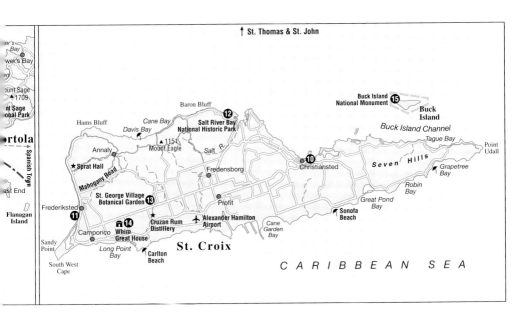

Feel the power of the wind in the sails of a catamaran or trimaran on a day, half-day, or sunset cruise (see page 361).

BELOW: a stroll past Fort Christian.

Museum (open daily; tel: 340-774 9295; entrance charge), a striking example of classic Danish West Indian domestic architecture, with a flower-filled courtyard where you can relax with your free drink.

To the yachting havens of the east

To break into the open country outside Charlotte Amalie might take you some time. Traffic jams are a constant factor in the town. But they are peculiarly "island" traffic jams – not so much the result of too many cars as they are of the relaxed attitude of locals who come upon a friend for a chat through the car window. Once outside of town, the roads twist and tumble drastically, and seem to want to pull you seaward to the little lanes that lead off to yet another posh resort. As you drive, you'll get two views of the island. At first, it's an extension of America; a nice little island dream that the large continent is having. After a while, you have the pleasant realization that it's a place unto itself, completely dependent upon tourism – the only vital industry, besides rum-making, left to these islands.

Leaving the town along the Waterfront you quickly come to **Havensight Mall**, another major shopping center where the cruise ships dock; Denmark owned all this until 1993. Nearby is the **St Thomas Skyride** (open 9am–5pm; tel: 340-774 9809; entrance charge; *see page 357*), a cable car that will take you up to a beautiful view point. From **Yacht Haven Marina** you can charter a yacht for the day, go light-tackle fishing, or deep-sea fishing for blue marlin – St Thomas is often referred to as the Blue Marlin Capital of the World – take a seaplane to St Croix or explore spectacular reefs in the Atlantis Submarine. Past the turn-offs to the dazzling **Morningstar Beach** (where the people dazzle

as well) and the idyllic **Secret Harbour**, after half an hour you come to **Red Hook ②**, at East End, and the **American Yacht Harbor** offering more sailing of all sorts and a choice of ferries running regularly to neighboring islands. Don't forget, the British Virgin Islands are another country and so passports need to be shown. There is a plethora of beautiful islands out there and you can explore them at speed but not in peace by renting a power boat from the marina.

Coral World – an underwater experience

A fascinating underwater observatory in which you the visitor become the contained curiosity, and the fish the passing curios, **Coral World ③** (open daily; tel: 340-775 1555; entrance charge; www.coralworldvi.com), is 20 minutes northeast from Charlotte Amalie at Coki Point. The marine complex includes an underwater observation tower on three levels, submarine tours, an aquarium, and colossal tanks featuring exotic reef life in one and sharks (there's a shark encounter program) and other predators in another. Small groups on a **Sea Trek** can follow a trail along the sea floor with the aid of a specially designed helmet.

And if that inspires you to swim down there among the exotic fish, the Orange Cup corals, and the colorful sponges in the underwater gardens off **Coki Beach**, Coki Beach Dive Club offers beginners' courses close by, with practice dives on the shallow reefs between St Thomas and St John. Many of the 15 dive companies on the island also give lessons in underwater photography (*see page 356*).

On the road back to the capital (a 20-minute drive away) lies **Tillett Gardens ④** (tel: 340-775 1929; www.tillettgardens.com) an old Danish farm that was converted into an arts and crafts center in 1959. Outbuildings in the grounds hold an art gallery, with local artists' work for sale, and screen-printing and crafts stu-

Map on pages 92–3

At Sandra's Terrace (tel: 340-775 2699), in Smith's Bay, close to Coral World on the east coast, you can enjoy creole cooking such as gutu, a sweet, steamed white fish, with fungi – a grit-like mixture of yellow cornmeal, okra, and butter – on an open wooden deck on stilts above nothing but jungle brush.

BELOW: St Thomas is a popular cruise-ship port.

A St Thomas pipe smoker.

dios, and you can combine a visit with lunch in the pretty garden restaurant. During the winter season, there is a series of chamber music concerts, and three times a year, the Arts Alive Arts and Crafts Festival is held here.

Back on the coast road, continue west for another 3 miles (5 km) or more, past the spectacular cliffside 18-hole **Mahogany Run Golf Course**, and you reach **Magen's Bay Beach** ❺ (entrance charge), a sheltered horseshoe bay voted "one of the 10 most beautiful beaches in the world" by *National Geographic*. All the fun of the beach can be had here on this mile-long stretch of sand that is perfect for children. Follow the marked trail to **Little Magen's Bay** for official sunbathing in the nude – but don't get burnt. The picturesque Route 35 back to Charlotte Amalie passes **Drake's Seat**, literally a concrete bench in a layby which is believed to be the spot used by Sir Francis Drake as his lookout.

For more views and the "world's best banana daiquiris" **Mountain Top** ❻ (open daily) the highest viewpoint on the island, nearly 2 miles (3 km) from the capital, offers more duty-free shopping. Once called Signal Hill, at 1,500 ft (457 meters), it was of strategic importance to the US in the 1940s. Now it's commercialised and best visited when there are few or no cruise ships in port. But it is still worth the trek for photos of the almost perverse beauty of Magen's Bay – a bright green teardrop of calm protected waters in a shell of white sand – toward St John and the British Virgin Islands.

Winding your way back down to Charlotte Amalie as evening falls, the boat lights in St Thomas Harbor look like felled constellations bobbing on the water. Island nightlife then kicks into gear as revellers gather to dance in the bayside bars around **Frenchtown** and the former World War II Sub Base to the west of the harbor – away from downtown which is not a desirable place at night.

BELOW: preparing the pool before a wedding party.

WEDDINGS IN PARADISE

The USVI has become a prime spot in which to get married. After all, what could be more romantic than a wedding ceremony on a white sandy beach or in an exotic tropical garden? What could be more original than tying the knot under the sea in a coral garden or on top of a mountain with a spectacular panorama as a backdrop? Of course you can get married the traditional way in a church, or at any time of day from sunrise to sunset – or how about chartering a luxurious yacht for you and your guests? The choice of settings in the USVI is endless.

As the islands are an American Territory, US marriage laws still apply, so there is just an eight-day waiting period after the Territorial Court of your chosen island has received your application. Then, with the help of the tourist office, which has long lists of addresses and telephone numbers, you can contact the army of wedding consultants, planners, florists, and photographers necessary to achieve the "wedding of your dreams."

Weddings are big business here and yacht charterers are used to working with wedding planners to enable a trouble-free ceremony and reception on the sea, even providing diving gear if desired. And you won't have to go far for your honeymoon – that can be laid on, too.

St John – a nature island

The ferry from Red Hook on St Thomas to St John takes you right across Pillsbury Sound into Cruz Bay in just 20 minutes. Essentially, St John's fate was sealed by the Caribbean itself, which lapped up enough of the island's coastline to render it a mere charm, larger than an atoll but not so large that one man couldn't buy up most of it, as Laurence Rockefeller did in the 1950s. He then deeded what amounts to about two thirds of the 28 sq. mile (70 sq. km) mountainous island to the National Park Service. There are no high-rise hotels here and a four-wheel drive is the best mode of transport. If you are over just for the day, taxis offer a two-hour trip around the island.

The main town of St John, **Cruz Bay ❼** is rather like a little town in Cape Cod: people come in to meet a friend at the ferry, pick up their mail, get some groceries, and then retreat back into the woods. The town square, opposite the ferry dock, is a raised curb bordering a patch of grass. To one side there is a fenced-in mound (either it's a sacred Amerindian site, or the town statue only works part time). Taxi drivers mill about and there are T-shirt shops, moped rental shops, open food stands, bars and restaurants. To the right is **Wharfside Village**, a beachfront shopping mall with a working spice factory. The road to the left goes to **Mongoose Junction**, another mall a few minutes' walk away, and the **National Park Visitors' Center**. Nothing is too far away in Cruz Bay.

Beautiful Northshore Road

Things seem pretty clear-cut on St John. People come here to hide away and feel good; businessmen falling off sailboards, college girls sneaking through the woods to isolated arches of white sand so they can get all-over tans (Solomon

Map on page 92–93

The dance styles that have developed in the US Virgin Islands are particularly interesting. During Carnival, look out for the Mokojumbies, dancers dressed in colorful costume who perform their art – on stilts.

BELOW: a bird's-eye view of St John.

Bay is an unofficial nudist beach). The **Northshore Road** follows the lush green coastline through the park to beach after beach of soft, white sand. At **Caneel Bay**, a few minutes drive outside town, the rich and famous enjoy going without their luxuries in the hotel on the beach; created by Rockefeller in 1956 as an "ecoresort", it is basic living here.

Hawksnest Beach in the next bay is another dream of a beach, popular with locals and film-makers alike, and at **Trunk Bay Beach** ❼ (entrance charge), the cream of the crop (so it does get crowded), snorkelers can follow the well-marked, 650-ft (200-meter) long National Park Underwater Trail. Around the corner are two campgrounds: Cinnamon Bay, run by the National Park Service, offers "the simple life" in canvas tents on the beach backed by tropical vegetation; and a little further on Maho Bay concentrates on deluxe camping with all mod cons.

Park trails and sugar-mill ruins

There are 22 hiking trails in the National Park and many of them start from the Northshore Road. From Leinster Bay, just past Maho Bay, you can take a 30-minute walking tour of the **Annaberg Historic Sugar Mill Ruins** ❾ (tel: 340-776 6201; entrance charge; www.nps.gov/viis), where there are the barest remains of old slave quarters and villages. The mortar between the stones of the buildings is made of flour, molasses, and sea shells, so you've essentially got very old, hard cakes in front of you. The trail back to the parking lot is lined with small, low-growing, fern-like plants known locally as *greeche greeche*. As if bearing some long-held grudge, the plant's tiny leaves fold up when touched.

The walking tours with rangers through the park are an eye opener, especially if you're curious about the indigenous flora (there are 800 varieties of plants and

BELOW: a colorful shop in St John.

160 species of birds) and their various medicinal uses. On the 3-mile (5-km) **Reef Bay Trail** (reservations at the Visitors' Center), you see a sugar-mill ruin and petroglyphs (prehistoric stone pictures) and have a boat ride back to Cruz Bay.

Map on pages 92–3

St Croix – an island with a difference

A sea plane – "It's fun to land on water" says the sign at the St Thomas terminal – takes you to St Croix (pronounced Croy as in toy), 40 miles (65 km) to the south of St Thomas. As you go through the main town of Christiansted to your hotel, condo, or villa, you'll get a notion of just how different St Croix is from St Thomas. For one thing, it takes longer to get around, and from east to west there is a dramatic change in the landscape – from low, grassy seaside hills that are reminiscent of Cornwall, England, to lush rainforests. Nearly 20 miles (33 km) long and at 84 sq. miles (210 sq. km), St Croix has room for changing climates; it's drier in the east and prone to drifting mists over the west end.

In the bars you'll hear many conversations comparing one island to another, declaring what one has over the other. You hear a lot of that from the resident aliens who make up one third of the population here – those from other Caribbean islands who've migrated to the USVI to find work and who are known as *garotes*, after a local bird that flies from island to island, and North Americans, called Continentals, who have made their home here. They say how they want to keep St Croix quiet and modest, not like St Thomas.

Bush teas are drinks made with medicinal plants from recipes handed down over the centuries. Many are still used for minor ailments: mango tea is taken for arthritis, soursop for insomnia, lime-bush for an upset stomach, and guava for coughs.

Christiansted – a Danish preserve

You can feel the Danish influence everywhere, especially in the main town of **Christiansted ⑩**, in the northeast, where the cream-colored buildings are made of bricks that the Danish ships brought over as ballast. Somehow, the Danes perfected a weighty architecture that barely interrupts the air. Christiansted is a town built to house its offshore breezes, with overhanging balconies and cool arcades, and walking along the streets you feel like one of those figures in a Chagall painting, too light, always floating up out of the frame.

BELOW: the perfect spot for a chat.

Many of the red-roofed buildings constructed in the properous years of the 18th century by rich merchants have been restored and the harbor front is now a historic site along with the majestic and colonial **Government House** on King Street where you can visit the ballroom, gardens, and the Court of Justice (open daily 8am–7pm; tel: 340-773 1404; free). In the square on the waterfront, the **Old Danish Scale House**, where sugar and molasses were weighed before being shipped out, serves as a visitors' center. Close by, **Fort Christiansvaern** (open daily 8am–4.45pm; tel: 340-773 1460; entrance charge; www.nps.gov/chri, which includes Steeple Building), built by the Danes in 1774, has been well preserved by the National Parks Service and you can see the dungeons and punishment cells plus an exhibit on how to fire a cannon. Across Hospital Street, the **Steeple Building** (open Mon–Fri 9am–4pm, Sat am; entrance charge includes admission to the fort), originally built as a Lutheran church in 1753, is now a museum of the island's early history. Since its deconsecration in 1831, the building has also been a bakery,

school, and hospital. Behind the Boardwalk where the sea plane checks in, **King's Alley Walk**, developed after the 1995 hurricanes, penetrates a fascinating maze of arcades and alleys lined with shops, restaurants and bars. Several times a year, whether it needs it or not, shopping is actively encouraged with "Jump Up," when bands play in the streets, Mokojumbie dancers (stilt walkers) chase away evil spirits and a party atmosphere pervades.

In tiny **Frederiksted ⓫**, 17 miles (27 km) away on the west coast, a small network of shops greets the cruise ships as they dock at the modern 1,500-ft (450-meter) pier, built after the old one was destroyed by Hurricane Hugo in 1989. This fortified town is not a stranger to disaster, as 100 years earlier it had been gutted by a fire and the islanders rebuilt it in wood…

Every plantation tells a story

If St Thomas is "Rock City", then St Croix might be considered its pastoral suburb. The island's expansiveness, its largely undeveloped inner landscape of old sugar plantations – with names like *Jealously*, *Upper* and *Lower Love* (names the Danish plantation owners gave as tributes, of sorts, to their different island mistresses, which makes you wonder about the plots called *Bold Slob* and *Barren Spot*) – all give the place a provincial feel. Many of the sugar mills have been restored as private homes.

Traveling northwest out of Christiansted for 4 miles (6 km), you reach **Salt River Bay ⓬**, where Columbus landed looking for fresh water (he found hostile Carib Amerindians instead) and which is now a National Park. **Northshore Road** runs along many of the island's beautiful beaches. Unprotected by reefs, the surfing is good off these shores and divers love the drop-off wall at Cane

Map on pages 92–3

Bay. Heading south on Route 69 past the **Carambola Golf Course**, Robert Trent Jones's pride and joy, you reach **Mahogany Road**, which leads west through the heart of the rainforest – a rich, bowered darkness with vines hanging from giant mahogany trees, kapoks, and the tidbit, also called the mother-in-law tongue for the way its long seed castings rattle in the wind.

On the way to Frederiksted, on Route 70, a collection of over 1,000 species of tropical and exotic flowering trees, vines, and shrubs can be seen among the ruins of a 19th-century plantation village in 16 beautiful acres (6.5 hectares) at **St George Village Botanical Garden** ⓭ (open daily in winter, Tues–Sat in summer; closed Sun and Mon June–Oct; tel: 340-692 2874; entrance charge; www.sgvbg.org). Two miles (3 km) farther on daily life on one of the island's 400 plantations during Danish rule is portrayed at the carefully restored **Whim Great House** ⓮ (open Mon–Sat Nov–Apr, Mon–Fri May–Oct; tel: 340-772 0598; entrance charge).

An underwater park

Buck Island National Monument ⓯ covers around 850 acres (340 hectares) of dry land, crystal-clear water and barrier reef just off St Croix's northeast shore. There's a stretch of beach to the west that boaters like to sail up to where there are changing facilities and picnic tables – charter a boat (there are plenty on offer) and it comes ready equipped with lunch, and snorkeling and diving gear – and two underwater trails. It is kind of a sunken china shop out there – the delicately designed fish float free from the coral shelves, and the sea's most exotic and psychedelic renderings pass you by like a pre-arranged fashion show: the dusky damselfish, the redbanded parrotfish, the yellowhead wrasses, and the lookdown moonfish – you can just check them off in your program. ❏

TIP

Guided nature horseback rides are arranged from the stables at Sprat Hall Plantation just north of Frederiksted (tel: 340-772 0305). For the more hale, the Tropical Mountain Bike Tour heads up through lush rainforest (St Croix Bike & Tours, tel: 340-772 2343).

BELOW: sail to Buck Island.

NOTICE

...MOVAL OF SAND FROM...
...IS BEACH IS PROHIBITED
...VIOLATORS WILL
...ED.
...NISTR... ...UR...
...SOURCES ...DB... ...EALTH.

THE BRITISH VIRGIN ISLANDS

*Once a pirates' refuge, today the crystal-clear waters that wash
the white powdery beaches of this peaceful archipelago are
a mecca for sailors and divers*

Map
on pages
106–7

O nly a few miles away from the glitz of the US Virgin Islands, the BVI, as the British Virgin Islands are affectionately referred to, do not cater for mass tourism. On the main islands of Tortola, Virgin Gorda, Jost Van Dyke and Anegada, out on a limb to the north, there are no high-rise developments, flashy hotels, or casinos and most of the other 50-plus islands are uninhabited. For a long time, they managed to evade the whirlwind of change that enveloped most of the Lesser Antilles and are now capitalizing on their simple treasures: a pleasant, gentle citizenry and long, unspoiled beaches of powdery white sand bordering clear seas that give new meaning to the word blue.

Here, all the action takes place above and beneath the surface of the water: sailors love the warm breezes that blow them from island to island where they can sample the secret coves only accessible by sea, and divers have a rich underworld of reefs to explore. This natural wealth forms the basis of the islands' economy and upmarket resorts have developed around marinas offering yacht and hotel accommodations combined – it's the yachties the government wants to attract, along with those seeking somewhere quiet and beautiful to escape to. Up on the mountain slopes, hairy lianas (vines) hang from ancient mahogany trees in snatches of remaining forest.

All the islands are of volcanic origin apart from Anegada, a flat coral and limestone atoll 30 miles (48 km) northeast of the largest island, Tortola (21 sq. miles/55 sq. km). Both Tortola and Virgin Gorda, 14 miles (20 km) away, rise steeply from the sea, each with a volcanic peak – Tortola's Mount Sage is 1,760 ft (540 meters) and Gorda Peak is 1,360 ft (415 meters). With coastlines only 3 miles (5 km) apart at their farthest point, getting anywhere in a hurry on Tortola is impossible. Some of the roads are easily on a par with alpine passes in Europe with altitude differences of nearly 1,000 ft (300 meters) within a couple of miles. The asphalt road encompassing most of Tortola was only completed towards the end of the 1980s; before then, anyone from Sea Cow Bay in the south who wanted to go to Cane Garden Bay in the north went by donkey.

Pirate haunts

Christopher Columbus may not have been all that impressed by these seemingly haphazardly located volcanic rocks when he discovered them in November 1493. Who was looking for good beaches at that time? Gold was what he was after, and there wasn't any. The predominantly steep terrain of Tortola provided the English with a handful of plantations later on, and there were enough fish in the sea to keep the slaves well fed. To protect the plantations and settlements from the incursions of pirates, forts were built along

PRECEDING PAGES:
beach at the Baths, Virgin Gorda.
LEFT: a seagrape tree hangs over a quiet beach.
BELOW: a friendly conversation.

Mrs Scatcliffe fills her verandah in Carrot Bay every night with people eager to feast on her papaya soup, home-made coconut bread, chicken in coconut milk, and soursop sherbert.

BELOW: hula at playtime in Tortola.

Tortola's south coast. One famous pirate dropped anchor here on numerous occasions: Sir Francis Drake, for whom the strait between Tortola and the southern islands is named. His fleet was often in the area from 1568 to 1595 to keep the Spanish and Dutch in check, which also entitled the English to plunder their gold. Sometimes the forces of nature helped by dashing the ships on to the reefs north of Anegada – more than 300 vessels lie on the seabed here. Other pirates roamed the southern islands feeding the imagination of story-tellers for years to come.

The BVI have been in British hands since 1666 and today are mainly self-governing as a British Overseas Territory.

Road Town – the capital on Tortola

The new yachting harbor, built around the artificial moles of Wickhams Cay 1 and 2, and the attractive marina beneath the renovated walls of the Fort Burt Hotel to the southwest have given **Road Town ❶** a bustling maritime character – "road" is the nautical name for a protected and safe place to drop anchor. The paved roads are never busy here and rush hour is an alien concept but, all the same, Waterfront Drive on the landfill area seems to be widened more each year.

On picturesque **Main Street**, once the waterfront road, the typical West Indian-style wooden houses are being carefully restored, and banks, insurance companies, boutiques and souvenir shops are mushrooming here and on **Wickhams Cay** across Waterfront Drive. Palm trees and shrubs are taking root on this once barren area of reclaimed land, and modern structures such as the Government Building came in for quite a bit of stick when first constructed. Caribbean T-shirts emblazoned with tropical patterns dangle from stalls in the **Crafts Market** close by, alongside colorful fish mobiles, napkin rings, and other delightfully

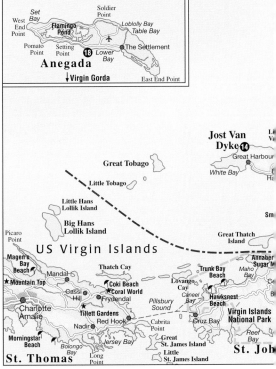

impractical items. Near the **ferry docks** a few minutes' walk southwards – where boats leave regularly for other islands including St Thomas and St John *(see pages 91–101)* – **Pusser's Co. Store & Pub**, an attractive gingerbread-style house that's hard to miss, has all the atmosphere of a British harbor pub. This is the place to try the Admiralty Rum, or Pusser's Painkiller, a notorious rum cocktail, and listen to maritime yarns. Through a door, Pusser's store (branches in Soper's Hole, Marina Cay and Leverick Bay) provides items with a nautical flavor.

Behind, the **Virgin Islands Folk Museum** (irregular opening hours; entrance charge) documents the colonial era alongside marine exhibits and Amerindian artifacts inside a typical old West Indian wooden building. At the bottom of Main Street, fronted by some spectacular flamboyant trees, the smart new government offices overlook the harbor. The **Old Government House** (open Mon–Fri 8.30am–4.30pm; tel: 284-494 3701; entrance charge) on Waterfront drive, is a national landmark and has been converted from the official governor's residence into a museum of local history.

To the north of the town, next to the police station, the **J.R. O'Neal Botanic Gardens** (open daily; donations welcome), with an avenue of palm trees, beautifully portrays the various vegetation zones of the islands and includes an orchid house, fern house, and medicinal herb garden.

Tortola's West End

Winter in the BVI means only a few hours of rain every now and then. It never gets cold or unpleasant; big warm raindrops fall on to the hot ground, and the sun's rays appear from time to time through dramatic cloud formations. Then in summer the islands look very exotic and green. Bougainvillea covers the houses

Map on pages 106–7

Great Thatch island off the western end of Tortola is being developed by the BVI government as a national park "in keeping with our unspoilt destination promotion."

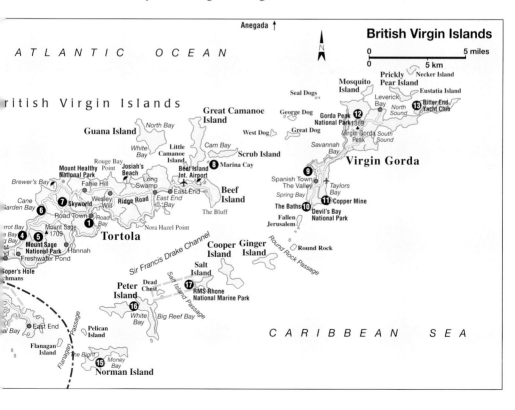

with its magnificent blossoms, and the gardens are full of bright red hibiscus. The marina at **Soper's Hole ❷** on Frenchman's Cay, 8 miles (13 km) west of Road Town, Pusser's Landing, the yacht charter buildings, the galleries and the shops all combine with the surrounding countryside to create a magnificently colorful scene, especially just before sunset. Ferries to the US Virgin Islands and Jost Van Dyke *(see page 112)*, 5 miles (8 km) away, leave from beside the **Jolly Roger Inn**, where two friendly women cook delicious Caribbean food.

All the beaches in the BVI are public, but you're certain to find a quiet spot near the elegant hotels in **Long Bay** at the end of the steep road over Zion Hill. The bumpy track westwards past Belmont leads to **Smugglers Cove ❸**, a delightful sandy inlet with sunshine practically guaranteed until evening and wonderful snorkeling. Around to the west, dramatic rocks rise from the sea at **Steele Point** and smart villas decorate the steep slope behind.

Trophies and shells

When Hurricane Luis passed this way in 1995, it seems to have had something of an effect on **Bomba's Surfside Shack**, in **Apple Bay ❹**. A venue popular with locals, yachties, and surfers jumping the waves in the bay, a few more oddities were added to the collection of trophies plastered over the ramshackle walls: an ancient bra, a pennant from New Zealand, T-shirts and other flotsam, many bearing personal dedications to the shack's owner. This place has become a real institution and one of the best-known nightspots in the BVI – the "full moon parties" and weekly reggae nights are quite an experience: hips sway amidst the barbecue smoke, and the fun spills out on to the road.

At the other end, in **Carrot Bay**, a more traditional collection can be seen at

ABOVE: a colorful spice shop on Soper's Hole Wharf.
BELOW: Bomba's Shack – *the* nightspot in the BVI.

the North Shore Shell Museum Bar & Restaurant where after a drink or a meal of cracked conch, grilled lobster, and good Caribbean cooking you can see exhibits of local crafts alongside the countless shells.

Panoramic hairpins around Mount Sage

The coast road winds up from Carrot Bay along spectacular Windy Ridge toward Cane Garden Bay and branches off into **Mount Sage National Park ❺**, a protected area of tropical forest spared from clearance in the plantation era. Giant mahogany trees with complex roots cling on to the rockface of the 1,780-ft (543-meter) **Mount Sage**, and lianas, moss, and numerous orchids leech moisture from tree trunks and hollows; tree frogs start their chorus just before sunset. As water takes longer to seep through volcanic rock than through limestone, the vegetation grows profusely here on an annual rainfall of less than 12 inches (300 mm).

Rum plays a major role in the BVI, but much of it actually comes from other islands. There were once seven family-run firms producing the "liquid gold" in **Cane Garden Bay ❻** but now only the fine Arundel Cane Rum is produced at the 200-year-old tumbledown **Callwood Distillery** (open Mon–Fri; free). The secret of the rum's high quality, according to owner Michael Callwood, is that it is made from the sugar-cane juice rather than molasses left behind in the sugar refining process *(see page 75)*.

The gently curving bay in front is one of the Virgin Islands' top beaches: deckchairs and sunshades are for rent, yachts move slowly past buoys on the turquoise sea, all types of watersports are on offer, and calypso bands strike up outside the bars just before sunset. **Brewer's Bay** farther north is far more provincial: the sand is much darker, and don't be surprised to see the odd cow

Map
on pages
106–7

TIP

The best surfing can be experienced from November along Tortola's north coast at Apple Bay, the eastern end of Cane Garden Bay and Josiah's Bay.

BELOW: walkers in Mount Sage National Park.

walking across it. The roads around here are very steep and signposts point to the ultimate viewing spot at **Skyworld**  on Ridge Road where there is a 360-degree panoramic view of Road Town, surrounding islands, and the rolling hills to the east: a perfect place for a picnic before hitting the challenging mountain road once more to Long Swamp and East End, 7 miles (11 km) away. From there turn steeply northward and over the summit to the new Lambert Beach Resort where, with a drink on the terrace, you can gaze in wonder at the creamy white beach edged by palms and ancient seagrapes around **Elizabeth Bay**.

From **Beef Island**, connected to East End by the Queen Elizabeth Bridge, the tiny 6-acre (2-hectare) island of **Marina Cay** ❽, only slightly higher than the surrounding coral, looks as if it could easily disappear under a large wave. Free ferries ply to and from the island, five minutes away, around 10 times a day from **Trellis Bay**, just east of the airport and a popular windsurfing spot. Once owned by the author Robb White, who used it as the setting for his book *Our Virgin Isle* and the film version *Two On The Isle* with Sidney Poitier in the 1950s, Marina Cay is now a private resort belonging to Pusser's and offers a wide variety of water-sports such as snorkeling, underwater safaris, kayaking, and deep-sea fishing.

The fat Virgin and her giant "marbles"

If Columbus had been thinking of St Ursula and her 11,000 virgins when he named this archipelago, why should a granite island have been named Virgin Gorda (fat virgin)? Speculation abounds, one notion being that, from afar, the 10-mile (16-km) long island looks like a reclining woman with a protruding stomach. **Spanish Town** ❾, also known as The Valley, is the main town on Virgin Gorda and until 1741 was the capital of the entire group of islands. The houses are dotted across various parks and gardens, and souvenir hunters will find a handful of colorful boutiques near the modern and well-equipped **Yacht Harbour**, south of the ferry dock.

From here taxis can take you across the southern part of the island past huge rounded granite blocks looking like giant marbles scattered all over the place to **The Baths** ❿, where the house-high boulders have formed natural grottoes and pools perfect for swimming and snorkeling. There's an easy trail between them with ladders and bridges over the tricky parts. Geologists refer to this phenomenon, which is part of the **Devil's Bay National Park**, as "woolsack weathering" – long ago, a thick layer of soil covered the stone, and acids from the humus gradually worked their way into hairline fissures in the rock wearing it away. As the topsoil gradually disappeared, wind, heat, and salt particles continued to erode the rough granite so that some look as if their shells are about to break.

Noticing that the granite southeastern coast of Virgin Gorda was similar to that of Cornwall, where copper mining was a lucrative industry in the early 19th century, the British speculated that there must be some copper here too. They were right and Cornish miners worked the **Copper Mine** ⓫, not far out of Spanish Town, for around 30 years. The chimney of the old mine, ruins of old stone buildings, a copper-ore pit, and remains of a smelting furnace can all still be seen.

Yachting in the north

Because of all the attention given to the southern bays, the north tends to get overlooked. Anyone with a boat will find this hard to fathom, because some of the finest beaches on Virgin Gorda are here. Just 5 minutes north of Spanish Town lies **Little Dix Bay**, where in 1964, after his success with Caneel Bay Resort in St John *(see page 97)*, Laurance Rockefeller opened the BVI's first hotel, geared expressly toward family vacations, and put Virgin Gorda on the map.

At the narrowest point of the island, less than 980 ft (300 meters) of land separate the spray-covered coast to the east from gorgeous **Savannah Bay**. On weekdays this coastline is like one long private beach – all yours. The road continues north, branching off to **Gorda Peak** ⑫ (1,369 ft/417 meters), a national park where the views from the observation point, reached after a short walk through some protected mahogany forest, are quite dizzying. Then it's downhill all the way to the happy and colorful Pusser's hotel at **Leverick Bay**.

The North Sound Express launch stops off at the hotel on its 45-minute journey eastward from Tortola (depending on the currents) across the unspoiled deep water of the North Sound to the **Bitter End Yacht Club** ⑬ at John O'Point. Here the yachties rule and the beach and watersports facilities are awe-inspiring. Instead of staying in any of the discreet-looking villas dotting the hillside or next to the beach, you can spend your holiday on one of their 30-ft (9-meter) yachts.

On the northeastern edge of North Sound lies **Prickly Pear Island**, which has a beautiful long white beach at **Vixen Point** and a small beach bar and watersports center. The island also has a nature refuge. No ferries stop here, so the most idyllic way to arrive is under your own sail.

Map on pages 106–7

TIP

Sailing, kiteboarding and windsurfing courses for all ages are available from the Bitter End Sailing School at Bitter End Yacht Club (tel: 284-494 2745/6) and you can also learn about live-aboard cruising (www.beyc.com).

BELOW: a beach hut at Biras Creek.

Foxy's reputation stretches far and wide. At his beach bar (tel: 284-495 9258) on Jost Van Dyke he always has a typically local song on his lips and his weekend parties are legendary with sailors.

BELOW: yachties meet up on the beach.

Jost Van Dyke – a tranquil retreat

The moment the speedboat to **Jost Van Dyke** 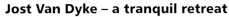 from Soper's Hole has docked, all the passengers disappear into Great Harbor except for the tourists, who stand gazing around them in astonishment. Time seems to stand still here: a handful of houses in a bay, and green hills under a scorching sun – indeed, electricity was only brought to the island in 1991. A few people stand in front of the Customs House, and goats graze peacefully in the cemetery. A pink sign bears the words "water-taxi" together with a phone number. What on earth do people spend their time doing here? Some, such as Foxy in his beach bar, have become accomplished storytellers *(see left)*.

The water-taxi quickly takes you westward round to White Bay where you have to paddle barefoot through the waves to the beach. Trousers and dress hems get wet, but dry out again almost as quickly while you're lying in the hammocks among the palm trees at the aptly named Soggy Dollar Bar. Every day feels like Sunday here. The atmosphere is perfect, and so romantic that it is almost a cliché: palm and seagrape trees, ultra-fine sand, gentle hills on the southern horizon, and all of it at the place where a painkiller (Pusser's Painkiller) was supposed to have been invented. What ailments needed to be cured in this paradise? Surely it can only have been the pain of having to leave.

Treasure islands

Forming the southern edge of the Sir Francis Drake Channel, south of Tortola, are a collection of tiny islands that provided perfect hiding places for pirates and inspired romantically inclined 19th-century authors such as Robert Louis Stevenson (1850–1894). This Scottish novelist and poet is supposed to have chosen the uninhabited **Norman Island** 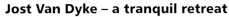 as the location for his *Treasure Island* (1883) and treasure hunters have done a great deal of digging ever since, to no avail. The real treasures, however, are under the water around the reefs of the protected bay known as **The Bight** which are bountiful in colorful fish; the caves along the rocky west coast, reached by boat, offer snorkelers a magnificent show. When it's time to come up for air, drinks and Caribbean food are served up by the galley team on the *William Thornton II* (tel: 284-496 8603; VHF channels 16 or 74; www.william thornton.com), a replica of an old Baltic trading vessel, in The Bight. More underwater caves and reefs give divers and photographers a fascinating few hours around **Pelican Island** and the pinnacles of rock called **The Indians**.

Despite the name, **Deadman's Bay** on the north coast of **Peter Island** 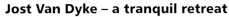 is often ranked as one of the top romantic beaches in the world – a white-sand beach fringed with palm trees and lapped by a gentle turquoise sea has to be irresistible. Cacti and enormous agaves cover the island, owned by the environmentally conscious Peter Island Resort. Gold medal-winning chef Alson Pont's Caribbean specialties can be sampled at the beach restaurant.

With a view of **Dead Chest**, where the pirate Blackbeard is said to have left 15 sailors to die – "*15 men on a dead man's chest/ Yo ho ho and a bottle of rum*" – the

diving boats set off toward the buoys surrounding the *RMS Rhone* in the **Rhone Marine Park** . In 1867, this 320-ft (100-meter) long Royal Mail vessel sank just to the west of **Salt Island** during a hurricane. One passenger and 20 crew members were rescued and to thank the Salt Island rescuers, Queen Victoria gave them ownership rights to it in return for one English pound of salt a year. Several of the boats that take divers out to explore the colonies of coral and sponge fore and aft of this ship – which lies 70 ft (20 meters) below the surface and has an enormous propeller – dock at Salt Island. In between dives, the last remaining elderly man, who still gathers salt to send to the Queen, demonstrates how it is produced and relates his life story over refreshments.

Map on pages 106–7

Anegada – an island of beaches and wrecks

The flat island of **Anegada** ⓲ at 11 by 3 miles (17 by 5 km) is easy to overlook: its highest point being a mere 28 ft (9 meters). But, with a continuous white beach from the Anegada Reef Hotel in the south, round West End along the north shore, where turtles nest, to East End, it would be a mistake if you did. For snorkelers, the reef offshore contains caves, drops and tunnels awash with colorful fish and turtles. Farther out, beyond the reef, scuba divers can explore several wrecks, home to angelfish, stingrays and grouper. Fishermen still provide the hotel with the best lobster in the BVI – it's also a top spot for bone fishing.

Two short strips of tarmac meet up in **The Settlement**, where most of the 300-strong population live. The controversial decision to introduce flamingos to the lagoon in 1992 proved a success when wild ones joined them and they reared some young. Anyone just here for a day would do well by hiring a jeep to visit **Loblolly Bay**, on the north coast, which is flanked by two bars. ❑

British entrepreneur and head of the Virgin empire Richard Branson couldn't resist the idea of owning a Virgin Island and his 64-acre (32-hectare) Necker Island, north-east of Virgin Gorda is available to rent – at a price.

BELOW: romantic Deadman's Bay.

LIFE ON THE OCEAN WAVE

The steady northeasterly trade winds which carried Columbus into the New World have made the Caribbean one of the top sailing destinations

The image of sailboats cruising in the gentle waters around the Grenadines seems like a dream – quiet sand-fringed bays below rolling hills, rustic harbor towns and lively beach bars. Visitors from all over the world flock to the Caribbean harbors during winter months with their own boats, but the international yacht charters also have a growing clientele in Europe, renting large yachts with a skipper and a crew. The old English seafaring tradition has influenced regatta competitions in the British Virgin Islands and in Antigua, with its annual Sailing Week at the end of April, preceded by the Antigua Classic Yacht Regatta, when beautiful schooners, ketches and sloops built as early as 1909 race off the southern coast of the island at English Harbour. Many yacht clubs on the bigger islands organize inter-island races which attract a more local crowd.

ISLAND HOPPING

Sailing during the night and funfilled days spent on different islands: cruises on the luxurious all-inclusive waterhotels are big business. Cruise ships mainly begin their routes in Miami, San Juan or Barbados and offer guests 24-hour entertainment with a break during the day to explore an island or shop in the tax-free malls which are popping up all over the Caribbean. Some cruise lines offer thematic holidays such as those for gay travelers or even romantic novelists.

▷ REGATTAS
The annual Antigua Sailing Week in April is one of the world's top five regattas, with five days of tough international competition and two days of harbor fun.

△ SEE THE SEA
Charter a yacht for a day, a week or a month – fully staffed with a crew including a cook to provide culinary delights at sea. Alternatively, join the crew yourself.

△ FLOATING HOTELS
Columbus's ship, the *Santa Maria* appears a nutshell compared to the cruise ships which carry one thousand or more people.

◁ CARIBBEAN CRUISING
The vessels carry happy passengers to almost all of the islands of the West Indies between the Bahamas and Aruba.

IT'S ALL IN THE GAME

When visiting the Carib Territory in Dominica you'll see large wooden canoes carved out of one tree trunk just like those of the Amerindian fishermen, who were skillful at killing fish using spears or by throwing branches of *matapisca* – the Papiamento name for *Jacquinia* tree – into the sea, which would slightly paralyse even big fish, but didn't harm humans. Today, big game fishing enthusiasts fight tuna, marlins and wahoo while strapped to comfortable seats on motor boats. Equipped with special rods, private charter boats offer day trips on many of the islands, but it is better to book from home. Smaller companies also provide angling gear, but the tale of the blue marlin or grouper that got away is up to you.

▷ **BARE BOATING**
Yachts are usually chartered for a week or two allowing anchorage in remote turquoise-colored bays.

△ **TRIMMING**
When racing, the highly technical, state of the art yachts still require the skills of a good crew for a good trim of the fibreglass sails.

◁ **HARD ON THE WIND**
Though mostly gentle the Caribbean sea can be a great challenge even to experienced skippers when tropical storms build up.

◁ **PIRATE STYLE**
Potent rum cocktails, food galore, music and lots of fun are guaranteed on the Jolly Roger party boat cruises.

▷ **WINDSURFING**
Aruba and the British Virgin Islands are top with international windsurfing buffs.

ANGUILLA

Map on page 120

Romantic, long white sandy beaches, exclusive hotels and a feeling of seclusion make this small British outpost, where the strong-minded people are welcoming and courteous, a paradise

Caribbean Sea — Anguilla

The low coral island of Anguilla sits at the top of the Leeward Islands chain, a serene, remote place of empty beaches with powdery white sand, and untouched cays and reefs, adrift in the wide blue sea. Nothing much happens on this tiny British territory, far from the mainstream of a busy world. And this tranquility is the island's main asset. Since it stood up and flexed its muscle against its governing partners St Kitts and Nevis in the late 1960s, Anguilla seems content to retain its sleepy character, proud and protective of its 12 miles (19 km) of well-kept beaches, crystalline waters, and exquisite coral reefs teeming with a wide variety of marine life – a magnet for sun worshippers, watersports enthusiasts (but no jet skis) and divers alike.

At 16 miles (26 km) long and 3 miles (5 km) wide, Anguilla (Spanish for eel) is one of the drier islands, covered in tangled vegetation and low tough scrub, foraged by hundreds of goats. Trees have never really been a feature here, especially after the ones they had were uprooted by Hurricane Luis in 1995 (a disaster the islanders have put well behind them), but now due to a concerted effort by a band of Anguillians to beautify the island, they are shooting up all over the island. Topsoil is scarce on this flat island, and only a few acres are fertile enough to support some hardy crops: pigeon peas, cassava, yams, corn and tropical fruits. However, modern technology, in the form of hydroponic agriculture, has permitted a small industry, growing vegetables for the local market as well as for the restaurants of St Martin *(see pages 127–34),* 5 miles (8 km) to the south.

A quirky history

This impoverished land endowed Anguillians with a social history that, like its political history, is quirky. Archeological digs have unearthed evidence of Amerindian presence on the island dating from 1300 BC, centuries before the Arawak-speaking tribes are believed to have settled the Caribbean chain at around the time of Christ. Remains from Amerindian villages have also been discovered at Rendezvous Bay, Sandy Ground and Island Harbour, making Anguilla one of the most archeologically interesting places in the region. By the time the first British settlers arrived in 1650, the Amerindians had gone.

The colonizers tried to plant tobacco and, later, sugar. Because of the dry climate and poor soil, these cash crops never took root and, to a large extent, neither did slavery. Still, slaves were duly imported, although they were freed long before Emancipation in 1834, as beleagured planters could barely feed themselves.

Thus, Anguilla's barren land left its people almost free of the scars of slavery, evolving into an extraordinarily egalitarian and color-blind society, where

PRECEDING PAGES: Rendezvous Bay. **LEFT:** Sandy Island before hurricanes blew the palm trees away. **BELOW:** a simple church with style.

*Goats roam
everywhere.*

everybody owned their land and helped each other through the frequent droughts and hurricanes, and to overcome the lack of fresh water and arable soil. Nevertheless, one resource, besides their character, was left to the Anguillians – the sea. Unlike other West Indians, landlocked by the success of plantations, Anguillians became expert boatbuilders, sailors, and fishermen.

Up in arms

Such strength of character, sense of community and loyalty, however, were severely tried when in 1967, against the Anguillians' wishes, Britain, in an attempt to divest itself of its dependencies, made Anguilla and the much-resented St Kitts and Nevis 70 miles (110 km) away an Associated State. More autonomy was directed from St Kitts, sparking the Anguilla Revolution *(see page 122)*.

Today, contentedly one of Britain's few remaining Overseas Territories, Anguilla's local government handles almost all domestic affairs, while a British governor takes care of the civil service, police, judiciary and foreign affairs.

Tasteful tourism

Much of Anguilla's charm lies in what it lacks. There is no mass tourism, although the extension of the runway at Wallblake Airport in 2004 now allows medium-sized jets to land in addition to the small island-hopping planes. Most visitors arrive by sea at **Blowing Point**, on the south coast, on swift ferries from Marigot in St Martin, just 20 minutes away. Not many people, only around 13,000 full-time residents, means courtesy reigns. Everybody knows one another and cars don't pass each other without a nod, a wave, or a honk. There are no casinos, scarcely any crime, and the Church – Methodist, Anglican, Baptist, and Seventh Day Adventist – is still the center of Anguillian life.

The islanders, as a whole, have adopted a tasteful approach to tourism, restricting development to small, expensive resort-hotels, such as the exclusive Cap Juluca at Maunday's Bay and Malliouhana (the Arawak name for the island) in Meads Bay, two of the Caribbean's most costly hotels. Moreover, they seem deeply committed to protecting their natural assets, introducing measures to assure the conservation of the island's fragile ecology, and enforcing strict regulations to protect the marine environment.

Map on page 120

When a major cruise line proposed to develop a cay as an island getaway for its passengers, the Anguillian owners of the land turned down the deal, worth millions of dollars, preferring to preserve the unspoiled islet for their children.

The Valley – a growing capital

Since the island has been reaping the financial rewards of tourism and a thriving offshore finance sector, **The Valley ❶** has grown from a few houses on a country crossroads to a small commercial center with banks, business places, and a shopping mall. Although shopping is minimal, young women dress fashionably off the racks of the Parisian boutiques on St Martin, and everyone gets their US, left-hand-drive cars there, too, even though driving here is on the left.

BELOW: roughhousing on the beach.

In the renovated old customs building across from Ronald Webster Park in The Valley is the **Anguilla National Trust Museum** (open Mon–Fri; tel: 264-497 5297) jointly set up by the Anguilla National Trust and the Anguilla Archaeological & Historical Society with natural history displays, Amerindian artifacts, and historical exhibits up to the Revolution. The National Trust plays a leading role in island conservation creating wildlife protection schemes and youth programs. The Archaeological & Historical Society (tel: 264-497 2263/2711) runs weekly tours of the old buildings in The Valley and Sandy Ground.

Heading south out of The Valley toward Sandy Ground, you come to **Wallblake House ❷** (open Mon, Wed, and Fri 10am–2pm; tel: 264-497 6613; www. wallblake.com; entrance charge; tours by appointment). Built in 1787 and recently restored, it is the oldest plantation house on the island. Cut stone had to be hauled across the island from the East End or Scrub Island and burnt coral, shells and molasses were mixed into the mortar. The restored house is home to the Roman Catholic priest of **St Gerard's**, the tiny modern chapel next door with walls of open stonework.

Farther along the road is the **Old House** (tel: 264-497 2228). Built around 1800, it was home to a succession of Magistrate-Doctors, representing the British Crown. The two-story wooden structure has been restored and is now an art gallery and restaurant.

The beautifully designed Anguillian postage stamps are very collectable. Issues such as Corals of Anguilla, Iguanas, and Fountain Cavern are on display at the Philatelic Bureau in The Valley Post Office (open Mon–Fri).

BELOW: Meads Bay beach in front of the Malliouhana.

A salty heritage

Anguilla was once famous for its salt, which was mined from saline ponds dotted around the island. They are home to a wide variety of birdlife, visiting and resident, such as the great blue heron and white-cheeked pintail. The last bag of salt was processed at Road Pond in **Sandy Ground ❸** in 1985, and at the northern end of the bay, which sweeps round in a horseshoe of white sand, the mini-museum in **The Pumphouse Bar**, once the old salt factory, documents the story of salt "picking". A few doors away **Johnno's** is said to be one of the best beach bars in the Caribbean, and literally jumps to live music at the weekends.

From Sandy Ground it's a five-minute boat ride (from the pier; on the hour 10am–3pm) to **Sandy Island ❹**, a veritable desert island of sand – with a beach bar and restaurant. The surrounding coral reef offers fascinating snorkeling, and farther out to sea, divers can explore the spectacular underwater canyon by **Prickly Pear Cays**, another short boat ride away.

Beautiful beaches

Many people come to Anguilla just for the beaches, and the west coast has an uncrowded long stretch of perfect, white sand. **Meads Bay ❺**, 3 miles (5 km) along from Sandy Ground, is one of the trendiest, attracting film stars and the super rich, while **Shoal Bay West** on the other side of West End Point is more remote. Sheltered **Rendezvous Bay** on the south coast looks over to St Martin and offers good windsurfing.

Reputed to be one of the best beaches of the Caribbean, **Shoal Bay East**, 3 miles (5 km) north of The Valley, is a perfect spot for swimming, snorkeling, and relaxing. Nearby, centuries before Columbus, Amerindians used to come to

"WE WANT ENGLAND!"

Animosity began between St Kitts and Anguilla after 1825 when Britain incorporated the two islands with Nevis into one colony. The Anguillians resented the St Kitts government which treated them as country bumpkins and did little to help them through some lengthy droughts.

Several pleas to London for direct British rule were ignored and the situation finally came to a head in 1967 when Britain tried to join the three islands together permanently as an Associated State of St Kitts-Nevis-Anguilla. Anguillians rebelled saying, "We don't want statehood, we want England", sent the 13-strong St Kittitian police force adrift in a boat and mounted an 18-man attack on St Kitts, which, in fact, fizzled out.

Until then, Anguilla had been poor and undeveloped with inadequate public and health facilities, such as no electricity or piped water, and high unemployment.

The St Kitts administration still didn't help and Britain remained blind to their plight, so the Anguillians took over their own management. Finally, in March 1969, 400 British paratroopers, marines and policemen invaded Anguilla to a great welcome, returning it to Britain. Today, the Revolution remains a crucial part of the islanders' psyche and they celebrate the anniversary every year.

the **Fountain Cavern** ❻ to perform religious rites to their god Johacu (giver of cassava). A natural spring in a large underground cavern, this is an important archeological site where magnificently preserved petroglyphs have been found alongside a 2,000-year-old stalagtite carved into the image of Johacu. Closed to the public, the cavern and the area around it are being developed by a subsidiary of the Anguilla National Trust into the island's first National Park, with plans for an interpretive center, museum, and easy access into the cave. Fountain Cavern is a UNESCO World Heritage Site.

Map on page 120

Sailing – the national passion

Island Harbour ❼, 3 miles (8 km) to the north, is a pretty working fishing village where brightly painted, prosperous-looking fishing boats neatly line the beach. Nearby, **Big Spring** (tel: 264-497 5297), which served as the village's water source, is in a partially collapsed cave with Amerindian petroglyphs.

Fishing off Anguilla has always been a booming business where sweet and luscious spiny lobsters are so plentiful; they are exported to St Martin, Puerto Rico, and St Thomas. After the day's catch, sacks of them are spilled on to the sand for prospective buyers.

Now powered by outboard motor, the fishing fleet once flourished under sail when the fishermen would race home from their grounds 30 miles (50 km) out to sea. Consequently, racing became a passion and today, the traditional wooden boats are built and sailed solely for that purpose; sailing is on a par with cricket in popularity. On holidays and in Carnival Week in August, the whole island comes to watch and place bets on boats which race from Sandy Ground, Meads Bay, Blowing Point and Rendezvous Bay to a marker out at sea and back. ❑

Half-built houses dot Anguilla's landscape, because after a young islander leaves school, his main aim is to build a house. As soon as he's earned enough money, he lays down foundations, adding to it bit by bit as he can afford it. This can often take as long as 15 years.

BELOW: fishing boats at rest in Island Harbour.

ST MARTIN

A busy island shared between the Netherlands and France, it is a haven for shoppers and sunseekers. While the French side excels in gourmet restaurants, the Dutch part is a gambler's delight

Map on page 120

According to legend, St Martin's border was defined when a Dutchman and a Frenchman stood back to back, then walked around the island until they met face to face. The Dutch side is smaller supposedly because the Dutchman was fat, or slow, or drinking gin as he walked, or all three. Crossing the border today is an affair of total informality, quite in keeping with the character of this tiny "freeport" island, with nothing but a few solitary signposts monitoring the tourists and locals crossing back and forth all day. Despite such informality, the border holds great symbolic value to the islanders, marking 200 years of peaceful co-existence and distinguishing two communities which are the same and yet different. Above all, it celebrates the unique character of an island which is many things in one.

Whatever its origins, St Martin's border bisects the smallest landmass – 37 sq. miles (96 sq. km) – in the world shared by two countries. The smaller southern half – Sint Maarten – is part of the Netherlands Antilles, while the northern side belongs to France. As of 1946, French St-Martin is technically an *arrondissement* of Guadeloupe, which is a *département* of France (in the same way that Hawaii is a state of the US). And the difference between the two nations is immense: St-Martin is quintessentially French in style, developed on a small scale but including Parisian shopping, whereas Sint Maarten has large resorts, casinos and fast food chains.

PRECEDING PAGES: hot dog and religion. **LEFT:** Mullet Bay. **BELOW:** duty-free shopping in Marigot.

Contrasting landscapes

Fittingly, the island is also composed of two contrasting landscapes: the west end is an atoll of low land surrounding a lagoon, while the east end consists of a range of conical hills, like a plate of candy kisses. Actually, St Martin is folded into two parallel ranges. One stretches north-northeast from Cole Bay Hill and includes the highest peak, Pic du Paradis (1,390 ft/420 meters); the other runs from Pointe Blanche to Oyster Pond, creating the steep rocky cliffs along the weathered southeast coast. Between them lie Great Bay and Salt Pond, the valley of Belle Plaine and the smaller salt ponds at Le Galion.

There is no drama here. The hills are low and easy to climb, the beautiful white beaches are sheltered, the feral boars of Terres Basses (western lowlands) are long gone. It's a fertile landscape of soft hills and pasture, cattle and horses. Green and hawksbill turtles nest on the shores and the fishing is good.

A cosmopolitan stew

There is a sly elusiveness about identities on this island. For instance, it's unclear whether residents are to be called St-Martinois or Sint Maarteners. Even the population figures are mysterious: various sources

estimate that there are at least 75,000 legal residents – 39,000 on the Dutch side and 36,000 on the French – along with thousands of illegal aliens from all corners of the world. While the French side is decidedly French, the Dutch side is anything but Dutch. Although a significant Dutch influence remains, most of the population represents a cosmopolitan mix in which American, Caribbean and Asian segments play equally important roles.

One result of this cosmopolitan nature is an extraordinary linguistic situation. The principal languages are Dutch, French, English, Spanish, patois, and papiamento (which was not spoken on the island until after 1960 when it arrived as the language of an imported labor force, *see page 53*). As a rule English (like French) is viewed as the conqueror's language, and some form of creole as the mother tongue, the "national language". In French St-Martin, everyone speaks French whereas in Sint Maarten, although Dutch is the official language and taught in schools, everyone speaks English and signposts and notices are all in English too. As the early commercial language of the region, gaining importance when the US became a major trading partner, English has always functioned as a neutral *lingua franca* amid the raging hostilities of the colonizers.

A sharing mentality

Remains of a half dozen or so Amerindian camps have been unearthed to date, especially around the beaches of Terres Basses, on the southwestern shore of Simpson Bay Lagoon, revealing that St Martin was used by the Caribs as a resort or hunting ground. They referred to the island as Sualiga, "a place to get salt" and Oualichi, "a place to get women." There were probably a few Caribs on the beach just after the hurricane season in 1493, when Columbus passed by

BELOW: school children in Philipsburg.

somewhere to the south. He is supposed to have missed St Martin completely, mistaking it for Nevis, or possibly St Kitts.

It was the salt, finally, that led the Dutch to lay claim to the island in 1631. Holland was at war with Spain, and Spain had a monopoly on European salt, an essential commodity for the preservation of food in the days before refrigeration. However, the Spanish soon snatched it away and it was while the Dutch were trying to recapture the island in 1644 that the young Peter Stuyvesant, then governor of Curaçao, lost his leg to a Spanish cannonball at Cay Bay (three years later he became governor of the Dutch colony on present-day Manhattan). The Spanish abandoned the island four years later, and the Dutch moved back with the French, dividing the territory between them. The border has survived unchanged to this day, despite several armed incursions in both directions and persistent attempts by the Dutch in the 18th century to buy the French side outright.

At the height of colonialism, sugar and salt became the island's most important exports until slavery was abolished and the plantations went into decline. Salt was shipped to the US and to Holland where it was used in the herring industry until that too ground to a halt in 1949.

Modern-day pirates' den

While St Martin is not entirely averse to its present or past colonial connections, the rhetoric of independence has been increasingly in vogue, particularly on the Dutch side, due to unhappiness over controls exerted by the Curaçao-based Antillean government and the influence of The Hague. Tax-free status and lax controls brought rapid tourism development on both sides of the island which spiraled to a peak in the early 1990s with undesirable side effects. To counteract

Map on page 120

Tourism in St Martin took off after World War II as the island had been left with a ready-made airport. Juliana Airport was built as a military airfield by the US in 1943 while St Martin was occupied by the Allies, during the Occupation by Germany of France and the Netherlands.

BELOW: Marina Port La Royale in Marigot buzzes with life.

these, new regimes such as customs controls and new taxes were imposed by Curaçao, which did not go down well with the islanders, who had survived decades of benign neglect from Europe earlier in the 20th century by relying on traditional activities such as subsistence farming and smuggling.

This rapid growth in tourism brought instant wealth to many, making the island the envy of several of its Caribbean neighbors, and Sint Maarteners today still take a certain pride in their island's image as a sort of modern-day pirates' den. Opinion in the bars and cafés on both sides of the island leans toward a preference for more direct self-governance, while maintaining all the benefits of ties with Europe – a happy solution indeed which would permit St Martin to enjoy the best of both worlds. Some islanders are particularly eloquent in their irritation at being ruled via another small island. After all, 600 miles (970 km) separate Sint Maarten from Curaçao, while five English islands and two Dutch intervene in the 150 miles (240 km) between Marigot and Guadeloupe. Marigot seems actually to have lost some autonomy, and there is a general, if rather nostalgic, sentiment that under direct rule St-Martin would be less encumbered by bureaucracy and at the same time would have better access to real executive authority and resources.

Philipsburg – the Dutch capital

In 1733, a town was founded on the sand bar that separates the Great Salt Pond from Great Bay. It was named **Philipsburg ❽**, in honor of John Philips, the Scotsman who did so much for the early development of Sint Maarten. The sand is still very much in evidence; all over town there are unobtrusive welcome mats to keep as much of it outdoors as possible. But what's left of the pond is easy to ignore – a stretch of stagnant water with some long-term plans to clean it up and make it a bird sanctuary – so who would realize that when Back Street takes a strange course behind the Sea Palace Hotel, it's avoiding the ghost of a huge storage pile of salt?

By day, Philipsburg is a lively, commercial town – its two main roads, Front Street and Back Street, are linked by a series of narrow alleys supporting a cruise-ship port, and "the shopping center of the Leewards". In the middle of everything is the **Courthouse**, built on **Wathey Square** in 1793, and still in use. A whole book has been written about its history, but now this is the place to pose for photos and pay parking tickets. The square is lined with former merchant residences that became shops as the population moved back out of the developing town. Directly in front of it, the town's characteristic excitement begins as ships' tenders, sometimes four at a time, unload crowds of passengers on to the pier, all bent on the task of spending money for pleasure.

The main shopping area, **Front Street**, is undergoing a beautification program including tree-planting and benches for weary shoppers. The duty-free shops are stocked with designer goods such as Gucci, Kohinoor and Little Switzerland, but soon buildings with ornamental fretwork known as West Indian "gingerbread" *(see pages 76–77)* come into view. The characteristic architecture that developed in the 18th and

19th centuries is still evident in a few two-story structures around Wathey Square with a warehouse or shop below, living quarters above, and steps from the street up to a front gallery or verandah. But since Hurricane Luis swept through in 1995 there are not many left.

A fascinating video showing the devastating effects of the hurricane can be seen at the small **Sint Maarten Museum** (open Mon–Sat; entrance charge) at the eastern end of Front Street and you can stop off for a drink at the **Pasanggrahan**, originally a government guest house, and now the oldest inn on the island, which has an atmosphere of disheveled charm. Queen Wilhelmina and her daughter Juliana stayed here during World War II and their bedroom is now the Sydney Greenstreet Bar. While relaxing with a drink, perhaps the island's famous Guavaberry liqueur – a rum-based cocktail mixed with the wild red berries that grow on the hills – you can watch the boats going in and out of the marinas on trips around the island and to St Barths, St Eustatius, and Saba.

Great Bay Beach is a wonderful place with an attractive boardwalk that stretches along the entire length of the sand. Restaurants, bars and stalls entice promenaders to pause and take in the view. While the tiny Wathey Square cannot match Marigot's wide-open waterfront, efforts to make it more "people friendly" have been successful and have given Philipsburg a much-needed focal point.

Around the popular west coast

Getting in and out of Philipsburg and Marigot, the capital of the French side, at rush hour, or traveling the main routes between Philipsburg, Simpson Bay, and Marigot can be nothing short of a bother and the historical sites around Philipsburg are only worth visiting for their views: from Fort Hill, the site of

TIP

Out of the 9 casinos in Sint Maarten, the Casino Royale in Sonesta Maho Beach Hotel has the highest table limit at US$2,000. The slot machines at the Golden Casino in Great Bay Beach Hotel can cough up as much as US$2,500 in one win.

BELOW: planes swoop low over Maho Beach.

Spiny lobster is caught on the Saba Bank, a shallow part of the sea between Saba, about 25 miles (40 km) south of St Martin, which is also a good breeding ground for fish like grouper.

BELOW: market day in Marigot.

Fort Willem to the west, you can look over the capital below; **Fort Amsterdam** commands Great Bay from the west, looking across to the **Old Spanish Fort** on Pointe Blanche, and over Little Bay on the other side.

The forts guarded the earliest Dutch settlements, which were located on the sand bar and around **Little Bay ❾**. Now sprawling along the peninsula in direct contrast to the historic ruins of Fort Amsterdam is the modern 220-room Divi Little Bay Resort.

The road continues round to the brow of Cole Bay Hill from where there is a justly famous vista of **Simpson Bay Lagoon** and neighboring islands. Beyond, the road drops to **Simpson Bay** and to the hotels and white beaches that circle the west end: the built-up resorts of **Maho** – over which the planes swoop down into Juliana Airport – and **Mullet**, the most popular; limestone and marl sediment laid in nearly horizontal beds has created low, richly colored cliffs along the shore of the quieter **Cupecoy Beach**, where clothes are optional. Across the border, beaches are unspoiled and secluded with **Baie Longue** stretching for 1 sandy mile (nearly 2 km), graced by one small, upmarket hotel, **La Samanna**.

Marigot – a touch of southern France

After the sometimes crass commercialism of Philipsburg, **Marigot ❿** seems more European and more Caribbean at the same time; more appealing, more colourful, and equally lively. There's more than a touch of southern France here, especially in the morning fruit and vegetable market (best on Wednesdays and especially Saturdays) on the quay. Wide open to the sea, the quay is a welcoming recess where, unlike its Dutch counterpart, it invites you to stop and watch in the cafés, bars, and excellent restaurants that spill out on to the

streets. It seems entirely right to sit and watch the ferries loading for Anguilla while eating chicken barbecued over a halved oil drum, or salt cod (once the food of slaves) served with rice and peas, or fresh fish with lime and garlic and spices – delicious Caribbean fare. Or, if you prefer, you can survey the market square over espresso and *pâtisserie* in a cafe like **La Vie en Rose**, opposite the harbor. It is then a 15-minute walk (or a car ride) up to the ruins of **Fort St Louis** for some magnificent views of the town and Anguilla 5 miles (8 km) away.

There is fine shopping to be done along **Rue de la République** and in the chic boutiques around the **Marina Port La Royale**, which embraces the boat-filled northernmost finger of Simpson Bay Lagoon with elegant shops and cafés. On Thursday nights a carnival atmosphere pervades as shops stay open late, bands play, and the restaurants fill up with onlookers and satisfied shoppers. Those too busy to sit down and eat can grab a barbecued snack at one of the many *lolos* (food stalls) scattered around the town. Significantly, much of the town still takes a siesta from noon until 2 or 3pm, unthinkable among the driven merchants of Philipsburg, where midday belongs to the cruise ships.

On the Route de Sandy-Ground, beside the tourist office, is an interesting museum, **On the Trail of the Arawaks** (open Mon–Sat 9am–1pm, 3–7pm; tel: 0590-292284; entrance charge), which includes exhibits from pre-Columbian times up to the 20th century and provides excellent information about the island.

Into the hills

Stretching to the west of Marigot along the northern shores of the lagoon is a strip of hotels and shopping centers. The beaches along **Baie Nettlé** are not much to write home about, but the area makes a good base. Leaving Marigot to

Map on page 120

BELOW: cacti grows in the craggier parts.

Map on page 120

The most popular dive site in St Martin is the 200-year-old British frigate HMS Proselyte, *just south of Philipsburg which provides excellent viewing for all levels.*

RIGHT: a cockfight in Marigot.
BELOW: restaurants in Grand Case.

the north, the road skirts past the central hills where there is a network of hiking trails punctuated by viewing points. Several lead to the **Pic du Paradis**, which is densely wooded and alive with colorful forest birds. The country to the north, around Grand Case, supported many of the sugar plantations in the 18th century and it is apparent that cane was planted virtually on the hilltops. It ushered in a long period of prosperity, which lasted until slavery was abolished in 1848 on the French side and 15 years later in the south, causing a lot of grief, especially where several plantations straddled the border.

Grand Case – the gastronomic capital

It has been said of the little town of **Grand Case** ⑪ that its only industry is eating, but there are also art galleries here and, of course, a beach. The most touted creole creativity in St-Martin is culinary, and this village alone offers dozens of choices, lined up along the beachfront road.

The sand at Grand Case and **Friar's Bay**, just to the south, is golden not white, and the light seems different in this part of the island, with tones of ochre and gold. The road leads round to the east, south of the salt pond which attracts an abundance of bird life, through the rolling countryside and mangrove swamps of **Cul de Sac**, where there are boats over to **Ilet Pinel** ⑫, an offshore island that offers excellent snorkeling and a choice of places for lunch. Sheltered **Anse Marcel** to the northwest is a favorite spot with yachties who take advantage of the large Meridien resort there, the shopping mall, and yacht charterers.

Acquiring an all-over tan

Along the rough Atlantic shores of the east coast, there are several isolated beaches off the road to Orléans and windsurfing is popular here – as is the odd cockfight in specially designated pits around St-Martin, which, incidentally is not encouraged. At **Baie Orientale** the Club Orient is a naturist resort claiming a section of beach for those who wish to acquire an all-over tan. On the bandstand next to the club, calypso and reggae bands play in the afternoons, creating a party mood.

On the western bank of the Etang aux Poissons is the **Ferme aux Papillons** ⑬ (butterfly farm; open daily; tel: 0590-873121; entrance charge; www.the butterflyfarm.com), which has a fascinating collection of the beautiful creatures. The best time to visit is in the morning when they are most active. **Orléans** ⑭, farther south, was the capital of French St-Martin until 1768, but only graves and a dueling ground recall those days. Local artist Roland Richardson lives here. He has a gallery in the former *mairie* (town hall), a restored West Indian building on the rue de la République in Marigot.

Beyond are the beaches of **Oyster Pond**, and reefs that lure scuba divers to their caves and cliffs. Oyster Pond is also home to a yacht club and the bay is busy with boats. The coast itself is wild, with windswept scrub and cacti, including the striking Pope's Head, growing around **Guana Bay** (named for the iguanas once found here); the beach here is where body surfer's come for the best rides.   ❏

ST-BARTHÉLEMY

Known affectionately as St-Barths, this ultra chic French haunt of the rich and famous is a Caribbean St Tropez, with magnificent yachts in the harbor and Parisian chefs in the restaurants

Map on page 140

St Barthélemy

Caribbean Sea

With an international renown that far outstrips its 10 sq. miles (25 sq. km) of white beaches and craggy hills, this tiny French island at the top of the Leeward Islands, less than half the size of Manhattan, is a magnet to the rich and famous. As a result St-Barthélemy harbors some of the world's most sought-after real estate. Like St Tropez in southern France, sky-high prices only serve to enhance the allure of St-Barths, as it is popularly known.

During Christmas, the likes of Madonna, Sylvester Stallone, Steven Seagal, and Sharon Stone can be found hiding out here, along with assorted billionaires, supermodels, royalty, and the scores of daytrippers who come over from St-Martin every day to try to spot them.

The essence of France in a tropical haven, St-Barths' convoluted coastline is sewn full of blue pockets trimmed with exceptional hideaway beaches; steep-sided mountains – the Pyrenees in miniature – are brindled with torch cactus and stunted wild frangipani; kaleidoscopic panoramas create a feeling of endless topography. St-Barths, with a rugged and irregular beauty, creates a natural environmental home for a wide variety of fascinating flora and fauna, including the pelican, which has become the island's unofficial mascot.

It smells of France, too – *baguettes* baking in the *boulangeries* and coffee wafting from the street cafés. The island is covered in a network of narrow roads which has given rise to the sensible use of the now ubiquitous compact Smart car. It is perfect for the terrain of St-Barths, particularly in the high season when the place is crowded and parking spaces are at a premium.

French settlers and pirates

Christopher Columbus sighted the island in 1496, naming it for his younger brother, Bartholomew, and it first appeared as a mere flyspeck on a Spanish map in 1523, identified as San Bartolemé.

In a sea of fecund, resource-laden islands, St-Barths was inimitably undiscoverable, bypassed even by the Caribs except as an overnight rest stop on their raids to other islands. However, a party of French settlers from St Kitts set up home here in 1648 only to be massacred by a passing band of Carib warriors several years later.

Undeterred, a group of Huguenots from Brittany and Normandy arrived, establishing the first permanent settlement, which thrived, not on farming and fishing, but on piracy. St-Barths became a clandestine rendezvous for pirates, plundering the passing Spanish galleons laden with treasure. The island's rocky, arid hills, with no fresh-water supply and lack of savannah, made a sugar and syrup industry unthinkable, although some cotton and tobacco were

PRECEDING PAGES: a windswept hillside. **LEFT:** only the locals are allowed to spear fish in St-Barths. **BELOW:** preparing the fishing boats.

cultivated. Few slaves were imported and the people continued to live the peasant life they had in France. The French government reported them to be "good people, very poor, honest, rather ignorant, and quite quarrelsome." This latter contentiousness and feistiness survives to this day in what seems to be an intramural sport.

Sold out to the Swedes

Nevertheless, in a most unexpected and bizarre trade, in 1784, the neglectful government of Louis XVI gave St-Barths to King Gustaf III of Sweden in exchange for trading rights in the port of Göteborg (Gothenburg). The Swedes immediately got down to turning the island into a model possession. The capital was given its decidedly non-Gallic name of Gustavia while the port was declared duty free.

Spared the terror and dissolution about to overtake her French sister islands, Martinique *(see pages 218–27)*, Guadeloupe *(see pages 194–203)*, and St Martin *(see pages 126–35)*, in the French Revolution (1789–95), the island flourished. The local administration worked to organize the indigenous population, not as Swedes, but as people of St-Barths with their own traditions and heritage. A rational pattern of streets was laid out around the harbor, warehouses were built, the roadways cobbled.

By 1806 the island wallowed in relative prosperity, with a population bloated to about 6,000. However, during the following decades St-Barthélemy experienced a series of devastating disasters – natural and economic – and in 1878 Sweden sold the island, with the 1,000 remaining French descendants, back to France.

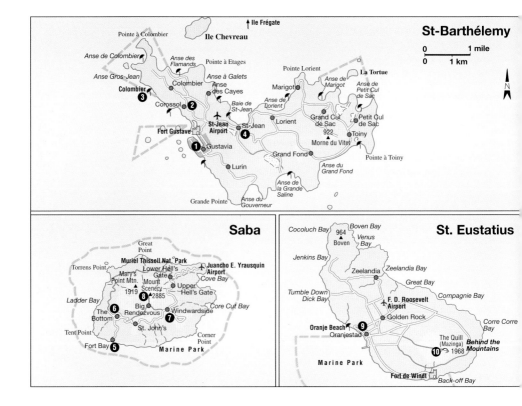

Content to be French

Today, St-Barths, together with St-Martin 15 miles (24 km) away, comes under the administrative umbrella of Guadeloupe, an overseas department of France *(see page 42)*, each with their own mayor. Candidates for the local administration are perennially right wing, but the islanders are not banking the fires of autonomy. "It's good to have a nation like France looking out for you," says a shop clerk in Gustavia. "Independence? Don't speak about that. Crazy people want it."

Here there is no underclass to be placated, suppressed, or promised, for unemployment is virtually non-existent. Fishermen, businessmen, builders, and laborers all have plenty to do, and they know how to enjoy life, too. Long lunches and plenty of breaks for surfing, fishing, and hanging out in Le Select in Gustavia is the order of things – so there is little crime to speak of. As once happened when Sweden took control, people are trying to get on the island, not off.

A hair-raising arrival

Around 170,000 visitors a year come to St-Barths, half of them by catamaran shuttle on daytrips from neighboring St-Martin. Those that fly in on the tiny eight- or 12-seater planes have an experience akin to a theme-park ride. The hills loom up in front at the approach to the 875-yard (800-meter) runway like an impenetrable wall and suddenly the plane dives steeply and lands, with brakes squealing, stopping just short of the sea. It wasn't long ago that two approaches had to be made – to clear the then grass airstrip of sheep before actually landing.

St-Barths is also a stop-over for yachts sailing the Caribbean between Antigua in the south and the Virgin Islands. Gustavia and the scattered islets around provide beautiful natural harbors, attracting the serious yachtsmen and leisure

Map on page 140

On St-Barths, a two-story, three-bedroom villa with a few acres of land is likely to set you back more than $7 million (5 million euros). A square meter of space in St Jean is more expensive than its equivalent on the Champs-Elysees in Paris.

BELOW: landing on the runway is like a theme-park ride.

Rudolf Nureyev (above) *built a house on the Pointe à Toiny on the rocks where the waves often sprayed him on his sundeck. The house is available to rent as a holiday villa,*

LEFT: flying high.
RIGHT: some secluded coasts.

palaces alike. Around the islets, such as **Isle Fourche**, the sea is rich in marine life and coral, and the marinas in Gustavia offer dive packages to small groups of up to 10. Deep-sea fishing for marlin, wahoo, and tuna on boats providing lunch and an open bar can also be arranged there, although visitors are not allowed to spear the fish.

Gustavia – a Gallic town with a Swedish heritage

Set around a yacht-filled harbor and careenage too small for cruise ships (small ships can anchor in the outer harbor), the picturesque buildings of the capital climb up the steep hillside behind. **Gustavia ❶** is still a free port and the latest Paris fashions from Versace to Gaultier are all available right here in the exclusive boutiques, along with Gucci leathers, Vuitton suitcases, and Charles Jourdan footwear. Boat-loads of shoppers arrive from St Martin, and cafés spill out on to the streets Parisian style, buzzing with a young, chic French crowd. There are no beggars or hucksters here; no ramshackle shops or rums, and no colorful, aromatic market clogs the waterfront – only four makeshift vegetable stalls on a side *rue*, operated by a half dozen women who sail the 125 miles (200 km) from Guadeloupe weekly.

The Swedes bequeathed three forts – Oscar, Karl and Gustav – at strategic points around the town and beneath Fort Oscar is the **Musée Municipal de Saint-Barthélemy** (open Tues–Fri, closed for lunch, Mon afternoon and Sat morning; tel: 0590 29 71 55; entrance charge). On rue Avater in the **Wall House** building, the museum has exhibitions of local history and island crafts. A five-minute walk past the ruins of Fort Karl brings you to **Anse de Grand Galets**, also called **Shell Beach**, which is simply a beach covered with shells.

Plentiful beaches

Going west out of Gustavia, you soon reach the tradition-bound, fishing village of **Corossol** ❷, on a brown sand beach lined with colorful fishing boats and lobster traps. The women sit outside their houses weaving hats, mats and baskets out of latania palms to sell.

St-Barths has at least 14 beautiful white sand beaches, and one of the best of the secluded ones is **Colombier** ❸ at the tip of the northwest peninsula, where sea turtles come back year after year to lay their eggs. The beach cannot be reached by car, but the 30-minute walk from the village is well worth it for the magnificent island views en route. Another way in is by boat from Gustavia. Around the point to the east, the wide stretch of sand edged with latania palms and seagrapes at **Flamands** is rarely crowded despite the few small hotels with all their watersports facilities.

St Jean ❹, on the northern shore, has the most popular beach, divided in two by a spit of rock on which stands the rebuilt **Eden Rock** hotel where Greta Garbo once stayed. Now you can lunch on freshly caught lobster, surrounded on three sides by a turquoise sea. Behind the beach are shops, hotels, and snack bars giving an atmosphere of the French Riviera.

Farther east, **Lorient**, where the first French settlers lived, offers good surfing or snorkeling depending on the mood of the sea. Windsurfers head for **Grand Cul de Sac** at the eastern end, which has a sandy bay protected by a coral reef and is backed by a large salt pond. Sand fleas can be a problem here as they sometimes are on **Anse de la Grande Saline**, in the south, a long white beach also next to a salt pond. Surfers gather here for the waves while waterfowl enjoy the pond. They know a good place to stay when they see one. ❑

Map on page 140

Lorient is the home of the annual St-Barths Music Festival, held here for two weeks every January. The festival includes a series of classical music and dance events at several locations on the island.

BELOW: a pelican fly-past.

SABA

A tiny volcanic peak jutting out of the crystal clear waters of the Caribbean and Atlantic, Saba's dramatic mountain scenery matches the magnificent underwater world around it

There are no white sandy beaches on the Dutch island of Saba (pronounced *Say*-bah). This miniature volcanic island's rocky slopes climb steeply out of the tropical sea rising to the highest point in the Netherlands at the top of cloud-covered Mount Scenery (2,885 ft/870 meters). Rugged cliffs, refuge to a variety of seabirds, support 5 sq. miles (13 sq. km) of green, mountainous terrain dotted with small villages of pretty, pristinely kept, white houses with red roofs, once linked only by hundreds of steps. Around 2,000 people live here, half of them light-skinned and the other half dark-skinned and they all speak English, although Dutch is the official language. As no plantation economy ever existed, slaves were only brought over to help on the small farms and carry goods up and down its paths.

Like St-Barths 30 miles (50 km) to the northeast, landing on Saba is a nerve-wracking experience. The pilot heads straight for a vertical rock face, only to fly a sharp, cool curve to the left just as you feel that your time has come and then lands seconds later on a runway the length of an aircraft carrier – 1,300 ft (398 meters) to be precise – so that his 10 or so passengers can disembark safely. Saba's airport, completed in 1963, is only open when the trade winds are gentle enough. In earlier days, arriving by sea was not much easier as there were no natural harbors for protection against the strong currents and fierce gusts of wind.

Shipwrecked

Christopher Columbus "discovered" Saba in 1493, but it was only in 1632 that the first Europeans – a couple of shipwrecked Englishmen – first set foot on the island. Later, eager Dutch settlers from St Eustatius, 17 miles (27 km) to the southeast, managed to brave the waves that crash regularly against the steep coastline. Ruled a dozen different times by the Spanish, French, and English, Saba was finally taken over for good by the Dutch in 1812, and the islanders have no plans to break away (see page 293).

The only inlet in the towering cliffs where boats can dock is at **Fort Bay** ❺, a relatively flat bay by Saban standards but with none of the luxuries of a proper harbor. Before 1972 when the pier was built, anyone who disembarked here – or at Ladder Bay on the west coast – always got their feet wet after being rowed ashore in wooden jolly-boats. The first vehicle on the island, a jeep, was landed in 1947 on two sloops lashed together to form a makeshift raft. These days, daytrippers from Sint Maarten, 28 miles (45 km) to the north, arrive on high-speed ferries almost daily and the dive shop in Fort Bay gets very busy.

The first part of the road that staggers across the craggy terrain to the airport was built in 1943, under

PRECEDING PAGES: monstrous moss on Mount Scenery. **LEFT:** Saban children. **BELOW:** shoals of colorful fish to see.

How much farther to the top?

BELOW: these hikers are determined to get there.

the auspices of Josephus Lambert Hassell. After Dutch engineers had declared any road construction to be impossible, Hassell took a correspondence course in civil engineering and proved them wrong. Before that, on landing at Fort Bay people had to walk up hundreds of stone steps to the main village of The Bottom, and cargo had to be carried, including once a piano that took 12 men to get it to its destination.

From The Bottom to the top

At 820 ft (250 meters) above the sea, **The Bottom ❻** does not live up to its name. In fact it is derived from *de botte*, the Dutch word for a bowl, as it stands on a small piece of flat land surrounded by mountains. With around 500 inhabitants, the village functions as the island's capital and the government building is surrounded by the hospital, school, **Cranston's Antique Inn** – the first guesthouse, established in the 1830s – and a few bars. American students from the small medical school there give it a youthful ambiance.

The road only reached the picturesque village of **Windwardside ❼**, 900 steps farther up, in 1951 and, despite the souvenir shops selling Saba lace, a bank, dive shops, and a few small hotels and restaurants, it is still very much a Dutch Caribbean idyll in its peaceful setting against a green mountain ridge between the haze-covered Mount Scenery and Booby Hill. Pretty white wooden houses on granite foundations, and gardens full of flowers in bloom decorate the village. The red roofs are all very clean – they have to be as they are used for collecting rainwater for there are no rivers on the island. What at first appears to be a family crypt in the vegetable gardens or orchards turns out to be the house's own cistern, crucial to survival, and you may see a grave beside it – there is little room for cemeteries here.

The **Harry L. Johnson Museum** (open Mon–Fri 10am–4pm; closed noon–1pm; entrance charge) was once a sea captain's house built in 1840 and still has the original kitchen. A wall covered with the masters' certificates shows how closely the Saban men are associated with the sea. For centuries, they earned a living as fishermen and mariners plying the Caribbean trading routes. One Saban sailor is reputed to have been paid in gold for smuggling escaped French prisoners from Guyana to Trinidad.

Nearby the home of road builder and engineer, Josephus Lambert Hassell, has been converted into a little shopping mall with an art gallery and a restaurant. Farther up the village the tourist office with helpful staff, a bank, shop and post office.

Foggy forest hikes

Waiting for a completely clear day before climbing **Mount Scenery ❽** is not a good idea, as the summit rarely peeks out of its thick cloud veil. The ascent begins on the outskirts of Windwardside (on the road to The Bottom) and you don't need to be an expert climber, although good shoes will make the three-hour tour easier because the 1,064 steps along the way are steep and often wet.

Lizards scurry across the path at the start of the trail and the bright red and yellow artificial-looking heliconia that grace the lobbies of smart hotels all over the world grow wild among the trees. The higher you climb, the more luxuriant the vegetation becomes: the trees are covered in lianas (tropical vines), massive leaves darken the path, and the fog closes in. Then, just beneath the summit, a 210-ft (64-meter) high radio tower (brought up in just one day by a helicopter) comes into view. The stormy wind whips through the trees and whistles through the steel structure, and behind it Mount Scenery drops away.

Other hiking trails around Saba may not be so dramatic but are just as satisfying. The **Muriel Thissell National Park**, which extends from Mount Scenery to the north coast and the Sulphur Mine, has a choice of trails in forest and scrubland.

Volcanic underwater landscapes

Cold hands after a 50-ft (15-meter) dive? No problem at the **Hot Springs** site where divers can plunge their hands into the warm sand there. From 1987, the waters around Saba have been protected as part of the **Saba Marine Park**, concealing a vast, spectacular volcanic landscape rich in sea life and open to divers. A small entrance charge to this colorful experience is charged by the diving schools, or by the organizers of boat excursions from Sint Maarten. The 26 diving grounds – only accessible by boat – provide divers at all levels with unbelievably beautiful spots such as **Tent Reef Wall**, encrusted with corals and sponges, or the gently sloping reefs where elegant stingrays cruise and nurse sharks sleep in the sand. At **Third Encounter** what must once have been an underwater volcano rears up to just 100 ft (30 meters) below the surface. A pillar of coral, called Needle's Eye, has grown up on its western flank over the millennia – a unique collection of tube and barrel sponges, star coral, elephant ears, and brain coral. ❑

Map on page 140

TIP

Everyone has a secret recipe for the aromatic dessert drink, Saba Spice. The main ingredient is always rum, while the mix of brown sugar, cloves, fennel, and other flavorings tends to vary. Try it and see.

BELOW: on a clear day – the view from Mount Scenery.

EXPLORING THE SPLENDORS OF THE DEEP

The dramatic seascape of the Caribbean is still a widely unexplored realm of beauty even though generations of settlers have changed the landscape.

Tourism has set off the spirits of invention: more and more tiny submarines seating about 20 or so passengers are being launched throughout the region to give the ordinary visitor a chance of sharing the kind of underwater experience previously only available to the rapidly growing crowd of scuba divers.

THE POOL IS OPEN

With its warm and shallow waters, 75°F (24°C) being the average temperature, the Caribbean Sea is an ideal spot to learn to scuba dive. Hundreds of dive shops certify beginners within five days of theory and practise in shallow grounds (PADI, NAUI courses). More advanced divers and budding marine biologists will also meet instructors to help them find the best sites and produce exquisite underwater photography.

Some of the most beautiful dive sites are located in protected marine areas. The boom in tourism – more fish to be caught, more sewage water to be dispensed with, more beach pollution and reef damage from ships anchors – has severely endangered the fragile and highly complex reef ecosystem. The tiny island of Bonaire was the first to protect the coastal waters around the island as a marine park, others such as Saba and the British Virgin Islands followed suit. Jacques Yves Cousteau initiated a marine park on the western shore of Guadeloupe, St Eustatius now protects its historic treasures below the water line, and Anguilla is about to start a reef care program.

▷ **HIDE AND SEEK**
Dimly lit caverns in the reef are favorite shelters for night hunters like snapper, found in rocky notches between corals and sponges.

△ **REEF CREST**
Where the waves are broken by the elkhorn corals in the shallower part of the reef, many fish search for prey.

▽ **NEW FRIENDS**
Dolphins are very friendly and communicative and occasionally swim alongside divers.

▽ **BRAINY**
Over centuries spherically growing brain corals can reach diameters of more than 6 ft (2 m).

▷ **FLEXIBLE**
Soft corals are perfect indicators of submarine currents, look for trumpetfish in the big Gorgonians.

RECAPTURED BY THE SEA

Off the western shores of Aruba, around 33 ft (10 m) below land is the *Pedernales*, the remnants of a tanker, torpedoed during World War II, it is only one of almost a dozen wrecks attracting divers close to the island. Aruba is the westernmost island of the Netherlands Antilles offering an assortment of underwater wrecks including planes. At 460 ft (140 m) long the *Antilla*, off the coast of Aruba, is the biggest wreck in the Caribbean and it is living proof of nature's rapid move to integrate: corals, sponges, anemones and other invertebrates have attached themselves on to the huge hull and transformed it into a multi-colored patchwork, where Spotlight Parrotfish and Queen Angelfish enhance the dazzling scene. Its storage room in the bow is as big as a church. There are plenty of books on each island documenting their shipwrecks and other man-made sites. Old anchors can be found around St Eustatius, explore the shipwreck *Proselyte* in Great Bay (St Maarten) or the *RMS Rhone* in the Rhone Marine Park, off Tortola or a load of old cars which tumbled from a barge off Vaersenbaai, Curaçao.

▽ WATCH OUT!
Tiny and big fish have developed clever tactics to hide from enemies and surprise their prey.

▷ DON'T TEASE
Crabs are very quick using their pincers, when searching the ground for organic food like worms.

▽ UNDERWATER TRAIL
Some marine parks, like this one at Buck Island, introduce snorkelers and divers to specific forms of local aquatic life by marked underwater trails.

ST EUSTATIUS

Peace and quiet is what you will find on this small Caribbean hideaway, along with a network of hiking trails and a vast underwater landscape just waiting to be explored

Map on page 140

Dominated by the dormant volcano called The Quill (1,970 ft/600 meters) with a lush rainforest center, this tiny Dutch island lazing in the Caribbean sunshine has so far avoided being on the beaten tourist track, making it a peaceful place to escape to. However, what it lacks in beaches and shopping this 11-sq. mile (28-sq. km) haven, with Oranjestad its only town, makes up for in dramatic scenery above and below the water. Colloquially called Statia, the island also has a fount of fascinating tales to tell of a more prosperous era.

In 1775, minuscule Statia was a thriving trading center, known as the Golden Rock, and had as many as 10 ships a day calling at Oranjestad, then a busy town. Janet Schaw, a touring Scottish gentlewoman strolled along this seafront and recorded her impressions in her *Journal of a Lady of Quality*: "From one end of the town of Eustatia to the other is a continued mart, where goods of the most different uses and qualities are displayed before the shop-doors. Here hang rich embroideries, painted silks, flowered Muslins, with all the Manufactures of the Indies. Next stall contains most exquisite silver plate, the most beautiful indeed I ever saw, and close by these iron-pots, kettles, and shovels. Perhaps the next presents you with French and English Millinary-wares. But it were endless to enumerate the variety of merchandize in such a place, for in every store you find everything…"

This "Lady of Quality" would have difficulty recognizing Statia today. A few crumbling ruins, some under water, are all that is left of the warehouses and merchants' offices along the sea front. Things are a lot quieter now.

PRECEDING PAGES: tidying up the backyard. **LEFT:** Oranjestad architecture. **BELOW:** island style in the sun.

Ill-gotten gains

St Eustatius was "discovered" by Columbus in 1493 and taken by the Dutch for the West India Company during the 1630s – 22 changes of flag later, the island finally succumbed to the Dutch.

Plantations on the central plain – where the airport now lies – gave the islanders a good living, but their jewel was the safe harbor. Well positioned on major trade routes, in the 18th century Statia was made a duty-free port and reaped the rewards. Valuable goods filled the coffers at the numerous local trading offices and the island became a center for the slave trade, too. During the American Revolution (1775–83) arms and gunpowder were smuggled through the island in barrels of rum and molasses via the merchant ships bound for New England – and the population is reported to have swelled to 20,000 – 10 times what it is today.

Such was the island's support of the rebellious British colonies in North America that in 1776 soldiers fired a salute when they sighted one of their

warships, the *Andrea Dorea*. This was the first salute ever fired by another land in honor of the recently formed United States of America and moved Statia to the front of the world stage. The Americans were delighted, but the British were absolutely furious.

However, historians now doubt whether love of freedom was actually the motive behind the ominous salute, because signals of that kind were normally only employed to greet trading vessels (and the Dutch Government also assured the seething British that they had had no intention of recognizing the sovereignty of the USA). Whether or not the guards up in Fort Oranje in Oranjestad did recognize the importance of the American flag, the ship was probably very welcome anyway because the American rebels were lucrative customers.

Rodney's revenge

Britain finally settled the score when Admiral George Rodney attacked St Eustatius in 1781 and ransacked the warehouses, banishing the merchants and capturing their ships. He sent back to England £5 million worth of booty. This started a steady decline in the fortunes of the island, precipitated by the end of slavery in 1863 which finished off the small plantation economy. The population dwindled to less than the 3,000 it is today and the island's main source of income is now an oil depot on the northwest coast where supertankers load and unload. Otherwise, the Statians live by subsistence farming, money sent home from relations abroad, and Dutch support.

However, poverty has not prevented the Statians, who mostly speak English, from generating their warmth and friendliness to visitors and there is very little crime to speak of. They are still proud of their historical gesture and on 16

In 1781, after invading St Eustatius, Admiral Rodney is supposed to have found most of his booty buried in the graveyard of the Dutch Reformed Church. He ordered the coffins to be opened after an abnormal spate of funerals had taken place.

BELOW: taking a break over a game of dominoes.

November each year, they celebrate Statia-America Day, when cannons are fired from Fort Oranje and the islanders get together and sing a hymn which includes the lines: "Statia's past you are admired/Though Rodney filled his bag/The first salute fired/To the American flag." The flags of the 13 American colonies are then hoisted above the fort to mark the occasion.

Oranjestad – a fallen town

Not long after Admiral Rodney's sojourn in **Oranjestad ⑨** a mighty undersea earthquake caused much of the lower part of the town, where all the ware-houses were, to crumble into the sea. Now some of the submerged ruins and sunken ships provide great snorkeling and there are plans to restore the parts of the Lower Town left on dry land. The Old Slave Road winds up to the top of the 130-ft (40-meter) high cliff where **Fort Oranje** (open daily), dating from 1636 and restored in 1976 for the US Bicentennial Independence celebrations, guards over the bay, the cannons pointing through the embrasures at imaginary enemies. There's a fine view down to the mile-long dark sand of **Oranje Beach**, Statia's best swimming spot. Memorial plaques on the fort from Franklin D. Roosevelt and the "St Eustatius Commission of the American Revolution" commemorate the island's fateful salute.

Close by in the 18th-century Doncker-De Graff House, once inhabited by an extremely wealthy Dutch merchant during Statia's heyday, is the **St Eustatius Historical Foundation Museum** (also known as Simon Doncker House; open Mon–Fri, Sat–Sun until noon; tel: 599-318 2288; entrance charge). This is where Admiral Rodney made his headquarters for 10 months in 1781 before the French pushed him out. Reputedly one of the best historical museums in the region, the house gives a genuine feel of what prosperous colonial life must have been like and has some excellently arranged archeological and historical collections of Amerindian pottery, tools used by the early settlers, and detailed documentation of the ignoble slave trade.

The plaques along the "Historical Walk" that continues on to the main sights in Oranjestad are rather worn-looking these days. **Honen Dalim**, the second-oldest synagogue in the western hemisphere (the oldest is in Willemstad, Curaçao), has been left to decay since the large Jewish population left with the arrival of Rodney. Built in 1739, its walls of yellow brick, brought over as ships' ballast and unusual at that time, enclose a broad, two-story room, but the outside steps lead to nowhere.

The congregation of the **Dutch Reformed Church**, the island's largest church, a few minutes farther on, also departed with the drop in prosperity. The massive tower made of dark volcanic stone in 1775 is still standing after renovation in 1981, but the broad nave is now roofed over by the blue of the sky. But the Seventh Day Adventist Church, just past Wilhelmina Park, bulges at the seams every Saturday morning and the narrow streets lined with houses with corrugated steel roofs are empty. The older houses have arcaded porches and balconies with gingerbread trim, many of which are being restored, whereas on the outskirts of town some of the modern concrete houses are not so pretty.

Map on page 140

TIP

The shore on the wild northeastern Atlantic coast has dark sand and a heavy surf only suitable for splashing about in. It is overlooked by La Maison Sur La Plage which offers fine French cooking and simple guest cottages.

BELOW: looking out over Zeelandia Bay.

Green giants in the crater

The Statians started shooting several worried glances at **The Quill ⑩** when Montserrat *(see pages 188–91)* started blowing up in 1995. Old paintings of the island show massive plumes of smoke above Mazinga, the old Amerindian name for the volcano. Geologists have soothed local anxieties, however, and both the slopes and the crater are accessible to hikers. A sometimes steep, but largely pleasant path, starts in the outskirts of Oranjestad on the road leading west out of town, and continues up to the edge of the crater. When you reach the edge, there are three possibilities: following the crater rim either to the right or the left (difficult because of hurricane damage), or actually descending into it and the untouched rainforest growing there. Small geckos race across the ground, and tiny hummingbirds dip into the orchids growing wild on the trees. Most startling are the hermit crabs that tumble to the sea inside their shells to reproduce, before making the arduous return journey back up to the crater.

In the early morning – the best time for the three–five-hour tour with guides provided by the tourist office in Oranjestad – swathes of fog hang above the gigantic trees inside the crater. Some of these ancient trees along the route have been given biblical names by the locals. Moses, for instance, is a mighty old tree covered with aerial roots.

Further hikes, all marked on the tourist-office map, are found in the area called **Behind the Mountain** on the southeastern slope of The Quill where the St Eustatius National Parks Foundation (STENAPA) is developing the **Miriam C. Schmidt Botanical Garden**, complete with an information center, to protect the secret habitat of the rare, pink-flowered morning glory. In the lonely bush and meadow landscape in the north more trails extend across the island as far as the **Boven** (964 ft/294 meters).

BELOW: passion-flowers grow in the wild.
RIGHT: hunting in The Quill rainforest.

Treasures in the deep

Statia has at least a dozen interesting dive sites with a historical slant, and is a very rewarding destination for underwater fans, however experienced or inexperienced they may be. Sometimes an ancient clay pipe may be seen on the ocean bed, but leave it there, it's against the law to remove historical artifacts. STENAPA has established a Marine Park on the leeward side of the island on the same scale as Saba's *(see page 149)*. Three dive centers in Lower Town offer, among other things, beginners' courses and snorkeling around the **Old City Wall** in the bay. Between the ruined walls of Lower Town's submerged buildings swim brightly colored parrotfish and angelfish.

The boat trip out to the other diving grounds only takes a few minutes. The finest ones are illuminated by the morning sun such as **Barracuda City**, where dozens of these silvery glinting fish glide around 65–80 ft (20–25 meters) down, beside a miniature precipice. An anchor has been lying here since the 18th century, and there are more at **Anchor Point** and **Lost Anchor**. Two wrecked ships at **Double Wreck** have undergone a sea change over the past 200 years and now stingrays, flying gurnards, and spotted morays live inside their hulls and cabins alongside vast communities of sponges and sea anemones. ❑

ST KITTS AND NEVIS

Map
on page
164

Two sleepy tropical islands in a sea of blue, St Kitts and Nevis have woken up to what they have to offer the discerning visitor – deserted beaches, a relaxed way of life and hotels in magnificent Great Houses

W hen the last Sugar Train tooted at the sugar factory at Needsmust on St Kitts on July 30, 2005, it signaled the end of a chapter in the Federation of St Kitts and Nevis. Certainly, it was the end of many years of toiling in the fields for the last 1,500 islanders employed in the industry. However, cane still grows around the island, since the crop protects the land from erosion, at least until another use is found for it.

As Kittitians waved goodbye to the sugar industry tourism was becoming a profitable prospect. But even with a growing number of tourists this is still a place to relax and enjoy the tranquility of an unrushed society. The sounds and moods that bring greetings at the crack of dawn range from the asthmatic braying of donkeys, the yap of dogs calling for their morning meal following a night on guard, to the sound of the refuse truck announcing its arrival to the tunes of the ice-cream truck – a trademark which visitors find delightful. The first hint of sun brings the crisp crack of thirsty volcanic sand hit by the unfurling ocean waves and the yawns and stretches of islanders rising at this same hour. The fishermen whose patched, wooden boats chart the waters just before dawn return with their catch, greeted by locals hoping for the best fish at a reasonable price. This kind of scene reflects life on the islands couched in the gentle northern arc of the Leeward Islands.

St Kitts & Nevis

*Caribbean
Sea*

PRECEDING PAGES:
Great Salt Pond on
St Kitts' southeast
peninsula.
LEFT: St Kitts farm-
land in Dieppe Bay.
BELOW: passing the
time of day.

Amid the freshness of flower gardens erupting in vivid bursts of colour, residents hurry to work in the business districts that are concentrated in the restored 18th-century towns of Basseterre in St Kitts and Charlestown in Nevis. These sun-drenched islands offer a cocooned feel of yesteryear – nostalgia for a simple past and a yearning for a modern, technologi-cally enriched future.

The Amerindians called St Kitts Liamuigua (the fer-tile isle). It sits on a land area of 65 sq. miles (168 sq. km), while Nevis, separated by a 2-mile (3-km) stretch of choppy sea, is smaller at 36 sq. miles (93 sq. km).

First British settlement

Columbus, who occasionally waxed poetical in his namings, bestowed the elegant title of *Nuestra Señora de las Nieves* (Our Lady of the Snows – in reality, clouds) upon Nevis in 1493, but then resorted to a little self-glorification by calling St Kitts St Chris-topher. As was often the case in those hectic colony-collecting days, claims of sovereignty were largely forgotten and the resident Carib population continued to smoke the "cohiba" tobacco, and delight in their diet of turtles and iguanas for at least another 30 years.

The arrival on St Kitts in 1623 of Sir Thomas Warner and the Caribbean's first bunch of hardy British settlers was followed closely by a group of French colonists and the peaceful island became a

microcosm of traditional Britain vs. France antagonisms, in which they joined forces only to eliminate the Caribs at Bloody Point in 1626. More than 150 years of conquests and counter-conquests ensued until the 1783 Treaty of Versailles acknowledged British sovereignty.

Queen of the Caribbees

By that time the islands were thriving sugar and cotton producers supported by a vast army of African slaves, which continued – with infrequent recessions – way beyond Emancipation in 1834. In the 1780s, tiny Nevis had become a more significant commercial center than New York, a veritable Caribbean social nexus ("The Queen of the Caribbees"), complete with palatial planter's mansions and a fashionable hotel-spa. Horatio Nelson *(see page 172)*, sent to enforce the Treaty of Versailles, was an attractive and eligible addition to the social whirl, despite annoying the planters by chasing away the "foreign" American traders vital to their economy.

The road to independence was a rather messy process. In 1967, the three islands of St Kitts, Nevis, and Anguilla, long jointly administered, became an Associated State of the United Kingdom. Almost immediately Anguilla ceded, eventually regaining its Crown Colony status *(see page 119)* and the islands of St Kitts and Nevis – never very compatible bedfellows – were left to sort out a joint constitution prior to their formal independence on September 19, 1983.

Nevis feared the economic dominance of St Kitts and made sure it had guarantees of partial self-government and even an "escape clause" if the union proved unworkable. According to many Nevisians today, that union has indeed proved unworkable and the specter of its secession has dominated political

At Nevis…a spa was established; and here, to this Tunbridge Wells of the Caribbees, came all the fashionable of the West Indies…

– SIR FREDERICK TREVES

The Cradle of the Deep

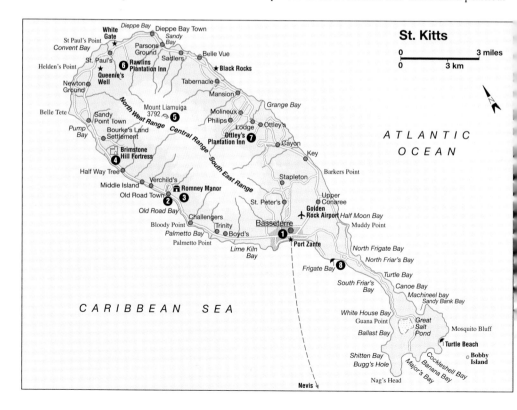

debate in the twin-island federation since 1996. Despite arguments that secession would be a "backward step" in an era of globalization and emerging trade blocs, those who wanted to break away remain undeterred. However, they narrowly missed their goal in August 1998 when 62 percent of Nevisians voted for secession, instead of the two thirds necessary.

The pulse of development

On 19 September 2008, St Kitts and Nevis celebrated their 25th birthday. The islands have experienced the full spectrum of challenges and achievements associated with "growing up" but the fact is that they are still really only teenagers and cannot lay claim to complete adulthood just yet. Make no mistake, the islands have experienced all the glamour of nationhood; a blossoming shopping port; unprecedented infrastructural development and an influx of investment interests, but the realities and challenges of development lurk ever so forebodingly just below the surface.

Among major developments are a brand new cricket stadium where the Indian, Australian, Scottish, Pakistan and West Indian cricket teams participated in the ICC Cricket World Cup. The Silver Jubilee Athletic Stadium also housed the region's major Olympic qualifier, the CARIFTA Games. Also commendable were recent efforts to ease the flow of traffic given the rising number of vehicles with the construction of the West Bypass, which will reduce traffic into and out of Basseterre.

It remains true that no one can really starve on these islands, with fruit trees at almost every corner. But Kittitians, like people elsewhere in the world, want more than subsistence living. Despite economic challenges the government ini-

TIP

The St Kitts Music Festival features well known artists from the Caribbean and all over the music world. This spectacular four-night event in June is held in the grounds of the Warner Park Stadium, which was refurbished for the Cricket World Cup in 2007.

BELOW: the day's catch waiting for a buyer.

POLITICAL MUD-SLINGERS

Islanders' energy is expounded in exuberantly heated political discourse – always colorful, often vitriolic, but often confined to diatribes on radio talk shows and in the two rival political newspapers in St Kitts, *The Labour Spokesman* and *The Democrat*.

Political affiliation is a major factor in everyday life – at work, at play and of course, in the choice of which of the latest crop of scandalous political rumors to believe or to reject as "blatant lies and propaganda."

In fact, many islanders possess an uncanny ability to relate everything to politics. For example, a gentleman's failure to show up for a date might be due to the government raising gasoline prices, rendering the poor fellow unable to fill his car's petrol tank so that he can pick up his girlfriend.

But while local-style politics is both highly polarized and passionate, the politicians and their supporters do tend to abide by the rules of democracy and free speech for the most part: the bitter verbal brawling rarely becomes physical.

The critics argue that if more effort were spent on social and economic development than political mudslinging, the islands could be better off.

tiated a fast-paced public-housing program so that today tiny, mostly well-kept dwellings speckle the landscape. Cable TV and the internet are no longer a luxury and almost everyone has a cell phone or two. The flimsy wooden cottages of the past are being replaced by "wall" (concrete) homes and SUVs (sports utility vehicles) are increasingly seen on the roads.

Basseterre – a gracefully revived town

This knack for patiently waiting to pick only the choicest fruits of progress, while preserving the best of the old ways, is nowhere more evident than in the bustle of a newly invigorated **Basseterre** ❶. After decades of sleepy existence and a long descent into downright shabbiness, this elegant old West Indian lady, which became the official British capital in 1727, is enjoying a second debut.

A campaign to restore the town's graceful but dilapidated commercial buildings and dwellings, some of them centuries old, has resulted in one of the greatest success stories in Caribbean architectural preservation. Careful and sensitive restorations have revealed all the original charm of the traditional buildings, with their lower floors of rough-cut volcanic stone and upper stories of fanciful wooden gingerbread. What began as a successful exercise in civic pride is rapidly turning out to be an economic success story as well. More and more cruise ship passengers are enjoying the town's charm and beauty, and business is growing, with attractive shops offering duty-free products opening up everywhere.

Yet Basseterre still booms with an irrepressible Caribbean vigor. Crisply dressed traffic police sort out the snarls at the intersections around the **Circus** where an ornate cast-iron clock tower, the **Berkeley Memorial**, regards the swirling scene with the pompous aloofness of a colonial plantocrat; bemused

Kittitian sprinter Kim Collins won the 100-meter sprint at the World Athletics Championship in Paris in 2003. And though he returned home without a medal after the Olympics in Athens, in 2004, he is a national hero and even has a highway named after him.

BELOW: a typical building at Independence Square.

visitors and locals peer down from the balcony of the **Ballahoo**, a meeting place and restaurant, at the frenetic salesmanship of the cab drivers ("Man, you gotta want a taxi – s'way too hot to walk, man").

Independence Square nearby is a pretty park, overlooked by 18th-century houses. Where once there was a slave market is now a network of paths in a Union Jack design with a fountain in the middle. The water feature, which is decorated with sculptures of naked women, was once the center of controversy. There were demands for its removal and replacement with a monument to slave emancipation.

Map on page 204-5

The bayfront

Just off the bayfront, **Port Zante** has emerged as if out of nowhere. Around 30 acres (12 hectares) of reclaimed land is now almost completely covered with stores and restaurants – a shoppers' paradise. Every kind of luxury item, souvenir, jewellery item, clothing or beverage imaginable are available on Port Zante. In fact locals fear that tourists arriving by ship will never move beyond the port where stores are mostly owned by foreigners. Certainly Kittitians hope that most tourists will make the effort to come further inland to get cultural experiences and to get a feel of real St Kitts life.

When cruise ships dock at the modern Port Zante in Basseterre on a Sunday, most shops open up especially for them.

Bay Road runs the full length of the ocean front in Basseterre, linking Port Zante to the downtown area where locals live and work. On Bay Road is the bus terminal and in the same complex is the ferry terminal, where ferries go back and forth between St Kitts and Nevis. In true Caribbean style, mangoes, soursop, pears, herbs and every type of tropical fruit and vegetable line the sidewalks just next to the terminal, wooing the discerning shopper towards the local market just steps away on the other side of the road.

LEFT: the fountain in Independence Square.
BELOW: Basseterre artifacts on display.

Large butterflies – orange sulfurs, malachites, mimics, and Caribbean buck- eyes – skim on fresh breezes after the familiar afternoon tropical downpour.

LEFT: creating a Caribelle batik.
BELOW: Romney Manor, where batiks are made.

The St Kitts circular

If Basseterre is basking in a vibrant new life, then the rest of St Kitts, as enjoyed on the 32-mile (51-km) loop drive, remains mostly in a sleepy haze, although there is evidence of an island in transition. The island's main road wriggles through villages of pastel-shaded wood and breeze-block cottages with tin roofs overlooking black sand beaches, and backed by fields of sugar cane climbing up to the fringes of the rainforest around Mount Liamuiga (once Mount Misery).

Remnants of old sugar mills abound, as on Nevis, a handful have found a more productive use as elite inns and private homes. But in spite of the busy little sugar-cane railroad, the slow demise of the sugar industry is evident everywhere.

The last of the Caribs

History interjects itself, sometimes subtly, in the form of Carib rock drawings at the side of the road in **Old Road Town ❷**, 5 miles (8 km) west of Basseterre, where the first British settlers landed. On the way, you pass the sad little ravine at **Bloody Point** where over 2,000 Carib Amerindians were massacred on a hot afternoon in 1626, as they were about to launch an attack on island settlers. Sir Thomas Warner, who led the first party of settlers, is buried further along the coast in St Thomas' churchyard at **Middle Island**, in an ornate tomb topped with his rather self-serving epitaph. Above Old Road Town are the ruins of Wingfield Sugar Estate and the lush rainforest gardens of **Romney Manor ❸**, the old estate house was destroyed by fire in 1995. Here are the workshops of **Caribelle Batik** (open Mon–Fri) where you can buy batik clothes and material and watch their creation.

Farther north, **Brimstone Hill ❹** (open daily; entrance charge), a Unesco World Heritage Site, is history preserved atop a huge volcanic plug of andesite edged by

Map on page 164

limestone protrusions. A great graystone fortress peers out over a panorama of ocean punctuated by the two cones of St Eustatius and Saba to the northwest. Begun in 1690, the fortress was confidently known as Britain's "Gibraltar of the West Indies," until its humiliating capture by the French in 1782, just prior to their final ejection a year later. Today a series of small museum rooms give a useful overview of island culture and history and a café provides a welcome rest.

A walk into Mount Liamuiga

High above the fort, the rainforest begins abruptly. Guided walking tours to the 3,792-ft (1,156-meter) picture-postcard volcanic crater of **Mount Liamuiga** ❺ are available from tour operators in Basseterre. Follow sinuous paths up through the cane and enter the gloom where the trade wind breezes suddenly cease. Buzzings and rustlings in the undergrowth and treetops suggest a lively retinue of residents and possible sightings of green vervet monkeys.

On the northern slope of the volcano, off the circular road, is **Rawlins Plantation Inn** ❻, a 17th-century plantation house and ruined mill which has been transformed into a lovely hotel surrounded by beautiful gardens. Farther along the Atlantic coast, **Ottley's Plantation Inn** ❼, another converted sugar estate, offers a spring-fed pool and short and easy rainforest walks.

The wild beauty of the southeast peninsula

At the entrance to the 14 mile (22-km) southeast peninsula, **Frigate Bay** ❽ embraces both the Atlantic and the Caribbean with pale sandy beaches offering watersports. This is the main island resort area. The construction of several spa resorts, hotel and condominium developments is now underway at what is affec-

Half Way Tree, on the Caribbean coast of St Kitts, is reputed to have got its name from the villagers cutting all of their trees halfway to ward off any jumbies (evil spirits) coming from Brimstone Hill.

BELOW: view from Brimstone Hill.

tionately known by most Kittitians as "the peninsula". **Ocean's Edge** covers 40 acres (16 hectares) of steep hillside just below the entrance to the peninsula, scattered with prestigious homes with superb views and seclusion.

A five-minute drive takes you to **The Estates on Sundance Ridge** – hidden away in the recesses of the peninsula's highest peak are several exclusive high-end properties. Further along, construction has begun on the $600 million **Christophe Harbour** project, which includes several five-star luxury hotels, a marina village, spas, beach clubs and a Tom Fazio golf course. One of the agreements between the developers and local government was that they maintain the environmental integrity of the island, including sensitivity to the salt ponds, lagoons, coral reefs, monkeys, tropical birds and vibrant sea life. Turtle Beach Bar and Restaurant, a long time favourite among seabathers in St Kitts, will be reconstructed as part of the Christophe Harbour.

The slow boat to Nevis

While regular short-hop flights are available between St Kitts and Nevis every day, ferries linking Basseterre to Charlestown provide an unforgettable 30- or 45-minute 12-mile (19-km), nautical experience – a slice of island life in its most chaotic and charismatic form. Whether you want to reach Nevis quickly and in style or on the slow cargo boat is up to you, since the number of vessels has increased there is no difference in the price, only in the experience.

The *M.V. Sea Hustler* wallows alongside Basseterre ferry dock by the side of the massive landfill development of Port Zante as the loading takes place – a mini-mountain of boxes, baskets, sacks of vegetables, even bicycles. The ride is choppy as the ferry rolls past the velvety hills of the southeast peninsula, skirt-

Alexander Hamilton (1757–1804), illegitimate son of a Scottish merchant, who grew up to be the first Secretary of the American Treasury alongside George Washington, kept his lowly start on Nevis quiet.

BELOW:
Charlestown, Nevis.

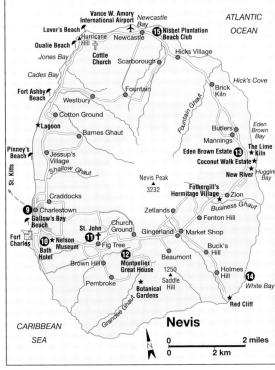

ing Ballast Bay, Bugg's Hole, and Nag's Head, catching the bigger waves in The Narrows between the islands. Outside the spray-splattered windows, the classic volcanic profile of Nevis Peak rises 3,232 ft (985 meters) into its perpetual cloud cap. Dense rainforest shrouds the higher slopes; lower down are tree-bounded fields and the remnants of old sugar mills and below that the long line of **Pinney's Beach** – 4 miles (6 km) of golden sand shaded by palms – backed by the luxury Four Seasons Resort. With bars and restaurants, this is the island's busiest beach and it still looks deserted. A new addition in transport to Nevis from St Kitts is the seabridge: owners drive their vehicles onto the barge and take an interesting journey to Nevis where they simply drive off when they arrive.

Map on page 170

A gingerbread capital

Emerging from its palmy setting, **Charlestown ❾** (pop. 1,800) is a colorful sprawl of pastel walls, tin roofs, and shady gardens. At the pier a hand-painted sign reads "Welcome to Nevis. Birthplace of Alexander Hamilton."

After Nevis' heyday in the 18th century, the town's fortunes fluctuated, hit by hurricanes and other disasters and the slackening demand for its sea-island cotton and sugar cane. However, Charlestown has retained a quaint dignity and architectural unity in its high-roofed, verandah-shaded, gingerbread-trimmed buildings on Main Street and around **D.R. Walwyn's Plaza**.

At the top end of Main Street is the **Museum of Nevis History** (open Mon–Fri, and Sat am; entrance charge) on the site where the 18th-century American statesman Alexander Hamilton was born (it is believed) 1757. Set in a beautiful garden by the sea, growing typical Nevisian plants and trees, the museum charts the life of Hamilton and the island's history.

BELOW: a ramshackle house in Charlestown.

Back at the Plaza, huckster ladies sell vegetables and trinkets near the **Nevis Handicraft Co-op**, where homemade fruit wines – pawpaw, sorrel, genip, and gooseberry – are for sale in old soda bottles along with some fiery pepper sauce. Around the corner at the **Nevis Philatelic Bureau**, visitors flock to buy first-day editions of colorful Nevis stamps (a useful source of revenue). And on Saturdays by 7.30am, the town is bursting with life as Nevisians crowd into the fish, meat, and vegetable market down by the docks.

Thanks to the ICC Cricket World Cup 2007, St Kitts and Nevis have a redeveloped sports stadium in Basseterre with a seating capacity of 12,000. The first cricket One Day International was played at the Warner Park Complex in 2006, the first of many.

The Nelson era

By comparison, the remainder of this 36-sq. mile (93-sq. km) volcanic island seems a sleepy, pastoral place. The 18-mile (30-km) road around Nevis meanders southward out of Charlestown to the shell of the once-fashionable **Bath Hotel ❿** (open Mon–Fri; entrance charge). Built in 1778 to accommodate the cream of colonial society visiting the natural sulfur spring nearby, the hotel spa is believed to be one of the first in the Caribbean. The British sea captain Horatio Nelson was a central attraction here in the mid-1780s when he married Fanny Nisbet, a Nevisian society widow, and the **Nelson Museum** (open Mon–Fri, and Sat am; entrance charge) has a marvellous collection of memorabilia of his time in the West Indies. Their marriage certificate is on display in the 300-year-old **St John's Fig Tree Church ⓫**, 2 miles (3 km) away, which over the centuries has been rebuilt twice and where there is a fascinating array of tombstones.

The road continues eastward, circling **Nevis Peak** whose forested slopes hide a web of hiking trails, and wriggles past bursting bushes of bauhinias and untidy bark-dripping gum trees. The spine-laden trunk of a sandbox rises out of a tangle of Mexican creepers and lantana. A turning to the right leads to

Below: schoolgirls in the shadow of Nevis Peak.

HORATIO AND FANNY

Horatio Nelson came to the Caribbean as Captain of the *Boreas* in 1784, to keep an eye out for any illegal trading. After American independence, the new nation's ships were no longer allowed to trade with British colonies, but when Nelson impounded the goods of four disguised American merchant ships lying off Nevis, the island's merchants, who were going to do business with them and whose livelihood depended on them, sued him for £40,000. Their anger was such that Nelson had to hide on his ship for eight weeks until John Herbert, the president of Nevis and Fanny Nisbet's uncle, bailed him out.

Based in Antigua in English Harbour *(see page 183)*, Nelson hated the "infernal heat" of the West Indies and sought diversion on Nevis which was the height of fashion at the time. His charm and his friendship with the future William IV, who was also based in Antigua for a time, made him a welcome guest in Nevis's Great Houses and he was soon seen with the attractive young widow, Fanny Nisbet on his arm. He married her in March 1787 and Prince William wrote: "*Poor Nelson is head over ears in love. I frequently laugh at him about it…he married Mrs Nisbet on the twelfth of March (it was the 11th) and I had, my Lord, the honour of giving her away…*"

Montpelier Great House , the sugar estate where Horatio and Fanny tied the knot. In the 1960s, a plantation house-style hotel was built on the site, which is now surrounded by lovely gardens, and past guests have included British royalty. It is one of several tastefully converted estates on the island, where you can recapture the atmosphere of the old plantocracy days, and is a perfect place to stop for lunch or a drink.

Map on page 170

If you believe in ghosts, the abandoned **Eden Brown Estate** (open daily; free), halfway up the east coast, is supposed to be haunted by a bereft bride whose husband-to-be was killed in a drunken duel on the eve of their wedding. She remained a recluse in the house until her death and islanders say that she has often been heard crying there still.

Hidden beaches

A narrow track winds down from the road at Gingerland past typical cameos of island life to the hidden beaches of **White Bay**. On the northeastern and west coasts beautiful sandy beaches fringed by palms and mangoes are quiet and deserted. Popular opinion has it that the **Nisbet Plantation Beach Club**, near Newcastle, has the best beach in Nevis.

A changing landscape

Life is picking up on Nevis but not everyone is invited to the party. Like St Kitts, most of the developments in the resort areas are catering to high-end clients. On the west coast beach, two and three-bedroom ocean-view condominiums and villas are being constructed, and new waterfront homes at Tamarind Bay mean that the coastline is changing rapidly. ❏

BELOW: the garden of Montpelier Great House.

ANTIGUA AND BARBUDA

With a white, sandy beach for every day of the year and waters licked by the steady northeasterlies these islands, set in the heart of the Caribbean, are a haven for beach lovers and sailors

Map on page 178

Shaped like a heart, the Leeward island of Antigua (pronounced An-*tee*-ga) shimmers in the heat of the Caribbean sun as the airplane comes in to land. For many, landing on this 108-sq. mile (270 sq. km) flat island of volcanic rock, coral and limestone is the first taste of the Antilles they have as they wend their way to other islands. At the heart of the Caribbean archipelago, Antigua, with islands Barbuda and the uninhabited Redonda, is edged by a beautiful coastline abundant with bays, coves and natural harbors: 365 white sandy beaches in all so the tourist brochures say, and water sparkling in every shade of blue and turquoise between the Caribbean and the open Atlantic.

The vegetation on Antigua is limited to low scrub and dry grassland – the forests that once covered the island had to make way for the plantations of European colonists, and the only real scenic variety is provided by a few green hills and scraps of forest in the southwest. But watersports enthusiasts love Antigua. Divers flock to the barrier reefs surrounding the island, while windsurfers and sailors enjoy the steady trade winds. Every April, the international yachting set breeze in for Antigua Sailing Week, when partying vies with sailing. The gentle Caribbean Sea on the leeward side is perfect for swimming and once, during a state visit, even enticed the Queen into its warm, soothing waters.

An experienced nation

The pale pink sands of Barbuda 25 miles (40 km) to the northeast offer a desert island remoteness for those who want to get away from it all and relax as Diana, Princess of Wales did in the February before she died. This tiny 60-sq. mile (160-sq. km) island has a population of only 1,300 contributing to the nation's 70,000, most of whom are dependent on tourism.

However, the self-confident islanders can look back on a lot more experience than most of their neighbors where tourism is concerned. During World War II, the USA used Antigua as a base for reinforcements and air power, building a modern airport which created a suitable infrastructure for tourism after the war. By 1965, there were over 50,000 visitors to the island, and, today, around 250,000 people arrive by air and some 525,000 come on cruise ships each year, contributing about two thirds of the country's revenue.

Wadadli and its "rulers"

In 1493, on his second journey to the New World, Christopher Columbus sighted the island and named it after a church in his home town of Seville in Spain: Santa María de la Antigua. It was first named Yarumaqui, meaning the island of canoe-making, by the Tainos and then the Caribs called it Wadadli, meaning eucalyptus oil, after the trees which the British cut

PRECEDING PAGES: colorful sails during Antigua Sailing Week. **LEFT:** Pigeon Point at sunset, English Harbour. **BELOW:** a photographer's simple studio.

down so that they could plant sugar cane. The name can still be seen today on the bottle caps of a local beer.

During the Anglo-French colonial wars in the 17th and 18th centuries, Antigua served as the Caribbean base for the British fleet. In 1666 the French briefly captured the island, after which it remained British when a white plantocracy was established feeding off sugar production. When sugar prices dropped in the late 1800s, and then dramatically collapsed in the late 1960s, the manor houses of the plantation owners fell into disrepair; these days, only the ruined windmills are left.

When Horatio Nelson (depicted above) was based in Antigua for three years in the 1780s, he was not enamored with the island or the heat, calling it "a vile spot" and "this infernal hell."

The big Birds

Part of the crown colony of the Leeward Islands until 1956, Antigua was given the status of an independent colony within the British Commonwealth in 1967, and in 1981 it finally became independent with Vere Cornwall "Papa" Bird as Prime Minister. From 1945, Bird and his Antigua Labour Party (ALP) had steered the fortunes of the island, and in 1994, he was "succeeded" by his son Lester.

The Bird clan's private fortune has been estimated at more than US$100 million, and critics have accused the Antigua and Barbuda "family business" of a level of corruption that is unique even by Caribbean standards, involving fraud, arms smuggling, drug running, money laundering and so on, interlaced with the fierce rivalry between two of Papa Bird's sons, Vere Jr and Lester. In her story *A Small Place* (1988) the Antiguan writer Jamaica Kincaid provides a particularly vivid account of this corruption. The Bird dynasty retained power until 2004, when unease about alleged corruption and vice connections in government circles finally led to the election of Baldwin Spencer, leading a coalition of opposition parties, the United Progressive Party (UPP), which won 12 of the 17 legislative seats.

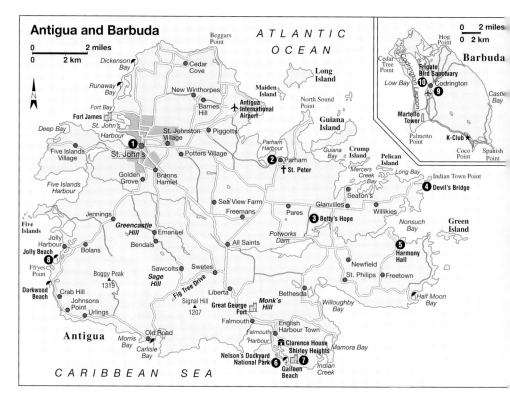

St John's – a thriving town and harbor

St John's ❶ (pop. 40,000) in the northwest is Antigua's capital and is set around its largest and most important natural harbor. The streets in the center are lined with typically Caribbean wooden houses; most of the historic buildings date from the late 19th and early 20th centuries, because a large part of the town was destroyed by a seaquake in 1843.

Old warehouses by the Deep Water Harbour have been converted into shopping centers within reach of the cruise ships: **Heritage Quay** offers a Las Vegas-style casino and duty-free shopping, and **Redcliffe Quay**, which used to accommodate enslaved Africans before they were auctioned off at the market, has been restored, retaining many of its historical features, and now has restaurants and souvenir shops. Both are pleasant places in which to relax in air-conditioned surroundings. A third quay, **Nevis Street Pier**, can accept the latest mega-ships.

At the southern end of Market Street a block or two up the hill, is the colorful **Public Market** where produce from the island is sold right on the street. The busiest days are Fridays and Saturdays. There is also a covered market here. No stroll through St John's would be complete without a visit to the **Museum of Antigua and Barbuda** (open Mon–Fri, and Sat am; tel: 268-462 1469; donations; www.antiguamuseums.org) on Long Street, at the other end of Market Street. Located in the Old Court House (1844), this collection of oddities provides an insight into local cultural history. It ranges from Siboney and Taino excavation finds to steel drums that you can try out for yourself. The most attractive items are in the geological section and include large coral skeletons.

The finest view of the busy capital is from **St John's Cathedral**, two blocks eastward on Church Street. Its distinctive twin towers can clearly be seen from

Map on page 178

TIP

Food City, Antigua's largest and most modern supermarket, is on Dickenson Bay Street on the way to the Deep Water Harbour in St John's. It is open daily from 7am to 11pm.

BELOW: Redcliffe Quay, St John's.

Wherever you see a huddle of men, you can be sure there will be a game of Warri (above) going on. Brought over from Africa by the slaves, it is played on a wooden board with 12 holes and 48 seeds. The aim is to capture your opponent's seeds.

BELOW: statues of St John on the cathedral gates.

all over the old town. This Anglican episcopal church is actually the third structure to be built on the site. The first church, built in 1682, was completely made of wood, while the second (built in 1789) fell victim to the quake of 1843. The present structure dates from 1845–48 and, despite its exposed location, it turned out to be sturdy enough to withstand Hurricane Hugo in 1989 and hurricanes Luis and Marilyn in 1995, which devastated the rest of the island. The two statues of St John on the south gate were actually planned for a church in Guadeloupe, but an English warship stole them during shipment.

The harbor entrance is protected by two 18th-century bastions: **Fort Barrington** to the south, and on the northern promontory **Fort James**, which still has cannon dating from the colonial era and has wonderful views. The beach in the bay below is St John's local beach and popular for beach parties at weekends. Otherwise the impoverished-looking huts along the northern suburbs make it clear that not everyone on Antigua has profited from tourism; and ironically, the streamlined luxury cruise liners still remain within full view, creating two worlds that could scarcely be more different from one another.

The white beaches of the north

While driving through Antigua you need to get used to two phenomena: amazingly fast minibuses, whose drivers prefer to hoot rather than brake, and almost no signposts. Make sure you are provided with a map by the car rental company and ask the locals for directions – bumpy tracks included, Antigua has no more than 60 miles (100 km) of road altogether.

The stretch of coast to the northwest of St John's provides perfect conditions for Antigua's number-one industry. **Runaway Bay** and **Dickenson Bay** are the

ST JOHN THE BAPTIST

ST JOHN THE DIVINE

names of the idyllic white beaches here, whose assets the hotel industry has not been slow to catch on to. The prices bear a direct relation to how far the hotel is from the water, with luxury establishments nearest the beach and medium-category ones farther back in the hills. Dickenson Bay is well equipped with glass-bottomed boats, various diving schools, jet-ski rental, and bars. The farther north you go, the quieter beach life becomes.

Quiet coasts and Betty's Hope

Broad, sandy bays nestle between weathered limestone crags along Antigua's eastern coastline, which is pounded by the Atlantic. It's advisable not to underestimate the power of the surf here, especially since no lifeguard assistance is at hand on these largely deserted beaches. The roads heading east out of St John's lead to **Parham ❷** where, in 1632, the first British colonists from St Kitts arrived and started clearing the land of trees to plant sugar cane. The village church of **St Peter's**, built in 1840, is an unusual octagonal shape. Nearby, the shoreline is bordered by several mangrove swamps which are now, owing to development, a rarity on Antigua. From Crabs Peninsula to the east, you can look over to Guiana Island, 100 yds (100 meters) offshore.

About 4 miles (6 km) away to the south and east, in the middle of dry bushland, on the other side of the small village of Pares, stands the remains of **Betty's Hope ❸** (open Mon, Wed–Sat; tel: 269-462 1469 for guided tour; entrance charge), the first sugar plantation to be established on a grand scale in Antigua in 1674, and now an open-air museum. In the midst of such a barren landscape, and plains dotted with husks of sugar mills it's not that hard to imagine vast fields of sugar cane here. The plantation was developed by the British officer Christopher

Map on page 178

Christopher Codrington Jr (1668–1710) was a leading slave owner whose family established Betty's Hope – the first sugar estate on the island. In 1702, he founded a theological seminary in Barbados (see page 270) and a year later he tried (and failed) to recapture Guadeloupe from the French.

BELOW: horseback riding on Runaway Beach.

An egret graces an Antiguan phone card.

Codrington, who came to Antigua as governor of the Leeward Islands. His family lived in the Great House, named for his daughter, for many generations until 1921 when they abandoned sugar and moved to the US. You can still see one of the old twin windmills working, and also the foundation walls of the former boiling house.

Devil's Bridge ❹, nearly 5 miles (8 km) away at the most eastern tip of the island near Long Bay, is a natural rock bridge with several blowholes formed by the incessant pounding of the Atlantic surf. Thought to have once been an Amerindian settlement, it is a popular weekend destination with the locals because the offshore reef acts as a breakwater, and the sea is calm.

Another good beach is **Half Moon Bay** in the south; because of its perfect almost circular shape, many consider it to be the finest on the island. Just before you get there, take a left turn to **Nonsuch Bay** 2 miles (3 km) away, to **Harmony Hall ❺** (open daily; tel: 268-460 4120; www.harmonyhall.com). A former plantation house, it is now known for its crafts and art gallery, and excellent Italian restaurant. The bar is tucked away in the old stone mill tower and moorings are available in the bay. The Antiguan Artists' Exhibition is held here in November.

Nelson's Dockyard and English Harbour

The quickest way to reach the southwest coast and **Nelson's Dockyard National Park ❻** (open daily; entrance charge), 12 miles (18 km) from St John's, is to take the much-used All Saints Road. The first small town you pass is **Liberta**, which commemorates the first slaves who settled here after they were freed by the British in 1834.

A 30-minute walk takes you up Monk's Hill to the ruins of **Great George Fort** and panoramic views across **Falmouth Harbour**, splattered with white

BELOW: Nelson's Dockyard, English Harbour.

sails. **English Harbour** is tucked away inside the bay, and was made a National Park in 1985. The potential of this magnificent, protected, natural harbor was realized as early as 1671, and while tropical storms damaged numerous Royal Navy vessels in most other parts of the West Indies, here in English Harbour and Falmouth Bay they were protected from the worst. Completely hidden away from the enemy out at sea, the dockyard was a safe place in which to repair the ships. Admirals Hood and Rodney stayed at **Admiral's House** on several occasions during their battles against France toward the end of the 18th century, and from 1784 to 1787, the young Horatio Nelson, commander of *HMS Boreas*, was based here *(see page 172)*.

Today, the former naval base is a picturesque yachting harbor. Warehouses and powder magazines have been restored with an affectionate eye for detail and transformed into a museum, romantic restaurants and nostalgic hotels. The **Admiral's Inn** and the **Copper and Lumber Store** are two sensitively restored and atmospheric hostelries, with walls of brick brought over from England as ships' ballast. A lively place at the best of times, Nelson's Dockyard really comes into its own during the big regattas, such as **Antigua Sailing Week**, when the bars and restaurants stay open all night and there's dancing till dawn.

Shirley Heights – a perfect lookout

Across the harbor high up on the hilltop stand the ruins of the once protective fortress of Shirley Heights. At the foot of the hill is **Clarence House,** which was built especially for Prince William, the Duke of Clarence, when he was transferred to Antigua in 1787 as commander of *HMS Pegasus*. This typically Georgian colonial building, with a pretty verandah and shuttered windows, now

Map
on page
178

TIP

Learn more about English Harbour on an historical boat trip (departs noon, daily from outside the Copper and Lumber Store), or during the multimedia show at the Dow Hill Interpretation Centre (open daily, entrance charge) on the way to Shirley Heights.

BELOW: boats docked in English Harbour.

ANTIGUA SAILING WEEK

Arriving in Antigua at the end of April you won't see suitcases on the luggage bands, just bulky sailor's bags by the hundred. Antigua Sailing Week (www.sailing week.com), four decades on, is one of the top five yachting events in the world, attracting more than 200 yachts, 1,500 participants and 5,000 spectators – from the world-class cup-winners to the amateur sailing enthusiast. Alongside the five days of racing off the shores of Antigua are seven days and nights of intensive partying.

Two days are wholly set aside for organized fun and frolics in Falmouth's shallow harbor waters: Lay Day falls after three days of racing, when climbing a greasy pole, tug of war, and a wet T-shirt competition judged by a "bishop" and other honorary majesties are all part of the festivities; Dockyard Day celebrates the finish in an even more raucous style.

Although to some sailing is just a sideline of the week, there is serious racing all around the island for a range of classes. All sorts of boats join in from the small (with a handicap) to the high-tech 58-footer (18-meter) with fiberglass sails and a crew of 20 plus. And at lookout points, it's a wonderful sight to see the boats turn into a westerly course and release their colorful spinnakers.

serves as the British Governor's guesthouse and country residence. But official visitors don't get exclusive access, as the rooms full of period antiques are open to the public when the governor is away (tours are free of charge, but a tip is appropriate and appreciated).

There's a perfect, 360-degree panoramic view from **Shirley Heights** ❼. In 1781 Governor Thomas Shirley instigated the construction of the fortifications to protect the harbor, and on clear days the excellent view extends as far as Montserrat, 28 miles (45 km) to the southwest, and Guadeloupe, 40 miles (64 km) to the south. The observation point and the restaurant at the top are both called **The Lookout** and every Thursday and Sunday there is a barbecue and live music here – steel bands from 4pm and reggae on Sunday after 7pm.

The feared attack by the French, which the bastion was supposed to prevent, never actually materialized. Most of the soldiers who died at English Harbour did so from tropical diseases rather than in battle. A marked path leads from The Lookout to the cemetery in which they lie buried; the ruins of several barracks, stables, and cisterns can also be seen, giving some idea of the harshness of garrison life. **Galleon Beach**, right beneath Shirley Heights, is an ideal place for a subsequent swim, although it is only accessible by car or water-taxi from English Harbour.

Green hills and soft sand

Just north of Liberta, **Fig Tree Drive**, the most scenic road on Antigua, winds its way down toward the southwest coast. The figs in question are not figs at all but the wild banana plants which, together with a few giant trees and lianas, provide a vague idea of what the rainforest here was once like. At Old Road, the trip

The Sir Vivian Richards Stadium in North Sound outside St John's was built to host the Super 8 matches in the ICC Cricket World Cup 2007. The large stadium has seating capacity for 10,000 people, with an additional 10,000 temporary seats.

BELOW: exclusivity is the name of the game on Barbuda.

Map on page 178

continues northwards, hugging the coast all the way, and soon **Boggy Peak** (1,319 ft/402 meters), the highest point on the island, comes into view.

Two of Antigua's finest beaches provide good rest-stops with a bar and restaurant along the way: **Cades Bay** and **Darkwood Beach** both have astonishingly few visitors. In contrast, just around the next point, **Jolly Beach ❽** (plus the yacht-filled Jolly Harbour) is full of commotion and good service; it's part of the Club Antigua, the island's largest holiday village, and the outskirts of St John's are only 5 miles (8 km) away.

Beautiful remote beaches of Barbuda

Barbuda is the ideal holiday island for those who love solitude, its sole attraction being the seemingly endless, shimmering and slightly pink-colored coral beach on the Caribbean side. The landscape on this 68-sq. mile (170-sq. km) island is flat as a pancake and scrubby apart from the eastern "Highlands", which rise to a maximum height of just 128 ft (40 meters).

There are at least two daily 10-minute flights from Antigua to Barbuda and you can arrange an all-in day trip with a visit to the frigate bird sanctuary, lunch, and some time on the beach included. Alternatively, take the catamaran, *Barbuda Express* (Wed–Mon from St John's), which also offers day tours of the island.

Situated on the eastern edge of the 8-mile (13-km) long lagoon, **Codrington ❾**, the main town (or village really), where most of the 1,300 inhabitants of Barbuda live, is named for Sir Christopher *(see page 183)*. The sugar baron was leased Barbuda by King Charles II in 1680 and the family kept it for 200 years. Here he resettled several powerfully built African slaves and their families, and today people say that Barbudans are taller than Antiguans.

Barbuda has just three "sights" worth mentioning: the **Martello Tower**, a 50-ft (17-meter) high former watchtower; **Highland House**, the ruins of Codrington's historical manor on the highest point of the island; and the **Frigate Bird Sanctuary ❿** to the north. Nesting sites of the unusually tame frigate birds are mainly located in the mangrove swamps, and can be reached by boat. On the southern tip of the island are two exclusive resorts, the luxurious Italianate **K-Club**, where an array of celebrities enjoy the private villas, and the relaxed **Coco Point Lodge**. Both pick up their guests from Antigua in private planes.

Redonda – a fantasy "monarchy"

The third island in this small nation, **Redonda**, 24 miles (38 km) southwest of Antigua, is uninhabited – except for birds. This half square mile (1 sq. km) rocky island, where guano was collected until the middle of the 20th century, has a history of its own: in 1865 an eccentric Irishman named Matthew Shiell had the unusual idea of crowning his son Philip "King of Redonda." He became a novelist and the title was passed on to the poet, John Gawsworth. As King Juan he liberally appointed new members of the Redondan aristocracy, such as Dylan Thomas, Diana Dors and Dirk Bogarde. Nowadays, the monarchy is hotly disputed with at least one king living in England and another in Spain. ❏

BELOW: an Antiguan beach lookout.

MONTSERRAT

Life under the shadow of the volcano is all but over. Today visitors can enjoy the spectacular volcanic scenery, picturesque walking trails in the northern mountains, and black sand beaches

Map on page 190

Montserrat

Caribbean Sea

The people of Montserrat are still rebuilding following the volcanic eruptions in the Soufriere Hills, that started in July 1995 and which destroyed much of the infrastructure in the southern part of the island. The mountain above Long Ground, which spewed pyroclastic flows of rocks, ash, and gases over the crater rim at 80 mph (130 kph) destroying many homes and livelihoods, continues to be active. After the initial explosion, subsequent flows devastated villages and towns, including the capital Plymouth, and in June 1997, 19 people died. Then, following a relatively quiet period, its dome collapsed again in May 2006, removing about 100 million cubic meters of lava and making it the second largest collapse of the eruption. The explosions sent ash nearly 12 miles (20 km) up into the air, the highest recorded so far. The island is still on the alert.

Before the eruption 11,000 people called the island home, now less than half remain. There is a resilience and determination within those who wouldn't, or couldn't leave, and those who returned to rebuild the island.

How Montserrat used to be

Life "before the volcano" had been normal. This tiny, pear-shaped island of 11 by 7 miles (18 by 11 km) – a British Overseas Territory – formed a gentle society. Its people were mainly farmers cultivating the rich volcanic soil, civil servants, construction workers, or in the tourist industry. Visitors loved "old-fashioned" Montserrat ("how the Caribbean used to be" was the marketing phrase) and, at one time, rock stars such as Paul McCartney and David Bowie came to record at Sir George Martin's Air Studios, a victim of Hurricane Hugo in 1989.

Plymouth had once been pastel pretty, with gingerbread houses in the Caribbean vernacular style. Everywhere had been green, except for the beaches which were volcanic black.

An Irish-Catholic sanctuary

By the time Columbus saw and named Montserrat during his second voyage to the New World – after the mountainous ridges near the abbey of Montserrat near Barcelona – the original Amerindian inhabitants were no more. The first recorded settlers in post-Columbian times were Irish and English Catholics finding sanctuary from Protestant persecution on St Kitts.

By the middle of the 17th century, a typical Caribbean colonial structure with an economy based on sugar had been established: a small Anglo-Irish planter class developing a social, economic, and political power base over a growing number of African slaves. When sugar collapsed, and a post-Emancipation society developed, limes and cotton were introduced, becoming the

PRECEDING PAGES: view of the volcano from Old Road Bay. **LEFT:** view from Montserrat to Redonda. **BELOW:** a Montserrat welcome.

backbone of the economy. Gradually, a greater degree of autonomy was won from the British. By the early 1990s most power lay with a locally elected government with a British governor responsible for security and external relations.

In 1907 Mrs Goodwin won a competition with her design for Montserrat's emblem (above). It portrays Ireland, as Erin, embracing Christianity with the Irish harp and reflects the island's early Irish connections.

BELOW: safe – an untouched estate house in the north.

Living in the "northern safe zone"

The islanders live in northern areas untouched by the volcano. Its wilder landscape ends in steep cliffs, and beyond the dark sea are the purple outlines of St Kitts and Nevis *(see pages 162–73)* on one side and Antigua *(see pages 177–85)*, on the other. The infrastructure has been rebuilt in this safe part of the island – protected from the volcano by the **Centre Hills** running from east to west through the middle of the country. Access to all areas south of **Richmond Hill** and Jack Boy Hill to Bramble Airport and beyond is prohibited. The daytime entry zone, including the top part of **St George's Hill** was closed in 2006. There is also a maritime exclusion zone around the south coast which has inadvertently benefited the local marine life. The dive sites off the north coast are also doing well with healthy coral teeming with fish and a variety of sponges.

Bramble Airport has been rebuilt at **Gerald's** in the north. Funded by the British government, the airport is the main link to other islands; the ferry service to Antigua ended in 2005 but there are plans to restart it one day.

An island tour

Signposting on the island isn't always as good as it should be, so if you rent a car don't be afraid to ask directions. Alternatively hire a taxi for a day.

A good place to start a tour is **Flemmings** where the **Montserrat Volcano Observatory ❶** (open Mon–Fri 8.30am–4.30pm; tours on Tues and Thurs pm;

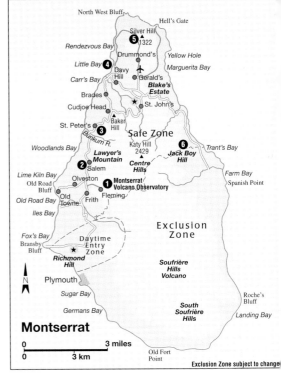

Montserrat

0   3 miles
0   3 km

Exclusion Zone subject to change

fee for guided tour; tel: 664-491 5647) is located in a purpose-built complex. The observatory provides amazing views of what nature can do and has an exhibition about the eruption and its devastating effect on the island.

The village of **Salem** ❷ is downhill from the observatory and worth a visit, especially on Friday night when its many bars are busy. The **Montserrat National Trust Visitor's Center** (open Mon–Fri and Sat am; tel: 664-491 3086) in Olveston, has a botanical garden and operates a series of nature trails in the hills.

The **Runaway Ghaut Gardens** are a mile from Salem, on the main road. Visitors walk the mile-long scenic track through the gardens to the west coast, following the line of the last retreat of the French who constantly fought the British for control of the island. It's an ideal spot for a picnic.

In a little cove off the main road, beyond the gardens, is the black sand **Woodlands Beach**, with changing and shower facilities maintained by the National Trust. The sea here is for strong swimmers only, because the beach shelves very quickly and the waves can be quite strong. Farther north is the hillside village of **St Peter's** ❸, whose four-square Anglican church dominates the clutch of houses spreading up the steep, main street. Climbing the hill from the village look left for a view of **Providence Estate House**.

The roads in northern Montserrat wiggle, climb and plunge, so proceed with caution. At the village of **Cudjoe Head**, whose bars get lively on Friday nights, turn right on to the twisty road for the breathtaking views at the top of **Baker Hill**.

Pass through **Manjack** before rejoining the main road about half a mile from where you left it at Cudjoe Head. You are now in **Brades**, where most of the island's shops are located. From Brades head north to **Carr's Bay**, and detour left near the cemetery, following the road for about a mile to **Little Bay** ❹. There are ambitious plans to develop this port and town to create a modern capital city. A cultural center (www.montserratculturalcentre.com) built by former record producer Sir George Martin, opened in 2007. Built into the hillside it is the largest building on the island and has an auditorium seating 500 and an amphitheatre with capacity for 2,500. Little Bay is also the location of **Festival Village**, an entertainment venue by the sea.

Uphill, past the residential district of Davy Hill, is the sprawling inland village of **St John's**, The Anglican church here is worth a visit. From St John's head downhill for about half a mile, turning right on to the road leading to the airport at Gerald's.

North and beyond the airport is the village of **Drummonds**, a good place to begin a walk to **Silver Hill** ❺ (1322 ft/403 meters). There is a communications tower at the top of the hill, and from here on a clear day you can see over Montserrat's northern coastline to Antigua 27 miles (44 km) away. Hikers can follow the signposted footpath to **Rendezvous Beach**, northwest of Drummonds. This is Montserrat's only white sand beach, but the trail to it is difficult and not for the faint hearted or unfit. There is a picnic spot and another excellent viewpoint at **Jack Boy Hill** ❻, on the east coast, where you can see the old airport in the valley below, and south to where the pyroclastic flow wiped out villages in its path. ❏

Map on page 190

TIP

The Montserrat Volcano Observatory (www.mvo.ms) issues weekly updates on volcanic activity with an archive of photos. By early 2007 the island was on alert level four (the highest is five), as the dome was growing rapidly producing lava flows and rockfalls.

BELOW: a forest ranger leads the way in Fogarty.

GUADELOUPE

French, but proudly Guadeloupean, this is an island of contrasts from the arid lowlands and white beaches of Grande-Terre to the mountain forests and diving grounds of Basse-Terre

Map on pages 196–7

Caribbean Sea

Butterflies have a short life span, but the two unequal wings of Guadeloupe – one dry and rocky, edged with its white ring of beaches, the other mountainous, luxuriant, and crisscrossed with crystal-cold rivers – have been spread for centuries. It is said that when Christopher Columbus first set eyes on Guadeloupe in 1493, he immediately encased it in a casket and presented the jewel to the very Catholic King of Spain.

At 555 sq. miles (1,438 sq. km) Guadeloupe is one of the larger islands of the Lesser Antilles and is not only diverse, but also complex. Beaches wash the sides of volcanoes wrapped in banana plantations, flat expanses of sugar cane grow alongside winding mangrove swamps, international hotels contrast with wooden huts perched on four stones, and major highways cross paths leading over the mountains amidst giant ferns and dense forests.

One section of the population defends its ties with France, the other, its African heritage. Some want to keep the political status of French overseas possession decreed in 1946. Others brandish a red and black flag, stamped with a crab, and demand independence. Some drive to work in a BMW. Others trundle along in an ox cart.

A piece of France

Guadeloupe, along with surrounding islands – Marie-Galante, Les Saintes, and La Désirade – St Martin *(see pages 127–34)* and St Barthélemy *(see pages 139–43)* is a *département* of France and therefore part of the EU. These islanders, like Martinicans, have French citizenship and French passports and have the same rights as those living in France, around 4,500 miles (7,000 km) away. Flying or sailing into Guadeloupe from another Caribbean island may make you wonder if you have taken a wrong turning somewhere: the four-lane highway from the airport is jammed with French cars, the large supermarkets and furniture stores are the same as those in France.

Guadeloupe's main export is bananas – most of which are eaten in France – and sugar cane, mainly used for making rum, still accounts for 40 percent of agricultural land. However, tourism is rapidly taking over as the country's biggest earner.

Land of beautiful waters

The Spanish made several attempts to settle the island after Columbus had dropped by long enough to name it for the Virgin of Guadelupe in Spain. However, they were foiled by the resident Caribs who tenaciously guarded their Land of Beautiful Waters (Karukera) until the arrival of the French in 1635. Within five years, the Amerindians had been suppressed and soon

PRECEDING PAGES: the magnificent cemetery at Morne à l'Eau.
LEFT: an Atlantic seascape,
BELOW: a fine place to relax.

Guadeloupe

0 _____ 5 miles
0 _____ 5 km

Pointe de la Grande Vigie

8

Anse Castalia

Pointe du Piton
Porte d'Enfer

Anse-Bertrand

Pointe d'Antigues

Massioux

Pointe des Gros Caps

Beaufond

Anse à la Barque

Haut de la
Montagne

Campêche

Ilet à
Kahouanne

Port-Louis

N8

Gros Cap

Anse des Corps

Anse de
la Perle   N2

Pointe Allègre

Pointe Gris-Gris

N6

Anse de la Savane Br

Grande
Anse

Duzer

Ste-Rose

Anse du Canal
Petit-Canal

Les Mangles

Deshaies

Montplaisir   Pointe Latanier

Pointe à Retz

Bazin

Anse Patate

Ilet à Fajou

Musée
du Rhum

Morne Rouge

Vieux Bourg

Morne
à l'Eau

La Rosette

7

Musée Arché
Edgar Clerc

Pointe de la
Grande Rivière

Anse Perrin

Bosredon

N5

Lasserre

Le

Domaine
de Séverin

La Boucan
Lamentin

Baie
Mahaut

Aéroport
Pôle
Caraïbes

Jabrun

Château-
Gaillard

Be

Pointe
Ferry

Têtê-Allègre
2345

Cadet

Karukères ★

Les Abymes

G r a n d e - T e r r e

Baille-
Argent

Castel

La Couronne
2480

N2

Baie-
Mahault

Bouliqui

Grands-Fonds

Douville

Châte

Pointe Noire

10

La Retraite

Pointe-à-Pitre

1

Cocoyer

Grands-Fonds

▲ 2440
Morne Jeanneton

Daubin

Petit
Cul-de-Sac Marin

Ste-Anne

4

Plage de
Bois Jol

Maison
du Bois

Prise d'Eau

Fort Fleur-d'Epée

2
3

St Félix

Mare Gaillard

N4

Caravelle

Anse
Guyonneau

Pointe Mahaut
Mahaut
Ilets
de Pigeon

N2

Route de la Traversée

Vernou

Montebello

Malendure

Maison de
la Forêt

9

Valombreuse
Floral Parc

Petit-Bourg

Le Gosier

Petit
Havre

Ilet du Gosier

Plage de Viard

G u a d e l o u p e

Reserve
Cousteau

11

Pigeon

**P a r c   N a t i o n a l
d e   l a   G u a d e l o u p e**

Anse à Douville
Goyave

Pointe à Lézard

▲ 3569
Pitons de Bouillante
▲ 3788
Morne Bel-Air

Bouillante

Anse de Sable

4257
Matéliane

Forêt de
Sainte-Marie

Ste-Marie

N1

Marigot

Maison du Café
★ "La Grivelière"

Grande Riv. de la Capesterre

Carangaise

Vieux-Habitants

B a s s e - T e r r e

Chutes
du Carbet

Pointe de la Capesterre

La Soufrière
4812

Routhiers

Capesterre-Belle-Eau

Baillif

St-Claude

13
Maison
du Volcan

Grand
Etang

L'Habituée

Basse-Terre

N1

Gourbeyre

Bananier

Anse

12

Trois-Rivières
Faubourg

St-Lo
Baie de St-Louis

Anse Turlet

Pointe
de la Grande Anse

Parc Archéologique
des Roches Gravées

Pointe de Folle Anse

Vieux-Fort
Pointe du Vieux-Fort

Anse Ballet
Pointe à Congré

Grand-

14

Ilet à
Cabrit

Les Saintes

Terre-de-Haut

Terre-de-Bas

Fort Napoléon

Terre-de-Haut
Grandè Anse

Terre-de-Bas

La Redonde

La Coche

Grand Ilet

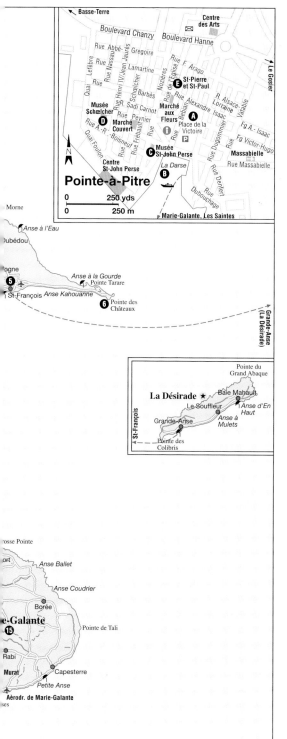

a thriving sugar economy was in operation, underpinned by the labor of African slaves.

The British cast a greedy eye on the island, invading twice and taking control in 1759. They agreed in the 1763 Treaty of Paris to return the island to Louis XV – in exchange for keeping Canada.

Life took a downward turn for the *békés* (rich, white planters), when during the French Revolution slavery was abolished in the French colonies and a revolutionary commissioner, Victor Hugues, was sent to Guadeloupe in 1794 to enforce it. This he did with gusto, defeating the British, who had been invited in by the *békés* to maintain the status quo, and then guillotining 850 royalist planters.

When Napoleon came to power, Hugues was replaced and slavery reinstated until abolition was decreed in the 1848 Revolution that established the Second Republic in France. After that, 40,000 East Indians came to work on the sugar plantations.

Guadeloupe and Martinique went into decline during the two world wars, thousands of islanders went to fight for France and in World War II they suffered an Allied blockade during the German Occupation of France, cutting off the import of basic essentials. Afterward, in 1946, integration into the Third Republic as *départements d'outre-mer* (overseas departments) of France seemed the only way toward economic recovery for the French islands.

There have been several groups advocating independence and many Guadeloupeans who, although not wanting to break away, resent France because of the way top jobs are given to incoming French when unemployment is high; they also feel that their creole culture – a mix of African, East Indian, and West Indian – is being swamped by all things French.

Pointe-à-Pitre – the unofficial capital

Every day jet liners from France arrive in the modern airport of Pôle Caraïbes 2 miles (3 km) from Pointe-à-Pitre, on the southern end of the Rivière Salée. They unleash a flow of tourists and emigrants

The two "wings" of mainland Guadeloupe are divided by the Rivière Salée. Paradoxically, the smaller flatter eastern "wing" is called Grande-Terre, which means large or high land, and the large, mountainous western "wing" is Basse-Terre meaning low land. It is believed they were named by sailors for the winds that blow greater in the east and lower in the west.

BELOW: fresh country produce in the market.

returning home to savor a few weeks of sun and family affection (3–4 percent of the population leave each year to work in metropolitan France).

Pointe-à-Pitre ❶ *(see map inset on page 197)* is the main economic capital of Guadeloupe, whose population is inflated daily by workers from the suburbs. If you close your eyes to the low-cost housing developments and delve into the old town, you discover its appeal. In some places its balconied wooden houses rival those of the French Quarter in New Orleans.

Place de la Victoire ❹ is bordered by sidewalk cafés and old colonial buildings. This is the historical heart of Pointe-à-Pitre, and several monuments in honor of local personalities and events are exhibited here. In 1989 Hurricane Hugo destroyed many of the century-old trees that stood here, although new varieties have been planted. The square opens out on to **La Darse ❸** (harbor) and the boats that transport people from the eastern side of the harbor to the islands of Marie-Galante and Les Saintes have kept the magic of yesteryear's sailboats. La Darse continues along the wharf where for three centuries the import-export houses sold red herring, lard, and codfish and have now been transformed into the modern US$20 million **Centre St-John Perse**, housing 80 shops, restaurants, and a hotel. Cruise ships drop anchor at the cruise terminal several times a week.

Behind, on the Rue Nozières, the small **Musée St John Perse ❻** (open Mon–Sat; entrance charge) celebrates the life and work of the Guadeloupean poet who was born into a *béké* family as Alexis Saint-Léger in 1887. Although he left the island when he was 12 never to return again, he idealized the Caribbean in his poetry and was awarded the Nobel Prize for Literature in 1960.

Mingle with the crowd thronging the **Rue Frébault**, Pointe-à-Pitre's busiest

street, another block away from the harbor. Stop at the **Marché Couvert** (covered market) close by, where the women sell sugar apples, sweetsops, soursops, mangoes, passion fruit, and tubers such as yams, sweet potatoes, cassava and madera, as well as home-grown vegetables.

A few minutes to the west on Rue Peynier is the **Musée Schoelcher** ❷ (open Mon–Tues, Thur–Sat; closed for lunch and Sat pm; entrance charge), dedicated to the French politician, Victor Schoelcher, who persistently campaigned for the abolition of slavery in the French colonies and signed the decree in 1848. On the way back to Place de la Victoire turn left up Rue Nozières and, nearby, tucked away to the right, is the **Marché aux Fleurs** (flower market) fronting the sand-colored façade of the basilica of **St Pierre et St Paul** ❸. Built in the 1830s with metal supports, it successfully withstood the huge earthquake in 1845.

Exploring Grande-Terre

On Grande-Terre the flat landscape of sugar-cane fields is dotted here and there with the massive stone silhouette of a sugar mill, the dark green foliage of a mango tree, or the scarlet splash of a flame tree. But on leaving Pointe-à-Pitre on the N4, the south coast road, you come to Guadeloupe's main resort area starting with one of the biggest marinas in the Caribbean at **Bas du Fort**, about 2 miles (3 km) from the center. On the hilltop above, looking across to Marie-Galante and the mountains of Basse-Terre, is the coral-built, 18th-century **Fort Fleur-d'Epée** ❷ (open daily; free) which holds art exhibitions and has lovely gardens.

Le Gosier ❸, 2 miles (3 km) farther on, is the hub of the holiday scene where there are countless little restaurants owned by the locals. The service is slow, but a Ti-punch (rum with sugar-cane syrup) helps to pass the time. Try the

Map on pages 196–7

TIP

To discover the islands' writers and artists, visit the Librairie Générale, 46 Rue Schoelcher, Pointe-à-Pitre. Here you will find books on every subject from fishing in Guadeloupe to local magic and architecture, and on the walls are paintings by local artists.

BELOW: jagged rocks at Pointe des Châteaux.

The island's only golf course is at St François, 25 miles (40 km) from Pointe-à-Pitre on the south coast of Grande-Terre. Designed by Robert Trent Jones, the course is being renovated but is still open for play.

LEFT: the waterfront at Basse-Terre.
RIGHT: sunset in Grande-Terre.

humbler dishes not to be found on every menu such as breadfruit *migan* (breadfruit slices cooked slowly with lemon juice and salt pork) and *bébélé* (plaintains, green bananas, congo peas, tripe with salt pork) from Marie-Galante, or try a *bokit*, a large round fried sandwich, the local answer to fast food. This is the real Guadeloupe. The town comes alive at night to the sound of zouk *(see page 62)* emanating from the nightclubs.

There are several sandy beaches along the south Atlantic coast but the typical French West Indian village of **Ste Anne ❹**, 9 miles (14 km) away, sits on one of the best, while the Club Med resort enjoys another fine beach at Caravelle. The road slopes down a farther 9 miles (14 km) to **St François ❺**, once a quiet little fishing village and now an upmarket resort with its own airport for light aircraft and private jets, and a golf course. Ferries depart regularly from the opulent marina for the island of La Désirade 6 miles (10 km) away. The road out of the town ends 7 miles (11 km) on at the craggy **Pointe des Châteaux ❻** where, as a final gesture, the rocks have been lashed by the Atlantic at its juncture with the Caribbean into spectacular castle-like formations. You can walk up to the cross planted at the Pointe des Colibris in 1951 for some fine views.

Pre-Columbian treasures

Back on the N5 heading north, after about 8 miles (13 km) you reach **Le Moule**, once the capital and now the surfing capital of the island. The beach restaurants are perfect for lingering in over a plate of seafood. Just outside at La Rosette is the **Musée Archéologique Edgar Clerc ❼** (open Mon–Sat; closed for lunch; entrance charge) which houses one of the Caribbean's largest collections of pre-Columbian items, among other treasures. The museum is the

work of Jack Berthelot, an architect known throughout the region and a figure in the independence movement, who died in 1984 in a car bomb explosion.

Instead of following the coast road and taking a swim in one of the many sheltered, hidden coves, push on farther north, on the N8, which cuts across country of thornbushes and acacias for about 15 miles (24 km) to the **Pointe de la Grande Vigie ❻**. Here the land ends in the dazzling realm of azure and the sea meets the sky. Only a few years back this area was a wild and desolate place. Still undiscovered by Club Med, it has become the haunt of scuba divers and the strong swimmer who is not duped by the apparent calm of the blue, blue water.

On your way back to Pointe-à-Pitre, stop off at **Morne-à-l'Eau**, faithful companion to the island's most magnificent cemetery, which is a true city of the dead with funeral palaces of black and white checkered tiles. On All Saints Day in November the cemetery at night is aglow with the flickering of tiny candles.

To the mountains of Basse-Terre

Now for the western wing, the mountainous **Basse-Terre**. Modern art lovers should stop in the town of **Lamentin**, a 15-minute drive west of Pointe-à-Pitre along the N2. Here, the mayor, José Toribio, is transforming the town into the cultural capital of Guadeloupe. Massive modern art sculptures, called Karuptures, pop up at intersections, in school yards, in the countryside and at the fishing port. The Théatre de la Verdure (Theatre in the Green) is an open-air theatre with excellent acoustics set in the middle of sugar cane fields. Taking the N1 out of Pointe-à-Pitre, cut across the 60,000 acres (30,000 hectares) of the **Parc National de la Guadeloupe** (also known as the Parc Naturel) on the dramatic **Route de la Traversée**, 5 miles (8 km) down the road. About halfway along the

Map on pages 196–7

The raccoon is a rare sight in Guadeloupe and is the emblem of Basse-Terre's massive Parc Naturel.

BELOW: the *Nautilus* in Basse-Terre waters.

COUSTEAU'S SILENT WORLD

When Jacques-Yves Cousteau (1910–97) was filming his award-winning film *Le Monde du Silence* (1955) at Ilets Pigeon, he discovered what he considered to be one of the best dive sites in the world. As a result of the enthusiasm of this French underwater explorer and cameraman *extraordinaire*, the Réserve Cousteau, a large 150-acre (300-hectare) submarine park was set up around the tiny islands off Malendure on the western coast of Basse-Terre. Why this site should be so much more beautiful than most others is because the hot volcanic springs around the islands have created a wonderful warm environment for a much wider variety of sea life than other Caribbean coasts. Forests of hard and soft corals and large communities of magnificent tube and barrel sea sponges in violets, yellows, flaming red, and greens give shelter to a universe of fish in all shapes, sizes, and color schemes. Gorgonias gently sway in the silvery gentle sea in temperatures of around 82°F (28°C), and the visibility is still perfect at depths of 65–130 ft (20–40 meters).

To experience such a spectacular site, well-equipped dive shops with licensed instructors at Malendure organize individual dives or courses. You can also rent tanks for beach dives, as the underwater scenery starts close by.

Map on pages 196–7

The Parc Naturel has very few wild animals at all, and definitely no poisonous snakes, just plenty of birds, butterflies – and some beautiful flowers.

BELOW: lunch outdoors.
RIGHT: heliconia dangle in the forest.

15-mile (24-km) route, edged with giant ferns, bright red flamboyants, and rainforest, is the **Maison de la Forêt ❾** (open daily; free), a good information center which provides maps for well sign-posted walks, some lasting 20 minutes – such as the one to the beautiful **Cascade de l'Ecrevisse** – or three hours such as the Pigeon Trail. The route reaches the west coast at **Mahaut** where you can turn right on the N2 and visit the **Maison du Bois ❿** (open daily; entrance charge) at **Pointe Noire**, 4 miles (6 km) away, a woodworking center which has an exhibition of wooden household implements. Turn left and you quickly come to the dark sands of **Malendure**, the launching pad for the **Réserve Cousteau ⓫**, a marine park around the Ilets Pigeon *(see box on page 201)*.

The N2 twists and turns along the coast for about 16 miles (26 km) to **Basse-Terre ⓬**, the administrative capital of the *département* of Guadeloupe. Under the shadow of the smoking **La Soufrière**, which last yawned and fell back to sleep in 1976, the old, colonial port, founded in 1634, has neatly planned squares, narrow streets and, on the south side, the ruins of an old fort.

Several roads lead up through lush countryside to the smart resort of **St Claude**, 4 miles (6 km) into the foothills of La Soufrière, where there is an informative **Maison du Volcan ⓭** (open Tues–Sun; closed for lunch) and the start of some scenic trails. You can drive farther up the mountain to a parking area by steaming fumaroles and the fit can tackle the arduous 90-minute climb to the often cloud-covered crater.

Trips to the islands

At **Trois Rivières** on the coast south of the volcano, two ferries a day make the 25-minute trip to **Les Saintes ⓮** where, in 1872, Britain's Admiral Rodney foiled the French fleet's planned attack on Jamaica in the Battle of the Saints. A huddle of eight islands, only two – **Terre-de-Haut** and **Terre-de-Bas** – are inhabited. Their tiny population is said to be of Breton origin, descended from the pirates who used to stake out the seas. Today, they are skilled sailors or fishermen, identifiable by their wide hats called *salakos*. It is worth staying the night in one of the several small hotels and inns on Terre-de-Haut to experience the tranquility of a beautiful island with white sand beaches. Try the delicious seafood after the daytrippers have left, or buy *torment d'amour* (torment of love) cakes at the ferry port.

From Pointe-à-Pitre two boats go daily to Les Saintes and three to the circular 60-sq. mile (155-sq. km) island of **Marie-Galante ⓯**, which Columbus named for his own ship. Bordered by white sandy beaches, one of the most secluded being the hidden coves of **Anse Canot** on the northwest coast, the island still grows sugar for rum. Tour one of the rum distilleries and visit the atelier of local sculptor Armand Baptiste.

La Désirade, a melancholy place not typical of Guadeloupe, is reached by ferry from St François, on the southern coast of Grande-Terre (an hour's drive from Pointe-à-Pitre along the N4); the island served as a leper colony and was often a final destination for its inhabitants. ❏

DOMINICA

Map
on page
208

*The magnificent volcanic landscape of this rugged
island provides bird-filled rainforests, spectacular waterfalls, a lake
of boiling water, and lovingly tended gardens everywhere*

A s Mr Rochester, the hero of Jean Rhys's novel, *Wide Sargasso Sea*, toiled up the path toward his honeymoon home half way up a Dominican mountainside, he lamented: "Too much blue, too much purple, too much green. The flowers too red, the mountains too high, the hills too near." Perhaps he might have said in more prosaic words: "Too beautiful for its own good." Not only fictional characters have been overwhelmed by Dominica's (pronounced Dom-in-*ee*ka) physical presence. From Columbus, who sailed into Prince Rupert Bay in 1493, to the 19th-century British imperialist J.A. Froude and the 20th-century travel writer, Patrick Leigh Fermor: all have been somewhat in awe of the rugged island of Dominica.

The largest of the Windward Islands (15 by 29 miles/25 by 46 km), Dominica lies between Guadeloupe and Martinique. From the air, it has a dark presence: volcanic mountains disappearing into its dense, cloud-covered spine, forested ribs of ridge and valley, carved out by the numerous rivers rushing down to the sea, while the odd road threads a parallel to the coastline. With much of its surface still covered in some of the finest rainforest in the region, its 70,000 people live in scattered communities beside the sea, mainly on the sheltered leeward side, or along the ridges.

A protecting environment

The magnificent environment of this "Nature Island" has been both a protection and a constraint. In the past, it protected the island from total exploitation by even the most grasping of European adventurers and settlers as there were no great riches to be made with only small patches of flat land.

Although the colonizers managed to drive the resident Caribs from the leeward coast into the mountain fastnesses and to the remote northeast, they were not entirely wiped out. The environment protected them. Again, in the 18th century, the forests provided a sanctuary for the maroons (escaped slaves) and it also enabled a strong-minded independent peasantry to develop, cultivating "gardens", as they still do, in forest clearings.

The early settlers, at the end of the 17th century, were small-timers, Frenchmen from Martinique, who traded with the Amerindians, cultivated tobacco, and later coffee and cocoa on estates whose names alone – *Temps Perdu* or *Malgré Tout* – evoke a sense of loss and resignation.

When the British finally took control in 1783, wrestling the island from the French (who continued to skirmish with the British through the Napoleonic Wars) sugar, then limes and eventually bananas in the 1930s became the main crops. The banana industry

PRECEDING PAGES:
well cared for
church in
Portsmouth.
LEFT: craggy cliffs
of the north.
BELOW: dramatic
Trafalgar Falls.

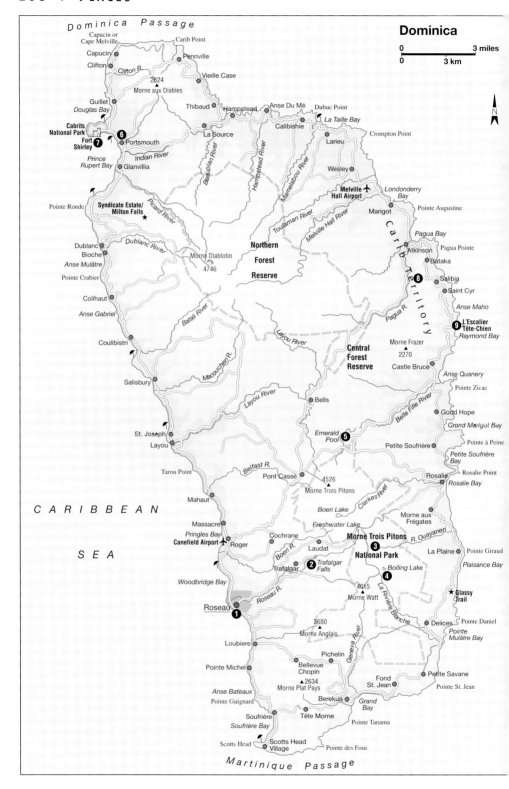

Dominica

Dominica Passage

Capucin or
Cape Melville
Capucin
Clifton
Clifton R.
2824
Morne aux Diables
Guillet
Douglas Bay
Cabrits
National Park
Fort
Shirley
6
Portsmouth
Prince
Rupert Bay
Glanvillia
Indian River

Carib Point
Pennville
Vieille Case
Thibaud
Hampstead
Anse Du Mé
Dubuc Point
La Taille Bay
Calibishie
Crompton Point
La Source
Larieu
Wesley

Pointe Ronde
Syndicate Estate/
Milton Falls
★

Dublanc
Bioche
Anse Mulâtre
Pointe Crabier

Dublanc River
Picard River
Beaulieu River
Hampstead River
Mamelabou River
Toulaman River
Melville Hall River

Melville
Hall Airport
Londonderry
Bay
Marigot
Pointe Augustine
Pagua Bay
Atkinson
Pagua Pointe
Bataka

Morne Diablotin
4746

Northern
Forest
Reserve

Colihaut
Anse Gabriel

Batali River

Coulibistri

Macoucheri R.

Salisbury

St. Joseph
Layou

Layou River

Belfast R.

Tarou Point
Pont Cassé
4526
Morne Trois Pitons

Mahaut

C A R I B B E A N

Massacre
Pringles Bay
Canefield Airport ✈
Roger

Cochrane
Boeri R.
Laudat

S E A

Woodbridge Bay

Roseau R.

Roseau
1

Loubiere

3680
Morne Anglais

Pointe Michel
Bellevue
Chopin
2634
Morne Plat Pays
Anse Bateaux
Pointe Guignard
Berekua

Soufrière
Soufrière Bay

Scotts Head

Scotts Head
Village

Pichelin

Fond
St. Jean

Tête Morne
Pointe Tanama

Pointe des Fous

M a r t i n i q u e   P a s s a g e

Pagua R.
8
Salibia
Saint Cyr
Anse Maho
L'Escalier
Tête-Chien
9
Raymond Bay
Morne Frazer
2270
Castle Bruce

C a r i b   T e r r i t o r y

Anse Quanery
Pointe Zicac

Bells

Emerald
Pool
5

Good Hope
Grand Marigot Bay
Petite Soufrière
Pointe à Peine
Petite Soufrière
Bay
Rosalie
Rosalie Point
Rosalie Bay

Belle Fille River
Clarkes River

Boeri Lake
Freshwater Lake

Morne aux
Frégates
R. Ouayaneri

Morne Trois Pitons
National Park
3

Trafalgar
Falls
2
Trafalgar

Boiling Lake
4

4015
Morne Watt

La Plaine
Pointe Giraud
Plaisance Bay

★ Glassy
Trail

La Rivière Blanche

Delices
Pointe Daniel
Pointe
Mulâtre Bay

Geneva River

Grand
Bay

Petite Savane
Pointe St. Jean

0   3 miles
0   3 km

N

grew spectacularly in the 1960s becoming known as "green gold" *(see box on page 44)*. Now challenged by the large Latin American competitors, modern Dominica, independent from Britain since 1978, is looking to tourism as a main provider of income and employment.

Unlike other islands dominated by tourism, Dominica has no casinos; no multi-national chains, all-inclusive resorts with white marble pillars, golf buggies, "limbo nights," and Jacuzzis. At least, not yet. For visitors to Dominica glory in its otherness. Instead of lounging on sunbeds on white sand beaches, they dive into pools at the base of rainforest waterfalls or bathe in rivers whose cliffs are smothered in vines, giant ferns, and the yellow-red claws of the dramatic heliconia plant. They hike into the forests, up trails that are still used by Dominicans to reach their forest "gardens", past the buttressed trunks of great trees, such as the chatanier, or the giant of the forest, the gommier, from which the Caribs still make their canoes.

On the banks of the Roseau River

Not even **Roseau ❶** (pronounced Ro-zo) – with a new shopping mall and supermarkets – can escape the impact of the island's hinterland, the essentially agricultural base of Dominican society. For every Saturday – from before first light until mid-morning – the capital (pop. 8,000) hosts market day. There, beside the mouth of the Roseau River with its backdrop of mountain and forest, is laid out the bounty of the land. From armfuls of ginger lilies, to sacks of yams, from coffee beans to avocados, watercress to coconuts, all are gathered into this place of plenty, an endlessly festive endorsement of Dominica's national motto: *Apres Bondie Cest La Ter* (After God it is the land).

Map on page 208

TIP

For a scuba site with a difference head for Champagne by Scotts Head in the southeast where you can swim through underwater hot-spring bubbles and watch myriad sea life – it's even better at night.

BELOW: a typical shop in Roseau.

The blending of Carib, French and British cultures are celebrated on Creole Day in November, when Roseau comes alive with the swirl of 18th-century petticoats and the jangle of gold jewelry.

Roseau is a bustling little town with a small, 18th-century French quarter, surrounded by 19th-century streets, their wood and stone houses supporting overhanging verandahs and gingerbread fretwork. Now that middle-class Dominicans (known in the old days as the *gros bourg*) prefer to live in the cooler suburbs, many of the old townhouses and their gardens have been pulled down and replaced by somewhat charmless concrete buildings. The once narrow waterfront has been extended to create the Bay Front, which includes the cruise ship pier. Opposite the pier is the imaginative **Dominica Museum** (open Mon–Fri, Sat am; tel: 767-448 2401; entrance charge) housed in the old post office.

A short walk from the waterfront, between Valley and Bath roads, are the splendid **Botanical Gardens** (open daily; free). There is still evidence of the destruction wrought by Hurricane David, in 1979, which reduced the 40-acre (16-hectare) site to a "junkyard of tree limbs" – the remains of a school bus can be seen beneath the large baobab tree that crushed it. Successfully restored, the gardens, on the eastern edge of the town, make the perfect setting for a cricket match and there is an aviary for Dominica's endangered sisserou and jacquot parrots.

Volcanic wonders

Heading inland for 5 miles (8 km) past the Botanical Gardens, you reach **Trafalgar Falls ❷** (open daily; entrance charge – tickets to attractions are also available from travel agents, car-hire companies and tour operators), two spectacular waterfalls. They are a 10-minute walk from the tropical gardens and inn at **Papillote Wilderness Retreat** *(see box below)*. You may be besieged by guides here but you will only need one if you want to go farther than the viewing platform.

Trafalgar Falls is on the western edge of the magnificent **Morne Trois Pitons**

BELOW: a carefully tended Carib garden.

ISLAND GARDENS

All Dominicans are wedded to the land, from the first Amerindians, who brought with them many of the fruit and vegetables now native to the island; the maroons, who survived by farming in the forests; and the slaves, with their provision grounds; to the colonizers, who saw that plants from other parts of the world could flourish in the Caribbean. This was particularly true of Dominica whose dramatic landscape provides a different miniclimate in every corner – it seems that every flower, fruit and vegetable can prosper here.

Dominicans welcome visitors to their lovingly tended patches whether they be the market gardens of **Giraudel** or a beautifully laid out Roseau backyard. But it's important to call first. This you can do through the **Papillote Wilderness Retreat**, near Trafalgar Falls (open daily; tel: 767-448 2287; garden tour fee; www.papillote.dm), where an array of tropical flowers complement the natural contours and vegetation of the rainforest. "They blend from nurtured collections into wilderness," says creator Anne Jno Baptiste.

Close by is **D'Auchamps Estate** (tel: 767-448 3346; tours by appointment) where the Honychurch family has made delightful walkways through natural dry forest.

National Park ❸, a UNESCO World Heritage site, which covers 17,000 acres (6,800 hectares) of the southern central part of the island. Those with more than an average dose of energy can hike to the **Boiling Lake** ❹, the second-largest cauldron of bubbling hot water (220 ft/66 meters wide) in the world, which lies in the heart of the park. This geological phenomenon is, in fact, a flooded fumarole, from where hot gases escape through vents in the earth's molten crust. It's a tough but extraordinary journey (an 8-hour round trip), which starts at **Titou Gorge**, close to the village of **Laudat**, 6 miles (10 km) northeast of Roseau. The track plunges and rises, crosses streams and climbs up to narrow ridges opening up into a lunar landscape of steaming vents and geysers, hot pools of boiling mud and mineral streams streaked with blue, orange, black, and yellow. This is the **Valley of Desolation** – and beyond that the Boiling Lake itself.

Rainforest birdlife

On the northeastern edge of the park, off the Castle Bruce road, lies the pretty **Emerald Pool** ❺ in the heart of lush green rainforest where you can have a picnic, stand behind the 40-ft (12-meter) waterfall and cool off with a dip.

Along the lower reaches of the **Central Forest Reserve**, travelers are sometimes accompanied by the sound of a squeaking gate. This, in fact, is the melancholic call of the rufous-throated solitaire (known locally as sifflé moutayn) echoing across the forest canopy. Local lore has it that this perky-looking thrush is a magical spirit whose call tempts travelers farther and farther into the forest.

Dominica is home to 172 species of birds, plenty to keep birdwatchers happy. Such an assortment within the confines of a small island is a reflection of the remarkable diversity of vegetation.

Map on page 208

TIP

If you are lucky you may see female whales and their young swim close to your boat on a whale-watching trip off the west coast, as well as schools of dolphin. Contact local dive shops for information.

BELOW: Indian River.

Map on page 208

Dominica's two endangered parrots, the sisserou and red-necked jacquot, live on the slopes of Morne Diablotin in the north. You may spot one with the help of the Forestry Division (tel: 767-448-2401), who can provide a guide.

BELOW: Dominica's endangered sisserou parrot.

Fortifications in spectacular surroundings

In dramatic contrast to the gnarled and battered elfin woodland – high, windy, and watered by 300 inches (760 cm) of rain annually – there is, for example, the dry tropical forest of the Caribbean coast. The spectacular headland of the **Cabrits National Park**, 25 miles (40 km) north of Roseau and close to the second town of **Portsmouth ❻**, is covered with bay, mahogany, sandbox, white cedar, and logwood. And there in the heat among the silent trees are the ruins of the 18th-century British fortifications, **Fort Shirley ❼** (open daily; entrance charge), once one of the most important military sites in the West Indies, complete with gun batteries, storehouses, and officers' quarters. During the colonial wars, it housed up to 600 men, protecting both the north of the island and Prince Rupert Bay to the south. The Cabrits Peninsula has the added attraction of being surrounded by a **marine park**, rich in underwater life and excellent for snorkeling and diving.

Another habitat, close by the Cabrits and with yet another story to tell, is the wetlands around the **Indian River**, just south of **Prince Rupert Bay**. It was into this bay that Columbus sailed on November 3, 1493, the day he first sighted Dominica, and it was the Caribs of the Indian River area who provided subsequent European sailors with water and shelter, pineapples and cassava. The boat trip from the coastal road at the river mouth (avoid boats with outboard motors which disturb the vegetation) up this haunting gray-green waterway follows the route European sea captains took to greet the Carib chief.

A remaining Carib settlement

Today, the surviving Caribs live along the northeastern seaboard (take the road east from Portsmouth to Pagua Bay) in coconut and banana country– although

they still grow cassava – edging the wild Atlantic. The **Carib Territory ❽** was set aside for them in 1903 by a well-meaning British administrator called Hesketh Bell, who thought they would die out unless they were guaranteed a "reservation" of their own. Today, the area is not in itself distinctive but you will see houses built on stilts, and stalls on the roadside display the unique basketwork of the Caribs (finely woven in three colors from a forest reed), the lingering legacy of an ancient culture.

L'Escalier Tête-Chien ❾ (the snake's staircase), a rock formation that looks like a stone serpent slithering up out of the ocean, farther southward along this dramatic coastline, features extensively in Carib folklore.

But while modernity has been embraced by wealthier Dominicans – the internet, vacations abroad, and American TV soaps (electricity only reached the east coast in the mid-1980s) – there is a characteristic gentleness about Dominican villages, from a southeastern community such as **Petit Savanne**, set among sweet-smelling bay trees, to the breezy hillside of remote **Capucin** in the north. Church, school, and store are the public face of village life, while the yard remains the center of the family's economic and social activity: a place to make brooms from the vines, to store provisions, such as yam and dasheen, to hang green bananas, or to gossip in the cooler hours of the day. ❑

Carib Indians

When the first European settlers came face to face with the Caribs already living on the islands of the Eastern Caribbean at the beginning of the 17th century, it was not a time for exchanging pleasantries. These Amerindians had made their way up from South America a few centuries earlier in 75-ft (23-meter) boats, hewn from massive gommier trees, which held 50 people apiece, and had competed with the resident Tainos for their land.

They were not going to give in to the new invaders easily. After all, as one Carib chief remarked ironically to French soldiers, "We have not gone over to your country to take it, so why have you come over to take ours?"

When Christopher Columbus had arrived in the Bahamas in 1492, the Indians (as he called the Lucayans, for he thought he was in India) for the most part had been friendly and provided sailors with food and water. His first impressions of them, recorded in his journal, were that they were timid and unwarlike: "They should be good servants and intelligent, for I observed that they quickly took in what was said to them." And he set about enslaving them to help in the Spanish quest for gold.

Word also spread that there were other tribes living on islands farther south, who ate their captives, roasted on a spit. These were the Caribs, but historians now say this was a scurrilous tale put about by the Spanish who wanted to justify their un-Christian methods of slavery and cruelty. However, it is understood they may have practised some form of ritual cannibalism in that they would eat a piece of heart of a courageous enemy or beloved chieftain, believing they would receive a portion of their courage or goodness.

Rebelling against European invaders, the Caribs took cover in the island's impenetrable mountain forests, from where they were able to launch attacks on other islands such as Antigua and Barbuda. During the 17th century, Carib tribes were also living on St Lucia and Grenada, keeping the colonists at bay with showers of arrows tipped with poison from the manchineel tree. Eventually, European weaponry and disease won the day and any that were left were beaten back to the protective arm of Dominica where a small enclave still remains.

Caribs painted their bodies red and wore feathers and beads of stone, bone, and teeth for decoration; the chiefs wore crowns and gold ornaments. They participated in a trade network that stretched for thousands of miles between the islands and South America. They grew cassava (manioc), maize, beans, squash, and peppers for food, along with tobacco, cotton (for hammocks), and annatto (for body paint). They fished, hunted, and gathered shells, crabs, and turtle eggs and the women planted, weeded, harvested, and prepared meals which included turtles, iguanas, and "pepperpot" stews *(see pages 71–72)*.

Early European travelers wrote about a Utopian life of ease, in which the Caribs saw each other as equal, none richer nor poorer than another. "Each man does what pleases him," wrote one 16th-century traveler, "and permits no one to give him orders." ❑

RIGHT: making basketware in the Carib Territory on Dominica.

TROPICAL BOUNTY OF THE ISLANDS

Flowers of the forest, fruit of the trees, vegetables from the ground – under the blazing sun there's a treasure trove of color, dazzling greenery and food

Like the people of the Eastern Caribbean, the flora of the region is a great melting pot. There were plants that were here before man, plants brought by the Caribs in their canoes when they paddled from South America, those which came from Africa during slavery and those brought from all over the world by the adventuresome Europeans.

For visitors to the region from North America or northern Europe, familiar only with expensive houseplants nurtured in a centrally heated room or the exotic fruit and vegetable section in the supermarket, the sudden sight of these magnificent plants growing naturally in a tropical landscape is intoxicating.

MARKET DAY

Venture into a local market in the rainier, more mountainous islands and explore the unfamiliar: the knobbly soursop (it makes an excellent juice); the pale green christophene or cho-cho of the squash family; tiny green and red peppers, some fiendishly hot. Drier islands will not have such a range, but there will be "ground provisions" – the root vegetables such as yams, which are part of the staple diet. And there are the cut flowers: the amazing red or pink gingers, artificial-looking anthurium and dramatic torch gingers. Everyone grows something somewhere.

And while there are the formal botanical gardens, or gardens of former estate houses to visit, don't forget to admire the ordinary backyard garden growing an amazing range of vegetables, fruit and exotic flowers often in just a tiny space.

△ **PINEAPPLE PUNCH**
"None pleases my tastes as does the pine," wrote George Washington in his diary during a visit to Barbados in 1751.

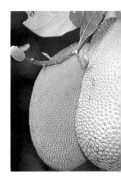

◁ **REALLY REAL**
The anthurium, part of the aroid family, looks more plastic than alive. It comes in many colors.

◁ SPOT COLOR
The winter-flowering immortelle is an exquisite tree of the forests, splashing the surrounding greenery with its color.

△ RICH IN ORCHIDS
Native orchids are found on all the islands, growing on trees in rainforests. Trinidad has some 200 species.

▽ FLOWERING FUN
A handsome shrub, known colloquially as Christmas candle or, less seasonally, as "ringworm bush".

SPICE AND ALL THINGS NICE

There is a sweetness in the Caribbean air which romantics might attribute to spice and, in particular to the vanilla plant (above), a straggly plant from the orchid family, with an exquisite-smelling flower that opens only for a few hours in the mornings. Pollinating is done by hand and it's the pods that give the much sought after vanilla flavor.

Although spices such as vanilla and nutmeg were once an important export crop, most arrived in the Caribbean in the 18th century from the Far East "spice islands". Once, Grenada grew some 25 percent of the world's nutmeg. You can still see the warehouses at Gouyave on the west coast where the spice is sorted. The outer lacy red covering is ground down into a powder and becomes mace. Visit local markets throughout the region for supplies of nutmeg and cinnamon (dried strips of bark), pale gold rhizomes of ginger, black pepper (grown on a vine) and cloves (dried flower buds).

◁ CHOCOLATE DROPS
The large orange pod of the cacao tree grows on the trunk and turns dark brown. The beans inside are dried to make cocoa.

▽ BREAD OF LIFE
The distinctive breadfruit first arrived in the Caribbean in St Vincent, thanks to Captain Bligh. It is best eaten roasted.

◁ ALOE, ALOE
Aloe vera, a large spiny succulent, grows in dry, thin soils. Break a leaf, and use the oozing "gel" for treating sunburn and skin problems.

▷ ONE-OFF GLORY
The delicate hibiscus flower comes in myriad colors, but lasts only a day. Hummingbirds love the blossoms, too.

MARTINIQUE

A piece of France transported to the tropics, this beautiful, mountainous island famous for its exotic flowers exudes a kind of sophistication from the black and white beaches to the rainforest

Map on page 220

Martinique
Caribbean
Sea

W hen Christopher Columbus landed on Martinique in 1502, he commented, "It is the best, the most fertile, the softest, the most even, the most charming spot in the world. It is the most beautiful thing I have ever seen. My eyes never tire of contemplating such greenery." But he continued on his travels and another century went by before the first French settlers arrived in 1635, led by the corsair Pierre Belain d'Esnambuc, to found St Pierre and begin the colonization of the island.

Apart from a few short-lived occupations by the British, Martinique has remained steadfastly French. It is actually a part of France, a *département* – a nail-polished fingertip on the end of an invisible arm stretching across the Atlantic. And the first impression visitors have of the island is of a tropical France: amid the palm-fringed beaches, hillside banana plantations, valleys of pineapples, and volcanic mountains, the essence of the motherland can be found in the *boulangeries*, the pavement cafés, the noisy mopeds, the hypermarkets and Parisian shops in the capital Fort-de-France. Trinidadian writer V.S. Naipaul wrote in *The Middle Passage* (1962): "Unlike the other islands, which have one main town to which everything gravitates, Martinique is full of little French villages each with its church, *mairie* and war memorial…"

PRECEDING PAGES: an isolated farmhouse in the foothills of Pelée. **LEFT:** Grand Anse du Diamant and Rocher du Diamant in the background. **BELOW:** a splash of local art.

Tropical France

At 417 sq. miles (1,085 sq. km) – 40 miles (65 km) at its longest, 19 miles (31 km) at its widest – Martinique is almost one-third the size of Long Island, New York. To the west lies the Caribbean Sea, placid, even lake-like; to the east, the rough Atlantic Ocean has created a dramatic coastline.

A mountainous island, it feeds the eye with its contours that ascend gradually from the irregular coastline and culminate dramatically, in the north in Montagne Pelée (4,583 ft/1,397 meters), the now dormant volcano that erupted with a shattering violence in 1902. Pelée is linked to other mountains – Les Pitons du Carbet (3,960 ft/1,205 meters) in the center, and La Montagne du Vauclin (1,653 ft/504 meters) in the south – by a series of gentler hills, or *mornes*. The temperature, with a yearly mean of 79°F (26°C), fulfils all expectations, while the winds blowing in off the sea make for comfortable evenings. Add a thick coating of vegetation and one can understand Columbus's enthusiasm.

Today, Martinique is a largely agricultural island with a racially mixed population of 430,000. Like the other Caribbean islands, it has been through the historical horrors of colonialism and slavery; but while most of the British West Indies have sought their own paths in independence, Martinique, with its sister island of Guadeloupe *(see pages 195–202)*, has been

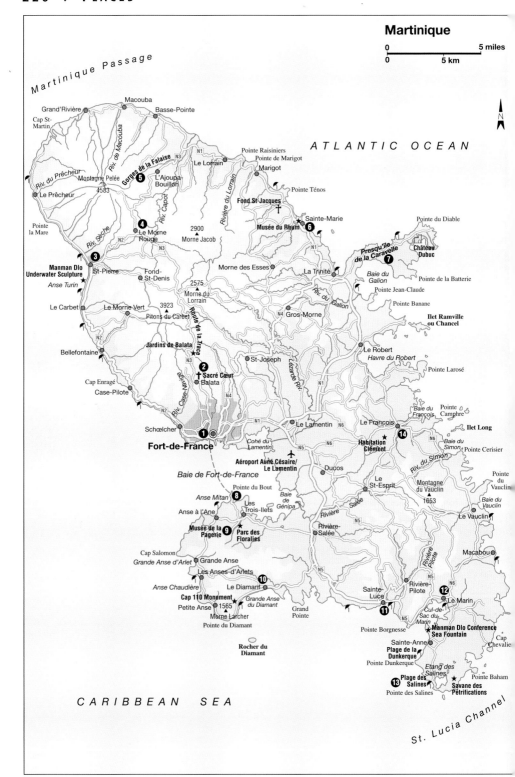

Martinique

0 _____ 5 miles
0 _____ 5 km

Martinique Passage

ATLANTIC OCEAN

Grand'Rivière
Macouba
Basse-Pointe
Cap St-Martin
Riv. du Prêcheur
Riv. de Macouba
Montagne Pelée
4583
Le Prêcheur
Gorges de la Falaise
5
L'Ajoupa-Bouillon
Le Lorrain
Pointe Raisiniers
Pointe de Marigot
Marigot
Pointe Ténos
Fond St-Jacques
Pointe la Mare
Riv. Seche
Riv. Capot
4
Le Morne Rouge
2900
Morne Jacob
Rivière du Lorrain
Musée du Rhum
6
Sainte-Marie
Pointe du Diable
Château Dubuc
Manman Dlo Underwater Sculpture
★
Anse Turin
3
St-Pierre
Fond-St-Denis
Morne des Esses
La Trinité
Presqu'île de la Caravelle
7
Baie du Galion
Pointe de la Batterie
Pointe Jean-Claude
Pointe Banane
Le Carbet
Le Morne Vert
3923
Pitons du Carbet
2575
Morne du Lorrain
Riv. du Galion
Gros-Morne
N4
Ilet Ramville ou Chancel
Jardins de Balata
★
N3
Route de la Trace
St-Joseph
Lézarde Riv.
Le Robert
Havre du Robert
Bellefontaine
N2
2
† Sacré Cœur
Balata
Pointe Larosé
Cap Enragé
Case-Pilote
Riv. Case-Nav.
N2
N4
Schœlcher
1
Fort-de-France
Cohé du Lamentin
N1
Le Lamentin
N6
Le François
Baie du François
Pointe Camphre
Ilet Long
Baie de Fort-de-France
Aéroport Aimé Césaire/ Le Lamentin
N5
N6
Ducos
Habitation Clément
★
14
N6
Baie du Simon
Pointe Cerisier
Pointe du Bout
8
Anse Mitan
Les Trois-Ilets
Baie de Génipa
Le St-Esprit
Montagne du Vauclin
1653
Pointe du Vauclin
Anse à l'Ane
Rivière
Salée
Riv. du Simon
Baie du Vauclin
Le Vauclin
Musée de la Pagerie
9
★
Parc des Floralies
Rivière-Salée
N5
Rivière Pilote
Macabou
Cap Salomon
Grande Anse d'Arlet
Grande Anse
Les Anses-d'Arlets
10
Le Diamant
Grande Anse du Diamant
Grand Pointe
N5
N5
Sainte-Luce
Rivière Pilote
N5
N6
12
Le Marin
Anse Chaudière
Cap 110 Monument
★
Petite Anse
1565
Morne Larcher
Pointe du Diamant
11
Cul-de-Sac du Marin
Pointe Borgnesse
Manman Dlo Conference Sea Fountain
★
Cap Chevalie
Rocher du Diamant
Sainte-Anne
Plage de la Dunkerque
Pointe Dunkerque
Etang des Salines
Pointe Baham
Plage des Salines
13
★
Savane des Pétrifications
Pointe des Salines

CARIBBEAN SEA

St. Lucia Channel

N

absorbed politically and economically into France as a full *département d'outre-mer* (overseas department) and *région* of the Republic.

Escape from the French Revolution

The first French settlers wasted no time in establishing sugar plantations, despite resistance from the Carib population who moved to the Atlantic coast until they were eventually wiped out by more sophisticated French weaponry and unfamiliar diseases. Slaves were imported and the economy thrived, driven by the *békés*, the traditional white élite. In 1789 at the onset of the French Revolution, their security was threatened by slave unrest and they invited the British to occupy the island to preserve the status quo. As a result, between 1794 and 1802, unlike Guadeloupe, Martinique's *békés* avoided the guillotine.

After Emancipation in 1848, fought for by French abolitionist Victor Schoelcher, the sugar industry went into decline, although remaining the island's main export with its liquid-gold by-product, rum. Nevertheless, St Pierre, the capital, grew into a cultural town with a "saucy" reputation, until it was obliterated on May 8 1902 when a volcanic eruption killed the entire population of 30,000.

Supporters of the Vichy government in World War II, the Martinicans were deprived of their essential imports by the Allied Naval blockade and learned to live off their natural resources. Afterward, the black radical Martinican poet, Aimé Cesaire, who had been educated in Paris and was a member of the French Communist Party, was elected both mayor of the new capital Fort-de-France and *député* to the French Assembly on a tide of anti-*béké* feeling. He and many others (not all Communists) were keen to divert power from the local aristocracy to the Republic, and in 1946 Martinique and her sister islands joined the club.

Map on page 220

Aimé Cesaire, born in dire poverty in Martinique in 1913, became part of the intellectual café society in Paris between the wars. There he published his anti-colonial views and started a new black pride movement, called "négritude." Mayor of Fort-de-France for more than 50 years, he died in 2008.

BELOW: Fort St Louis stands guard over the capital.

Parc Floral, on Place José Marti, is beautifully laid out and shady, with botanical galleries (open Tues–Sat, but gardens and workshops are being renovated so expect closures). The aquarium here is also being renovated and is closed to the public.

BELOW: tying up in Fort-de-France.

Fort-de-France – the island's "new" capital

Martinique's capital, **Fort-de-France ❶**, is not a large town but, with a population of over 170,000, it bustles with people, traffic, and noise until the closing of stores and restaurants in the mid-afternoon heat imposes a somnolence on its narrow, crowded streets. There is a seedy, tropical feel to the town; buildings quickly lose their newness and cloak themselves in a black mildew born of heat and the humidity wafting in across the **Baie des Flamands** (Flamingo Bay). Old and new blend together to create a slightly askew colonial vision of a graying town melting in the bubbling humidity and burgeoning vegetation.

The centerpiece of the town is **La Savane,** a 12-acre (5-hectare) park of lawn, shady palms, footpaths and benches which is currently being renovated and modernized. A wide boardwalk runs along the seafront; called the Malecon, it is ambitiously named for Cuba's historical boardwalk in Havana. It adds a spacious dimension to the capital for those arriving by the ferries from Pointe du Bout and Trois Ilets.

At the northern end of La Savane stands the headless statue of Napoleon's Josephine, who was born at Les Trois-Ilets on Pointe du Bout across the Baie de Fort-de-France. Her pedestal shows a relief of Napoleon about to crown her; her date of birth (June 23, 1763); and the date of her marriage (May 9, 1796). Birth, marriage, coronation: they are her most notable achievements; however, many believe that she was behind her husband's decision to reintroduce slavery in 1802 after the Revolutionary Convention banned it in 1794, hence the monument's decapitation. And it remains defaced, a potent symbol of Martinique's tortured past.

A library and cathedral in metal

Just across Rue de la Liberté to the right is the magnificent **Bibliothèque Schoelcher** (library: open all day Mon–Thurs and Fri and Sat am; free), a colorful baroque building crazy with Roman, Egyptian, and majolican tiles, and named for the man most responsible for the final abolition of slavery in the French West Indies. Designed by Henri Picq, a contemporary of Gustav Eiffel, it was built in metal in Paris in 1887 and then shipped out to Martinique piece by piece. **St Louis Cathedral**, on Rue Schoelcher a few minutes away, is another of his metal constructions, built to withstand the fiercest hurricanes and earthquakes.

On the way back down Rue de la Liberté toward the bay, you will find the **Musée d'Archéologie** (open Mon–Fri and Sat am; closed for lunch; entrance charge) with three floors of remnants from Taino and Carib Amerindian tribes who survive only in historical writings and glass cases. It has the finest collection of pre-Colombian artifacts in the Caribbean.

To the east of the bay looms **Fort St Louis**, originally built in 1640 and added to over the years. The fort is still used as a military base and is closed to visitors, except on special occasions such as the annual Journées du Patrimoine, when all the island's historical monuments are open to the public free of charge. These Heritage Days are held over the third weekend in September. Opposite at **Pointe Simon**, the cruise ships dock within easy walking distance of the center.

Downtown can be a hot, humid, traffic-dominated place, but it is dotted with colorful markets that take place in its streets. The **Marché aux Poissons** (fish market), by Place Clemenceau and next to the river, is the scene of constant activity, as fishermen unload their catch from small boats. In surrounding streets

Map on page 220

French is the official language, but many Martinicans speak Creole consisting of a West African grammatical structure with a basic Africanized French vocabulary.

BELOW: easy riding on the ferry from Fort-de-France.

TIP

Fort-de-France's street markets start early, at dawn. It is a good idea to visit as early as possible in order to see or buy the best – and freshest – produce.

there are several other less pungent markets specializing in flowers, fruit, and vegetables. The **Grand Marché** on Rue Blénac is the most tourist-oriented and is full of attractively packaged spices and sauces; open every day, all day, but busiest on Friday afternoon and Saturday.

To higher ground in the north

Heading north out of town for the hills, you pass through the prosperous suburb of Didier and, a mile (2 km) or so farther on, join the spectacular **Route de la Trace**, which zigzags across the the mountainous spine of the island to Morne Rouge. You may do a double take at the sight of the **Sacré Coeur de Balata ❷** peering out of the hillside, as the church is a shrunken copy of the Sacré Coeur in Paris, but not so white. The stone walls and the statue of Christ are as if licked by fire, blackened in the greater humidity of the tropical rainforest.

Nearby, the **Jardins de Balata** (open daily; entrance charge) are tropical botanical gardens with a difference. Isolated in the hills, with distant views of both mountain and water, the calm and quiet of a monastery follow in your footsteps as you wander the meandering paths among the flowerbeds thick with plants of unfamiliar shape and color. There are things growing here that might easily form part of the set of a science fiction movie, a vegetation wondrous and mesmerizing. Indeed Martinique has a wealth of parks and gardens to discover – over 30 dotted around the island.

Originally carved out by Jesuits, the Route de la Trace is slight; it winds upward into the mountains, through vegetation thick and varied, creating a green background for the explosions of pink and orange bougainvillea, pink bells, and pink and yellow hibiscus.

BELOW: the Pitons du Carbet behind the Sacré Coeur.

A Caribbean Pompeii

In the wet twilight of the rainforest, high above **St Pierre** ❸, the Caribbean spreads out dramatically and the road forks left at Le Morne Rouge descending in sunlight to the little ghost town hugging the coast. St Pierre: the former cultural and economic center of Martinique that was once known as the "little Paris of the West Indies." Behind looms **Montagne Pelée**, the sleeping volcano (now constantly monitored) that, after grumbling for a few days, finally awoke on May 8, 1902, at 7.50am, in a fireball of seething lava and superheated gases. Fires erupted in the town and the sea boiled. Within seconds, 30,000 people were dead. It is somehow appropriate that, on entering the town, the road passes the cemetery with its large white mausoleum containing the remains of the victims.

Map on page 220

A relic of the volcano

St Pierre never recovered and lost its status as its principal city. Today it is a quiet little town, clean and pretty with resurgent foliage, but distinguished only by its former self and violent end. Ruins offer their mute testimony: the burnt, broken stone walls of seaside warehouses; the foundations and stairways that lead nowhere; the vanished theater (a replica of Bordeaux's), and on the hill that rises behind it is the cell of the sole survivor, Antoine Ciparis, a drunkard locked away the day before and protected by the strength of his dungeon. After such a reprieve, Ciparis ended up traveling the US in a replica of his cell with the Barnum & Bailey circus. Today, much of the town is being excavated.

The **Musée Vulcanologique** (open daily; entrance charge) in Rue Victor-Hugo, presents personal evidence of the disaster: large clumps of nails and screws fused by heat, melted bottles, a large church bell deformed by fire, containers of scorched food. In the sunlight outside, with the knowledge that deep down Pelée still seethes, it is a chilling display.

BELOW: an Antillean crested hummingbird at home.

Through the Gorges de la Falaise

Backtracking 5 miles (8 km), **Le Morne Rouge** ❹ sits at the foot of Mont Pelée from where a rough road leads up to within 1,600 ft (488 meters) of the volcano summit where the mountain air is cool. Only experienced climbers with guides may want to attempt the peak where it rains a lot and is full of hidden dangers. However, there are many trails leading from the village around the mountain suitable for different levels of fitness and experience. A hike along the River Falaise leads to the **Gorges de la Falaise** ❺, a series of impressive canyons and dramatic waterfalls.

The Rum Museum

Taking the dramatic Atlantic coast road, peppered with beautiful beaches which are battered by an angry sea (swimming is dangerous), it is worth stopping off in **Ste Marie** ❻ to visit the **Musée du Rhum** (open Mon–Fri and Sat, Sun am; free) in the St James rum distillery. Here, exhibits tell the story of sugar and rum from 1765 and there is plenty to sample and buy. Martinican rum is considered to be among the finest in the world. In 1996 it was awarded the AOC (*Appellation d'Origine Contrôllée*) label, bestowed only on fine French wines. Rum flavors vary according to climate and soil conditions and all of the island's distil-

Islanders are proud of their fine rum. Most of the sugar cane is transformed into white rum and enjoyed in Ti-Punch, the traditional aperitif. Some rum is aged to make a rich liqueur.

leries offer *dégustation*, or rum-tasting. Further south in Le François is the **Habitation Clément** (open daily; tel: 596-54 62 07; www.rhum-clement.com), a restored 18th-century plantation house with distillery and rum aging facilities producing Rhum Clément. If you are going to do a little tasting be aware that the traffic police carry out regular patrols of the island's roads.

The road meanders on down past **La Trinité** to the 8-mile (13-km) long **Presqu'île de la Caravelle ❼** which, protected by the Parc Naturel de la Martinique, is criss-crossed by nature trails. There are plenty of good beaches here offering an assortment of watersports, particularly surfing. At its tip are the ruins of the **Château Dubuc**, perfectly positioned for the pirate and smuggler who once lived there.

Josephine and the south

It takes 15 minutes for the *Somatour* (ferries depart every half-hour from the quay in front of La Savane) to cross the Baie de Fort-de-France to **Pointe du Bout ❽** where it ties up in another Martinique. The beaches here in the south are pristine with smart yachts moored in the marina, restaurants, the Créole Village Shopping Plaza, and a cluster of luxury hotels.

Taxis eagerly await the ferry to drive you to the **Musée de la Pagerie ❾** (open Tues–Sun but closed 1–2.30pm at weekends; entrance charge) just outside Les Trois-Ilets. A rusted metal sign points the way to the birthplace of Empress Josephine. Marie-Josèphe Rose Tascher de la Pagerie, later rechristened Josephine by her famous husband, left Martinique for Paris at the age of 16 in 1779, to marry the Viscount of Beauharnais. Two years after his death during the French Revolution, at the age of 33, she married Napoleon Bonaparte.

A 15-minute walk past open fields brings you to the lush greenery of the **Parc des Floralies** (open daily; closed public hols; entrance charge), a botanical garden where picnic tables sprout up among the profusion of flowers and trees with a good view of the Trois Ilets golf course, a Robert Trent Jones 18-hole championship facility. Farther along the road is the town of **Trois Ilets**, where the sidewalks and roofs are made from clay bricks and tiles manufactured at the Poterie de Trois Ilets, which you can visit (daily; tel: 596-68 03 44). Situated on the main road leading to Rivière Salée, Château Gaillard (daily; tel: 596-68 15 68) has a coffee and cocoa museum, and sells fine pottery made from local clay.

Across the southwestern peninsula, on the Caribbean coast, the pretty village of **Anse d'Arlets**, has a fine sandy beach dotted with seaside restaurants. Next is Petite Anse, and a few miles and many bends later is **Le Diamant ⑩**, a larger village with a good choice of hotels and restaurants and a long beach of soft, white sand. At **Anse Cafard** at the western end of Le Diamant stands the CAP 110 sculpture by Martinican artist Laurent Valère. Overlooking the sea where a slave ship sank in 1830, the 15 large bowed figures are a memorial to the 300 enslaved Africans who perished in the wreck; the sculpture also commemorates the 150th anniversary of the French abolition of slavery.

About a mile out to sea is the unmistakable hump of the **Rocher du Diamant** (Diamond Rock), an outcrop of volcanic stone which was curiously once a small part of the British Empire. In 1805, a party of 100 British soldiers, complete with cannons, took possession of the rock to control the channel between Martinique and St Lucia to the south. After 18 months the French ejected them from their uncomfortable position, which they had named HMS *Diamond*.

Map
on page
220

Marin is a cultural hub with its own resident artist, Habdaphaï, whose art studio is on the hillside overlooking the sea, opposite the 18th century church. Hadaphaï organises art fairs and exhibitions that attract artists from all over the Caribbean.

BELOW: Empress Josephine – a local who made a good marriage.

Southern splendour

The best beaches in Martinique are on the southern coast. In Diamant, Grand Anse is a lovely stretch of sand but the sea can be treacherous. For calmer waters, head towards **St Luce ⑪**, the neighboring village, where several beaches are tucked away in calm coves. Further along is the town of **Marin ⑫**, a bustling seaside town and the centre of all yachting activity in Martinique. Marin has a pleasant arty feel *(see margin)*; on the seafront, restaurants and bars add to the atmosphere with live music and late night sessions.

La Plage des Salines ⑬, the finest stretch of white sand beach and calm turquoise sea on the island, wraps itself for miles around the town of St Anne and the surrounding littoral forest. **François ⑭**, further up the Atlantic Coast, is protected by an immense barrier reef; maritime excursions offer picnics on the islets in the shallow lagoon. Martinicans say that you have not really visited the island until you have drunk a midday T-Punch in the Baignade de Josephine (Josephine's bathing area), a stretch of clear, shallow water situated between two islands.

The town of François is home to **Habitation Clément**, an old plantation house (open Oct–Aug 9am–5.30pm; tel: 596-54 62 07; www.habitation-clement.fr), which has an on-site rum distillery, an art gallery, and an arboretum with an important palm tree collection containing specimens from all over the world. ❏

ST LUCIA

Map on page 232

A luxuriant, tropical island indented with sandy coves exploding out of the surrounding crystalline waters in a volcanic heap, beautiful St Lucia is a destination for nature lovers

Caribbean Sea   St Lucia

Fought over for more than 200 years, St Lucia (*Loo*-sha), lying between Martinique to the north and St Vincent in the south, has earned the grand-sounding title "Helen of the West Indies". A veritable treasure during colonial times for its strategic position, and caught in a power struggle between the British and French, this Caribbean classic is an incredibly beautiful and enchanting island, whose mixture of luxuriant tropical vegetation on a mountainous landscape, stunning beaches, and typically creole culture now attracts a different kind of invader, keen to share in its natural splendors.

The most spectacular of these are the Pitons. The two majestic, cone-shaped peaks on the southwest coast, coated with lush forest, appear on the covers of holiday brochures and postcards all over the world. Rising straight out of the Caribbean Sea to a height of 2,600 ft (795 meters), these twin peaks are proof that St Lucia actually is a pile of lava that reached the earth's surface millions of years ago after a series of mighty eruptions. So is the sand which shimmers in all kinds of shades: snow-white, cream, anthracite gray, and even black.

But it is the color green that predominates as you go inland. At least one fifth of the 238-sq. mile (617-sq. km) island is covered by a thick carpet of luxuriant tropical rainforest, home to a colorful assortment of wildlife such as the St Lucia parrot *(Amazona versicolor)* and pygmy gecko, and with orchids, anthurium, and the heavily scented frangipani just growing wild. The highest peak, Mount Gimie (3,116 ft/950 meters), is almost permanently hung with cloud, which provides the fertile interior, rivers, and streams with enough water and moisture the whole year round. Banana plantations sweep down to the craggy east coast, dramatically buffeted by the wild Atlantic.

Tourism, dollars, and bananas

Until the 1980s, agriculture was the island's most important source of revenue. Bananas were export article number one, despite a great many problems with pricing and marketing. Since then, tourism has outstripped all other income sources, and now more than 300,000 visitors holiday on St Lucia each year, making the sector the island's most important foreign exchange earner.

Even though the idyll has not been destroyed by ugly high-rise hotels, tourism still causes problems: the all-inclusive resorts on the island own one third of its beds, and even though they create jobs through providing sports, entertainment, and even shopping, they are simultaneously making life very difficult for small restaurants, souvenir shops, and local tour offices. Marketing initiatives to promote locally run businesses like "The Inns of St Lucia" and "Heritage Tourism" programmes have attempted to even out the

PRECEDING PAGES: a misty, moist morning.
LEFT: a water-taxi outside Soufrière.
BELOW: a Lucian smile.

At the Marquis Estate, northeast of Castries, you can watch copra being produced.

distribution of the sector's profits; nonetheless, the push for foreign revenue at national level has also dramatically increased cruise-ship arrivals – holiday-makers who traditionally spend little in smaller establishments during their few hours ashore.

One development, which caused huge divisions among islanders, was the all-inclusive Jalousie Plantation Resort and Spa, on a spot believed to be a Taino burial ground right between the emblematic Pitons. It was immediately branded an act of desecration by its critics, who included the St Lucian poet and Nobel Laureate for Literature in 1992, Derek Walcott *(see pages 66–7)*; he likened it to opening "a casino in the Vatican or a take-away concession inside Stonehenge." The complex remained under-booked after it opened in 1992, and, following a series of ownership negotiations, was eventually bought out by the Hilton group. Opponents of the scheme would no doubt have been dis-heartened to know that Jalousie set a precedent for the future; much of St Lucia's remaining undeveloped coastline, particularly the beaches on the eastern,

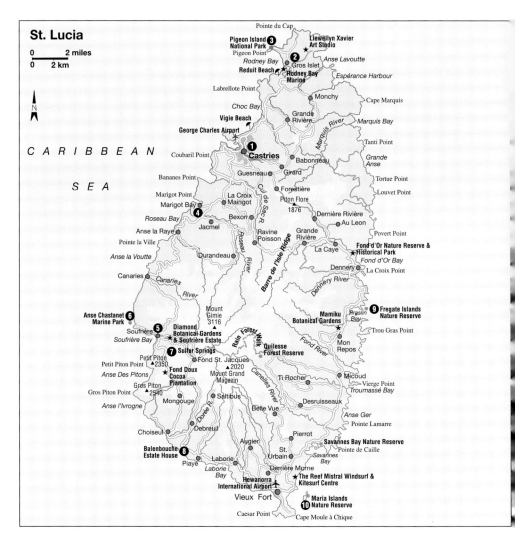

Atlantic side, have now either been built on or are slated for new resort and golf course developments.

Colorful changes of flag

St Lucia's landscapes aren't its only classically Caribbean feature: even the history of the island is typical of the region. Columbus and the Spanish probably noticed the Pitons from a distance, but were too busy heading for South America to bother with the island. After that the Caribs used guerrilla warfare to defend their "Hewanorra" (land of iguanas) very successfully against half-hearted attempts at invasion by the British and Dutch. It was only in 1650 that some French settlers finally managed to establish a long-term base on the second largest of the Windward Islands. In the years that followed the French flag and the Union Jack alternated with each other at least 14 times, until the island finally became British for good in 1814. In 1979, the island was granted independence while remaining within the British Commonwealth.

However, French cultural influences have remained a strong factor in St Lucia. English is the official language but the mother tongue is a melodic creole patois – a mix of West African influences and French *(see page 53)* – known as kwéyòl, which is spoken in formal and informal arenas. A good 75 percent of the inhabitants are Roman Catholic rather than Anglican and although cricket is played here, as elsewhere in the British Caribbean, the people also love dancing the *beguine* from Martinique *(see page 62)* or the *merengue* from the Dominican Republic.

Novelist and poet, Derek Walcott has revealed this complexity in his ironical writing about his creole background and multiple identity.

Map on page 232

The St Lucia Jazz Festival (www.stlucia jazz.org) every May is claimed to be the most successful in the Caribbean, drawing around 18,000 people. Started in 1992 to fill hotel rooms in low season, the event attracts scores of international big names.

BELOW: working and gossiping on the beach.

Castries – risen from the ashes

Apart from its attractive position in the natural harbor bay, **Castries ❶** (pop. 62,000), St Lucia's modern capital, has little in the way of interesting sights to offer. The town was named after the French naval minister Marechal de Castries, who did a great deal to help the colony's economic development at the end of the 18th century. In 1927 and 1948 two major fires reduced the entire old part of the town to ashes and most of the rebuilding was done in concrete. A stroll through the center, however, provides an exciting glimpse of everyday Caribbean life.

On Fridays and Saturdays the large **Castries Market** spills out on to Jeremie Street and Peynier Street, heaving with a noisy seething mass of country folk, townies, and visitors. The local farmers pile up the fruits of their labors – rose-colored sweet potatoes, papayas, bananas, heavy breadfruit, and all the aromatic spices that flourish in the fertile volcanic soil. Craftsmen lay out their work alongside the fishermen's catch or stalls selling local furniture, and old men play dominoes as bystanders noisily egg them on.

At the southern end of Peynier Street stands the somber-looking **Minor Basilica of the Immaculate Conception** whose interior walls are lined with colorful murals by the acclaimed St Lucian artist Dunstan St Omer. The main square in front, still bordered by the only 19th-century buildings that escaped the fires, was renamed by the proud city fathers in 1993 in honor of their son Derek Walcott, after he put St Lucia on the literary map, and is pleasantly shaded by a 400-year-old Saman tree. The very best view of the town and island is from Fort Charlotte on **Morne Fortune**, or the "Hill of Luck", 3 miles (5 km) south of Castries. Renovated and used as a college, the fort was built by the French and British in the 18th century and has witnessed many a battle between the two

BELOW: the rich interior of the Minor Basilica of the Immaculate Conception.

colonial powers. Today, you can watch the larger-than-life cruise ships battle it out for the prime spot in the port next to **Pointe Seraphine** and **La Place Carenage**, duty-free, shopping centers.

Beaches and nightlife in the north

The island's best white beaches stretch northward from where the island-hopping planes take off at Vigie Airport, just outside Castries and are edged with hotels and all-inclusive resorts. Sleek catamarans and luxurious windjammers lie at anchor in the 1,000-berth marina tucked away behind **Rodney Bay**, once a US naval base built to protect the Panama Canal, while close by on **Reduit Beach**, young people dressed rasta-style hawk their wares between the sunbeds. At sunset the sound of reggae and steel bands begins, inviting everyone back for the Manager's Cocktail at the hotel pool.

There's a very special kind of party every Friday night from 10pm when the otherwise rather sleepy fishing village of **Gros Islet ❷**, on the north side of the marina, wakes up for a "jump-up" lasting well into the early hours. Anyone can come and the smell of grilled chicken fills the streets together with the steady thump from sound systems. Everyone loves a party on St Lucia.

Connected to the mainland by a causeway near Gros Islet is the **Pigeon Island National Park ❸** (daily 9am–5pm; tel: 758-452 5005; charge; www.slunatrust.org) with inviting beaches and well-tended footpaths. The ruins of **Fort Rodney** overlooking the bay and a small museum commemorate Admiral George Rodney's departure from here in 1782 just before he inflicted his crushing defeat on the French at the Battle of the Saints, off the coast of Guadeloupe *(see page 202)*. You can also see the northernmost **Pointe du Cap** where the St

Map on page 232

TIP

Several boat tours sail down the west coast to Soufrière for lunch and a visit to the volcano, Diamond Falls, and Botanical Gardens. *The Unicorn*, a replica of a 19th-century brig, leaves from Rodney Bay Boatyard several times a week (tel: 758-456 9100).

BELOW: Government House on historic Morne Fortune.

A mural in Choiseul, on the southwest coast between Soufrière and Vieux Fort, brightens up the quaint Caribbean village where visitors can watch furniture being made at the Arts and Craft Development Centre (tel: 758-459 9941).

BELOW: leaving church in Soufrière.

Lucia Golf Resort and Country Club is located. It's worth stopping off at the **Llewellyn Xavier Art Studio**, a majestic building set in the Cap Estate hills. Xavier's work is exhibited in some of the world's finest museums.

The scenic route to Soufrière

Beyond Morne Fortune south of Castries, the road twists and turns and goes up and down through spectacular scenery to **Marigot Bay ❹**, 8 miles (13 km) away, through jungle vegetation, up mountains and down past the broad banana plantations dominating the valley. "Yachties" flock to the natural harbor and large marina, where once Admiral Rodney bamboozled the French by disguising his fleet with palm fronds, and you can enjoy a drink in Doolittle's, a boat ride across the bay, named for the 1966 movie *Dr Doolittle* shot here.

The main road now winds its way south across the mountains in a series of hair-raising hairpins; several rivers have formed natural harbor bays along the coast, and the villages of **Anse La Raye** (from where it's just a 15-minute walk to a wonderful waterfall) and **Canaries** are filled with colorful fishermen's houses. Every Friday night, Anse La Raye residents put on a "fish fry" where you can eat fresh seafood accompanied by DJs and dancing in the streets.

At **Soufrière ❺**, the first capital of St Lucia, about 5 miles (8 km) farther south, old wooden buildings line the streets, slender coconut palms border the dark volcanic sand, fishing boats and yachts bob in the emerald-green bay, and the dark-green wooded peaks of **Petit Piton** (2,414 ft/736 meters) and **Gros Piton** (2,600 ft/795 meters) create a magnificent backdrop. This Caribbean landscape seems too good to be true; not even the rain, frequent on the west coast, can spoil the joy of being in a place like this.

The dramatic scenery continues underwater at the **Anse Chastanet Marine Park 6**, north of Soufrière, where the diving and snorkeling is reputedly the best on the island, with more than 25 different types of coral in the reefs.

Sulfurous springs and charming plantations

Not far from the Pitons you may notice the pungent odour of hydrogen sulfide in the air, a smell similar to bad eggs. The crater region of **Sulfur Springs 7** (open daily; tel: 758-459 7686; entrance charge) just outside Soufrière is praised by the guides from the town as "the only drive-in volcano in the world", because car parking was possible between the two bubbling springs for quite some time. Now the last few yards have to be covered on foot. In 2004, the Pitons, the marine park, and the Sulfur Springs were made a Unesco World Heritage Site.

The restorative powers of the steamy springs are harnessed in the water at the historic **Diamond Botanical Gardens and Soufrière Estate** (open daily, Sun 10am–3pm; tel: 758-459 7565; entrance charge; www.diamondstlucia.com) close by, which Louis XVI presented to the three plantation-owning Devaux brothers just before the French Revolution for their services to the colony. In the middle of a splendid garden, where colorful orchids, flame trees, and hibiscus bushes bloom, the hot water streams out of the ground into tiled basins at a temperature of around 100°C (212°F). A commemorative plaque announces that a creole girl from Martinique named Marie-Josèphe Rose Tascher de la Pagerie *(see page 227)*, Napoleon Bonaparte's wife-to-be, used to spend her holidays here in the 18th century because her father owned a plantation near Soufrière. Still owned by the Devaux family today, the estate also features a restored water mill (1765), which used to crush sugar cane and provide Soufrière with electricity. Candle-lit "Planter's Dinners" are

Map on page 232

TIP

Experienced climbers can try their hand at scaling Gros Piton, but the difficult ascent may only be made in the company of local guides familiar with the terrain. Call the Tour Guides Association on 758-489 0136.

BELOW: playing on the beach.

Map on page 232

TIP

You can join a turtle-watching camp on Grande Anse Beach on the east coast (Mon–Sat by arrangement mid-March to mid-Aug), where the leatherback sea turtles come ashore at night to lay their eggs. Tel: 758-451 6058; www.heritagetours stlucia.org.

BELOW: typical St Lucian cottage. **RIGHT:** red roof.

available for hungry visitors after they've toured the property (book in advance).

The region around Soufrière as a whole is just the right place to get a feel for what life must have been like on plantations during colonial times. An increasing number of the traditional old manors are opening their doors to the public. The **Fond Doux Estate** (tel: 758-459 7545; www.fonddouxestate.com), between Soufrière and the fishing village of Choiseul, offers tours around its 250-year-old cocoa plantation, local cuisine at the restaurant and accommodations in the estate cottages.

Halfway between Choiseul and Laborie, inside an enchanting 70-acre (30-hectare) park, lies 200-year-old **Balenbouche Estate House** ❽ (tel: 758-455 1244; www.balenbouche.com). Always atmospheric with ghostly remains of sugar production throughout, the estate also manages to be supremely peaceful.

The green heart of the island

The only way to penetrate the heart of the island is to join an organized hike through one of the main tour agencies – hiking alone is not permitted, both for safety reasons and to safeguard the forest's sensitive ecology. The **Barre de l'Isle Trail**, named after the spinal mountain range dividing the island, is a pleasant 2–3 hour tour providing unforgettable views of sea and forest. In contrast, you have to be very fit to enjoy the **Central Rainforest Walk**, which is 6 miles (10 km) long and goes straight through the central highlands, beneath Mount Gimie. With a bit of luck, especially if you are with a small, quiet group, you may spot a rare St Lucian Parrot. It nearly became extinct in the 1970s, but after strict protective measures, several hundred of them are thriving on the island again. The **Union Trail** is much easier and, beginning inland from Rodney Bay, lasts just an hour and includes a medicinal herb garden. Another good bet for getting to know the island's flora is **Mamiku Gardens** (daily 9am–5pm; tel: 758-455 3729; charge; www.mamiku.com), close to Mon Repos on the east coast. With easy walking trails, bright orchids, and a plethora of visiting bird species, Mamiku is perfect for a relaxed afternoon.

Frigate birds and whales

The east coast, which has plenty of rainfall, few inhabitants, and a raw Atlantic atmosphere, is the most rewarding part of the island for nature lovers. At the **Fregate Islands Nature Reserve** ❾ (guided tours only; tel: 758-455 3163) near Dennery, vast colonies of frigate birds have made their home. With a wingspan of nearly 7 ft (2 meters), they are true acrobats to watch as they force other seabirds to drop their prey.

The **Maria Islands Nature Reserve** ❿ (open on request; guided tours only; call the National Trust on 758-452 5005), just off the southern cape near **Vieux Fort**, is a bird-watchers' dream, home to, among others, the sooty tern, the red-billed tropic bird, and the brown noddy, which tucks its nests under the prickly pear cactus. Also living there are two endemic reptiles: the large, colorful ground lizard and a non-venomous snake.

Another increasingly popular local attraction is whale-watching. Humpback whales, sperm whales, and dolphins can be spotted, if you are lucky, swimming off the Atlantic coast almost year-round, but the main season is November to April. ❑

ST VINCENT AND THE GRENADINES

Map on page 244

An area of time-warped quaintness, numerous islands, some of the world's finest beaches, and a sea of such incredible blues remains a prized discovery for the more adventurous traveler

A savored retreat for West Indians themselves, St Vincent and its 32 sister islands and cays, scattered like shells dropped from a child's overflowing bucket as she walks along the beach, are still untouched by the overt hand of tourism. There are no neon lights, no high-rise buildings, no traffic jams, no brand-name fast-food joints, no crowds, no noise.

Completing the lower arc of the Lesser Antilles and the Windward Islands, between St Lucia in the north and Grenada to the south, only eight of the islands are inhabited, accounting for a population of 120,000, most of whom live on St Vincent. The largest, at 18 miles (30 km) long and 11 miles (18 km) wide, the lush, craggy island of St Vincent looms out of crystalline waters presided over by the somnolent volcano La Soufrière (4,048 ft/1,234 meters). The "untouched" islands of the Grenadines, encompassing only 17 sq. miles (44 sq. km) all together, are havens of natural beauty whose charms extend across some of the most beautiful beaches in the world into seas of many hues rich in marine life – perfect for sailors and divers, and beachcombers in search of privacy.

Among the populated islands, the manicured Mustique and Petit St Vincent are the hideaways of the rich and famous while the teeming coral reefs of Bequia, Canouan, and Mayreau offer spectacular diving and snorkeling. Union Island, the most southerly, is the sailing gateway to the region.

In searching for new and interesting destinations unspoiled by the inevitable flood of packaged holidaymakers, travelers discover that the benefits of visiting "untouched" islands can be tempered by the accompanying disadvantages of remoteness. St Vincent and the Grenadines, which receives around 160,000 visitors every year, does not fall into this category and offers a delightful compromise for those who feel more at home with the beauty of nature but also enjoy creature comforts such as easy accessibility, a comfortable place to sleep, and the occasional pleasure of a good meal in a restaurant.

Caribbean Sea

St Vincent and the Grenadines

PRECEDING PAGES: Palm Island – loved by Caribbeans. **LEFT:** leatherback turtle on a mission. **BELOW:** view from the hills.

Forceful Caribs

It was not until the early 18th century that St Vincent was finally settled by the French after many wrangles with the resident Caribs. Having already eliminated the Tainos, keeping their women, the Caribs were not going to let go of their domain without a fight. However, in 1675 they took in some African slaves found shipwrecked between Bequia and St Vincent. Intermarriage produced the "Black Caribs", distinct from the indigenous "Yellow Caribs", and eyewitness reports of the time describe many a battle between them. But united

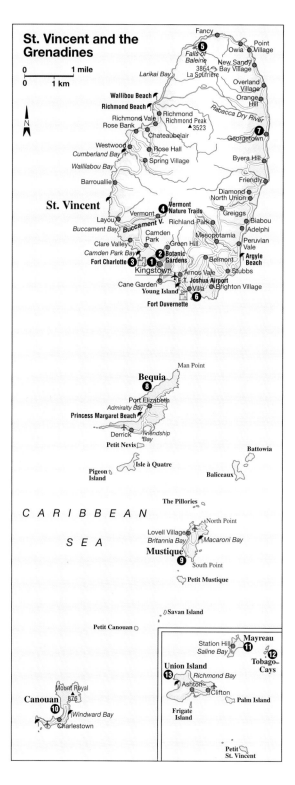

St. Vincent and the Grenadines

in their fight against the European intruders, they lived alongside the French in an uneasy truce.

In 1722, the British moved in and throughout the rest of the century the two countries were involved in a tug of war over the island, already planted with indigo, cotton, tobacco, and sugar. Alongside this conflict the Black Caribs waged war against the British colonists in what is known as the Carib Wars, followed by the Brigand Wars that were finally ended in 1797 when 5,000 Caribs were deported to Roatán, an island off Honduras. There is still a small settlement of the Black Carib descendants in Sandy Bay in the north of St Vincent.

British landlords

With the British at the helm, by 1829 St Vincent contained 98 sugar estates manned by slaves. Most of these were run by landowners who lived in Britain. By the end of the century, most of the arable lands in St Vincent were in the possession of just five owners, using a labor force largely of Portuguese and East Indian immigrants.

However, natural disasters took their toll in the form of a hurricane in 1898 and an eruption of La Soufrière in 1902 – two days before the catastrophic eruption of Montagne Pelée on Martinique *(see page 225)* – which killed around 2,000 people and finished off the plantation economy.

Run down and poor, St Vincent, along with the Grenadines, was granted independence in 1979, just a few months after another volcanic eruption had wrecked the island's agriculture, already suffering from a series of hurricanes. As a result, modern civilization has taken a little longer to arrive here.

Island cultures tend to blur on a rationale loosely based on the length of the airport runway. The small one at St Vincent's E.T. Joshua Airport allows only small planes to land here, meaning fewer tourists and a culture, island, and people spared from the forces that have homogenized many other parts of the Lesser Antilles.

Kingstown – the heart of a nation

In the mornings, the cobblestone streets of **Kingstown ❶** are full of uniformed school children, government workers, dollar taxi cab drivers, people peddling sandals, and old women selling from upside-down cardboard boxes the oddest collection of goods. Hustlers appear out of alleyways to coax tourists on rides to the volcano or to the Falls of Baleine, or to sell recordings of local calypsonians and bands such as Blaksand and New Direction. As the afternoon heat grips the town, government officers, bankers, and lawyers take their lunch at the **Bounty**, a café on Halifax Street, or at the more cosmopolitan rooftop restaurant in the **Cobblestone Inn**, a converted sugar and arrowroot warehouse in Upper Bay Street.

Nonetheless, this town, little more than several dusty blocks carved in a rugged shoreline, is the heart of St Vincent and the Grenadines. There are no buildings of colonial grandeur here, but the Roman Catholic **St Mary's Cathedral**, beside Victoria Park to the west, makes up for this by providing a fascinating selection of architectural styles and features in one – Romanesque, Moorish, Byzantine, and Flemish spires, turrets, towers, belfries, crenellations, and castellations are all here – built throughout the 19th century and renovated in 1940. Opposite, the old Anglican **St George's Cathedral** has some wonderful stained-glass windows, which feature red angels.

Although Kingstown may be the most visible source of activity in this tiny nation, the real power comes from the rich volcanic soil. This is an island of farmers, a world where practically everyone knows how to furrow a hillside to plant sweet potatoes. Agriculture is part of the school day and the more fortunate students go away to study it further in one of the Caribbean universities.

On Fridays and Saturdays you can get an idea of just how productive that soil

Map on page 244

Hairoun was the Carib name for St Vincent.

BELOW: St Mary's – an architectural mish mash.

is when the farmers ride dollar taxis into town loaded down with their produce of fruit and vegetables such as ginger, breadfruit, cashews, dates, and cassava. Trade in the large, colorful **Central Market** on Upper Bay Street is brisk, but the market building caused a great deal of controversy when it was constructed because of its lack of aesthetic appeal.

On the reclaimed land on the harbor in front stands the concrete **Little Tokyo Fish Market**, built with Japanese aid, to nurture support for continued whaling in the region. Minibuses bound for the rest of the island depart from here.

In the port, the dockside hubbub reaches a crescendo once a week when the Geest Industries freighter arrives to ship the week's crop of bananas to the rest of the world. The banana industry suffered when the preferential agreement with the EU ended in 2006, but the crop still accounts for around 35 percent of St Vincent's exports and makes a significant contribution to the island's economy.

The oldest botanic gardens in the West

Leaving Kingstown via the Leeward Highway to the west, on the edge of town you come to the **Botanic Gardens ❷** (open daily; free), founded in 1765 to propagate spices and medicinal plants, and the oldest in the western hemisphere. Chances are young men – unofficial guides – will approach you at the entrance and offer you a tour of the 20-acre (9-hectare) gardens that contain teak and mahogany trees, and nearly every flower and tree that can grow in the Caribbean, including a 50-ft (15-meter) breadfruit tree, one of the original seedlings brought to the West Indies in 1793 by Captain Bligh on his famous ship *The Bounty*.

Perched some 600 ft (180 meters) on a promontory above the town, 15 minutes' drive to the west, the ruins of **Fort Charlotte ❸**, built in 1805, command

spectacular views across the Caribbean to the Grenadines and, on a clear day, as far as Grenada 60 miles (95 km) away. In the barracks a series of paintings (1972) portrays the early history of St Vincent.

Map
on page
244

In search of the St Vincent parrot

The Leeward Highway provides a dramatic two-hour drive along the west coast with beaches of gold or black sand. What would take 10 minutes to drive in a flatter world can take hours here, as you circumvent mountains and jungles. In the **Buccament Valley** about 2 miles (3 km) from Kingstown you can wander through rainforests along the **Vermont Nature Trails ❹**. Maps of hikes are provided at the information center and you may see the endangered St Vincent parrot or the whistling warbler, both unique to the island. **Richmond Beach**, under the dark gaze of La Soufrière, marks the end of this beautiful winding road and a boat is necessary to go on any farther. Many boat operators offer trips – which can include snorkeling and a lunch stop – to the **Falls of Baleine ❺**, 7 miles (11 km) to the northern tip of the island. There you can swim in the pools filled by these freshwater falls on a river that flows from the volcano.

The St Vincent parrot hides in the rainforest.

Along the Windward coast

The Vigie Highway leaves Kingstown from the east to the airport about 15 minutes away. Close by is the **Arnos Vale cricket ground**, the home (or shrine) of Vincentian cricket. The stadium was refurbished and expanded to host warm up matches for the ICC Cricket World Cup in 2007. Vincentians love their cricket and support their team in droves, making a match a festive social occasion with loud music and dancing no matter which team wins or loses.

BELOW: on the front deck of a cat in Tobago Cays in the Grenadines.

A little farther east, on the south coast road, **Villa ❻**, colloquially known as "The Strip", is the island's main resort area with several hotels, guest houses, restaurants, bars, and watersports facilities. Just 200 yards (180 meters) off shore, the tiny, privately owned resort on **Young Island**, linked to the mainland by a small water-taxi, becomes officially child free between January 15 and March 15. Beside it on a rock is the 19th-century **Fort Duvernette**.

The Vigie Highway winds through what the Vincentians call the "breadbasket" of their island. On the Atlantic side the soil is more fertile and from the unbarricaded road you have views, somewhat frightening, of deep valleys dotted with small farms and banana plantations. You may experience the odd traffic jam on the narrow coastal road that leads north to Georgetown, but they are usually only caused by drivers stopping for a chat, or someone going over to inspect a fish for sale on the roadside. Such impromptu markets are common.

Georgetown ❼, the second-largest town on St Vincent, was once the prosperous sugar capital of the island: when the price of sugar fell, the sugar plant, which employed most of the laborers in this valley, was closed. Now there's a sense of driving through a ghost town, although rum is still produced nearby by **St Vincent Distillers** (open Mon–Fri; visits by appointment; tel: 784-458 6221; free). Formerly the Mount Bentinck refinery, the distillery bottles and exports local rums.

A little farther on is the **Rabacca Dry River**, once a hot river of lava. You can drive or walk along here to well-marked trails that lead to the crater of La Soufrière. A six-hour round trip, it is an arduous hike best started as early in the morning as possible only by the fit and healthy, but it is worth the effort when you finally crest the rim and look down into that awesome volcano. It is often cloudy, cold, and wet at the top so come well equipped and take a guide.

At least three times a day banana farmers will inspect each stalk to see if there are leaves pressing against the fruit. Bruised fruit will not be accepted by the buyers.

BELOW: a whole island to yourself.

Island-hopping in the Grenadines

Most people arriving on an island in the Grenadines do so by sea, and many are under sail either on their own private yacht, or they have chartered a yacht or are bare boating *(see pages 114–15)*. More and more anchorages are being provided to protect the coral reefs surrounding the islands from damage. Water-taxis zip around the bays waiting to take yachtsmen on shore and boys often come out to the boats with goods for sale. Ferries regularly leave Kingstown for the islands, and Bequia, Mustique, Canouan, and Union Island all have small airports for light aircraft.

Map on page 244

The focal point of **Bequia** ❽ (*Bek*-way), 9 miles (14 km) from St Vincent, is the stunningly beautiful **Admiralty Bay**, an enormous, clear harbor bordered by steep green cliffs, holding several yacht anchorages. Around the island is a Marine Protected Area looking after 30 superb dive sites, many of which are suitable for snorkeling too. **Port Elizabeth** is a thriving little community with guest houses and a full range of stores including a yacht chandler, bank, and internet café. Along the shore sloops are built by the skilful local boatbuilders.

During the 19th century, the New Bedford whalers used Bequia as a whaling station. The island's last whale harpoonist, the late Aytheneal Oliverre, lived in a small house in the south which he turned into a **whaling museum**. The front door is framed by a whale jawbone and inside is a vertebra of the first one he killed in 1958. When and if a whale is caught (Oliverre caught his last one in 1992 – the International Whaling Foundation permits the islanders to harpoon two a year), the whole island comes to watch.

Conch shells on the beach on Mustique.

Visitors to **Mustique** ❾, 15 miles (24 km) south of St Vincent, are often greeted by the island's only policeman checking that everyone has a proper destination. Not that there are many places to go. There are approximately 80 houses on the 3-sq. mile (8-sq. km) island. More than half of these properties belong to the rich and famous. However, on the western shore, fishermen have set up camp on the beach near **Basil's Bar**, the only public restaurant, and they eat the conch they fish for, leaving behind a mountain of shells.

BELOW: island-hopping offered on Bequia.

The small, crescent-shaped island of **Canouan** ❿ has some of the Caribbean's best and most private beaches. There is also a luxury resort, complete with the Grenadines' only golf course. Tiny **Mayreau** ⓫ is less than 2 sq. miles (4.5 sq. km) and is inhabited by about 250 people. There are no roads, a small salt pond, and one very quiet resort. Nearby a tiny clutch of five uninhabited islands, known as the **Tobago Cays** ⓬, offers spectacular snorkeling and diving. In order to preserve the area a national marine park is being developed around the islands.

Mountainous **Union Island** ⓭, the most developed of the smaller Grenadines, is the sailing center of the region, and is an ideal starting point for trips to the surrounding islands. Across the bay is beautiful **Palm Island**, once known as Prune Island and now a popular resort with Caribbean islanders seeking peace.

Farthest south is **Petit St Vincent**, an island resort considered to be one of the best in the region, where exclusive privacy is the order of the day. ❑

GRENADA

To the south of the Grenadines, this aromatic island is known as the Spice Island of the Caribbean, most famous for nutmeg. Grenada is alluring, with lush rainforest and pretty beaches too

Map on page 254

Caribbean Sea

Grenada

A colorful gem of an island, Grenada (Gre-*nay*-dah) is, by any definition, small. Only 21 by 12 miles (35 by 20 km) in size, it seems bigger than it really is, partly because its mountainous interior looms large and is slow to cross and partly because its landscape is so varied. Its fertility is largely thanks to the 160 inches (4,060 mm) of rain deposited on the island's interior each year by the trade winds. This creates lush and often impenetrable rainforest, streams that cascade down to the sea, and ideal conditions for the generations of small farmers who have worked their smallholdings since the British freed the slaves in 1834.

In 2004, the island was struck directly by Hurricane Ivan, which uprooted trees, caused damage to 90 percent of the buildings and devastated crops. However, the land is astonishingly fertile; bananas, cocoa, citrus, mangoes, and coconuts grow in dense groves or by the roadside. Farther up in the interior, ferns and mahogany trees drip in the humidity.

Known as the Spice Island of the Caribbean, it is nutmeg *(see page 215)* which gives Grenada its most delicious and distinctive aroma. Nutmeg has been grown here since the 1780s when the British brought it over from East India and, together with cinnamon, ginger, and cloves, replaced sugar as the island's main export. Mature nutmeg trees were destroyed by the hurricane but replanting and recovery was swift and the crop still accounts for a significant proportion of Grenada's export earnings and provides a living for small farmers. Known affectionately as the "retirement tree" as it is thought to guarantee a comfortable old age, the nutmeg tree drops an apricot-like fruit which splits when ripe to reveal its seed and the surrounding red membrane which makes the separate spice, mace.

The prettiest capital

Few would disagree that the capital, **St George's ❶**, is a fine town. In a region regularly ravaged by natural disaster or crass development, it has retained its picturesque charm and small-town warmth.

The geography of St George's is unusually attractive, as the town is built around the rim of a volcanic crater which forms its almost landlocked harbor. From around the waterfront Carenage, edged with solid stone warehouses, the town rises steeply, houses, churches, and forts ringing the inner horseshoe bay. Over the promontory, where the French-built **Fort George** (open daily; entrance charge) commands panoramic views of the town and harbor, is another part of town, joined to the Carenage by the 100-year-old Sendall Tunnel. Here, **Market Square** is the scene of hectic and colorful activity on Saturday morning as farmers bring their vanloads of yams, mangoes, and bananas to town.

PRECEDING PAGES: Hurricane Ivan devastated the island. **LEFT:** nutmeg and mace in the raw. **BELOW:** youngsters survey Dougaldston Plantation.

The Queen's Park Stadium, just north of St George's, was refurbished and its seating capacity increased to 20,000 for the ICC Cricket World Cup in 2007. The island is also home to the West Indies' Cricket Academy.

Delicate French provincial architecture rubs shoulders with robust Georgian stonework, a happy consequence of Grenada changing colonial hands several times in the 18th century. Pink fish-scale roof tiles date from the time when they crossed the Atlantic as ballast in French ships. Pastel-colored wooden houses clinging to the hillsides contrast with the dour stone ruins of **St Andrew's** Presbyterian Kirk's belfry and the imposing walls of **Fort George**.

The small **Grenada National Museum** (open Mon–Fri and Sat am; entrance charge), near the Sendall Tunnel, is housed in the former prison cells of 18th-century French barracks. One of the best ways to pass the time is simply to sit and admire the view, toward sea or mountains, preferably from the shady terrace of the waterside **Nutmeg**, famous for its rum punches.

The "intervention"

The town exudes history, but most Grenadians prefer not to discuss the events of October 1983 which brought their island brief notoriety. In 1979, a group of

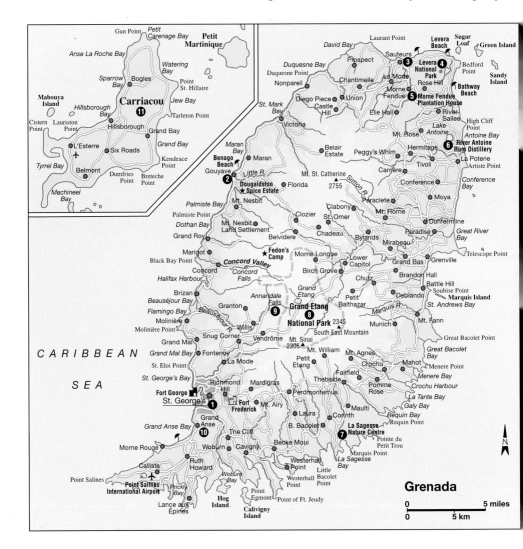

Grenada

0   5 miles

0   5 km

Map on page 254

young radicals turfed out the eccentric and dictatorial Prime Minister Eric Gairy in a bloodless coup. Four and a half years of People's Revolutionary Government, led by the charismatic Maurice Bishop, ensued in which long overdue reforms were introduced. But Grenada's "revo" disintegrated as a hardline faction tried to snatch power. Bishop was arrested, freed by a crowd and then, in scenes of appalling brutality, was executed with several supporters in the courtyard of Fort George. The US, long suspicious of Grenada's links with Castro's Cuba, seized the opportunity to invade. More than 6,000 US Marines landed in what is euphemistically known as "the intervention".

It seems long ago, but the scars remain. Several of those convicted of the murders have been released, while some remain in jail in **Fort Frederick** on Richmond Hill. Others still mourn their dead.

Spice of Grenadian life

The center of Grenada's nutmeg industry is the west-coast town of **Gouyave** ❷ (pronounced Warve), about 6 miles (10 km) north of St George's. A ramshackle one-street fishing community, populated by as many goats as people, it has a pungent **Nutmeg Processing Station** (open Mon–Fri; entrance charge), where visitors can see the grading, drying, and packing process. The town is also home to a weekly laid back evening fish fry, known as Fish Friday, where visitors can enjoy Grenadian fish specialties and local music. Just before Gouyave, down a dirt track, is the crumbling **Dougaldston Spice Estate** (open Mon–Fri; free), once a prosperous plantation but now fallen on hard times. Small bags of nutmeg, cinnamon, or cloves are on sale here for a few dollars.

From Gouyave the road follows the coast northward, providing spectacular sea views, before turning inland through several poor villages to the small north-coast town of **Sauteurs** ❸. The French name (literally "leapers") recalls a grisly moment in Grenada's colonial past when French forces surrounded the last community of indigenous Caribs in 1651. Rather than surrender, the 40 Caribs jumped from the 100-ft (30-meter) cliff into the sea below. On the promontory by **St Patrick's** church there you can peer down on to the rocks and spray.

A rough road leads eastward out of Sauteurs to the **Levera National Park** ❹, a wild and varied area of scrubland, mangrove, and palm-lined beach. From the hilltop, there are spectacular views of the offshore and uninhabited **Sugar Loaf**, **Green**, and **Sandy Islands**. **Bathway Beach**, looking out to Sandy Island, is a normally deserted expanse of white sand, where seagrapes provide welcome shade. Currents are reportedly strong, despite a protective reef, but there is a natural 33-ft (10-meter) long natural rock pool perfect for swimming.

A pepperpot lunch

The main road south of Sauteurs takes you to the **Morne Fendue Plantation House** ❺ (tel: 473-442 9330), a gray stone house. Here, for a reasonable price, the owner provides a traditional Grenadian lunch of pepperpot *(see page 72)*, complete with rum

In October 1961, a fire ripped through the Italian liner, Bianca C, in St George's Harbour. Boats of all types rushed to the rescue, saving the 400 passengers, and the ship's owners erected a bronze statue, Christ of the Deep, in their honor. The ship is now the largest wreck dive in the Caribbean.

BELOW: taking the mace off the nutmegs.

TIP

Serious hikers can
take a five-hour walk
in the Grand Etang
National Park to
Concord Falls, where
it's possible to swim,
and on to Fedon's
Camp, where a rebel
planter held out
against the British in
1795. The good news
is there is a bus back
to St George's from
nearby Concord.

punches *(see page 75)*. It is essential to phone in advance. Heading south through **Mount Rose** village there is a turn-off to the **River Antoine Rum Distillery** ❻ (open Mon–Fri; entrance charge) where guided tours demonstrate 18th-century rum distilling techniques based on a water-powered cane crusher. From the distillery it is a short drive to **Lake Antoine**, a lonely crater lake teeming with birdlife.

Nature in the raw

At **Grenville**, a sprawling, rather unattractive town with a dirty beach on the east coast, the picturesque coastal road leads to **La Sagesse Nature Centre** ❼, about 10 miles (16 km) south. Here, you drive through a banana plantation before arriving at a shaded beach, overlooked by a small guesthouse and restaurant terrace. Within walking distance is a microcosm of Caribbean coastal ecology: a mangrove estuary, salt pond, coral reefs, and cactus woodlands.

But Grenada's natural *tour de force* is the **Grand Etang National Park** ❽, an area which covers the mountainous backbone of the island, from Mount St Catherine (2,755 ft/840 meters) to Mount Sinai (2,306 ft/703 meters). The Grenville–St George's road winds tortuously up into rainforest and occasional warm mist. About halfway is Grand Etang itself, a water-filled volcanic crater at 1,900 ft (580 meters). Legend has it that the lake is bottomless, and certainly few feel the urge to swim in the strangely still water.

A **Visitors' Center** has information on the surrounding flora and fauna, and there are well-marked hiking trails which take from 15 minutes to three hours to complete. It is wet, sweaty, and sometimes slippery high in the mountains, but

BELOW: there is
dense rainforest in
Grand Etang Park.

walkers will be rewarded with panoramic views and sightings of orchids, hawks, and even opossums (considered a delicacy locally).

On the way back to St George's it is worth making a half-mile detour to **Annandale Falls** ❾, where a cold stream drops 50 ft (15 meters) into a pool used by locals and tourists alike for swimming. The site has attracted fair numbers of self-appointed "guides" as well as those eager to sell spices.

The southern tail of the island is comprised of a series of inlets, promontories, and beaches. The most celebrated of these is **Grand Anse** ❿, several miles of perfect white sand fringed with palm trees and hibiscus hedges. This is the tourist strip, with hotels bordering the beach and a road of restaurants and shops running parallel. Smaller and more secluded is **Morne Rouge**, lying in a protected cove farther round, east of **Point Salines** airport (claimed by the US, in the heady Cold War days of 1983, to have been built by Cuba as part of its expansionist designs in the Caribbean) is **Prickly Bay**. Here is the popular **Spice Island Marina** alongside smart hotels such as **The Calabash**, whose lawns sweep down to the beach.

Yachting hideaways

Grenada's two even smaller island dependencies, **Carriacou** ⓫ and **Petit Martinique**, a three to four-hour boat ride off the northeastern coast are a haven for those who want to get away from it all. Boats leave twice weekly and express ferries daily from the Carenage or you can fly, but sailing into Carriacou's natural harbor is an experience to be savored. Carriacou is famous for wooden boatbuilding, the African-influenced Big Drum Dance and (some say) smuggling; tiny, volcanic Petit Martinique also has a reputation for illicit supplies of whisky. ❑

Map on page 254

Carriacou Regatta, held every August, was started in 1965 to show off the hand-crafted schooners built by the descendants of Scottish settlers. It is now a huge festival with street parties and Big Drum Dances.

BELOW: hauling in the nets at Gouyave.

BARBADOS

A coral island set apart from the rest of the Eastern Caribbean chain, this "singular" island has a character and landscape of its own with an emphasis on beauty, fun and friendliness

Map on pages 262–63

Caribbean Sea

Barbados

The breakers of the Atlantic – "white horses" as the Bajans call them – slam against the jagged cliffs of River Bay, a vast, barren plateau and dry river bed at the isolated northern tip of Barbados.

Ordinarily it is deserted here. But today is Boxing Day. A lengthening line of public buses curves along the road that leads to this rugged area, intruding on the landscape like a monstrous blue and yellow snake. Clusters of people swarm toward a hillside shaded by a grove of long-needled casuarina trees. Women wearing their Sunday best – brilliant turquoise skirts or scarlet dresses that look even brighter next to the muted browns and greens of the landscape – step gingerly across a narrow stream and stake out the best picnic spots on the hillside. The few trees, gnarled and stunted by the ever-present trade winds, provide a canopy under which the women unveil their elaborate holiday fare.

With a total area of only 166 sq. miles (431 sq. km), Barbados has some of the most varied terrain in the Caribbean. Divided into 11 parishes, each has its own character and landscape. The north is the least populated section; its shores punctuated by dramatic cliffs and crashing waves. Equally unspoiled is the scenic east with miles of windswept beaches along the Atlantic coast fringing the hilly "Scotland District." As the Atlantic Ocean rushes wildly along the south coast westward toward the Caribbean Sea, the sand becomes whiter, hidden away in rocky coves edged by palm trees, washed by the breakers that are finally lulled into submission on the heavenly beaches of the west coast. The center of the island is covered with gently rolling cane fields, rural villages, and lush tropical vegetation.

Although some of the hills are very steep, Barbados is considered a flat island. Coral rather than volcanic, its highest point, Mount Hillaby, is just 1,115 ft (340 meters) above sea level. Off the beaten track, 100 miles (160 km) to the east of the rest of the Lesser Antilles, Barbados is often referred to as "the singular island." During the days of sailing conquerors and Caribbean settlement, this isolation provided Barbados with an unwitting defense: it is difficult to sail here from the other islands because of the prevailing easterly winds.

The first Bajans

Once a British colony and nicknamed "Little England," Barbados can appear very British with afternoon teas and starched school uniforms. One 19th-century visitor declared it "more English than England itself." However, any ties to the mother country could be broken, if plans for the island to become a republic are implemented. Bridgetown's Trafalgar Square has been renamed National Heroes Square and the statue of Lord Nelson may be replaced with one of a national hero.

PRECEDING PAGES: repairing the fishing boats on the beach. **LEFT:** the beach at Bathsheba. **BELOW:** a happy face in the sun.

North Point
Cluffs
Bay
Archer's
Bay
Animal 18
Flower Cave
Middle Bay
Flatfield
River Bay
Crab
Hill
Greenidge
Hope
St. Clement
The Duppies
Harrison
Point
Harrisons
Friendship
St. LUCY
Broomfield
Hannays
Durham
Cave Hill
Gay's Cove
Maycock's
Bay
St. Lucy
Nesfield
Date Tree Hill
Pico Teneriffe
80
Fort
Maycock
Alexandra
Boscobelle
Checker
Hall
Castle
Cherry
Tree Hill
804
Colleton
Alleynedale
Diamond
Corner
St. Nicholas
Abbey
19
Grenade Hall
Signal Station
Mile and
a Quarter
Six Mens
Maynards
All Saints
Farley Hill
Nat. Park
Barbados
Wildlife
Reserve
20
Morgan
Lewis
Morgan Lewis
Beach
Shorey
Village
Walker's
Beach
ATLANTIC
Six Mens Bay
Port St. Charles Marina
Heywoods Beach
The
Whim
St. PETER
The Rock
Breedy's
St. Andrew
OCEAN
Speightstown
17
Richmond
Hall
Bawdens
Belleplaine
Lakes
Beach
Heyman's
Factory
Black Bess
Four Hills
Rock Hall
St. ANDREW
Sleeping
Napoleon
548
Ermie Bourne Hwy
Mullins Beach
Four Winds
Rock
Dundo
Sion Hill
St. Simons
The Potteries
Chalky
Mount
Barclays Park
Lower Carlton
Weston
Read's Bay
Westmoreland
Mose
Bottom
Bissex Hill
Cattlewash
Alleynes Bay
Mount Standfast
St. JAMES
Orange Hill
1115
Mount
Hillaby
Boarded
Hall
St. JOSEPH
Bathsheba
Andromeda
Botanic Gardens
Tent Bay
Atlantis Hotel 9
Flower
Forest 13
Melvin Hill
Foster Hall
Lancaster
Endeavour
Mount
Misery
1076
Chapman
Horse Hill
Hackleton's Cliff
Malvern
Great House
Hothersal
Martin's Bay
Newcastle
Folkestone
Folkestone Park and
Marine Reserve 16
Greenwich
Trents
Portvale Sugar
Factory
and Museum
Rock Hall
Porey
Spring
Welchman
Hall Gully 12
Welchman
Hall
Chimborazo
1105
3A
Cotton Tower
Signal Station
Venture
St. John
Coach Hill
Conset
Bay
15
Holetown
Sunset Crest
St. THOMAS
Harrison's
Cave 11
Coffee
Gully
Villa Nova
Sherbourne
Mt. Tabor
Church
Eastmont
Codrington
College 8
Sealy
Hall
Sandy
Lane Bay 14
Sandy Lane
Hotel
Vaucluse
Factory
St. THOMAS
Parris
Hill
St. JOHN
Ashfold
Steward Hill
Paynes Bay
Bagatelle
Great House
Fisher Pond
Four Cross Roads
Cherry
Cove
Massiah
Street
Thic
Platinum
Durants
Bailey
Hill
Bridgefield
Proutes
Market Hill
3B
Kendal
Church
Village
St. Ph
Thorpes
Arthurs Seat
Belair
Retreat
Prerogative
Greens
Hill View
Summervale
Fitts Village
Husbands
Locust
Hall
Bibbys
Lane
Jackson
Salisbury
Cottage Vale
Coast
Prospect
Warrens
Great House
Gun Hill
Signal Station
Gun Hill
Drax Hall
Bushy Park
Lazaretto
University
Eden
Lodge
Green Hill
Francia Plantation
House 10
Valley
St. George
Ellerton
St. GEORGE
Melverton
4B
Sunbury
Plantation House 6
Fresh
Water
Bay
Cave Hill
Tyrol
Cot
Hothersal
Turning
Foster Hall
Bulkeley Sugar
Factory (closed)
Marchfield
Six Cross
Roads
Stro
Mount Gay Rum
Visitor Center
ABC Highway
Turnpike
St. George Valley
Brereton
Rum Factory and
Heritage Park 7
BELFIELD
Brighton
Beach
St. MICHAEL
Salters
Watts Village
Highland
Woodbourne
5
Mangrove
DEACONS
Emancipation
Monument
Mapp Hill
Free
Pilgrim
Lower Gray
Yorkshire
Fairview
St. Patricks
Foul E
NEW ORLEANS
Government
House
Mount
Friendship
Staple
Cove
Cave
Hill
Christ Church
St.
Bridgetown 1
BELLEVILLE
WILDEY
Clapham
Upton
St. David's
Bannatyne
Newton
Plantation
Searles
Village
Walronds
Carlisle
Bay
The Garrison
Savannah 3
Barbados
Museum
BRITTONS HILL
2
Vauxhall
Newton
Terrace
Charnocks
Gemswick
Needham's
Point
Rendezyous
Hastings
Graeme Hall
Bird Sanctuary
Kendal Hill
Pilgrim Place
Grantley Adams
International Airport
Rockley Beach
Worthing
Maxwell
Durants
Wiloox
Sandy Beach
St. Lawrence
Dover
Maxwell
Coast
Casuarina
Beach 4
Oistins
Chancery Lane
Long
Bay
Miami Beach
Oistins Bay
Enterprise
Chancery
Lane Swamp
Goodland
Silver
Sands
South Point

CARIBBEAN SEA

CHEAPSID
Cheapside
General
Post
Office
Cheaps
Marke
Princes
Hwy
Fish Mark
Pelican Craft Centre
Fishing H
Emmerto
School Ln.

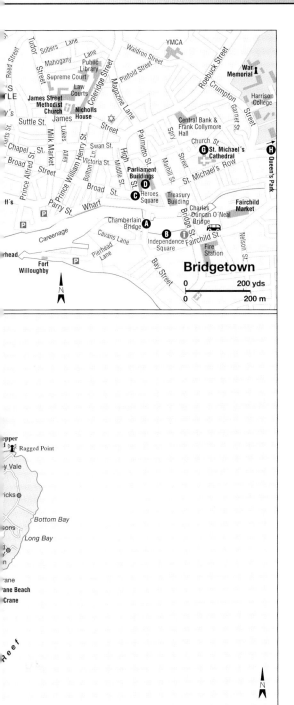

Bridgetown

0   200 yds
0   200 m

Barbados

0   2 miles
0   2 km

This tiny coral island is densely populated – about 265,000 people live in a space just 14 miles (22 km) wide and 21 miles (33 km) long, yet Barbadians, or Bajans, as they are generally known, have one of the highest incomes per head in the West Indies and a literacy rate of over 98 percent.

The first Bajans were Amerindians, who came in canoes from Venezuela in around – it has recently been discovered – 1600 BC. Different tribes came and went, with the Tainos remaining most evident, but these gentle fishermen and farmers are believed to have been captured by the Spanish at the beginning of the 16th century and taken as slaves to Hispaniola – no archeological evidence has been found that Caribs ever lived here. When the English arrived in 1625, all they found was a population of wild hogs left by Portuguese explorers who had anchored briefly in 1536.

The brightest jewel

In 1627, on 17 February, 80 English settlers and 10 African slaves, captured from trading vessels en route, landed on the calm west coast of the island, which became the first English possession to cultivate sugar on a large scale. By the 1650s, Barbados had a booming economy based solely on sugar cane and became known as "the Brightest Jewel in the English Crowne." As the sugar cane plantation system evolved, the institution of slavery *(see pages 33–35)* became firmly entrenched, but not without some notable uprisings – in 1675, 1695, and 1702 – cruelly quashed by the planters. The final 5,000-strong rebellion came in 1816 after the abolition of the slave trade had not given the slaves the freedom they, mistakenly, thought they were due. That didn't come until 1834–38.

New challenges

Between 1850 and 1914, around 20,000 adventurous laborers left for Panama to help build the canal, and many returned wearing flashy clothes, their pockets stuffed with US currency, with which they bought land, educated their children, and increased their standard of living. However, afterward there were few opportunities for black Bajans and most returned to

Many believe that the island was named in 1536 by Portuguese explorers calling it Los Barbudos ("the bearded ones") after the bearded fig trees (above) *which grew there. But this name had appeared in a Spanish document dated 1511.*

BELOW: engrossed in a game of Warri.

the plantations as laborers. The poor conditions there and a lack of political power sparked a half century of intense political and social change.

Perhaps the most noteworthy figure to challenge the ruling white planter class was Grantley Adams, the acknowledged leader of the Barbados Progressive League, the island's first mass movement political party formed in 1938, which over the course of 30 years and eventually under the title of the Barbados Labour Party (BLP) helped attain fair labor laws and universal voting rights.

Political independence from Britain finally came in 1966, with Errol Barrow of the Democratic Labour Party (DLP) at the helm. Remaining in the British Commonwealth, the island has continued with a Westminster-style parliament consisting of a Senate and a democratically elected House of Assembly and now the government swings between the BLP and DLP.

Creation of a new culture

While Barbados has managed to forge a political identity, it has taken much longer to escape a cultural limbo and develop its own indigenous culture. Alongside its African heritage, brought over by the slaves, and long known for its "Britishness" and the old-fashioned lifestyle of its people, Barbados's reputation began to change in the 1970s, when the Black Power movement and Rastafarianism had a profound impact on island identity. At the same time, the tourist industry was rapidly growing, widening its appeal across the board, attracting visitors who were not rich and famous and who congregated around an increasingly lively south coast.

Another powerful influence on Bajan culture in the past four decades has been US television and music. One of the island's most famous calypsonians, the

Mighty Gabby, has sung about the negative effect of commercial programs on society, advocating instead, more worthy Barbadian subjects such as George Lamming's *Castle of My Skin*.

Now, after 40 years as an independent nation, Barbados is finally coming into its own culturally. There is a growing appreciation of things Bajan, and a movement to preserve aspects of the folk culture that have been dying out. The enthusiasm the revived annual Crop Over Festival in July and August generates is one sign of the new cultural pride and the wildly popular calypsonians are a major force in Bajan society. The festival, a five-week long traditional celebration of the end of the sugar-cane harvest, is the highlight of a virtual 12-month calendar of events, which reflects a boom period in Barbados enhancing its reputation that there is always something exciting going on.

Bridgetown – colorful contrasts

It is in **Bridgetown ❶**, the bustling capital of Barbados, that the contrasts characterizing the island are most evident. While duty-free shops sell luxury items like cameras, crystal, and cashmere, a Rastaman peddles coconuts from a wooden cart outside and country women, or hucksters, sit by their stalls of fresh fruit and vegetables picked from their gardens. Old ramshackle colonial buildings stand next to multi-million dollar office blocks and the strains of calypso emanate from juke boxes in back-alley cafés.

Early British colonists established a settlement here in what was no more than a swamp, where they found a bridge left by the Amerindians – hence the name. The first harbor was built in the outer basin, called the Careenage where the boats were "careened" or keeled over so that their hulls could be repaired and cleaned.

Map on pages 262–63

Bussa, the monument to freedom at the top of Two Mile Hill in Bridgetown.

BELOW: colonial grandeur.

Baxter's Road, in Bridgetown, is called The Street That Never Sleeps. It comes alive at night with meals grilled by the roadside and rum shops selling beer and rum, resounding to the steady throb of calypso and reggae.

BELOW: cricket commentators at the Oval.

Now there are two bridges across the river, which in fact is just an inlet of sea: the wider Charles Duncan O'Neal Bridge and **Chamberlain Bridge** Ⓐ, the gateway to Bridgetown, which used to swing back to allow boats to pass through, and is now closed to traffic. Down on the south bank, as part of a major renovation program, the old warehouses are being converted into shops and cafés, such as the **Waterfront Café** where you can relax and watch the water world and city life unfold in front of you. At night the tempo rises with a jazz band to dance to. In the Careenage, where the island's trading center once was, large catamarans offer sightseeing trips along the coast, and sportfishing boats are all set to hunt down the big wahoo and marlin.

Nelson – a controversial monument

Between the two bridges sprawls **Independence Square** Ⓑ, a city park dominated by a statue of the first prime minister and National Hero, Errol Barrow. Walking over Chamberlain Bridge past the stalls of colorful fruit and vegetables, visitors come face to face with a bronze statue of Nelson located in what was known as Trafalgar Square, renamed **National Heroes Square** Ⓒ. The monument to Nelson, erected in 1813 (17 years before Nelson's Column in London's Trafalgar Square) was a controversial figure as early as 1833. Seen as a symbol of colonialism, many local people want a Barbadian hero in its place.

The island's 10 National Heroes can be seen immortalized in stone in the **Museum of Parliament** and the **National Heroes Gallery** (open Mon, Wed–Sat; entrance charge; tel: 246-427-2019) in the **Parliament Buildings** Ⓓ, opened to commemorate 40 years of independence. The Parliament Buildings were built in the 1870s to accommodate the Houses of Parliament, which were

CRICKET, LOVELY CRICKET

Cricket is much more than a game in Barbados; it is a national religion, inspiring the islanders with a fierce passion, particularly when the West Indies meets England, their old colonial masters, in a Test Match.

For five days, the **Kensington Oval**, the island's cricketing headquarters and national shrine, takes on a carnival atmosphere as supporters of both teams (Barbados almost sinks under the weight of the English fans who fly out for the event) pack the stands. With a "We must win but if we don't, then we must still have a good time" attitude, the West Indians welcome their visitors, encouraging them to join in the fun and share their picnics and "liquid sunshine".

The game of cricket has been described as "like abstract art – you only understand it when you have watched it for a long time". Introduced to the island almost 200 years ago by the British as a character builder, cricket now has no class boundaries and Barbados has produced many heroes: the "Three Ws" – Clyde Walcott, Frank Worrell, and Everton Weekes – were knighted in the 1960s; Gordon Greenidge and Desmond Haynes, one of the world's best opening pairs; several fast bowlers, and the greatest cricketer of all time, Garfield "Gary" Sobers, who was knighted in 1975, having scored 8,032 runs, taken 235 wickets and held 110 catches.

Map on pages 262–63

founded in 1639, making them the third oldest parliamentary body in the Commonwealth after Bermuda and Britain.

Broad Street is the main shopping area with several large duty-free stores; many of the buildings, such as Barclays Bank and Da Costa's, retain their old colonial grandeur. The **Verandah Art Gallery** (open Mon–Fri and Sat am), where local artists' work is on sale at reasonable prices, is located in the Old Spirit Bond Mall, facing the Careenage. At the far end is the Georgian **St Mary's Church ❺** (open daily; donations welcome), which also serves as a hurricane shelter, surrounded by beautiful gardens. Opposite, the concrete facade of **Cheapside Market** fronts a typically colorful Caribbean scene on Saturday mornings.

Westward along the seafront is **Pelican Craft Center ❻** in a purpose-built center where Barbadian artists and craftspeople can be seen at work, and where you can buy their wares – a handy spot for the passengers of the cruise ships that dock in the **Deep Water Harbour**. Before the docks were built in 1961, passengers and freight had to be rowed ashore. Today, around 500,000 visitors arrive on cruise ships each year, usually for a one-night stopover.

From National Heroes Square, take the road east to **St Michael's Cathedral ❼** (open daily; donations welcome). Dating from 1665, the original building was destroyed by a hurricane in 1780. However it was rebuilt in solid limestone coral nine years later, with the help of lottery money, ironically lending a church blessing to gambling. Inside is a single-hand clock. A few blocks farther to the east lies the tranquil oasis of **Queen's Park ❽** with the magnificent **Queen's Park House** (1780) as its centerpiece. This fine Georgian building, with an impressive wooden balcony, houses a small theater that puts on plays with a Caribbean flavor, and an art gallery exhibiting the work of local artists.

The Nidhe Israel Synagogue, founded in 1634, has a new museum (open Mon–Sat).

BELOW: horseplay at the racetrack.

The Garrison Historical Area

Leaving Bridgetown via the Charles Duncan O'Neal Bridge, you pass the bus terminal for the south and **Fairchild Street Market** and continue along Bay Street to the **Garrison Historical Area**, where the **Garrison Savannah ②**, once a parade ground for the British West Indian forces, is now a busy race-course and sports venue. Nearby is **George Washington House** (open Mon–Fri; entrance charge; tel: 246-228-5461), the recently restored Barbadian residence where the first American president stayed for two months in 1751.

East of the Garrison is the **Barbados Museum ❸** (open Mon–Sat and Sun pm, closed public hols; entrance charge; tel: 246-427-0201) housed in an early 19th century British military prison. Beautifully presented in the old preserved prison cells, this portrayal of island history with an art gallery and children's hands-on gallery is one of the best in the Caribbean. There is also a café in the shady courtyard and a well-stocked museum shop.

Southern hot spots

The road hugging the south coast leads through a built up area of hotels, shops, and restaurants punctuated with glorious white beaches which offer plenty of fun and water sports but no seclusion. This part of Barbados is literally "jump-ing" after dark with islanders and visitors all after some nocturnal action, from **Harbour Lights** and **The Boatyard** on Bay Street, open-air nightclubs on the beach outside Bridgetown brimming with Caribbean atmosphere, to the cluster of bars and restaurants at **St Lawrence Gap**, 3 miles (5 km) away off Highway 7. Each nightspot is unique with its own ambiance and following, but they all rock with the sounds of live soca, calypso, reggae, soul, or jazz.

Tyrol Cot, the former home of the first Premier of Barbados, Sir Grantley Adams, and his son Tom, the second Prime Minister, is part of a Heritage Village (open Mon–Fri; entrance charge) northwest of Bridgetown.

BELOW: a portrait of a flying fish.

Oistins ❹, farther on, the fishing "capital" of Barbados, is another hot spot to try out on Friday nights, but of a different kind. Here, the **Oistins Fish Fry** – fish and chips cooked outside in enormous pans over burning coals – is held in an area of bars and stalls, which has had a facelift, adjacent to the fish market on Fridays and Saturdays. Rum and beer is sold by the bottle and the music is turned up loud for dancing. You can still find a good fish supper here on other, quieter, nights. On weekdays, the fishermen take their catch of dolphin (dorado or mahi mahi), snapper, king fish, tuna, and the national delicacy, flying fish, to the market, where you can watch the women deftly gut and fillet them for sale.

Oistins also has an historical tale to tell: in 1652 the Royalist islanders had been besieged for weeks by Cromwell's Roundheads. The contretemps was finally settled in the Charter of Barbados which pledged the islanders to obedience to the hated Cromwell and his Commonwealth Parliament in exchange for the right to religious freedom and consultation over taxation.

Plantation house and the Crane

Heading inland from Oistins into the parish of St Philip, you reach **The Heritage Park and Rum Factory** ❺ (open daily; entrance charge) at Foursquare off Highway 6, for a tour of the most modern rum distillery in the world. In the adjoining Heritage Park is an amphitheater, an art gallery, and several craft shops selling locally made products. Farther north off Highway 5 is **Sunbury Plantation House** ❻ (open daily; entrance charge), a beautifully restored 300-year-old plantation house, full of colonial antiques, which gives a real feel of what it must have been like to be a wealthy plantation owner. You can stop for lunch here in the café at the back and return for a typical lavish evening banquet.

Back across Six Cross Roads to the southeast coast are two beaches and an old hotel where it is worth spending some time; all three are notable for their beauty and stunning location. Head south toward the first beach, **Harrismith**, where narrow steps lead down to a small secluded cove lined with tall palms. Farther along the coast a left turn leads down to **Bottom Bay**, a fine stretch of wide sandy beach that is perfect for picnics. It is here that the Atlantic meets the Caribbean and the waves build up some force making the sea ideal for body surfing.

The waves are especially good around the **Crane Resort** ❼ (open daily, entrance charge for non-guests redeemable in the bar or restaurant). Opened in 1887, it was the island's first exclusive hotel and was patronized by the wealthy. Before that the bay contained a small port where boats arrived with goods from Bridgetown. A crane at the top of the cliff unloaded the boats, giving the area its name. The resort with its beautiful cliff-top view is undergoing rapid expansion. Several five-story blocks of time-share apartments have been built alongside the original hotel and a glass lift takes people down to the pink-sand beach.

Sam Lord's Castle stands farther along this craggy coastline. Now closed, the 18th-century house was a hotel for many years, but before that it was the home of Sam Lord, a notorious planter and pirate who is one of the most colorful characters in Bajan folklore.

Map on pages 262–63

TIP

The Barbados National Trust (tel: 246-426-2421) runs an Open House scheme in which private houses – old and new – are open to the public for one afternoon a week in high season.

BELOW: new view points from a horse.

The wild and rugged east

To explore Barbados's magnificent, windswept east coast, it is a good idea to make a day of it, and you could stay overnight in one of the old Barbadian hotels traditionally used by the islanders for their holidays. From west to east across the island may not be very far in miles but along the hilly network of roads it can take time, especially if you get lost.

The scenery changes dramatically along the East Coast Road compared to the flat pastureland of the south and as it cuts through tropical woodland, the impressive entrance of **Codrington College ❽** (open daily, entrance charge), with a long drive lined with majestic royal palms, hoves into view. Founded in 1702 by Christopher Codrington, the Barbados-born governor general of the Leeward Islands and de facto owner of Barbuda *(see page 181)*, the limestone coral theological college has a fascinating nature trail in the grounds, leading through primeval forest. The adventurer and travel writer Patrick Leigh Fermor described it in the late 1940s as "in a hollow beyond a spinney of tall mahogany, south of the township of Bathsheba, a beautiful Palladian building, reclining dreamily on the shores of a lake among lawns and balustrades and great shady trees, suddenly appeared, its columns and pediments conjuring up, in the afternoon sunlight, some enormous country seat in the Dukeries." And it has barely changed.

Continuing north on the East Coast Road, the undulating sugar-cane fields change to steep hillsides of banana plantations that drop to the sea. A right turning plunges down to **Bathsheba** and the **Andromeda Botanic Gardens ❾** (open daily; closed public hols; entrance charge) which has one of the finest displays of tropical flowers and shrubs in the Caribbean. Created in 1954 on a rocky hillside by amateur horticulturist Iris Bannochie, who died in 1988, the garden

Watch the surfers in the Soup Bowl while you tuck into delicious Bajan fare at the Bonito Bar and Restaurant in Bathsheba. This breezy restaurant is open for lunch Sunday to Friday, tel: 246 4339034.

BELOW: waiting for the bus to town.

is intelligently designed and harbors exotic tropical plants that she collected on her travels around the world. There is a splendid example of a bearded fig tree alongside collections of orchids and bromeliads. A stream cuts through the 6-acre (2-hectare) profusion of tropical flora, now run by the Barbados National Trust.

At Bathsheba is the wind-battered **Atlantis Hotel**, where Barbados's most famous author, George Lamming, sometimes stays when he returns. It is one of the oldest hotels on the island, and serves local dishes. Surfers flock to Bathsheba for the Soup Bowl, where the waves are a challenge.

You have to go back up the hill and down again at the next turn to Cattlewash where the road runs beside a long golden beach washed by Atlantic rollers. Usually deserted during the week, the sea is dangerous for swimmers. You pass two more typically Barbadian establishments offering excellent local food – the **Edgwater Inn**, which provides a good Sunday lunch buffet, and the **Round House** whose specialty is flying fish paté.

The hills of the Scotland District

Homesick British colonists likened the lush landscapes of Barbados to England and the rolling hills and bizarre rock formations to the Scottish Highlands, earning the nicknames Little England and the Scotland District. An excursion into the island's interior will take you through open countryside, past acres of cane fields and small hamlets of chattel houses *(see page 77)* each with a rum shop-cum-store. Leaving the ABC Highway in Bridgetown on Highway 3, follow the signposts to **Gun Hill** – a former military signal station where there is a small museum (open daily; entrance charge) and a white, stone lion – and just over a mile farther on you reach **Orchid World ❿** (open daily; entrance charge;

Map on pages 262–63

TIP

The Morgan Lewis Sugar Mill in the northeast is the largest working windmill in the Caribbean. Restored and run by the National Trust, the mill can be see in action on certain days. Call 426-2421 for more information.

BELOW: Colony Club hotel on the Platinum Coast.

246-0433-0306). Created on a disused chicken farm, this magnificent tropical garden has benefited from its rich soil and around 20,000 orchids of all sizes and species flourish here. The landscaped paths take you past a waterfall and through a coral grotto, and enable you to take in views of the surrounding countryside.

Farther north, **Harrison's Cave** ⓫ (open daily; entrance charge; tel: 246-438 6640) is a geological feast for the eyes, a crystallized limestone underworld of gorges, grottoes, streams, and waterfalls encrusted with spectacular stalactites and stalagmites which you can marvel at from an electric tram.

For tranquil, natural beauty above ground, walk through the luxuriant jungle greenery of **Welchman Hall Gully** ⓬ (tel: 246-426 2421 for tours) nearby. The half-mile (1-km) long ravine was once part of a series of caves, whose roofs fell in, and connected with Harrison's Cave. Now owned by the Barbados National Trust *(see page 269)*, there are over 200 species of plants, flowers, and trees, plus large families of green monkeys who snap up the fruit.

Another botanical delight is the **Flower Forest** ⓭ (open daily; entrance charge) a little farther north, where you can touch and smell the wonderful array of tropical flowers and plants set against magnificent views of the east coast. In the center is a young baobab tree, traditionally grown in the middle of African villages.

White beaches on the Platinum Coast

The west coast of Barbados is lapped by the deep azure blue of the tranquil Caribbean Sea with pinky white coral sand beaches edged with casuarina trees and palms, living up to the tropical island dream. Earning the tag Platinum Coast, this is where the smart hotels jostle for the best sea view each in their own landscaped paradise and sporting such tantalizing names as Glitter Bay, Coral

Reef, and Tamarind Cove. As no one can own a beach in Barbados, it is possible to walk for miles along the water's edge, stopping at the beach bars for a rum punch and trying out the wide variety of water sports on offer.

The world-renowned **Sandy Lane Hotel** ⓮, refuge of the rich and famous, is tucked away in Sandy Lane Bay just south of Holetown (about 3 miles/5 km north of Bridgetown on Highway 1). Built in 1961, the original hotel was demolished and the site redeveloped into a large luxurious resort, which has a spa and three spectacular golf courses.

Captain Henry Powell accidentally landed in **Holetown** ⓯ in May 1625 on his way to somewhere else. He took a fancy to what he saw as a nice piece of real estate and, as any true Englishman would have done in those days, he stuck his country's flag in the ground and claimed it on behalf of the King. In February 1627 an expedition to settle the island arrived and, today, the Holetown Festival celebrates the anniversary with street parties and a waterski show.

Farther on you can learn how a coral reef is formed at the **Folkestone Park and Marine Reserve** ⓰ (open Mon–Fri; entrance charge) and go snorkeling along an underwater trail around Dottins Reef. Out to sea is a shipwrecked Greek freighter deliberately sunk to form a coral reef.

Around the spectacular north

Speightstown ⓱, the island's second town, was once an important port for transporting sugar to Bristol in England, earning it the moniker of Little Bristol. Its story is imaginatively told in the restored three-story, 18th-century balconied **Arlington House** (open Mon–Sat; entrance charge; tel: 246-422-4064). In contrast is the modern **Port St Charles Marina**, just to the north, an upmarket, environmentally friendly development, with a berth for a yacht attached to each luxury residence.

Highway 1 continues through the pretty fishing village of **Six Men's Bay** and into the rugged, sparsely populated northernmost parish of St Lucy. Here you will find the best picnic spots on the island, such as **Archer's Bay**, a peaceful, grassy area shaded by a grove of casuarina trees, which is usually deserted, and **River Bay**. At the very northern tip of the island is the **Animal Flower Cave** ⓲ (open daily; entrance charge), named for the few tiny sea anemones that may be seen in the pools. The view of the sea from the cave is tremendous but it has to be closed in rough weather. The ocean's relentless pounding has created steep, jagged cliffs and rocky, barren land that resembles a moonscape. A café sells snacks and drinks.

From here the road cuts inland to the Jacobean plantation house **St Nicholas Abbey** ⓳ (open Sun–Fri; entrance charge). Thought to be the oldest original building on the island, it has never been a religious institution, despite the name, and is full of fascinating features (note the chimney) and antiques.

Farther south you reach the main road back to the west coast and **Barbados Wildlife Reserve** ⓴ (open daily; entrance charge). Here the only caged creatures are pythons and boas – the green monkeys, tortoises, iguana et al roam free alongside the visitors in a mahogany woodland. ❑

The Story of Sugar is told at the Sir Frank Hutson Sugar Museum (open Mon–Sat; entrance charge) just east of Holetown. The sequel is at Mount Gay Rum Visitors Center (open Mon–Fri; tel: 246-425 9066) north of Bridgetown.

BELOW: flamingos in the Wildlife Reserve.

TRINIDAD

Geologically part of South America and politically the stronger half of a twin-island republic, this exhilarating, cosmopolitan, tropical island is also a land of natural beauty

Map on page 278

Caribbean Sea

Trinidad

Pulsating with life, Trinidad is a noisy, vibrant island, much noisier than Tobago, its more tranquil partner, 21 miles (33 km) away, in the republic of Trinidad and Tobago. And it reaches a crescendo every February (or March) at Carnival time when the capital Port-of-Spain, the birthplace of steel pan and capital of calypso, throbs to the rhythms of the bands and the dancing in the streets. Whether Trin-bagonian or foreign visitor, all revellers are welcome to join the flamboyant costumed parades and have a ball in the "greatest street party on earth" *(see pages 282–83)*.

The music permeates the very heart of the countryside where more than 400 species of birds take up the tune, silently accompanied by myriad butterflies. Trinidad was not called Land of the Hummingbird by the Amerindians for nothing. In the mountain rainforests of the north, the coastal swamps and the flat palm-fringed beaches of the east, it is easy to escape the west coast's modern hubbub of industrialized life, spawned by the riches of offshore oil fields.

The oil booms of the 1970s and 2000s have created an economic climate comfortable enough for Trinidad not to encourage tourism, unlike its sister islands in the rest of the Antillean chain, which means that many of its stunning beaches are deserted and inaccessible except by boat or on foot. Nonetheless, outside the hurricane belt, the sheltered bays of the northwest have become a haven for yachties who buy permanent moorings for their boats in the top-class marinas that were developed there in the 1980s and '90s.

PRECEDING PAGES: early morning in Queen's Park Savannah. **LEFT:** dancing in Emancipation Day parade. **BELOW:** Shivetha Verma in traditional dress.

South American influences

It would be wrong to eulogize the beautiful blue waters that surround Trinidad, because on all but the northern coastline, they are distinctly brown. The southernmost and largest island in the Eastern Caribbean chain (1,864 sq. miles/4,660 sq. km), it is washed by the waters of the Orinoco delta just 7 miles (11-km) away in Venezuela, but the sea is still mostly warm, clear, and pleasant to swim in. Sailing or flying across to Tobago, halfway you can see the color of the water dramatically change to blue.

Long before Christopher Columbus sighted three mountain peaks on the horizon on July 31, 1498, and named the island they belonged to "La Trinidad" (Trinity), Amerindians had canoed across from the Orinoco region and settled its shores. The Spanish colonizers failed to find the gold of El Dorado here, but they did use the island for tobacco plantations. To cultivate them they enslaved the local Amerindians, who practically died out within a century as a result.

English sailors, Spanish farmers, French planters and their families, adventurers, thousands of African slaves and, from the 19th century onward, numerous

Asian, Portuguese and Chinese laborers, and a small minority of Syrian and Lebanese merchants, have formed the basis of today's multicultural society of just over a million people, who now live largely at peace with one another. During Carnival in particular all social and ethnic barriers fall – reputedly resulting in a sharp rise in the birth rate during late autumn.

Rich resources

The acrobatic limbo you see (and attempt) in hotels comes from a symbolic dance guiding the soul to the next world.

After full Emancipation in 1838, cheap labor was suddenly in demand on the sugar plantations – and East Indian and Chinese contract laborers were lured to the Caribbean by clever promises. The harsh terms of many of their contracts were such that they often had to work in the fields for up to 10 years just to pay their transport costs. Soon villages with their own Hindu temples and their own social order began to appear in the sugar belt of the central plain and southern Trinidad.

As oil replaced sugar as king, a multiracial middle class in the industrial centers of the west coast administered the profits from lucrative wells near La Brea.

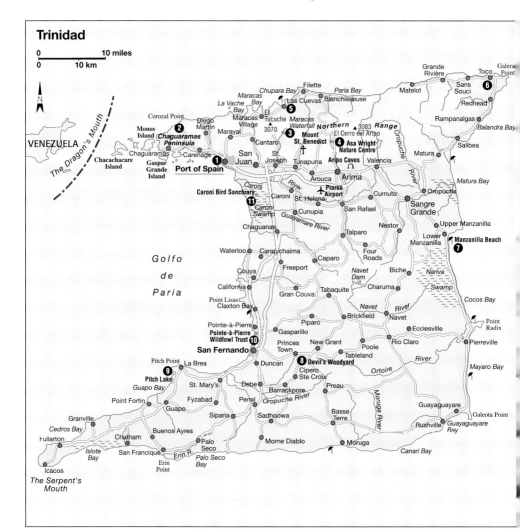

Manufactured products for export to the whole of the Caribbean grew sharply through the post-war years and onwards, and the discovery of further rich oil and gas reserves in the 1970s nourished the island's hopes of a future free from economic worries. The new prosperity also helped ensure Trinidad's rise to having one of the highest literacy rates in the Americas.

Politically, Trinidad and Tobago were governed by Britain between 1888 and 1962. In the 1950s local politics flourished under the leadership of the brilliant historian Dr Eric Williams, who founded the People's National Movement (PNM) and became the first Prime Minister after independence in 1962. The Republic was created in 1976. Between 1995 and 2001 the largely East Indian United National Congress formed the government under the ageing but charismatic Basdeo Panday, with the PNM maintaining control since 2002.

Port-of-Spain – a modern city

Colorful and turbulent, **Port-of-Spain ❶**, the capital of the island republic is situated at the foot of the Northern Range. Established in 1754 by the Spanish, today modern skyscrapers, such as the 300-ft (92-meter) high Twin Towers, and elegant shopping centers contrast sharply with dilapidated gingerbread-style villas, wooden huts, and rusty fences. A stroll during the daytime through Independence Square and Queen's Park Savannah to the attractive buildings of the Magnificent Seven *(see right)* is not too strenuous. In the evenings, however, walking downtown should be avoided, and the eastern suburbs should only be visited if accompanied by a local.

Independence Square is bordered to the east by the neo-Gothic cathedral of the **Immaculate Conception**. Extending away westward toward the cruise terminal on both sides of this long square are shopping centers, banks, a statue of Christopher Columbus, and the Twin Towers, containing government offices. The attractive promenade along the center is named for Brian Lara, who has done much to make Trinidad famous as a cricket-playing nation.

Frederick Street, lined with street traders, leads on to the park on **Woodford Square**. This is where dissatisfied citizens keep the Speaker's Corner tradition alive by loudly criticizing the various decisions made in the imposing **Red House**, the seat of parliament, at the western end of the square. The Anglican cathedral of the Holy Trinity, the Supreme Court, the Town Hall and police headquarters surround the park and its magnificent old trees. At the southwest corner rises the striking modern National Library.

To the north, a 15-minute walk away, Frederick Street ends at Port-of-Spain's giant park, the **Queen's Park Savannah**. Nearby, in the **National Museum and Art Gallery** (corner of Frederick and Keate streets; open Tues–Sat 10am–6pm, Sun 2–6pm; tel: 868-623 5941; free), you can see documents dating from the colonial era and also a collection of glitzy Carnival costumes.

West of the Savannah, the **Magnificent Seven** – a line of very fine (if partly dilapidated) colonial buildings dating from the turn of the 20th century – give Maraval Road a great deal of flair and elegance. In the early morning, the sun shows them at their best.

Map on page 278

North to south the Magnificent Seven are: Stollmeyer's Castle (1904); White Hall, the prime minister's office; Archbishop's House; Mille Fleurs; Roomor; Hayes Court, the Anglican bishop's residence; and Queen's Royal College with an eye-catching clock tower.

BELOW: the city Financial Complex.

The Hindu temple of Sewdass Sadhu Mandir built right next to the sea, near the village of Waterloo, is a beautiful spot.

BELOW: a guide at the Asa Wright Nature Centre.

To the northern rainforest

The rugged coast of the **Chaguaramas Peninsula** , a US naval base (1945–64) to the northwest of Port-of-Spain, is a popular sailing area. On the island of **Gaspar Grande**, a 20-minute boat ride away from Chaguaramas town, guided tours of the **Gasparee** limestone caverns are available (open Mon–Fri 8am–4pm; book in advance on tel: 868-634 4227; www.chagdev.com).

The mountainous hinterland of the Northern Range arrives quite suddenly when leaving the urban sprawl north and east of Port-of-Spain. The Eastern Main Road passes through a number of towns including Trinidad's first capital when under Spanish rule, **St Joseph** – a turn northwards at the prominent Al Jinnah mosque brings you past the town's church, the current structure dating from 1815. Continuing north from here, the Royal Road meanders through rainforest and near to the 320-ft (100-metre) high **Maracas Waterfall** , twenty minutes walk from the road, which is especially impressive after rainfall.

Back on the main road, some good Chinese and East Indian roti restaurants mark your arrival in **Tunapuna**. High on the hill above lies **Mount St Benedict**, the oldest Benedictine monastery in the region (founded 1912), and 8 miles (13 km) further east, you reach **Arima**, the island's third-largest town. From here the road north twists and turns through orchards and rainforest to the **Asa Wright Nature Centre** (open daily 9am–5pm; tel: 868-667 4655; entrance charge; www.asawright.org). This 182-acre (74-hectare) site contains a vast amount of fascinating tropical flora and fauna. Over 100 different species of bird, including several rare hummingbirds, can be observed here. For a guided dawn or evening birdwatching hike, you can stay in lodges near the plantation manor.

The wildly romantic coastline near **Blanchisseuse** on the northern coast is reached via 23 miles (37 km) of hairpin bends with stunning views and dangerous potholes. The glorious sands and waterfall at **Paria Bay** lie a two-hour hike from here, while more easily accessible is the half-moon-shaped sandy bay at the fishing village of **Las Cuevas** to the west. **Maracas Bay** is the busier beach, though equally attractive.

Never-ending palm-fringed bays

At the northeastern tip of the island are the dramatic cliffs of **Toco** , a three-hour drive from the capital via the Eastern Main Road and a rather bumpy route through some mountain rainforest. Leatherback turtles lay their eggs on the secluded beaches here between April and June, when swimming is forbidden.

The East Coast Road leads back down to **Matura** from where three sandy bays sweep southwards for 40 miles (64 km). Edged by dense coconut plantations, **Manzanilla Beach** in the middle has some modern public amenities and **Mayaro** at the southern end has houses to rent. However, swimming in the sea here is dangerous, due to a strong undertow and high waves. Behind the palm trees is the mangrove swamp of **Nariva**, and young boys can often be seen driving their water buffalo out into the fields. The rural south of Trinidad is mainly inhabited by East Indian families, who, if not connected to the energy industry, earn just enough as farmers and sugar-cane workers to live.

Where the earth bubbles

At **Devil's Woodyard** ❽, about 8 miles (13 km) east of Trinidad's second-largest city, San Fernando on the southwest coast, gas bubbles can be seen inside the mud holes of one of the island's 18 mud volcanoes. This is a holy site for Hindus, who leave sacrificial offerings here such as flowers and coconut oil. These mud volcanoes, and also the **Pitch Lake** ❾ at La Brea (daily 9am–5pm; tel: 868-651 1232), 13 miles (20 km) southwest of San Fernando, are connected with the crude oil and natural gas beneath the South American continental shelf that were discovered in 1897. The largest natural lake of asphalt in the world and up to 320 ft (100 meters) deep in places, the Pitch Lake was a spiritual site for Amerindians before being found in 1595 by the English captain Sir Walter Ralcigh, who used the sticky substance to help keep his ship waterproof. You can walk on parts of the surface of the lake, but don't explore it without an experienced guide.

Just to the north of San Fernando, some rare wildfowl have found a refuge right at the center of a crude oil refinery. The **Pointe-à-Pierre Wildfowl Trust** ❿ (daily by appointment; tel: 868-658 4200; www.trinwetlands.org) devotes itself to breeding threatened species and preserving natural habitats. The national bird of Trinidad is the scarlet ibis, and every evening flocks of these elegant creatures with long curved beaks can be seen settling on trees for the night in the peaceful bird sanctuary and mangrove swamp at **Caroni** ⓫ (tours by boat; daily 4pm).

Halfway between these two wildlife attractions lies **Carapichaima**, famous for its 85-ft (26-metre) high statue of the Hindu monkey-God, Hanuman, its impressive Waterloo Temple-in-the-Sea – joined to the mainland by a causeway – as well as the **Maha Sabha Museum** (Wed–Sun 10am–5pm; tel: 868-673 7007), documenting the East Indian Caribbean experience since the 1830s. ❑

Map on page 278

A colorful bird from the Northern Range where the wonders of the Aripo Caves can be seen by potholers with the help of a knowledgeable guide.

BELOW: a boatload of goats going to market.

THE GREATEST STREET PARTY ON EARTH

Carnival in the Lesser Antilles is alive and well and getting bigger every year as the islands fill up with revelers from all over the world

Neither age nor profession, nor money or skin color matter when every February, thousands of Trinidadians and visitors seem to drown in a sea of colors, feathers, rhythm, and rum. From Jouvay, the wild street party from dawn on the Monday before Ash Wednesday until King Momo's fire death in the last hours of the Tuesday, Port of Spain is one big anarchic Carnival party. The heroes are soca stars and ingenious costume designers highly revered by a hip-swinging crowd dizzy with the beat and pulsating rhythm of the steel pans.

NEW CARNIVALS

Trinidad hosts the biggest Caribbean Carnival, which originated out of the Christian tradition of having a last big feast before fasting during Lent. In Guadeloupe and Martinique people dress in black and white on Ash Wednesday and bury King Vaval. On St Barthélemy King Moui Moui is burnt, and on St Kitts Christmas and the New Year are the best times to enjoy parades and street fetes. Other so-called carnivals in the summer months have developed from the harvest festivals after the sugar cane had been cut, such as Crop Over in Barbados, which includes the ceremonial delivery of the last canes. Some islands have only recently established carnivals for tourism's sake – any excuse for an extended street party…

▽▷ **BIRDS OF PARADISE**
Feats of engineering, some of the magnificent outfits are so cumbersome that wheels have to be fixed on to facilitate movement.

▽ **STEELY COMPETITION**
Months before, steel bands compete with their Carnival songs, and calypso singers prepare to fight for the title of "Calypso Monarch".

◁ **MOKOJUMBIES**
An old African tradition, Mokojumbies dance away evil spirits on stilts at carnivals and festivals all over the region.

▷ **JUMP UP**
All the parades – be it in Trinidad or in Barbados at Crop Over – are bouncing musical events with everyone joining in with the jump up (dancing) in the streets.

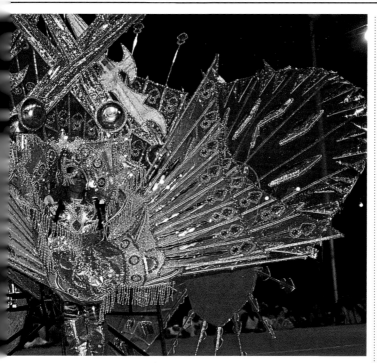

▷ MUDDERS
Early Monday morning, Jouvay (joo-vay) begins when groups of revelers smear themselves with mud and hug anyone they can.

▽ KIDDIES CARNIVAL
Many of the island carnivals have a special day set aside for the children just before the official start. Their costumes are often made in the Mas Camps of Trinidad.

PLAYING MAS IN TRINIDAD

As soon as one Carnival ends the designers' imaginations are hard at work on the next one. Great Carnival designers such as Trinidadian Peter Minshall – whose renowned costumes led him to design the costumes for the opening of the Olympic Games in 1992 and 1996 – set up Mas Camps (workshops) in which vast numbers of costumes are made on a theme for their bands. Each band has a Carnival King and Queen who wear the masterpieces which are judged on Dimanche Gras, the night before Carnival officially begins.

The Mas tradition started in the late 18th century with French plantation owners organizing masquerades (mas) and balls before they had to endure the fasting of Lent. Slaves copied and lampooned their masters, and once set free from forced labor, their frustrations found a platform in clever calypso lyrics mocking their former masters.

▷ BEAUTIFUL DEVIL
When the slaves started creating their costumes the mythology of their African ancestors inspired them to figures of good and evil. Over the years even nasty devils have been clad in shiny robes and jewels.

TOBAGO

Only a 20-minute plane flight away from frenetic Port-of-Spain, Tobago is an oasis of calm in a bright blue sea of tranquility offering copious white beaches, sheltered coves, and a wild forest interior

Map on page 286

Caribbean Sea

Tobago

Trinidad's other half in the Republic of Trinidad and Tobago, this small tropical island 21 miles (34 km) to the northeast provides a complete contrast to its twin's cosmopolitan bustle, industrialization, and magnitude. Rural tranquility and Caribbean enjoyment of life go hand in hand in Tobago and the magnificent beaches and colorful coral landscape just offshore are an effective means of dispelling stress.

At only 26 miles (42 km) long and 7 miles (11 km) wide, Tobago is a continual feast for the eyes: picturesque, bumpy roads wind around the coast past unspoiled bays of white sand and bright blue sea, and climb up across the mountainous backbone through high stands of creaking bamboo and dense rainforest, alive with colorful birdlife, before plunging into panoramic views on the other side. No wonder Columbus named it *Bellaforma* (beautiful shape) in 1498.

Tobago does not share the cultural mix that enriches Trinidad, despite having changed colonial hands 29 times in 160 years; the population of around 55,000 are mainly descendants of African slaves and make a living from tourism and agriculture. Despite the steadily increasing flow of visitors to their island, Tobagonians are friendly and development remains notably low-key.

LEFT: seventh heaven at Arnos Vale.
BELOW: tropical idyll at Pigeon Point.

Tobago's colonial past

Hope, Courland, Shirvan, Les Coteaux – the place-names are all reminders of Tobago's past colonial phases. At the beginning of the 17th century, the first Dutch and English settlers arrived only to be wiped out or chased off by the Caribs. Eventually, 80 families from Latvia succeeded in settling on Courland Bay in 1654 and planted sugar cane, tobacco, pepper, and cotton. Adventurers, smallholders, and pirates from all over Europe followed in their footsteps, and many were killed either by tropical diseases or by Carib arrows.

Slaves were set to work on the first sugar cane and cotton plantations 100 years later. In 1793, when the English had managed to seize control of Tobago yet again, the island was inhabited by 14,170 blacks, 850 whites, and five Amerindians. Numerous slave rebellions were dealt with ruthlessly by plantation owners – Tobago became one of the most profitable colonies by area, with around 80 estates.

After full Emancipation in 1838, most of the plantations went broke as freed slaves left to begin subsistence farming. French planters in particular took the opportunity to buy up land very cheaply and started several coconut plantations – later settling very comfortably on Trinidad.

To save money, the British decided from 1888 onward to treat their two southernmost islands in the Caribbean as a collective administrative unit. In 1962,

the twin-island state was given independence *(see page 279)*, and since 1987 Tobago has had an internal autonomy separate from Trinidad, though it is still heavily dependent on subsidies from Port-of-Spain. There are no major industrial centers on the island, and tourism is only growing slowly due to other Caribbean competition.

Scarborough – a village capital

The little town of **Scarborough ❶** (pop. 18,000) on Rockly Bay is Tobago's main harbor as well as the island's center of trade and administration. It was founded by Dutch settlers (who named the site Lampsinburg) in 1654, and has been the island's capital since 1769. A dusty, commerical place, the center consists of two road junctions and concrete structures housing the post office, the market, the ferry and cruise ship harbor, Scarborough Mall, and the bus station. On market days half of Tobago meets up here to go shopping.

An oasis of calm behind the mall is the **Botanic Gardens** (free), where native trees, bushes, and flowers can be found in graceful and shady arrangements. From the harbor, Carnett Street leads up steeply past several tradesmen's stands to **James Park**; at the top end is the imposing-looking, Georgian-style **Court House**, built between 1821 and 1825.

Follow Fort Street uphill, and a few steep curves later you reach the impressive **Fort King George**, built in the late 18th century 490 ft (150 meters) above Rockly Bay. Severely damaged by a whirlwind in 1847, the fort was rebuilt according to old plans. Today, the complex contains not only the excellent though small **National Museum** (open Mon–Fri; entrance charge), holding Amerindian artifacts and artwork from the slave period, but also the town's hospital and prison.

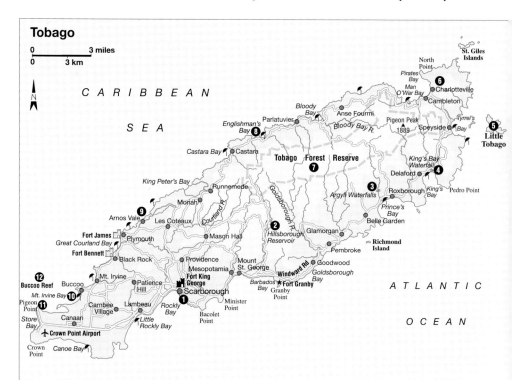

Tobago

Rugged coasts and dense forests

Keen car drivers with good nerves will adore **Windward Road**, which winds its way along the southeast coast of Tobago in steep curves. Spectacular views of the Atlantic, potholes which are often knee-deep, and idyllic villages at the roadside all make this route an unforgettable experience. Leave Scarborough via Bacolet Street and **Gun Bridge**, named after the two old cannon there.

Map on page 286

The only reminder that **Mount St George**, about 4 miles (6 km) along the road, was once the British seat of government is the renovated court building dating from 1788. A left turn shortly afterwards leads inland 2 miles (3 km) to the **Hillsborough Reservoir** ❷, an artificial lake providing the islanders with drinking water and also the natural habitat of many rare species of bird; the dragonflies are very colorful, and you may even see a cayman (alligator).

Back on Windward Road, all that remains of **Fort Granby** is a weathered-looking gravestone. During the 18th century this once-proud structure, looking across Barbados Bay, was home to the English 62nd Regiment; now it makes a perfect picnic spot. The road winds along the coast, between the dark fringes of the rainforest and the spray of the Atlantic, passing through picturesque villages like **Pembroke** and **Belle Garden**. Outside village bars, at road junctions, and in mini-markets, Tobagonians enjoy their spare time "liming" – the local word for "hanging out".

A hummingbird gathers nectar.

Seasonable waterfalls

Standing out amongst the tropical greenery high above the rocky coast (just before you reach Belle Garden) is **Richmond Great House** (tel: 868-660 4444; www.richmondgreathouse.com), a renovated manor house dating from 1766,

BELOW: King Peter's Bay from afar.

TIP

When driving in
Tobago remember that
the locals are familiar
with every pothole and
hairpin bend and are
prone to overtaking at
dangerous places. To
avoid stress, slow
down and when it's
safe to do so, cheer-
fully wave past any
traffic behind you.

which today is a popular guest house with New York intellectuals. Just before Roxborough 3 miles (5 km) on, the road branches left to the **Argyll Water-falls ❸** (open 9am–5pm; charge; www.argylewaterfall.com), which pours out of the mountainside in two separate cascades during the rainy season, the highest on the island at 177 ft (54 metres). Even though they're reduced to trickles at other times of year, there's still enough water for a refreshing shower after the muddy 15-minute walk to get there. Another 3 miles (5 km) past **Roxborough**, the largest settlement on the southeast coast – where badly paid black workers led the Belmanna Uprising in 1876 – is **King's Bay ❹**, a picturesque coconut plantation and waterfall with a cool and wild beach nestled beneath.

In the fishing village of Speyside, nearly 3 miles (5 km) away, tucked in a beautiful broad blue bay, young men offer excursions to the bird sanctuary on **Little Tobago ❺** just offshore. It's also known as Bird of Paradise Island, as those birds flourished on the island from 1909 – when 48 were brought over from New Guinea – until 1963 when the colony was destroyed by Hurricane Flora. It is more rewarding, therefore, to go diving and snorkeling along the spectacular reefs around there. Glass-bottomed boats (plenty to choose from) are the most comfortable way on calm days to admire the marine life on show.

The picturesque northeast

Windward Road leaves the coast at Speyside and winds its way up a steep incline to a good viewpoint of the rough northeastern tip of the island. The houses and huts of **Charlotteville ❻** on the other side cling to the steep slope above **Man O'War Bay** rather like birds' nests. The town's 600 or so inhabitants live mainly off fishing and tourism – visitors here appreciate simplicity and idyllic tranquility

BELOW: top-class
golf at Mount Irvine.

though the introduction of a proposed small cruise-ship terminal may change the village's face in the near future. For now, however, a flight of 68 steps leads down to **Pirates Bay**, where local women spread out their clothes on the rocks to dry. Just offshore is a reef teeming with life and elegant yachts moor in the bay.

Map on page 286

The oldest nature reserve in the world

From Charlotteville, a new (if winding) stretch of road navigates the northern Caribbean coast to Bloody Bay, from where another route cuts back across the island through the **Tobago Forest Reserve** ❼. This thick jungle in myriad shades of green spreads along the Main Ridge between Hillsborough and Charlotteville and is the oldest section of protected rainforest, unaltered by man, in the world; the British declared it a nature reserve on April 8, 1776. The road and the several hiking routes here only allow visitors to cover a very small proportion of the entire area; the green thickets contain black-and-yellow weavers, green parrots and dazzlingly colorful hummingbirds, and the tropical vegetation is fascinating. Yellow poui and red flame trees stand out against the green forested hillsides. The paths are sometimes steep and muddy, which is why it's best to go with an experienced guide.

The cocrico is the national bird of Tobago and tends to descend on gardens in enormous flocks. When the pheasant-like bird starts squawking loudly it is considered a sure sign that rain is on the way.

At Bloody Bay, the road follows the coastline westward for 2 miles (3 km) to **Englishman's Bay** ❽, a magnificent beach where the forest comes down to the edge, coconut palms wave gently in the breeze, and the waves lap against the (usually) deserted beach. Almost as enchanting are the sands at pretty **Castara**, which also offers a smattering of guesthouses and a large party called the **Fisherman's Fete** in August. A track branches off at Runnemede, 2 miles (3 km) down the coast, to stunning panoramic views over **King Peter's Bay**.

Several more small bays are tucked away at the end of **Arnos Vale** ❾, down a small road farther west, which offer excellent snorkeling and birdwatching. Not far from the village, surrounded by forest, is the **Arnos Vale Waterwheel Park** (daily 9am–10pm; tel: 868-660 0815; charge) which has a small museum, shop, and restaurant around an old waterwheel which used to provide power to the plantation estates.

BELOW: the waterwheel at Arnos Vale.

Buccoo – an endangered reef

Black Rock marks the beginning of the southwestern, vacation side of Tobago. There are several expensive hotels as well as private rooms for rent around the broad beaches here, including **Mount Irvine Bay** ❿ where there is a championship golf course and good waves for surfers. Locals and tourists all meet up in **Buccoo** every Sunday evening for the "Sunday School" open-air disco – especially lively at Easter when the amusing (yet deadly serious) **goat races** are held.

At the incredibly idyllic **Pigeon Point** ⓫, one of the most-photographed beaches in the Caribbean, the glass-bottomed boats can be seen taking snorkelers to the largely destroyed coral gardens at the now protected **Buccoo Reef** ⓬. Boats offer trips that include a barbecue and a wallow in the shallow turquoise waters of the **Nylon Pool**. However, this is one place where it's obvious that promoting tourism isn't always in the best interests of an island like Tobago.   ❏

THE ABC ISLANDS

Fascinating as much in their differences as in their common Dutch, African, and Amerindian origins, Aruba, Bonaire and Curaçao have excellent diving and welcoming people

Off the coast of Venezuela are Aruba, Bonaire and Curaçao, otherwise known as the ABC Islands, three of the six islands which comprised the Netherlands Antilles until the administrative unit's break up in 2008. Aruba became a self-governing nation within the Kingdom of the Netherlands in 1986, a status Curaçao attained in 2008, where only defence and certain foreign policy matters remain in Dutch hands. Conversely, Bonaire has opted for closer ties, becoming something like a Dutch "city state". The remaining Dutch-affiliated territories, Saba, St Eustatius and Sint Maarten lie at the northern end of the Lesser Antilles chain.

The official language is Dutch, but papiamento, an intriguing mix of European and African tongues, is widely spoken throughout this part of the Caribbean. This blend of Dutch, Spanish, Portuguese, English, French, and African dialects reveals much about the nations which have shaped the islands and influenced their heritage. Spanish and English are also spoken.

Physically, the ABC Islands' landscapes are similar with a hilly and desert-like terrain, which is a stark contrast to the shimmering turquoise oceans which lap at the fine sandy coastlines. The similarity ends right there though because each island provides travelers with an individual experience. If you crave water sports action, hectic nightlife, casinos, and shopping then Aruba is for you. Bonaire on the other hand, offers peace and tranquility with flocks of pink flamingos, marine parks, and excellent diving. Curaçao may just offer a little of all of this, with some extra heritage tourism and Carnival culture thrown in too.

The choice is yours… ❑

PRECEDING PAGES: a swirl of Aruban gulls.
LEFT: fading beauty, Willemstad.

CURAÇAO

The largest of the former Dutch Antilles is a cosmopolitan kaleidoscope of people, and with sheltered bays, turquoise water, and coral reefs it offers a world of discovery for divers

Map
on pages
298–99

Caribbean
Sea

Curaçao

Achieving independence from the Netherlands in 2008, Curaçao is home to around 133,000 people from over 60 nations, together with many attractive bays with shimmering water – and a bizarre and wonderful world for divers to discover beside the coral reefs offshore. With Unesco World Heritage site status, Willemstad, the island's capital, is like a small tropical Amsterdam – a fascinating mixture of the Caribbean and attractive Dutch-style colonial architecture.

Long before the arrival of Spaniard Alonso de Ojeda, the first European to set foot on this rocky island off the north coast of South America in 1499, the land was settled by tall Amerindians from the Caiquetío tribe. Which is why today's Curaçao was called the "Island of Giants" by its Spanish conquerors who came in search of treasure. They failed to find the legendary gold of El Dorado here, and limited their colonization of the island to a few cattle farms. In the 17th century, the Dutch built a military base at Schottegat, a natural harbor with a deepwater entrance, and it soon became an important trading center.

Since agriculture on the dry soil was both exhausting and unprofitable, the settlers – who included numerous Jewish families from Amsterdam and northeastern Brazil – switched to trading in indigo, cotton, tobacco… and slaves. After suffering the rigors and inhuman conditions of their transatlantic voyage, hundreds of thousands of African slaves were "freshened up" in the camps around Willemstad, and then sold like cattle at the slave market – a practice which continued until well into the late 18th century. A bloody slave uprising in 1795 did nothing to alter the situation: the leaders of the rebellion, named Tula and Carpata, were executed by Dutch soldiers in Punda together with 25 other slaves. It was only in 1863 that the Netherlands finally abolished slavery for good.

The island experienced an economic upswing through the opening of a massive oil refinery on the flat "isola" in the Schottegat, where crude oil from Lake Maracaibo in Venezuela was refined. However, since the oil crisis of the 1980s, Curaçao has been earning a great deal less in petrodollars than it would have hoped for. Tourism has become another important earner here alongside lucrative finance business, international services, and a flourishing harbor with ultra-modern docks. Around 230,000 vacationers and 300,000 cruise-ship passengers visit this exotic island with its dash of Dutchness every year.

LEFT: old and new meet in Willemstad.
BELOW: sunny smile.

A tropical mini-Amsterdam

Willemstad ❶, the busy capital of Curaçao (pop. 125,000), impresses visitors most with its candy-colored, renovated colonial buildings dating from the 16th to the 19th century. Magnificent merchants' houses with steep, red-tiled roofs, townhouses with beautiful

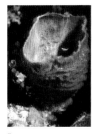

Strange sponge.

stucco facades, three well-preserved forts, picturesque little streets, and large airy churches all stand as reminders of the prosperity of the first European settlers.

The town is one huge sprawling development around the **Schottegat**, a large, deep inlet of water creating a perfect hidden harbor, with **Sint Annabaai** as the narrow entrance. Take a stroll through the historic center of **Punda** ("point") and you won't find it difficult to locate its hub. The streets here and in **Otrobanda** ("other side") on either side of Sint Annabaai are mainly pedestrianized, and lined with attractive cafés and snack bars.

Sacred treasures

An important sight to see is the **Mikveh Israel Emanuel Synagogue**, which has been in continuous use since it first opened at the Passover Festival in 1732. Sephardic settlers from Amsterdam and northern Brazil founded the community of "Mikveh Israel" (Hope of Israel) in the 17th century. The guard at the gate in the **Hanchi di Snoa** is the only outward sign that something special is hidden behind the high yellow walls with their decorative gables. White walls, blue windows, and dark-brown mahogany furniture contrast pleasantly with each other in the three-aisled prayer room of the synagogue; the enormous brass chandeliers come from an Amsterdam workshop, and the fine sand on the floor is a reminder of the Israelites' march through the Sinai Desert.

The central courtyard is surrounded by the 200-year-old ritual bath, or mikvah, and two renovated residential buildings which today house the **Jewish History Museum** (open Mon–Fri 9am–4.30pm; closed Jewish and public hols; tel: 5999-461 1067; entrance charge). An interesting display here includes valuable torah rolls, seven-branched candlesticks, and numerous ancestral objects belonging to the influential Luckmann and Maduro families. Along the walls of the courtyard you can see copies of ancient gravestones from the Jewish cemetery of Beth Chaim on the outskirts of the town, across the Schottegat, where the originals have been severely eroded by sulfurous vapors from the nearby oil refinery.

Renovated magnificence

Around the **Waaigat** are several markets that reveal a colorful picture of island life. The circular concrete structure houses the main market where the female traders are almost completely concealed from view behind mountains of fresh fruit and vegetables. At the **Marsh Biev**, by the post office, is the old market hall where cooks serve enormous helpings of stew (*stoba*) and other delicacies for the lunchtime crowd. Visitors can also buy fresh fish from the Venezuelan coast boats at the **Floating Market** (Sha Caprileskade).

Next to the main market, the **Queen Wilhelmina Drawbridge** leads across to the old Jewish quarter of **Scharloo**. Take a walk along **Scharlooweg**, where the dilapidated charm of crumbling walls alternates with magnificent renovated villas. Stars of David on some of the garden fences here serve as reminders of the buildings' former owners. Today, these attractive structures are largely occupied by banks, legal practices, and administrative offices. Impressive examples of the elaborate architecture typical of the 19th century include the yellow-and-white Kranshi, the registry office, and the "Wedding Cake" or *Bolo di Bruid*, as the very decorative green-and-white building at number 77 is referred to in papiamento, the colorful language of the ABC islands *(see page 53)*. Today it is home to the **National Archive**.

The gently swaying **Queen Emma Bridge**, with the colorful façade of the **Handelskade** in the background, is the most photographed scene in the whole town. This pontoon bridge has connected the business center of Punda with the picturesque old residential quarter of Otrobanda since 1888. Whenever a freighter or cruise ship needs to enter or leave the harbor through the Sint Annabaai, a powerful motor pulls the bridge aside; at the same time, a bell rings to warn pedestrians. Two ferries transport passengers across the bay while cars roar across the spectacular 175-ft (55-meter) arch of the **Queen Juliana Bridge** (1974) to the north, flying high above the massive ships below.

Enormous forts are situated on either side of the harbor entrance. Iron rings were set into their walls in order to prevent access to the harbor with a heavy chain or metal net. The **Riffort** in Otrobanda today provides an atmospheric backdrop for pleasant dining in the Bistro Le Clochard; in contrast, on the opposite bank a large and rather ugly hotel building towers above the walls of the Waterfort. Beside it is yellow **Fort Amsterdam**, built in 1641 and now the seat of the island's government. The inner courtyard houses the Protestant church, **Fortkerk** (1769), and a small **museum** (open Mon–Fri; tel: 5999-461 1139; entrance charge) with religious artifacts. A cannonball is still lodged in the masonry here: in 1804, during a 26-day long siege of Willemstad, the English Captain Bligh's men fired on the fort.

The stylish shop windows along **Heerenstraat** and **Breedestraat** contain expensive cameras, watches, and cosmetics; designer clothes, perfumes, and

Map on pages 298–99

TIP

Architect Anko van de Woude, art historian Jenny Smit, and historian Joopi Hart give regular tours of the old part of Willemstad. Call 5999-461 3554 or 5999-767 3798 for details.

LEFT: the floating market.
BELOW: all roads lead to Willemstad.

There is always time for sailing.

elegant household items are sold duty-free in the local boutiques. The gables above, like many façades in this area, have been renovated. Pay special attention to the magnificent yellow-ochre **Penha Building** in Punda, which dates from 1708, next to the pontoon bridge. Initially the gallery on the upper story was left open so that air could circulate freely through the house.

Stroll back through the centuries

The winding streets of Otrobanda were the site of the most remarkable renovation, however, which led to Willemstad joining the Unesco global cultural heritage list in 1997. Previously a run-down area, the Brionplein was the site of riots in May 1969, when a mob of unemployed refinery and harbour workers gave vent to their frustration at social injustice. With burnt-out buildings remaining until the late 1990s, it is hard to imagine this chic district in its former state.

The owner and architect of the **Kura Hulanda Hotel** off Klipstraat deserve much credit for the area's rejuvenation; the city's most luxurious accommodation option features a restored 18th-century Dutch village, with narrow cobbled streets separated by leafy courtyards with high-end dining, a casino and spa. Perhaps of even greater significance is the addition of the **Kura Hulanda Museum** (Klipstraat 9; daily; tel: 5999-434 7765; charge; www.kurahulanda.com), the Caribbean's largest permanent exhibition on the trans-Atlantic slave trade and African civilisations, built around a courtyard used for slave auctions centuries ago. The impressive and moving collection includes a life-size model of the hold of a slave ship, alongside photographs and documents pertaining to the Dutch- and Portuguese-managed trade.

During the day a stroll along **De Rouvilleweg** and busy **Breedestraat**, past

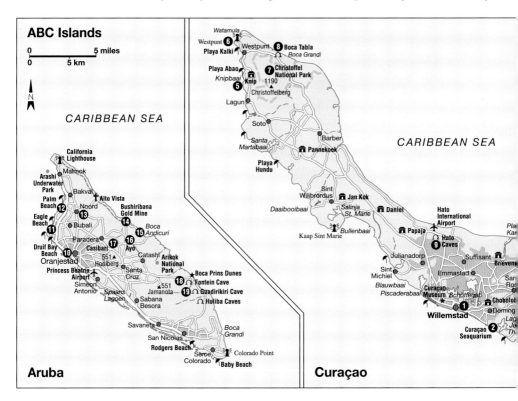

the attractive Haus Sebastopol and the picturesque buildings on Nanniestraat as far as the elaborately renovated Haus Belvedere, takes you back through two centuries of history. At night, visit the numerous bars and terraces at the **Koral Agostini** or the **Keizershof**. The **Kas di Alma Blou** in the cruise-ship terminal contains a good selection of souvenirs.

Just outside Otrobanda, inside the former Dutch military hospital on Van Leeuwenhoekstraat, is the **Curaçao Museum** (open Mon–Fri, Sun 10am–4pm; closed Sat; tel: 5999-462 3873; entrance charge) with an unusual and eclectic collection of antique furniture, old kitchen equipment, and modern art.

From Bolívar to beer

Pietermaai, the district to the southeast of Punda, is undergoing a similar development to Otrobanda. Expensively renovated office buildings and the attractive **Avila Beach Hotel**, once the governor's residence, are certainly worth inspecting. The South American freedom fighter Simón Bolívar is commemorated in a small museum in the **Octagon** (daily; tel: 5999-461 4377; charge); he took refuge here with his two sisters for a while in the early 19th century.

In the Landhuis Chobolobo in the Saliòa quarter, the Senior family has been distilling the world-famous **Curaçao Blue** liqueur for over 110 years (open Mon–Fri; www.curacaoliqueur.com), and in the modern Amstel Brewery on the Schottegat, the island's delicious beer is produced using desalinated sea water and imported ingredients. Many international hotels are located on the Piscaderabaai or the Jan Thielbaai, west and east of town respectively.

The latter is famous for the **Curaçao Seaquarium ❷** (open daily; tel: 5999-461 6666; entrance charge; www.curacao-sea-aquarium.com) where rare and

Genuine Curaçao liqueur is distilled in the ancient copper vats at the Landhuis Chobolobo from the dried peel of local oranges and then refined with the addition of several secret ingredients. Taste some on a tour (open Mon–Fri; free).

Map on pages 298–99

BELOW: an example of Dutch West Indian architecture.

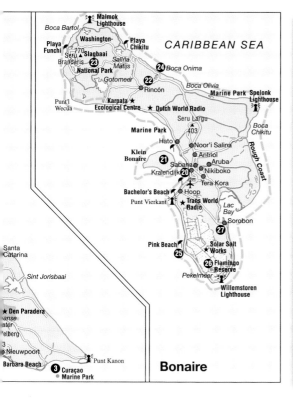

exotic tropical fish, turtles, and crustaceans can be seen from a boardwalk. In the "Animal Encounter" section, divers and snorkelers can feed sharks from behind a Plexiglass screen while having their photograph taken.

Although Bonaire is the most famous diving spot in the Caribbean, Curaçao does have several spectacular diving grounds for the experienced diver. The **Curaçao Marine Park ❸** extends from the Oostpunt and along the southwest coast as far as Jan Thielbaai. Most of the diving areas can be reached directly from the shore, and the clear water is also excellent for snorkeling, with colorful coral reefs, massive sponges, and tropical fish. Anyone eager to discover the underwater world in all its magnificence and also visit the wreck of a Dutch steamer without getting their feet wet should board *Seaworld Explorer,* the glass-bottomed, semi-submarine operated by Atlantis Adventures (tel: 5999-461 0011; www.atlantisadventures.com).

Kunuku – wild and beautiful hinterland

Banda Riba, the southeastern part of Curaçao, has numerous attractions including broad, flat, and sandy **Santa Barbara Beach ❹**, where children can splash about and play quite safely in the clear warm water, and also the hidden bay of **Playa Kanoa**, where courageous surfers brave the waves and local bands congregate for dancing parties at weekends. If you are interested in medicinal herbs, visit schoolteacher Dinah Verijs and her beautiful garden, **Den Paradera**, located at the foot of the Tafelberg: she'll give you all kinds of ideas from curing hair thinning to upset stomachs (call in advance: 767 5608).

During any trip through the hinterland, or kunuku, to Westpunt you'll notice several magnificent, mostly yellow-ochre plantation manors – some close to the

TIP

Dance the night away to local bands at the salsa and *merengue* parties on the broad terraces of Landhuis Brievengat just north of Schottegat. An ideal way to keep fit. Call 737 8344 for details.

BELOW: tranquil beauty of a Curaçao hidden bay.

road, others nestling among hills. These residential and administrative buildings once belonged to influential families who kept them as country estates alongside their business premises in Willemstad. Today they have been converted into restaurants, small hotels, and museums. **Landhuis Jan Kok** (tel: 5999-869 4965), for instance, has a fine art gallery; **Landhuis Groot Sint Martha** contains workshops for the disabled; the **Landhuis Daniel** (tel: 5999-864 8400) is a gourmet restaurant – the other majestic buildings along the road are either privately owned or the property of official institutions. Back on the eastern side of the Schottegat, the **Landhuis Groot Davelaar** contains the renowned De Taveerne restaurant with its excellent local and international cuisineu (tel: 5999-737 0669).

Rough wilderness

With a bit of luck, on a tour through the **Banda Abao** – the western part of the island – you may see some of the shy flamingos which live on the **Salinja St Marie**, or sea turtles on the **Knipbaai ❺**. Here the sandy beaches, the best on the island, are surrounded by rocks, making an attractive setting for a rest stop. The majestic **Landhuis Knip**, once at the center of the wealthiest plantation on Curaçao, now holds a fascinating museum, and hosts cultural events on a regular basis (open daily; tel: 5999-864 0244; entrance charge).

Pelicans are the only creatures courageous enough to brave the waves off the **Westpunt ❻**, where the sea crashes down with unbelievable force onto the rocky shoreline off Watamula. Just a few miles to the east of the sleepy fishing village of Westpunt, a fence on either side of the road marks the **Christoffel National Park ❼**. This large nature reserve was opened in 1978 on land formerly occupied by three vast plantations; it can be explored by jeep, mountain bike, or on foot. Guided tours led by expert rangers introduce visitors to the typical local flora and fauna. Keep an eye out for the green parrots native to the island: they usually fly in pairs and enjoy landing on the enormous cacti. A short but exhausting climb leads to the top of the 1,230-ft (375-meter) high **Christoffelberg**, where the view extends as far as Bonaire. Further attractions in the park include Amerindian rock drawings, spectacular stretches of coastline on the Boca Grandi, and numerous rare palm trees and fragrant orchids in the wilderness of Zevenbergen.

To the northeast, the Christoffel National Park is bordered by the Die Shete Boka, a beautifully atmospheric piece of coast with its hidden grotto of **Boca Tabla ❽** and breathtaking scenery whenever the powerful breakers smash down on the cliffs. It was breakers similar to those which created the original cave system of **Hato ❾** (open daily; tel: 5999-868 0379; entrance charge) not far from the airport. These limestone caves contain ancient Amerindian drawings rumored to date back more than 1,000 years. Guided tours are available (last tour 4pm).

Since the ABC Islands rose up from the sea on several occasions during their genesis, the landscape comprises a whole series of terraces filled with countless grottoes and caverns. The graceful walls of stalagmites and curtains of stalactites, combined with an underground waterfall, make these limestone caverns a fascinating but crowded place to visit. ❑

Map on pages 298–99

Kas di Pali Maishi, near Tera Kora, on the road to Westpunt, is a reconstructed hut thatched with straw showing how simply the country folk used to live (and some still do). Surrounded by a prickly cactus fence, the open-air museum is open daily; tel: 5999-864 2742; entrance charge.

BELOW: Watamula natural bridge, Noordpunt.

ARUBA

Explore an underwater shipwreck and natural reefs, laze on miles of white sandy beach, swim in gentle blue ocean, and shop in modern malls – Aruba has something for everybody

Map on pages 298–99

Caribbean Sea

Aruba

Aruba, the smallest and richest of the ABC Islands, has cosmopolitan shopping centers, elegant restaurants, and a refreshingly deserted hinterland which all go to providing highly attractive alternatives to lazing away happily under the palms all day long on the island's 7 miles (11 km) of white sand lapped by gentle turquoise and dark-blue waters.

For more than 50 years, the massive Lago oil refinery at San Nicolas was Aruba's main source of foreign revenue and not only as the biggest employer on the tiny island. Lago financed schools, doctors, houses, streets, and even a golf course for its workforce. When the refinery was unexpectedly closed down in early 1985 it came as a great shock not just to Arubans but also to the numerous workers from all over the Caribbean. On an island with a population of around 100,000 people, unemployment rose dramatically and affected thousands. The refinery reopened in the early 1990s, but by then the island had changed.

The closure caused potentially devastating economic problems, which struck just as Aruba officially assumed special autonomous status. Tourism was seen as a way of attracting much-needed foreign currency and this gamble has paid off. Today, visitors arrive from all over the world but especially from the Netherlands, the US, and nearby South America. High-rise hotels appeared above the palm trees on Eagle Beach and Palm Beach, and the small town of Oranjestad developed a colorful shopping center. Cunning entrepreneurs created a holiday industry that catered to every taste, whether on water or land: undersea diving along the natural reef, with spectacular underwater scenery around wrecked ships and airplanes; romantic candlelit dinners on board sailing ships; tours on party buses, and Las Vegas-style shows on the stage of the Alhambra – plus casinos where visitors can try their luck at roulette tables.

LEFT: all kinds of watersports in Aruba. **BELOW:** Las Vegas style at the Alhambra.

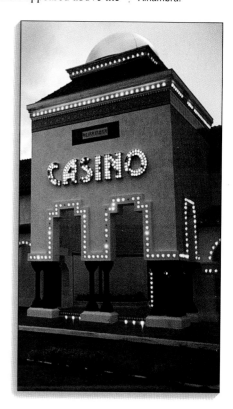

A holiday bonanza

The customer is definitely king here, as long as they have enough dollars in their pockets to pay for it, because perfect service does come at a high price. Well over half a million vacationers spend a few pleasant days each year at Eagle Beach and Palm Beach, and that figure doesn't include the 500,000 or so passengers from cruise ships who visit the bars and boutiques in Oranjestad, eager to take advantage of the bounty of duty-free goods and impressed by the relaxed and polite service. Shopping can be an expensive business especially when you're after European goods such as English and German porcelain, Belgian chocolates and Swiss watches.

The horrors of the colonial era largely passed Aruba by, because the island was only inhabited by a handful of settlers, soldiers and Caiquetío Amerindians.

Practically every type of watersport is on offer on the beaches from sailing to parasailing. And you can have a go on an assortment of "toys" such as jet skis, wave runners, and banana boats.

BELOW: modern shopping malls in Oranjestad.

Agriculture, animal husbandry, the cultivation of aloes, and the export of tree bark containing tannin enabled the islanders to lead a largely self-sufficient existence. Papiamento *(see page 53)*, the local creole language, sounds far more Spanish here than elsewhere and is also very melodious.

Spruced up: Oranjestad

A handful of shopping streets, administrative buildings, and churches, a small harbor with a cruise-ship pier, and some magnificently restored hotels complete with shopping malls and casinos – that just about sums up the center of **Oranjestad ⑩**. If you feel like taking a break from the numerous cafés and bars around the yachting harbor where you can enjoy the view and soak up some local atmosphere and the sunshine, take a stroll past the colorful, Dutch-style façades and visit the few sights Aruba's capital has to offer.

The most noticeable relic of colonial times here is the small **Fort Zoutman** and **Willem III Tower**, the oldest surviving structure on the island. The fort was built right beside the **Paardenbaai** in 1796, and since then land reclamation at the harbor has pushed it around 300 ft (100 meters) inland. Its ancient walls contain the **Aruba Historical Museum** (open Mon–Fri; tel: 297-582 6099; entrance charge) where the exhibits include sea shells, sections of coral, 19th-century household items, and a mechanical barrel organ from Italy that still works. From the clock tower there's a fine view across the island, which is only 22 miles (30 km) long and 4 miles (9 km) across at its widest point. At 6.30pm every Tuesday the well-organised **Bonbini Festival** is held inside the fort, where you can sample local culinary and liquid specialties and learn some traditional dances like the energetic Latin American *tumba* and *merengue*.

Funeral urns, jewelry, and simple artifacts in the **Archeological Museum** (Zoutmanstraat, adjoining the Protestant church of St Francis of Assisi; open Mon–Fri; tel: 297-582 8979) document the largely unresearched culture of the Caiquetío Amerindians and other pre-Columbian peoples, who settled the ABC Islands long before the Europeans arrived. Unfortunately, the exhibits provide rather scant information about the Caiquetío. The streets around the busy main street – **Caya G.F. (Betico) Croes** (formerly Nassaustraat) – are where the locals tend to do most of their shopping. They still contain a few traditional-style Aruban houses with typically steep and flat torto-style roofs.

Craggy coastline and stunning beaches

The terrace-shaped northeast coast of Aruba, with rough landscape, hidden sand dunes, large limestone caverns, and thorny scrubland is a striking contrast to the tourist regions of the west coast. **Eagle Beach ⓫**, 380 ft (120 meters) wide in some places, is lined by so-called Low-Rise Hotels, which blend in harmoniously with the landscape despite their colorful mix of styles. Powdery white **Palm Beach ⓬** is just as beautiful, but high-rises predominate here. Both beaches are signposted from the multi-lane highway that runs north from Oranjestad: most hotels here provide total luxury and the best of entertainment, and anyone who gets tired of the beach can invest any sum they like in air-conditioned boutiques, restaurants and casinos.

Farther north the sea becomes rougher, but that is welcomed by the windsurfers off **Malmok**, and doesn't affect the divers down at the wreck of the German warship *Antilla* either *(see page 151)*. It was surrounded off Aruba by the Dutch Navy on May 10, 1940, during World War II, and rather than hoist the white flag, the captain set the ship alight and sank it. The crew were interned in the Caribbean for the rest of the war, and at the end several of them were allowed to settle on the ABC Islands for good.

Rocky attractions

The 100-ft (32-meter) high **California Lighthouse** towers above the craggy Noordpunt and the sand dunes around it. Built between 1914 and 1916, it stands close to the bright green **Tierra del Sol** golf course, set in the midst of the reddish-brown scrubland. A dusty track, which should only be attempted in a (preferably four-wheel drive) jeep, leads along the east coast, passing the **Alto Vista Pilgrimage Chapel** and a section of rocky landscape. The divi-divi trees here, bent by the northeasterly trade winds, are like natural signposts always pointing southwest.

Art and architecture lovers should take a detour to the unpretentious little church of **Sint Annakerk** in **Noord ⓭**. It contains a surprisingly good neo-Gothic altar of carved oak by Hendrik van der Geld (1870) from Antwerp, as well as stained-glass windows from the Wilhelm Heinrich workshop in Kevelaer. The ruins of the **Bushiribana Gold Mine ⓮** are another popular and also very photogenic destination. They stand in memory of the gold rush that took place here in 1820 when a young boy found some nuggets in the dry valleys on the northeast coast.

Map on pages 298–99

Cacti are a common sight in the arid countryside.

BELOW: sand dunes at Boca Prins.

The romantic spot that was formerly the site of a natural bridge at **Boca Andi-curi ⓕ** is still worth a visit for its seclusion and raging surf – though the bridge itself collapsed in 2007.

Diorite boulders – a geological rarity – can be seen up close in **Ayo ⓰** and **Casibari ⓱**: enormous, cushion-like rocks with large sections gouged out of them, some of them decorated with Amerindian rock drawings. The 551-ft (168-meter) high **Hooiberg** provides a fine view of the **Arikok National Park**, with its fascinatingly desolate wilderness of cactus fields. Near a small renovated farmhouse called **Kunuku Arikok** you can see wooden troughs in which the green juice of the aloe vera plant was collected and boiled. The juice from this plant is believed to purify the blood and regenerate the skin, and is highly treasured worldwide as an ingredient for health foods, skin creams, and sunburn balms.

Mysterious spirals

The cave systems of **Fontein ⓲** and **Quadirikiri ⓳** contain several strange and largely inexplicable Amerindian symbols such as spirals, circles, and lines of dots; in addition there are rare bats, bizarre rock formations, and the odd piece of graffiti left behind by ignorant visitors. The cave walls and roof have been cleaned by experts, and guards and grilles are in position to ensure no further damage is done.

While surfers balance on the high waves out at Colorado Point, a good place to relax from a tour of southern Aruba is in the shallow waters at **Baby Beach**, where there is also good, secluded diving and snorkeling. Alternatively, visit **Charlie's Bar** (tel: 297-584 5086; www.charliesbararuba.com), which is right

The large iguana, indigenous to the island, is protected but it has a long history of making a very tasty and nutritious soup – and today some locals are not averse to bagging the odd one or two for the pot.

BELOW: Cas di Flor, a house decorated Italian style.

beside the refinery at San Nicolas on Main Street. This bar is a virtual institution. Over the past 50 years, guests from all over the world have lined the walls and ceiling with a scurrilous collection of personal mementoes. Such a unique setting is the hangout of local thespians, artists, and musicians, as well as tourists who enjoy coming here for a drink and a chat with the owner.

Aruba made its giant leap from small island to international industrial nation in 1924, when the Lago Oil & Transport Company from the US built a massive refinery in a bay near the southwestern point of the island, not far from San Nicolas. The large oil companies chose Aruba and also Curaçao as safe and easily accessible locations due to political instability in nearby Venezuela. After the oil crisis of the 1980s, parts of the refinery were shut down, but smoking chimneys still dominate daily life in San Nicolas, and enormous tankers can be seen most days coming into port.

Italian inspiration

On the other side of the main road between Oranjestad and the island's former capital of Savaneta, a turn-off leads to the ruins of the **Balashi gold mine**, and through the narrow path known as **Frenchman's Pass**, where legend claims that French soldiers surrounded and shot a group of Amerindian warriors. The village of **Sabana Besora** still contains some typical small houses, such as the Cas di Figura and Cas di Flor, with decorative patterned strips. Italian construction workers probably scratched the attractive ornamentation into the plaster around the turn of the 20th century. Colorfully painted flowers, stars, and other decorations can also be seen in the church of St Francis of Assisi in Oranjestad. ❏

Map on pages 298–99

Paardenbaai (Horses' Bay) off Oranjestad got its name from the colonial merchants who used to unload horses from the boats by tying one to the beach and then shoving the rest overboard. They swam straight to their companion on the shore.

BELOW: Aruba's coastline.

BONAIRE

The waters around this island are a diver's paradise with spectacular views of a magical underwater world, a stark contrast to its cacti-strewn desert and national park

Map on pages 298–99

Caribbean Sea

☐ Bonaire

Parts of the tiny boomerang-shaped desert island of Bonaire lie just a few feet above the seemingly endless blue of the Caribbean Sea – the top of an underwater mountain. Most of its delights can be found under the sea, in the diving grounds of the Bonaire National Marine Park. Despite all the marine marvels, there is also life above the water: there's picturesque Kralendijk (pronounced *Kral*-en-dike), the cactus-filled wilderness of the Washington-Slagbaai National Park, the endless channels in the mangroves of Lac Bay, hiking and biking trails in the thorny back country, and the graceful sight of more than 10,000 pink flamingos in the salt pans of the Pekelmeer.

Below as well as above the water, Bonaire takes ecotourism and environmental issues seriously, in fact the environment is a required subject in primary schools. The surrounding sea to a depth of 200 ft (60 meters) is protected as a Marine Park, the oldest in the Caribbean, and about 40 percent of the total land area is preserved as either national or private park land.

In 1634 the Dutch established a small military base on a coral dike, the *kralendijk*, on the west coast of the island. Bonaire was only interesting to the colonizers because of its dyewood and grazing land for livestock. The slaughtered animals were loaded on to ships at Slagbaai ("Slaughter Bay") in the north, to be taken to market in Curaçao. It was during the 17th century that the Dutch West India Company first discovered the possibility of evaporating seawater in shallow basins to produce salt cheaply, which at that time was much in demand as a preservative for fish and meat. The arduous labor involved was carried out under the scorching sun by so-called "government slaves."

Today, salt from the Pekelmeer remains a major export for the chemical industry, but over the past 35 years tourism has steadily grown to become the most important foreign-currency earner. Since the island is thinly populated (14,000 inhabitants in 111 sq. miles/288 sq. km) and has no other industry to speak of, nature is still largely intact.

A friendly and colorful capital

Kralendijk ❷⓪, the island's picturesque capital, is a serene throwback to the time when tourists had yet to discover the Caribbean. Many of the public buildings and restaurants are located along two streets on or behind the waterfront. On **Kaya Grandi** colorfully painted façades and coral mosaics shaped like flamingos create a tropical atmosphere, and the 1-mile (1.5-km) long harbor promenade is a pleasant place to stroll.

Bonaire is the least densely populated of the ABC islands, with a cosmopolitan mix of 42 nationalities living in relative safety, free from all but petty crime.

LEFT: Bonaire is host to more than 10,000 flamingos. **BELOW:** coral is well-protected on the reefs.

Iguanas of all sizes love the arid conditions.

The capital is compact and easy to tour on foot. Start at **Fort Oranje** – built in the 17th century – beside the cruise ship pier. The small lighthouse built in 1932, is the Harbor Office, while the other fort buildings have been restored and house the courthouse. **Plaza Reina Wilhelmina**, in the center, contains a Protestant church (1847) and the **Pasangrahan**, an attractive neoclassical colonial-era building, which was once the residence of the governor.

In the funky pseudo-Greek market pavilion on the waterfront, traders from Venezuela sell tropical fruit and vegetables. The best views of Kralendijk can be had either from **Karel's Beach Bar** or from the terrace restaurants at the harbor side. It is only when a cruise ship docks (twice a week in the winter) that things get busy. On the edge of town is the **Museo Boneriano** (open Mon–Fri; tel: 5997-717 8868; entrance charge), with an amazing collection of furniture, pictures, colonial household items, and bric-a-brac. The town's only art gallery is the **Richter Gallery** (open Mon–Fri; tel: 5997-717 4112; www.richterart.com) on Kaya Van Eps, which features the work of local artists.

Underwater magic

The entire west coast of Bonaire is lined by coral reefs *(see page 150)* and with unmatched underwater visibility it provides some of the best diving anywhere in the Caribbean. The sea right round the island is part of the **Bonaire National Marine Park**, and since 1979 has been strictly protected. The adjacent island of **Klein Bonaire ㉑**, a quarter mile offshore, is a wilderness preserve that is also managed by the Marine Park. Spear fishing is forbidden here, and it is also illegal to touch – let alone collect – the coral. Bonaire's west coast is full of spectacular dive sites, mostly situated where the reefs gradually slope down into

BELOW: conch shells lie discarded in Lac Bay.

the deep. Snorkelers swimming close to the coast will easily find themselves above magnificent elkhorn, staghorn or brain coral and colorful fish.

Map on pages 298–99

Thorns, salt, and pink feathers

Unspoiled nature begins a few miles beyond the former slave settlement of **Rincón ㉒**, a collection of yellowish-brown houses among the flat hills of the *mondi* (countryside). With rocky volcanic upthrusts in the north, swamps in the center, and salt pans in the south, Bonaire's landscape is varied.

The **Washington-Slagbaai National Park ㉓** (open daily, no entry after 3pm; tel:5997-788 9015; entrance charge; www.washingtonparkbonaire.org) was established on the site of two former plantations in 1979. It takes up the entire northern part of the island, and its brackish salt flats are an important stopover for birds migrating between North and South America. Depending on the season you may see wild geese or ospreys here, and the conures, parrots, and pelicans native to the island can be observed the whole year round. The idyllic beach of **Playa Chikitu** is an excellent place to relax – swimming is discouraged because of the dangerous currents. Two routes for car drivers and cyclists and several hiking paths lead through the scenery and around the base of 791-ft (241-meter) high **Seru Brandaris**, the highest point on the island.

Queen angelfish.

A short, slightly bumpy road leads to **Boca Onima ㉔**. Here, beneath a rocky outcrop in the limestone terrace along the north coast are partially fenced off Amerindian drawings. Painted in a reddish color, they include spirals, circles, and stylized birds. No one is certain of their precise origin, though it is believed that centuries ago, Arawak-speaking Amerindians prayed to the goddess Onima for calm seas here before rowing across to Venezuela.

BELOW: these tiny dwellings each slept six slaves.

In the flat, southern part of the island, the scenery is dominated by conical white mounds of salt and flocks of pink flamingos. A popular viewing spot is the **salt works ㉕** which extracts salt from seawater. Nearby there are a number of peaked-roof buildings, the size of dog kennels, where enslaved salt workers stored their gear, slept and sheltered from rainstorms.

Flamingo Reserve

The entire southern quarter of the island is taken up by the **Flamingo Reserve ㉖**, one of only four nesting-grounds for pink flamingos in the Caribbean. The birds are disturbed by noisy visitors, and may only be observed from afar. During the morning many of these elegant creatures fly to Venezuela or Curaçao to feed on algae, shrimps, and other crustaceans (which give the older flamingos their striking pink hue), so to see them, get there early with a good pair of binoculars. **Jibe City** at Sorobon ㉗, on the east coast, is bordered by mangroves and is popular with kitesurfers, windsurfers and kayakers. Bonaire offers ideal conditions for such watersports with typical winds of 15–25 knots from December through August and 12–18 knots the rest of the year. Its waters are a breeding ground for many reef and pelagic fish as well as the endangered Queen conch. Conch shells can be found lying at the entrance to the bay at **Kai** (a good beach for families). However, the shells are protected and must not be removed. ❑

INSIGHT GUIDES

TRAVEL TIPS

CARIBBEAN

TRAVEL TIPS

T RANSPORTATION

GETTING THERE
AND GETTING AROUND

GETTING THERE

By Air

As far as accessibility goes, the islands fall fairly neatly into two groups: those that can be reached by direct flights from North America, South America, and Europe, and those that cannot. Islands that can be reached by direct flight are as follows:

- Antigua
- Aruba
- Barbados
- Curaçao
- Grenada
- Guadeloupe
- Martinique
- St Kitts
- St Lucia
- St Martin
- Trinidad
- Tobago
- US Virgin Islands

All other destinations must be reached by inter-island airline from the nearest direct-flight island. All the islands, including those listed, can be reached from various points in the Caribbean via numerous carriers, on a tangled spider's web of routes *(see Inter-Island Carriers, page 317 and 318)*. If you want to know which islands can be reached from a particular island, see the listing for that island. Note that inter-island schedules and itineraries are liable to change. Once you have decided on all the places you want to visit, talk to a travel agent, your tourist board representative or airline company to determine the most efficient way to get to your destinations.

A good travel agent will help you plan your trip and find the flights that best suit your pocket and your timetable. Fare prices can vary according to the season and special offers from airlines, so shop around. Many scheduled services are supplemented by charter flights, but even so, flights become heavily booked during high season. Budget fares to Martinique and Guadeloupe are available if you fly with Air France or Aéromaritime from an international airport in France.

Cruise Lines

A large proportion of visitors to the Caribbean arrive by cruise ship, the combination of staying in a luxurious floating hotel and making short visits to different exotic locations being increasingly popular. The days on which cruise ships call see hundreds of passengers flooding into usually low-key ports, and in many places shopping complexes, such as Heritage Quay in St John's, Antigua, have sprung up to accommodate them.

The Lesser Antilles are on the itineraries of several cruise lines, though frequency of service to the different islands in the group varies widely – from hundreds of port visits each year to the US Virgin Islands, to no stops at all at certain other smaller islands. Itineraries change constantly. The best way to plan your trip is to decide first where you would like to go, then visit the web, contact a cruise operator or travel agent to see if there is a current itinerary that covers all or most of your destinations.

The following cruise ship companies have ships that call at islands in the Lesser Antilles:
Carnival Cruise Lines, 3655 NW 87th Avenue, Miami, FL 33178, tel:

800-327 9501 (US); Carnival House, 5 Gainsford Street, London SE1 2NE, tel: 020-7940 4466 (UK); www.carnival.com.
Celebrity Cruises, 1050 Caribbean Way, Miami, FL 33132, tel: 800-722 5941 (US); Addlestone Road, Weybridge, Surrey KT15 2UE, tel: 0800-018 2020/2525 (UK); www.celebrity.com.
Costa Cruises, Venture Corporate Centre, 200 South Park Road, Suite 200, Hollywood, FL 33021, tel: 800-447 6877/954-266 5600 (US); 5 Gainsford Street, London SE1 2NE, tel: 020-7940 4499 (UK); www.costacruises.co.uk.
Cunard Line, 24305 Town Center Drive, Santa Clarita, CA 91355, tel: 800-728 6273 (US); Richmond House, Terminus Terrace, Southampton SO14 3PN, tel: 0845-071 0300 (UK); www.cunardline.com.
Holland America Line, 300 Elliott Avenue West, Seattle, WA 98119, tel: 206-281 3535 (US); 5 Gainsford Street, London SE1 2NE, tel: 020-7940 4477 (UK); www.hollandamerica.com.

Air Passes

Several airlines offer air passes that allow travel to three or more islands in the Antilles; some tickets extend to parts of Central and South America. Call regional airlines such as Air Jamaica, LIAT and larger carriers such as American Airlines for the latest information about the types of passes available and the conditions of purchase.

Fred Olsen Cruise Lines, Fred Olsen House, White House Road, Ipswich, Suffolk IP1 5LL, tel: 01473-742424; www.fredolsen.co.uk.
Norwegian Cruise Line, 7665 Corporate Center Drive, Miami, FL 33126, tel: 800-327 7030 (US); 1 Derry Street, Kensington, London W8 5NN, tel: 0845-658 8010 (UK); www.ncl.com; www.uk.ncl.com.
Ocean Village, Richmond House, Terminus Terrace, Southampton SO14 3PN, tel: 0845-358 5000; www.oceanvillageholidays.co.uk.
P & O Cruises, North America c/o Princess Cruises, 24305 Town Center Drive, Santa Clarita, CA 91355-4999, tel: 800-252 0158 (California only), 800-421 0522; 213-553 1770 (US); Richmond House, Terminus Terrace, Southampton SO14 3PN, tel: 0845-355 5333 (UK); www.pocruises.com.
Princess Cruises, 24844 Avenue Rockefeller, Santa Clarita, CA 91355 California, tel: 1-800-PRINCESS (1-800-774 62377); Richmond House, Terminus Terrace, Southampton SO14 3PN, tel: 0845-355 5800 (UK); www.princess.com.
Royal Caribbean International, Addlestone Road, Weybridge, Surrey KT15 2UE, tel: 0800-018 2020, 01932-820 230; 800-398 9819 (US Reservations); www.royalcaribbean.com.
Seabourn Cruise Line, 6100 Blue Lagoon Drive, Suite 400, Miami, FL 33126, tel: 800-9299391 (US); 0845-070 0500 (UK); www.seabourn.com.
Silversea Cruises, 110 Broward Boulevard, Fort Lauderdale, FL 33301, tel: 800-722 9955 (US); 77–79 Great Eastern Street, London EC2A 3HU, tel: 0844-770 9030 (UK); www.silversea.com.
Star Clippers, 7200 NW 19th Street, Suite 206, Miami, FL 33126, tel: 305-442 0550 (US); c/o Fred Olsen, Fred Olsen House, White House Road, Ipswich, Suffolk IP1 5LL, tel: 01473-292029 (UK); www.starclippers.com.
Windstar Cruises, 2101 4th Avenue, Suite 1150, Seattle, WA 98121,

tel: 206-292 9606 (US); Carnival House, 5 Gainsford Street, London SE1 2NE, tel: 020-7940 4480/8 (UK); www.windstarcruises.com.

Cargo Ships

For the traveler in search of something out of the ordinary, a cargo ship offers a different type of cruise: comfortable cabins for only a handful of passengers (evening meals are generally taken with the officers) on a working cargo ship. Geest "banana boats", for example, leave Southampton on a round trip lasting 25 days, and call at Antigua, Barbados, Dominica, Grenada, Guadeloupe, Martinique, St Kitts, St Lucia, St Vincent, and Trinidad. Enquiries to the following:
Cargo Ship Voyages Ltd (agents for Geest), Hemley, Woodbridge, Suffolk, IP12 4QF, tel: 01473-736265.
Freighter World Cruises, 180 South Lake Avenue, Suite 340, Pasadena, CA 91101, tel: 818-449 3106.

GETTING AROUND

By Car

The islands are well stocked with auto-rental agencies. Travel by car allows great freedom and flexibility to explore the nooks and crannies of the islands, but there are a few things the driver should be aware of. Many of the islands are mountainous, and on all of them roads are narrower than most US and European drivers will be familiar with. Driving thus may be a little more harrowing than at home – not for the faint-hearted. Also, in some areas yearly rainfall is quite light and this allows a film of oil to build up on road surfaces. When it does rain on these roads, they become especially slick, requiring extra caution. All in all, drivers should prepare to drive defensively and with caution, perhaps following the advice of one of the islands' tourist agencies to "sound the horn frequently," especially when approaching bends. Regulations on driver's licenses vary

from island to island – see under listings for individual islands.

By Taxi

Perhaps the most common means of transportation for visitors to the islands is the taxi. Not only are taxis convenient, and relatively inexpensive, but taking a taxi also gives you access to the resources of the driver. Where else could you chat with an island expert for the price of a cab ride? Most taxi drivers will gladly help you find things you are looking for, or that you aren't looking for but may be delighted to find. It is usually possible to find a taxi driver who is willing to give you a tour of his or her island and, in some places, drivers are specially trained to do this.

Another positive feature of taxi travel for island visitors is that rates are generally fixed and published. Often, printed sheets with detailed rates are available from points of entry, drivers, and tourist offices. If you plan to travel much by taxi, one of the first things to do upon arrival is to familiarize yourself with the rates to different destinations and at different times of day. You can often negotiate for longer excursions out of town.

Taxi drivers are usually friendly and extremely helpful. If you receive good service, return the favor with a good tip – say, 15–20 percent.

By Bus

Most of the islands have local bus services that many residents use to get around. Though they are not as flexible as taxis and rental cars, buses are quite inexpensive and have the advantage of allowing travelers to get a small taste of how local residents live. Your hotel, a tourist office, or a police station should be able to supply information on schedules, and fellow riders and drivers are friendly and helpful in making sure that bewildered visitors get off at the right stop.

Tour buses (both mini and full-sized), vans, jeeps, and "communal taxis" are available on all the islands for taking groups sightseeing.

Inter-Island Carriers

Inter-island airlines include the following:

- BVI Airlines
- Air Caraibes
- Air St Thomas
- Air Sunshine
- American Eagle
- Caribbean Airlines
- LIAT
- Trans Island Air
- Seaborne Airlines
- SVG Air
- Windward Express
- Winair

Yachting Information

For yachtsmen and women who want to stay put for a while, there are community anchorages in St Martin, Bequia (Grenadines), Grenada, and Trinidad. There are marinas with slips of different types and facilities for provisioning and repairs. Several of the larger ones have dry-dock facilities for boat storage.

Inter-Island Links

As you might expect in this region of islands cut off from one another by the sea, the options for getting around between islands are legion.

By Air

For the traveler desiring quick transfers (and perhaps the novelty of a ride in a seaplane), there are a number of airline companies operating inter-island routes. LIAT is probably the largest and best-known of these carriers, although ALM (Dutch Antillean Airlines) has a monopoly on flights between Aruba, Curaçao, Bonaire, and St Martin.

However, several Caribbean airlines have merged, reducing the number of companies operating in the region. For a short list of inter-island air carriers, *see Getting There, page 319*.

By Sea

On the sea, an armada of ferries operates regularly between islands, and there is even a regular run between Aruba, Curaçao, and Venezuela. Some of these ferries are the familiar steel-and-smokestack variety, while the inquisitive and adventurous traveler will find catamarans, hydrofoils, schooners, and other types of sailing vessel plying the waters between islands. *Voyager I & II*, for example, make regular runs between St-Barthélemy and St Martin, while *The Edge* runs between St Martin and Saba daily.

It is often possible for travelers to bargain with fishermen and other small boat owners to arrange rides out to the many small islands which lie off the shores of the major islands.

Sailing

Chartering a Yacht

One of the most exciting ways to explore the Caribbean is on a private yacht, either with your own crew to sail the boat for you or bareboat – just the boat – for experienced sailors. Popular destinations are the

Grenadines and the Virgin Islands as the islands are close together and easily explored in a week or two. A three-week trip might take you, for example, from Antigua to the Virgin Islands or Antigua to Grenada, making leisurely calls at the islands along the way. Short charters of just a few days can also be arranged, and for those who prefer to sleep on dry land, most islands have day-sail operators too. Whatever your itinerary, if you are at home on a boat, this is a wonderful way to see the islands.

If you want to rent a crewed yacht, make sure you are happy with your choice – that the yacht is safe, comfortable, and well-equipped and the crew congenial enough to share close quarters. Organize the trip with a reputable agency, which will match you with the right boat and crew. One long-established agency is: **Nicholson Yacht Charters,** 78 Bolton Street, Cambridge, MA 02140, tel: 800-662 6066.

An exhaustive list of companies offering bareboat Caribbean charters is published in the March issue of *Sail* magazine, while the August issue covers crewed yachts. *Sail* is available in many libraries, and back (or current) issues can also be ordered from the magazine's publisher. Contact: **SAIL Magazine**, www.sailmag.com.

THE ABC ISLANDS

By Car

International car-rental firms have offices at the airport as well as in many hotels. Those wishing to rent a car must be 21 years of age and in possession of a valid national driver's license. Car-rental companies include:
AB Car and Scooter Rental, Aruba, tel: 599-717 8980.
Amigo Car Rental, Aruba, tel: 297-583 8833.
Avis, Curaçao, tel: 5999-461 1255.
Budget, Bonaire, tel: 599-717 4700.
Budget, Curaçao, tel: 5999-868 3466.
Budget Rent-A-Car, Aruba, tel: 297-582 8600.
Orlando's Bonaire Motorcycle Shop, Bonaire, tel: 599-717 8429/ 599-717 7790.

By Taxi

Taxis are available for hire at the airport, cruise terminals, and other

central locations. In addition, on Aruba and Curaçao public transportation is provided by buses and taxis following fixed routes. Always agree the fare before beginning a taxi journey.

Inter-Island Links

Airlines operating scheduled flights between Hato International in Curaçao, Queen Beatrix International in Aruba and Flamingo Airport in Bonaire include: **Dutch Antilles Express** (www.flydae.com); **Divi Divi** (www.flydivi.com); **Tiara Air** (www.tiara-air.com), and **Insel Air** (www.inselair.com). **Air Jamaica**, **American Airlines**, **American Eagle**, **Continental Airlines** and **Delta** link the ABC Islands to North America and the Caribbean. **KLM** and **Arkefly** fly nonstop to The Netherlands once or twice daily.

ANGUILLA

By Car

Cars drive on the left, British-style. To purchase a temporary Anguillan driver's license, which is good for up to three months, present a valid driver's license from your country of origin, with a small fee, to the police station in The Valley. The ports of entry can also perform this service.
Car-rental companies include:
Avis Car Rental, The Quarter, tel: 264-497 2642.
Caribbean Rental Ltd, The Valley, tel: 264-497 4662.
Thrifty Car Rental, The Valley, tel: 264-497 2656.

By Taxi

Taxis are available at all points of entry including Wallblake Airport, which is located more or less at the center of Anguilla, a couple of miles from The Valley, the island's principal town. Passengers arriving by boat disembark further west at Blowing Point. Taxis are not metered, but there are fixed charges for taxi rides; confirm the price before you start.

Island tours take about three hours and start from the airport or Blowing Point.

Inter-Island Links

From Wallblake Airport you can fly to Sint Maarten, St Kitts, St Thomas, BVI, Antigua and Puerto Rico. Airlines include:

American Eagle, tel: 264-497 7300, www.aa.com
Caribbean Star, tel: 264-497 8690, www.flycaribbeanstar.com
LIAT, tel: 264-497 5000/2, www.liatairline.com
Winair, tel: 264-497 2748, www.fly-winair.com

Marigot in St-Martin is a 20-minute ferry ride away from Anguilla and makes a good day trip. Ferries leave Blowing Point every half hour, 7.30am–7pm. Don't forget your passport and immigration card to show in St-Martin.

Ferries from Marigot to Blowing Point depart every half hour, 8am–6.15pm.

A charter ferry service is also available from Blowing Point to Juliana in Sint Maarten by Link Ferries (www.link.ai).

ANTIGUA AND BARBUDA

By Car

Driving is on the left, British-style. Drivers should present their regular license, along with a small fee at a police station or car-rental office in order to be issued with a local driving permit. Vehicles can be picked up at the airport, or delivered to your hotel. Agencies include:
Avis, tel: 268-462 2840.
Budget, tel: 268-462 3009.
Dollar Rent-a-Car, tel: 268-462 0362.
Hertz, tel: 268-481 4440.
National, tel: 268-462 2113.

On Barbuda, jeeps are available from **Linton Thomas**, tel: 268-460 0081.

Some of the roads outside St John's are narrow and potholed with no sidewalk, so beware.

By Taxi

There are plenty of taxis to meet flights at V.C. Bird International Airport, and jeeps at Barbuda's Codrington Airport. Fares are pre-set (a list is posted in Arrivals at the airport, at the tourist office, and in hotels). Confirm the price before you start.

Inter-Island Links

Barbuda is just 10 minutes away from Antigua by air, or by ferry from St John's. Montserrat is 25 minutes away by air, and there is the odd ferry, check with the tourist board for details.

Antigua has direct air connections

from Europe, USA, and Canada, and frequent links with all Caribbean islands. For details, contact:
Air St Kitts/Nevis, tel: 268-465 8571.
Carib Aviation, tel: 268-481 2401/2/3.
Caribbean Airlines, tel: 800-744 2225.
Caribbean Star Airlines, tel: 268-480 2561.
LIAT, tel: 268-480 5601.

BARBADOS

By Car

Driving is on the left, and by Caribbean standards the roads are good, although driving at night can be difficult on narrow unlit country roads. So leave plenty of time to reach your destination. The maximum speed limit outside urban areas is 50 miles per hour. Bajan rush hour is from 7.30–8.30am and 4.30–5.30pm.

Visitors' driver's licenses are available from the airport, many car-rental companies, and most police stations. To obtain one you must present your own driver's license and BDS$10.

The following car-rental companies offer a wide choice of cars, including mini mokes (beach buggy-style vehicles), free pick up and delivery to and from your accommodations, and free road maps. They all accept Visa, American Express, and MasterCard credit cards:
Coconut Car Rentals, tel: 246-437 0297; fax: 228 9820; email: coconut@caribsurf.com.
Corbin's Car Rentals, tel: 246-427 9531; fax: 427 7975; email: corbins@ndl.net.
Courtesy Rent-a-Car, tel: 246-431 4160.
Stoutes Car Rental, tel: 246-416 4456; email: info@stoutescar.com.
Sunny Isle Motors, tel: 246-419 7498; email: sunisle@caribsurf.com.

By Taxi

Taxis are always in plentiful supply at the international airport, hotels, and in town. Make sure you agree the fare before beginning your journey. Enquire at the airport or the hotel reception for the official rates.

Inter-Island Links

There are frequent flights and boat trips to nearby islands such as

St Vincent and the Grenadines, St Lucia, and Grenada.
For details, contact:
Caribbean Safari Tours: Ship Inn, St Lawrence Gap, Christ Church, tel: 246-420 7600.
Chantours: Plaza 2, Sunset Crest, St James, tel: 246-432 5591.
LIAT: Grantley Adams Airport, tel: 246-428 0986/7101.
Sunlinc Barbados: Welches, St Thomas, tel: 246-436 1710.
Trans Island Air (TIA): Grantley Adams Airport, tel: 246-418 1654, fax: 246-428 0916.
WIIT Tours: Worthing, Christ Church, tel: 246-435 7051.

BRITISH VIRGIN ISLANDS

By Car

Driving is on the left, but many cars are Japanese or American and have the steering wheel on the left. To drive here, a temporary BVI driver's license is required. It can be obtained through the rental agency (for US$10) on presentation of your valid driver's license. Advance reservation is recommended in peak season. Hotels are very helpful in organizing car rental, and a car can be delivered to your hotel.

There are many international and local car-rental companies including:
Avis, Road Town, Tortola (opposite the Botanic Gardens), tel: 284-495 4973.
D.W. Jeep Rentals, The Settlement, Anegada, tel: 284-495 9677/8018.
International Car Rentals, Road Town, Tortola, tel: 284-494 2516.
Mahogany Car Rentals, Spanish Town, Virgin Gorda, tel: 284-495 5469.

By Taxi

Taxis are easy to find on the BVI. They stop if hailed on the road, and can be found waiting at the airports and at ferry docks. On Virgin Gorda small converted lorries with benches run a shuttle service between the main tourist points at a reasonable price.

Taxis have fixed prices, but it is always best to establish the fare before you start out on a journey.

Inter-Island Links
By Air

There are good connection flights from the international airports on St Martin and Puerto Rico; smaller

airlines connect BVI with the US Virgin Islands and Tortola with Anegada:
Air Sunshine, tel: 284-495 8900; in the US: 800-327 8900.
Air St Thomas, tel: 284-495 5935.
American Eagle, tel: 284-495 2559.
Cape Air, tel: 284-495 2100, in the US: 800-352 0714.
Caribbean Sun, tel: 284-494 2347.
Clair Aero, tel: 284-495 2271.
Caribbean Star, tel: 284-494 2347.
LIAT, tel: 284-495 1187/2577.
Winair, tel: 284-494 2347.
Charter companies include:
Caribbean Wings, tel: 284-495 6000.
Fly BVI, tel: 284-495 1747.
Island Birds, tel: 284-495 2002.
Island Helicopters, tel: 284-499 2663.

By Ferry

Timetables are available in hotels, at the tourist board, and in the *Welcome* magazine.
There are regular services:
● from Road Town, Tortola to Spanish Town, Virgin Gorda and Peter Island.
● from West End, Tortola to Jost Van Dyke.
● from Beef Island, Tortola to North Sound and Spanish Town, Virgin Gorda (North Sound Express).
● from Road Town, Tortola and West End to St Thomas and St John (both USVI).
● from Virgin Gorda to St Thomas (USVI).
There is also a free ferry from Beef Island, Tortola to Marina Cay (Pusser's).

DOMINICA

By Car

Driving is on the left-hand side, British-style. The speed limit in built-up areas is 20 miles per hour. Elsewhere there is no limit. Roads in Dominica are characteristically twisting and narrow, with steep gradients. Road surfaces vary from excellent to potholed.
There are various car-rental companies in and around Roseau. You need a national or international driver's license and a local visitor's permit. The latter can be obtained from your car-rental company.
Car-rental companies include:
Island Car, tel: 767-255 6844.
Budget, tel: 767-449 2080.
Cars can be picked up at and returned to the airport.
Hitchhiking is possible, but there is usually little traffic in rural areas.

By Taxi

Dominica's main airport, **Melville Hall**, is located near Marigot, on the island's northeast coast. Taxis are available there to take travelers on the long but scenic 36-mile (58-km) drive to Roseau, where many hotels and guesthouses are located.
There are numerous taxi services. On fixed routes the fares are set by the government. Otherwise, settle on a price before you start your journey. Taxis do not cruise the streets and are sometimes difficult to find at night. See the telephone directory or enquire at the tourist office for taxi telephone numbers, or ask your hotel or restaurant to order one.

By Bus

Minibuses are the local form of public transportation, from early in the morning to nightfall. They run mainly to and from Roseau. There are no fixed schedules; buses leave when they are full (in Roseau there are various departure points depending on the destination). There are frequent services to villages around Roseau, but making a round trip in one day from Roseau to more remote communities can be a problem. Coming into Roseau in the early morning from towns such as Plymouth or Marigot, and returning at lunch time or in the afternoon is easier.

Inter-Island Links

There are no direct flights from Europe to Dominica. Connections with Dominica are made with regional airlines, including LIAT, from neighboring Caribbean islands, including Antigua, Guadeloupe, and Martinique. American Eagle flies daily from San Juan, Puerto Rico (with connections to North America). The main airport is Melville Hall Airport. LIAT and air taxi services also use the smaller Canefield Airport, close to Roseau.
Try the following for interconnecting flights:
American Eagle, tel: 767-445 7242.
LIAT, tel: 767-445 7242.
If you prefer to travel by sea, efficient ferry services connect Dominica with Guadeloupe (to the north) and Martinique and St Lucia (to the south). Ferries depart from Roseau almost daily. For tickets and information, contact:
L'Express Des Isles: upstairs in the Whitchurch Centre, Roseau, tel: 767-448 2181.

GRENADA

By Car

Driving is on the left. Roads are sometimes in poor condition, especially in the mountains. Drivers must be over 21 and have a valid license as well as a local permit (available from the central police station). There is a good choice of rental firms, but cars are sometimes difficult to obtain, particularly in high season and during Carnival. Rental companies include:
Avis, tel: 473-440 3936.
David's, tel: 473-444 3399.
Maitlands, tel: 473-444 4022.
McIntyre Bros Ltd, tel: 473-444 3944/1550.
Y&R Rentals, tel: 473-444 4448.

In Carriacou
Sunkey's, tel:473-443 8382.

By Taxi

Taxis are available at the airport, the Carenage, and outside most hotels. They are not metered and there are no fixed charges, so it is advisable to establish the fare with the driver before setting off. Taxi drivers can normally be hired by the hour or day for sightseeing tours of the island. Allow most of a day for a tour of Grenada.

By Bus

There are bus services around the coastal roads to St George's, but Grenada's buses are normally very crowded and travel much too fast for many visitors' comfort.

By Bicycle

Bicycles can be rented from **Ride Grenada** (tel: 473-444 1157). The island's mountainous terrain, tropical climate, and sometimes erratic road conditions should be borne in mind if visitors plan to tour the island on two wheels.

Inter-Island Links

LIAT, St Vincent Grenada Air (SVG Air) and Airlines of Carriacou connect Grenada with Carriacou (six–eight flights daily). LIAT also provides services to all Eastern Caribbean destinations.
Airlines of Carriacou, tel: 473-444 3549/1475.
LIAT, tel: 473-444 4121/2; www.liatairline.com.

SVG Air, tel: 784-457 5124; www.svgair.com.

The most popular way to get to Carriacou is by the *Osprey Express* passenger ferry, which leaves from the Carenage. The journey takes 90 minutes. Check with your hotel for sailing times and fares.

GUADELOUPE

On Arrival

Seagoing passengers arrive in Guadeloupe at centrally located Pointe-à-Pitre, which, along with Basse-Terre, is one of the island's two major towns. Most air passengers touch down at the Pôle Caraïbes Airport outside Pointe-à-Pitre, although some traffic, including regional flights, passes through airports near Basse-Terre and St-François, as well as the old Le Raizet Airport.

By Car

To rent a car for 20 days or less, your current valid license is all you need. For longer periods, Guadeloupe requires an international driver's permit. Visiting drivers should have at least one year's driving experience. Pointe-à-Pitre and Pôle Caraïbes airports have car-rental agencies. Mopeds are also available for hire.

By Taxi

At all points of entry – air and sea – taxis are available. All taxis have meters, which are useful for short trips, but for longer excursions, negotiate a tariff. Many drivers speak English.

Inter-Island Links

Air links with neighboring Caribbean islands are available with the following airlines:
Air Caraïbes, tel: 0820-835 835
Air Saint-Martin, tel: 590-211 289.

MARTINIQUE

On Arrival

Travelers arriving in Martinique by cruise ship will dock at Pointe Simon in Fort-de-France, the island's principal town. Air passengers land at Aimé Césaire Airport, southeast of Fort-de-France, where both taxis and rental cars are available.

By Car

To rent a car, your current valid license is all you need. Visiting drivers should have at least one year's driving experience. Traffic is heavy, so avoid the main roads at rush hour.

By Taxi

All taxis are fitted with meters, which makes it easier for short journeys, but expensive for longer trips. It is advisable to negotiate a fixed rate for excursions. Many drivers speak English.

Inter-Island Links

Airlines connecting Martinique to Antigua, Barbados, Dominica, Grenada, Guadeloupe, Puerto Rico, St Lucia, St Martin, St Vincent, and Trinidad include:
Air Caraïbes, tel: 0820-83 58 35
LIAT, tel: 596-42 16 93
Jet Aviation Service, charter flights, tel: 596-42 22 00
Ferries link Martinique to Dominica, Guadeloupe and St Lucia. Contact:
Caribbean Express Des Iles, tel: 0825-35 90 00.

MONTSERRAT

By Car

Drive on the left, British-style. A local driver's license can be obtained from the police. Island-wide road improvements are ongoing.
Car rental: the island has car-, jeep-, and scooter-rental services.

By Taxi

Taxis are available; the Tourist Board should be able to supply visitors with company names and telephone numbers.

By Bus

A public bus service (using minibuses) serves the safe northern part of the island.

Inter-Island Links

The W. H. Bramble Airport closed because of volcanic activity in June 1997. Another airport was built at Gerald's in 2005.
Air Montserrat (www.airmontserrat.com) offers charter flights to neighboring islands.
Winair (tel: 664-491 6988; www.fly-winair.com) has flights to Montserrat from Antigua and Sint Maarten.

Charter flights can also be arranged through **Carib Aviation**, V.C. Bird International Airport, Antigua (tel: 268-481 2401; email: caribav@candw.ag) or **Norman Aviation**, St John's, Antigua (tel: 268-462 2445).

ST-BARTHÉLEMY, SABA, AND ST EUSTATIUS

By Car

All valid foreign drivers' licenses are accepted.

In **St-Barths** car rentals are available – with pick-ups at the airport. Advance reservations are particularly important on this little island. Most rental cars have standard transmissions. Rental agencies include:
Budget, tel: 590-27 66 30.
Europcar, tel: 590-27 74 34.
Hertz, tel: 590-27 71 14.
In **Saba** contact: **Caja's Enterprises NV,** The Bottom, tel: 599-416 3460.
In **Statia** contact: **ARC**, tel: 599-318 2595.

By Taxi

Taxis are available on all three islands for pick-ups at airports and ferry ports, and for island tours. Agree the price in advance.

Inter-Island Links

St-Barths is linked by air with Puerto Rico, St Martin, St Thomas, Saba, Antigua, Anguilla, Guadeloupe, St Kitts, Barbados, and St Croix; **Saba** is linked with St Martin, St Kitts, and Statia; and **Statia** is linked with St Martin, St Kitts, St-Barths, and Saba. Airlines include:
Winair, tel: 590-27 61 01 (St Barths); 599-318 2303 (Statia); 599-416 2255 (Saba).
St-Barths is served by catamarans and ferries.

ST KITTS AND NEVIS

By Car

Cars drive on the left, British-style. Visitors who wish to drive while on the islands must present a valid national or international license at the Traffic Department or the fire station, along with a small fee. A temporary license, valid on St Kitts and Nevis, will then be issued. Branches of the Traffic Department are located at the police stations in Basseterre on Cayon Street and Charlestown on the main road.

Saloon cars, jeeps, and mini-mokes (like a beach buggy) are available for rental but should be booked well in advance, especially in high season.

For more details contact:
Avis, South Independence Square, Basseterre, St Kitts, tel: 869-465 6507.
Avis, Nevis, tel: 869-469 5199.
Caines, Princes Street, Basseterre, St Kitts, tel: 869-465 2366.
TDC Car Rentals, Bay Front, Charlestown, Nevis, tel: 869-469 5690.

It is possible to split the rental between the two islands for the same price as renting a car on only one island.

By Taxi

St Kitts is served by Robert Llewellyn Bradshaw International Airport (RLB International), from which taxis are available for the 2½-mile (4-km) trip to Basseterre – the island's major town and capital of St Kitts. Taxis also serve the island's scattered hotels.

Travelers flying to **Nevis** land at Vance W. Amory International Airport, a 7-mile (11-km) jaunt from Nevis's principal and only town, Charlestown. Once again, taxis are on hand to bring visitors to their destinations. Tariffs are fixed, but be sure to confirm the total price of your journey before starting out.

By Bus

Local people tend to use the little minibuses which service both islands. The buses are usually reliable and inexpensive, but they don't generally travel the general tourist routes.

Inter-Island Links

St Kitts is linked by air with many islands including Puerto Rico, Antigua, Barbados, St Martin, Anguilla, St Barths, Saba, St Eustatius, USVI, BVI, Grenada, and St Lucia.

Nevis is linked with USVI, St Barths, Anguilla, Antigua, St Martin, and Puerto Rico.

Airlines serving the routes into and from St Kitts and Nevis include:
Carib Aviation, tel: 869-465 3055.
LIAT, tel: 869-465 8200/869-469 9333.

Nevis Express, tel: 869-469 9755/4756.
Winair, tel: 869-465 0810.

Scheduled carriers (with connecting flights):
From Europe: Air France, Iberia, KLM, Lufthansa, Martin Air.
From Canada: Air Canada, American Airlines, Caribbean Airlines.
From USA: American Airlines, Caribbean Airlines, US Airways (direct), Northwest, Air Jamaica, Universal Airlines (direct).

You can travel the short distance between St Kitts and Nevis either by air taxi or by the Basseterre to Charlestown ferry, a 30–45-minute journey that runs daily. The ferries cost EC$20 (US$8) one way. There is also a port fee of EC$1 each way. Tickets are purchased at the ferry terminals just before departure.

ST LUCIA

By Taxi

Taxis are available at Hewanorra International Airport in the south and Vigie Airport, near Castries. Most larger hotels lie in the northwest of the island; so if you land at Hewanorra, you are likely to have a long, albeit picturesque, journey to your destination. Always agree the fare before starting your journey.

By Car

Drive on the left. Visiting drivers must obtain a temporary driving permit, valid for three months, available from both of the island's airports and all car-rental companies for EC$54.
Car rentals:
Avis, tel: 758-452 2700
Ben's West Coast Jeeps and Taxis, tel: 758-459 5457/484 0708
Cool Breeze Jeep-Car Rental, tel: 758-459 7729
Hertz, tel: 758-454 9636

By Bus

Traveling on the bus in St Lucia costs very little and it can be fun, if fast. Minibuses run to and from the main towns throughout the day, but are less reliable at night.

Inter-Island Links

LIAT flights from George F.L. Charles (Vigie) Airport connect St Lucia to islands such as Antigua, Dominica, Grenada, Barbados, Martinique, St Vincent, and Trinidad. There is also

a high-speed catamaran service, L'Express des Iles, to Martinique, Guadeloupe, and Dominica.

ST MARTIN/SINT MAARTEN

On Arrival

Most visitors arrive at Juliana Airport on the Dutch side of the island. Sea passengers are likely to land at Philipsburg, in Sint Maarten, a popular cruise port, or at Marigot or Grand Case on the French side of the island. Take a taxi from the airport (see Getting Around, page 317).

By Car

Cars drive on the right on St Martin and foreign licenses are accepted. Car-rental companies operating on the island include:
Hertz: Baie Nettlé, St-Martin, tel: 590-87 83 71; Sint Maarten, tel: 590-545 4541, www.sxmrentacar.com.
Avis: Simpson Bay, Sint Maarten, tel: 590-545 3959; Grand Case, St-Martin, tel: 590-87 50 60, www.avis-sxm.com.

By Taxi

Taxis are available at the island's ports of entry. There are no meters, but there are fixed charges, so check the price before you start. A taxi tour is a good way of seeing the island.

By Bus

Buses travel regularly from 6am–midnight between Philipsburg and Marigot, and other principal routes. Ask at the tourist office for details of island tours by minibus.

Inter-Island Links

Destinations linked with St Martin by local airlines include Barbados, Trinidad and Tobago, Martinique, St-Barthélemy, Anguilla, BVI, St Kitts, Curaçao, Aruba, Bonaire, St Thomas, Saba, St Eustatius, and Jamaica. Inter-island airlines include:
LIAT, tel: 599-546 7621.
Winair, tel: 599-545 4237.

A ferry from Marigot serves Anguilla (7am–7pm). Voyager I & II run between St Martin (Marigot waterfront and Oyster Pond) and St-Barths (tel: 590-871 068, www.voyager-st-barths.com).

ST VINCENT AND THE GRENADINES

By Car

Driving is on the left, British-style. You will need an international license, or, failing that, for a moderate fee you can purchase a local license at the police station in Bay Street, Kingstown, or the Licensing Authority in Halifax Street. Rental companies on St Vincent include:
Avis, tel: 784-456 2929.
David's Auto Clinic, tel: 784-456 4026.
Phil's Rental Service, tel: 784-458 3304.
Rent & Drive, tel: 784-457 5601.

By Taxi

Flights arrive at St Vincent's E.T. Joshua Airport, where there are plenty of taxis to take you to your destination. Taxis and minibuses are also available on Bequia and Union Island. There are fixed tariffs for journeys, but check the price before you start.

By Bus

Local buses on St Vincent and the Grenadines tend to be both busy and noisy, but they are also inexpensive and run reasonably frequently.

Inter-Island Links

St Vincent is linked by air with other Caribbean islands including Barbados, Trinidad, St Lucia, Martinique, and Grenada. Petit St Vincent, Palm Island, and exclusive Mustique, all private islands, are also accessible with permission.

Short trips throughout the islands of the Grenadines – Bequia, Union Island, Canouan, and Mayreau – are readily available and usually very enjoyable. Generally speaking, boat trips tend to be the best option as they are usually easy and more economical. There are a number of inexpensive ferries and a mail boat that ply the local waters each week. Schedules can be erratic, so check carefully for departure times – the local tourist office can help plan the trip. Also contact:
Admiralty Transport: Port Elizabeth, Bequia, tel: 784-458 3348.
Email: admiraltrans@caribsurf.com, www.admiralty-transport.com.
If you prefer to island-hop by air, the following airlines have services:
LIAT, tel: 784-458 4841.

Mustique Airways, tel: 784-458 4380.
SVG Air, tel: 784-457 5124.
Trans Island Air (TIA), tel: 246-418 1654 (Barbados).

TRINIDAD AND TOBAGO

By Car

Visitors wishing to rent a car must be at least 21 years old and in possession of a valid driver's license. Traffic drives on the left in Trinidad and Tobago. Car rental companies:
Auto Rentals, Piarco Airport, tel: 868-669 0644. Crown Point Airport, tel: 868-639 0644; www.autorentalstt.com.
Econo-Car Rentals, 191–3 Western Main Road, Cocorite, tel: 868-622 8074. Crown Point Airport, tel: 868-660 8728.

Motorbike Rentals
Baird's Rentals Ltd, Crown Point and Scarborough, Tobago, tel: 868-639 7054, fax: 868-639 4126.

By Taxi and Bus

Taxis are available for hire at central points. There are also buses and route taxis running between most towns on the two islands. Some taxis follow set routes and minibus-taxis provide additional transportation.

Inter-Island Links

There is a twice-daily fast ferry service between the two islands. The crossing from Port-of-Spain to Scarborough takes about 2½ hours. Caribbean Airlines and Tobago Express also run a service linking the two islands. The journey takes 20 minutes and there are 13 flights every day.

US VIRGIN ISLANDS

By Car

Cars drive on the left, British-style, in the US Virgin Islands, despite the fact that most steering wheels are on the left, American-style.

A US driver's license is valid in the USVI. If your license is from another country and you wish to drive here, contact the USVI Division of Tourism in your home country before you go to see what arrangements need to be made. Vehicles available to rent

range from a standard saloon to an open jeep.

In St Thomas and St Croix, rental cars may be picked up at the airport. In St John hire vehicles are available in the main town of Cruz Bay. There are a variety of rental companies to choose from, which include:
St Croix: Avis, tel: 868-778 9355; Caribbean Jeep and Car Rental, tel: 868-773 4399.
St John: St John Car Rental, tel: 868-776 6103.
St Thomas: Budget, tel: 868-776 5774, 1-800 626 4516 (toll-free only when dialed in the country of origin); Dependable, tel: 868-774 2253, 1-800-522 3076.

By Taxi

Whether you arrive by plane, cruise ship or ferry, you will find taxis waiting for you at your point of entry to take you to your hotel or wherever else you want to go. Taxi fares are published by the Virgin Islands Taxi Association, but you should discuss the charge before getting in.

If taking a day trip to St John, an open-air taxi tour of the island is recommended. Taxi companies include:
St Croix: St Croix Taxi Association, tel: 868-778 1088.
St Thomas: VI Taxi Association, tel: 868-774 4550.

By Bus

There are regular services on St Thomas, St John and St Croix; look for the Vitran bus stop signs. On St Croix buses run every half hour between Christiansted and Frederiksted.

Inter-Island Links

There are airports on St Thomas and St Croix. You can fly between the US Virgin Islands on Cape Air (tel: 1-800 352 0714; www.flycapeair.com) or Seaborne Airlines (tel: 868-773 6442; www.seaborneairlines.com). There are regular ferry services from St Thomas (Charlotte Amalie) to St John, Tortola, and Virgin Gorda. Contact Ferry Transportation Services (tel: 868-776 6282). For further information about ferry services, visit www.vinow.com. Local airlines link the USVI with nearby islands including the British Virgin Islands, Anguilla, and St Martin. Airlines include:
American Eagle, tel: 800-433 7300.
LIAT, tel: 340-774 2313.

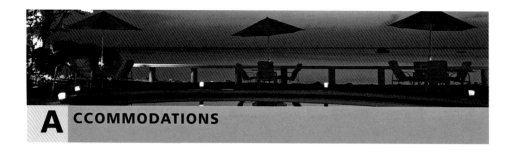

A CCOMMODATIONS

HOTELS, APARTMENTS, AND GUESTHOUSES

Choosing a Hotel

The range of accommodation choices in the Caribbean is as varied as the islands themselves, going from basic guesthouses and bed and breakfasts to ultra-exclusive eco-resorts and luxurious five-star hotels.

All-inclusive resort hotels are a popular choice; the appeal of not having to reach for your wallet every time you want a drink or a snack is strong, especially when you have children in tow. But there are two main disadvantages: you miss out on all the local food, drink, and color beyond the resort, and you do not put money back into the local community; most resort hotels are foreign-owned.

Self-catering apartments and villas are good value if you are traveling in a group or as a family; often you share the amenities such as a pool and restaurant with other visitors in the "village".

Prices can be considerably lower off-season (from May to late December), when it's worth negotiating for an upgrade or a price reduction. Bear in mind, however, that this is also hurricane season, so check the likelihood of your favored destination being affected *(see pages 365–6)*. Most major resort chains and some holiday packages offer hurricane protection; check before you book.

The internet is a useful tool for accommodation-hunting; try www.caribbeantravel.com. Alternatively, try the Caribbean tourist office in your home country *(see pages 373–5)*. As there is a variety of currencies in the islands, our price guide *(see opposite)* is given in US dollars.

ABOVE: Kura Hulanda Hotel, Curaçao.

ACCOMMODATIONS LISTINGS

ABC ISLANDS

High season in the Netherlands Antilles is from mid-December through mid-April. Apart from the hotels, there are numerous guesthouses and apartments, which are usually considerably less expensive (albeit more modest) than the hotels. The relevant tourist office can supply details. Some accommodations are only available for rent on a weekly or monthly basis.

August is Family Month in Bonaire, when many hotels, villas, and other accommodations and attractions offer free or reduced rates for children.

Aruba

Amsterdam Manor Resort
J.E. Irausquin Boulevard, 252
Eagle Beach
Tel: 297-527 1100
Fax: 297-527 1112
www.amsterdammanor.com
Elegant family hotel in the style of a Dutch canal house. Across from the beach. **$$**

Bucuti Beach Resort
L.G. Smith Boulevard, 55B
Eagle Beach
Tel: 297-583 1100
Fax: 297-582 5272
www.bucuti.com
Medium-sized luxury hotel complex in a top location; popular with Europeans. Children discouraged. **$$$**
Coconut Inn
Noord 31
Tel: 297-586 6288
Fax: 297-586 5433
www.coconutinn.com
Friendly bed-and-breakfast establishment with ·

comfortable rooms for self-caterers. **$–$$**
Hyatt Regency Aruba
J.E. Irausquin Boulevard, 85
Palm Beach
Tel: 297-586 1234
Fax: 297-586 1682
www.aruba.hyatt.com
Luxurious mini Las Vegas by the beach. Casino, aquatic fun park, an artificial ruined castle, and expensive boutiques. **$$$**
Manchebo Beach Resort and Spa
J.E. Irausquin Boulevard, 55
Eagle Beach

Tel: 297-582 3444
Fax: 297-583 2446
www.manchebo.com
Pleasant down-to-earth
hotel on a white-sand
beach. International
clientele. **$$–$$$**
Perle d'Or
Boegoeroei
Tel: 297-587 7710
www.perledoraruba.com
Student-oriented
apartments with air
conditioning, pool, and
lively bar. **$**
**Renaissance Aruba Resort
and Casino**
L.G. Smith Boulevard, 82
Oranjestad
Tel: 297-583 6000
Fax: 297-582 5317
www.marriott.com
Spacious, slightly
impersonal large luxury
hotel directly by the harbor,
with its own island and
marina. Shopping mall and
casino on site. **$$$**
Sea Breeze Apartments
5 Malohistraat, Pos Chiquito
Tel/Fax: 297-585 7140
www.sea-breezeappartments.com
Apartments set in tropical
gardens with pool. **$–$$**

Captain Don's Habitat
Kaya Gobernador N. Debrot 103,
Kralendijk
Tel: 599-717 8290
Fax: 599-717 8240
www.habitatdiveresorts.com
Built near the reef, this
hotel was established by
Bonaire's dive pioneer. Very
small beach. **$$–$$$**
Carib Inn
Boulevard J.A. Abraham 46,
Kralendijk

BELOW: the floral Carib Inn, Bonaire.

Tel: 599-717 8819
Fax: 599-717 5295
www.caribinn.com
Small family-owned hotel,
ideal for divers. **$$**
**Divi Flamingo Beach
Resort**
J.A. Abraham Boulevard 40,
Kralendijk
Tel: 599-717 8285
Fax: 599-717 8238
www.divibonaire.com
The oldest hotel on the
island; it also has the only
casino on Bonaire. **$$**
**Harbour Village Beach
Resort**
Kaya Gobernador N. Debrot 71,
Kralendijk
Tel: 599-717 7500
Fax: 599-717 7507
www.harbourvillage.com
Luxury resort with first-
class watersports facilities.
$$$
The Lizard Inn
Kaya America
Tel: 599-717 6877
www.lizardinnbonaire.com
Appealing to younger
travelers and divers, all
rooms have air conditioning
and fridge/kitchen, and
there's a courtyard with
hammocks. **$**
Plaza Resort
J.A. Abraham Boulevard 80,
Kralendijk
Tel: 599-717 2500
Fax: 599-717 7133
www.plazaresortbonaire.com
Villas and suites set in a
12-acre (5-hectare) garden.
There are a variety of land
and watersports available.
$$$
Sorobon Beach Resort
Lac Bay
Tel: 599-717 8080
Fax: 599-717 6080

ABOVE: Captain Don's Habitat, Bonaire.

www.sorobonbeachresort.com
Upscale naturist resort in a
remote location; relaxed
atmosphere. **$$–$$$**

Avila Beach Hotel
Penstraat 130, Willemstad
Tel: 5999-461 4377
Fax: 5999-461 1493
www.avilahotel.com
Tastefully extended former
governor's residence with
antique furniture and
colonial flair. **$$–$$$**
Buona Sera Inn
Kaya Godett 104, Pietermaai
Tel: 5999-465 8565
Fax: 5999-465 8344
Simple family-run
guesthouse in a renovated
colonial residence. **$**
**Curaçao Marriott Beach
Resort and Emerald Casino**
John F. Kennedy Boulevard,
Piscaderbaai
Tel: 5999-736 8800
Fax: 5999-462 7502
www.marriott.com
Pleasant luxury hotel with
Dutch-Caribbean
architecture. Sandy beach,
and perfect service. **$$$**
Habitat Curaçao
Coral Estate, Rif St Marie
Tel: 5999-864 8800
Fax: 5999-864 8464
www.habitatdiveresorts.com
Colorful complex with
practical cottages and
suites for divers. **$$–$$$**
Hilton Curaçao
John F. Kennedy Boulevard,
Piscaderbaai
Tel: 5999-462 5000
Fax: 5999-462 5846
www.hiltoncaribbean.com/curacao
Large American-style
resort. Attractive beach-
side location. **$$–$$$**

Kura Hulanda Hotel
Langestraat, Willemstad
Tel: 5999-434 7700
www.kurahulanda.com
Top-notch exclusive hotel
set in a maze of Dutch
village passageways with
numerous pools and
jacuzzis and the island's
best museum on site. **$$$**
**Lions Dive and Beach
Resort**
Dr Martin Luther King Boulevard
Tel: 5999-434 8888
www.lionsdive.com
Small beach-front resort
popular with divers.
$$–$$$
Hotel Park
Frederikstraat 84, Willemstad
Tel: 5999-462 3112
Friendly lodging in
Otrabanda. **$**
**Sunset Waters Beach
Hotel**
Santa Martha Bay
Tel: 5999-864 1233
www.sunsetwaters.com
Best all-inclusive option,
well out of town. Great
facilities, friendly, and
relaxed. **$$**
**SuperClubs Breezes
Curaçao Resort Spa
and Casino**
M.L. King Boulevard 8
Tel: 5999-738 7888
Fax: 5999-614 131
www.superclubs.com
Elegant beach hotel; the
social hub of the island.
$$–$$$

PRICE CATEGORIES

Price categories are for
a standard double room,
for one night:
$ = under US$100
$$ = US$100–200
$$$ = over US$200

ANGUILLA

Given Anguilla's size and population, the range of accommodations available around the island is astonishing. Further information is available through the Anguilla Department of Tourism *(see page 373).*

Altamer Resort
Shoal Bay West, Anguilla, BWI
Tel: 264-498 4000
Fax: 264-498 4010
www.altamer.com
Three luxurious five- to eight-bedroom beach-front villas with European-style furnishings, pool, and floodlit tennis court. **$$$**

Anguilla Great House
Rendezvous Bay, Anguilla, BWI
Tel: 264-497 6061
Fax: 264-497 6019
www.anguillagreathouse.com
A low-key hotel on a crescent of white sand. Colonial-style gingerbread cottages with fans in the rooms and beautiful gardens. **$$–$$$**

Arawak Beach Inn
Island Harbour, Anguilla, BWI
Mailing address: PO Box 1403, Anguilla, BWI

Tel: 264-497 4888
Fax: 264-497 4889
www.arawakbeach.com
Ocean-front rooms with balcony or terrace. A family-style restaurant features continental and Caribbean dishes. **$$–$$$**

Cap Juluca
Maunday's Bay, Anguilla, BWI
Mailing address: PO Box 240, Maunday's Bay, Leeward Islands, BWI
Tel: 264-497 6666
Fax: 264-497 6617
www.capjuluca.com
Luxury beach-front complex in tropical gardens. Aqua golf-driving range and three award-winning restaurants. **$$$**

CuisinArt Resort and Spa
Rendezvous Bay, Anguilla, BWI
Tel: 264-498 2000
Fax: 264-498 2010
www.cuisinartresort.com
Luxury suites and rooms. Guests enjoy fruit and vegetables from the hotel's hydroponic farm. **$$$**

Kú
Shoal Bay East, Anguilla, BWI
Tel: 264-497 2011
www.ku-anguilla.com
A beach hotel popular with

ABOVE: the ultra-stylish Cap Juluca.

a young, hip crowd. It has 27 minimalist-style suites, a dive shop, and spa. **$$–$$$**

Lloyd's B&B
Crocus Hill, Anguilla, BWI
Tel: 264-497 2351
Fax: 264-497 3028
www.lloyds.ai
Comfortable family-run bed and breakfast offering true Anguillan hospitality. Panoramic views. **$**

Malliouhana
Mead's Bay, Anguilla, BWI
Tel: 264-497 6111
Fax: 264-497 6011
www.malliouhana.com
This exclusive, jet-set haunt has huge rooms decorated with Haitian art. The cellar

has thousands of bottles of wine and the restaurant has a Michelin-awarded Parisian chef. **$$$**

La Palma
Sandy Ground, Anguilla, BWI
Tel: 264-497 3260/6620
Fax: 264-497 5381
A small, intimate inn with three apartments and a cottage, each with a kitchenette, fans, and TV. **$**

Shoal Bay Villas
Shoal Bay West, Anguilla, BWI
Tel: 264-497 2051
Fax: 264-497 3631
www.sbvillas.ai
Privately owned, individually decorated condos on the island's most gorgeous beach. **$$–$$$**

ANTIGUA AND BARBUDA

For budget-minded travelers, Antigua has plenty of villas, guesthouses, and apartments, some at weekly or monthly rates. On Barbuda there are three luxury hotels, and a few guesthouses.

Antigua

Admiral's Inn
Nelson's Dockyard, PO Box 713, St John's, Antigua, WI
Tel: 268-460 1027
Fax: 268-460 1153
www.admiralsantigua.com
Small, pretty hotel in a restored building at English Harbour. **$$–$$$**

Carlisle Bay
Old Road, Antigua, WI
Tel: 268-484 0002
www.carlisle-bay.com
Luxury hotel on a pretty bay with every comfort; style is minimalist. **$$$**

Coco's Antigua
Mount Prospect Estate, PO Box 2024, Valley Church, Antigua, WI
Tel: 268-460 2626
www.cocoshotel.com
Chattel-style wooden cottages overlooking Jolly Beach. Romantic and pretty. All-inclusive. **$$$**

Copper and Lumber Store
Nelson's Dockyard, PO Box 184, St John's, Antigua, WI
Tel: 268-460 1160
Fax: 268-460 1529
www.copperandlumberhotel.com
Hotel in a former warehouse directly on English Harbour. **$$–$$$**

Curtain Bluff Resort
Old Road, PO Box 288, St John's, Antigua, WI
Tel: 268-462 8400
Fax: 268-462 8409
www.curtainbluff.com
Exclusive hotel with all-inclusive prices and tropical garden. **$$$**

Falmouth Hillside Apartments
PO Box 713, St John's, Antigua, WI
Tel: 268-460 1027
Fax: 268-460 1534
Simple apartments near English Harbour with views of the harbor and the beach just minutes away. **$$**

Joe Mike's Hotel
PO Box 136, St John's, Antigua, WI
Tel: 268-462 1142
Basic but comfortable mid-town hotel, with restaurant, bar, and casino. **$**

Barbuda

The Beach House
Palmetto Point, Barbuda, WI
Tel: 268-725 4042
www.thebeachhousebarbuda.com
Upscale hotel on a glorious pink-sand beach, with 20 luxury suites. Price includes air transfers from Antigua. **$$$**

The Island Chalet
Codrington Village, Barbuda, WI
Tel: 268-773 0066
Three small rooms with shared kitchen and TV room. Run by a local family. **$**

K Club
Coco Beach, Barbuda, WI
Tel: 268-460 0300
Fax: 268-460 0305
www.kclubbarbuda.com
Exclusive resort hotel owned by a style-conscious Italian designer. Security is tight for celebrity guests. No children under 12 years old. **$$$**

PRICE CATEGORIES

Price categories are for a standard double room, for one night:
$ = under US$100
$$ = US$100–200
$$$ = over US$200

Most of Barbados's expensive hotels line the west coast, or Platinum coast, as it is known, and the lower-priced ones are generally located along the southeast coast. A few elegant, atmospheric old hotels are also dotted around the south and east coasts.

Renting a villa or an apartment is a good alternative to a hotel, especially for families with children, and many of them come with maid service. Several local real-estate agents provide a range of villas and apartments to rent, such as:
Altman Real Estate: St James, tel: 246-432 0840.
Atlantic Realty: Rockley, Christ Church, tel: 246-434 9283.
Bajan Services: St Peter, tel: 246-422 2618.

West Coast

Cobblers Cove
Road View, St Peter
Tel: 246-422 2291
Fax: 246-422 1460
www.cobblerscove.com
Elegant luxurious hotel built around a country house on a lovely white-sand beach. Friendly staff. Beautifully

furnished, spacious suites with ocean or garden view. **$$$**
Colony Club
Porters, St James
Tel: 246-422 2335
Fax: 246-422 0667
www.colonyclubhotel.com
A lovely hotel that suggests informal elegance, with tropical gardens, watersports, and fitness center included in the price. **$$$**
Coral Reef Club
Holetown
Tel: 246-422 2372
Fax: 246-422 1776
www.coralreefbarbados.com
Luxury accommodations including cottages set in beautiful gardens. **$$$**
Settlers Beach Villa Hotel
Holetown, St. James
Tel: 246-422 3052
Fax: 246-422 1937
www.settlersbeachhotel.com
Comfortable air-conditioned apartments and villas overlooking the beach. **$$–$$$**

South Coast

Accra Beach Hotel
Rockley, Christ Church
Tel: 246-435 8920
Fax: 246-435 6794
www.accrabeachhotel.com
Modern ocean-front hotel. Comfortable rooms with

ocean or island view. Wheelchair access. **$$**
Almond Casuarina Resort
Dover, Christ Church
Tel: 246-620 3600
Fax: 246-428 1970
www.almondresorts.com
Refurbished all-inclusive beach hotel in a beautiful palm garden. **$$$**
Divi Southwinds Beach Resort
St Lawrence Gap, Christ Church
Tel: 246-428 7181
Fax: 246-420 2673
www.divisouthwinds.com
Luxury complex with all mod cons close to lively nightlife in "The Gap".
$$–$$$
Magic Isle Beach Apartments
Rockley, Christ Church
Tel: 246-435 6760
www.magicislebarbados.com
Beach apartments, with sea view. Quiet. A choice of stores and eateries are within walking distance. **$$**
Sandy Bay Beach Club
Worthing, Christ Church
Tel: 246-435 8000
Fax: 246-435 8053
www.sandybaybeachclub.com
Pretty pink and blue hotel on a sandy beach. **$$$**
Silver Sands
Christ Church
Tel: 246-428 6001
Fax: 246-428 3758
www.silversandsbarbados.com

Off the beaten path, with basic rooms and apartments; good windsurfing. **$$**

Southeast and East Coast

The Crane Resort and Residences
St Philip
Tel: 246-423 6220
Fax: 246-423 5343
www.thecrane.com
A private residence resort built around a traditional hotel beautifully located on top of a cliff. A large and lengthy expansion program is in progress, which includes five-story blocks of time-share accommodations and a spa. **$$$**
New Edgewater
Bathsheba, St Joseph
Tel: 246-433 9900
Fax: 246-433 9902
www.newedgewater.com
Perched on a cliff overlooking the Atlantic Ocean. Some rooms with ocean views. **$**
Round House Inn
Bathsheba, St Joseph
Tel: 246-433 9678
Fax: 246-433 9079
www.roundhousebarbados.com
Cozy inn with friendly atmosphere, in a lovely country setting. The beach is a short drive away. **$–$$**

BELOW: preparing the beach-side barbecue at the Coral Reef Club.

THE BRITISH VIRGIN ISLANDS

It is easier to find a four- or five-star de luxe hotel on the BVI than a budget guesthouse. However, there are three camp grounds, one on Anegada, one at White Bay on Jost Van Dyke, and one at Brewer's Bay on Tortola.

All the hotels are surrounded by lovely gardens, and some of them have prize-winning chefs.

Tortola

Cane Garden Bay (Rhymer's) Beach
PO Box 570, Cane Garden Bay, Tortola, BVI
Tel: 284-495 4639
Fax: 284-495 4820
Simple, clean rooms close to the beach. Evening entertainment mainly at weekends. **$**

Fort Burt Hotel
PO Box 3380, Road Town, Tortola, BVI
Tel: 284-494 2587
Fax: 284-494 2002
The historic site of a fort tower has been converted into a romantic hotel with a pleasant restaurant overlooking Road Harbour. It is connected with Fort Burt Marina which has extensive yachting facilities. **$$–$$$**

Frenchman's Cay Hotel
PO Box 1054, West End, Tortola, BVI
Tel: 284-495 4844,
800-235 4077 (US)
Quiet resort overlooking Tortola's south coast, small beach. **$$–$$$**

Jolly Roger Inn
PO Box 21, West End, Tortola, BVI
Tel: 284-495 4559
Fax: 284-495 4184
www.jollyrogerbvi.com
Six colorfully decorated rooms, some with shared bathrooms. Friendly atmosphere. The restaurant serves creole cuisine and is popular with locals. Live music on weekends. **$**

Lambert Beach Resort
PO Box 534, East End, Tortola, BVI
Tel: 284-495 2877
Fax: 284-495 2876
www.lambertresort.com
Pleasantly furnished rooms in small villas scattered along the quiet, magnificent white beach of Elizabeth Bay with shady spots; pool, pretty gardens. Delicious Caribbean and international cuisine. Very friendly ambiance. **$$–$$$**

Long Bay Beach Resort
PO Box 433, Long Bay, Tortola, BVI
Tel: 284-495 4252,
800-858 4618 (US),
0870-160 9645 (UK)
www.longbay.com
Beautiful resort with elegantly furnished studios and villas. Good watersports facilities on a long white sandy beach; two restaurants. **$$–$$$**

Moorings – Mariner Inn
PO Box 139, Road Town, Tortola, BVI
Tel: 284-494 2332
Simple rooms with kitchenettes. There are dock-side moorings and facilities for bareboat charters. **$$**

Prospect Reef Resort
PO Box 104, Road Town, Tortola, BVI
Tel: 284-494 3311
Fax: 284-494 7600
www.prospectreefbvi.com
Large complex around a marina west of Road Town; good facilities for yachting and other watersports. **$$–$$$**

Sebastian's on the Beach
PO Box 441, Apple Bay, Tortola, BVI
Tel: 284-495 4212,
800-336 4870 (US)
www.sebastiansbvi.com
Friendly, informal place especially popular with young people and surfers, right on the beach. Caribbean dishes in the restaurant overlooking the bay. **$–$$**

Virgin Gorda

Biras Creek Hotel
PO Box 54, North Sound, Virgin Gorda, BVI
Tel: 284-494 3555, 877-883 0756 (US), 0800-883 0756 (UK)
Fax: 284-494 3557
www.biras.com
Thirty-two luxury suites in a secluded area with breath-taking views over the Atlantic and the North Sound. Excellent sports facilities plus a pool, quiet sandy beach, and renowned restaurant. **$$$**

ABOVE: a junior suite with views to die for, Little Dix Bay Hotel.

The Bitter End Yacht Club and Resort
PO Box 46, North Sound, Virgin Gorda, BVI
Tel: 284-494 2746,
800-872 2392 (US),
VHF Channel 16
www.beyc.com
Sailors' paradise, with a maritime atmosphere. Spacious rooms in villas spread over a hill with beautiful flowering plants. Windsurfing, sailing, and diving classes; pool and a sandy beach. The waterfront bar and restaurant has evening barbecues. **$$$**

Guavaberry Spring Bay
PO Box 20, Virgin Gorda, BVI
Tel: 284-495 5227
www.guavaberryspringbay.com
Lovely cottages located in beautiful gardens, close to The Baths. **$$–$$$**

Leverick Bay Resort Hotel
PO Box 63, The Valley, Virgin Gorda, BVI
Tel: 284-495 7421
Fax: 284-495 7367
www.leverickbay.com
Hill-side rooms on North Sound overlooking the sea and offshore islands. Lots of watersports at the marina, a spa on the property, and a range of other facilities including organized excursions. **$$**

Little Dix Bay Hotel
PO Box 70, 1150, Virgin Gorda, BVI
Tel: 284-495 5555
Fax: 284-495 5661
www.littledixbay.com
De luxe villas set in quiet, pretty gardens. The hotel offers some watersports activities and spa packages, as well as a water taxi to nearby beaches. International specialties. **$$$**

Outer Islands

Anegada Reef Hotel
Setting Point, Anegada, BVI
Tel: 284-495 8002
Fax: 284-495 9362
www.anegadareef.com
A perfect place to relax, only 18 rooms; mooring facilities, dive store. **$$–$$$**

Peter Island Resort
PO Box 211, Road Town, Tortola
Tel: 284-495 2000
www.peterisland.com
De luxe harbor and beach rooms and suites on a 1,000-acre (405-hectare) island. Exquisite restaurants next to the pool and under the palms of beautiful, secluded Deadman's Beach; walking/jogging and mountain-biking trails. Regular ferry service to and from Peter Island ferry dock, Tortola. **$$$**

White Bay Villas
White Bay, Jost Van Dyke, BVI
Tel: 410-571 6692,
800-778 8066 (US)
www.jostvandyke.com
Villas and cottages on one of the best beaches in the Caribbean, next to the Soggy Dollar bar with romantic candlelit dinners. **$$–$$$**

TRANSPORTATION · ACCOMMODATIONS · EATING OUT · ACTIVITIES · A–Z

DOMINICA

This selection of hotels offers a range of quality and price in different parts of the island. However, most accommodations are concentrated around Roseau.

Anchorage Hotel, Whale Watch and Dive Centre
PO Box 34, Roseau, Dominica, WI
Tel: 767-448 2638
Fax: 767-448 5680
www.anchoragehotel.dm
Long-established family-run hotel in Castle Comfort, just south of Roseau. **$$**

Beau Rive
PO Box 2424, Castle Bruce, Dominica, WI
Tel/Fax: 767-445 8992
www.beaurive.com
Situated on the rugged east coast, this stylish, small hotel is set in 3 acres (1.2 hectares) of tropical gardens. **$$**

Calibishie Lodges
Main Road, Calibishie, Dominica, WI
Tel/Fax: 767-445 8537
www.calbishie-lodges.com
Charming retreat in the northeast of the island, overlooking the Guadeloupe Channel. Near a beach; pool and a good restaurant on site. **$$**

The Carib Territory Guest House
Crayfish River, Dominica, WI
Tel: 767-445 7256
Owned by the current Carib chief, Charles Williams, this friendly guesthouse is in the heart of the Carib Territory and within striking distance of many of the island's natural treasures. **$**

Castle Comfort Lodge
PO Box 2253, Roseau, Dominica, WI
Tel: 767-448 2188
Fax: 767-448 6088
www.castlecomfortdivelodge.com
Traditional guesthouse on the seafront with restaurant, bar, and dive center. All-inclusive dive packages available. **$$**

Cherry Lodge Guesthouse
20 Kennedy Avenue, Roseau, Dominica, WI
Tel: 767-448 2366
Traditional building, with wooden veranda. **$**

D'Auchamps Cottage
PO Box 1889, Roseau, Dominica, WI
Tel: 767-448 3346
Self catering in a lovely old estate, with delightful garden trails. Near Trafalgar Village. **$$**

Evergreen Hotel
PO Box 309, Roseau, Dominica, WI
Tel: 767-448 3288
Fax: 767-448 6800
A family-run hotel on the seafront in Castle Comfort. **$$**

Fort Young Hotel
PO Box 519, Roseau, Dominica, WI
Tel: 767-448 5000
Fax: 767-448 5006
www.fortyounghotel.com
Dominica's smartest hotel, overlooking the sea, with mainly a business clientele. Swimming pool; pleasant atmosphere. **$$$**

Papillote Wilderness Retreat
PO Box 2287, Roseau, Dominica, WI
Tel: 767-448 2287
Fax: 767-448 2285
www.papillote.dm
Small secluded inn in the rainforest, with an acclaimed garden. Natural hot-water pools. Close to Trafalgar Falls. **$$**

Roxy's Mountain Lodge
PO Box 265, Roseau, Dominica, WI
Tel/Fax: 767-448 4845
Family-run guesthouse in the mountain village of Laudat, the starting point for the walk to the Boiling Lake. Popular with backpackers. **$**

3 Rivers
PO Box 1292, Rosalie, Dominica, WI
Tel: 767-446 1886
Fax: 1-510 578 6578
www.3riversdominica.com
Eco-friendly, east-coast lodge with cottages and a camp site, set in a lush rainforest valley and surrounded by pristine rivers. **$**

Zandoli Inn
PO Box 2099, Roseau, Dominica, WI
Tel: 767-446 3161
Fax: 767-446 3344
www.zandoli.com
On the south coast, this hotel is perched over the Martinique Channel. Delightful design and color schemes, surrounded by a developing arboretum. Plunge pool. **$$**

GRENADA

Most of Grenada's more expensive hotels are dotted around the southern tip of the island, especially along the Grand Anse beach. Guesthouses tend to be fairly rudimentary (as reflected in their prices), and there are also plenty of vacation apartments, designed for self-catering. Detailed information and price lists are available from Grenada Board of Tourism *(see page 374)*.

Blue Horizon Garden Resort
PO Box 41, Morne Rouge, St George's, Grenada, WI
Tel: 473-444 4316
Fax: 473-444 2815
www.grenadabluehorizons.com
Cottage-style buildings scattered around attractive grounds, with one of the island's best restaurants, La Belle Creole, attached. Residents are entitled to use the excellent beachside facilities of Spice Island Resort *(see page 330)*. **$$**

BELOW: pool bar of Le Phare Bleu, Grenada.

PRICE CATEGORIES

Price categories are for a standard double room, for one night:
$ = under US$100
$$ = US$100–200
$$$ = over US$200

The Calabash Hotel
PO Box 382, St George's,
Grenada, WI
Tel: 473-444 4334
Fax: 473-444 5050
www.calabashhotel.com
The most prestigious hotel
in Grenada, set in beautiful
gardens of calabash
(gourd) trees just outside
St George's at L'Anse aux
Epines. All the suites have
balconies and several have
their own private pools.
$$$

Coyaba Beach Resort
PO Box 336, Grand Anse,
St George's, Grenada, WI
Tel: 473-444 4129
Fax: 473-444 4808
www.coyaba.com
An attractive setting next to
Grand Anse beach.
Relatively small in
comparison to the less
intimate all-inclusives, but
with a good range of
facilities, including

watersports and a pool bar.
$$$

Grenadian
PO Box 893, Point Salines,
St George's, Grenada, WI
Tel: 473-444 3333
Fax: 473-444 1111
www.rexresorts.com
Grenada's biggest hotel,
refurbished after the
hurricane in 2004, has two
beaches and four
restaurants as well as 212
non-smoking rooms. Plenty
of amenities, but perhaps
lacking a little in intimacy.
$$$

Laluna
Morne Rouge, St George's,
Grenada, WI
Tel: 473-439 0001
Fax: 473-439 0600
www.laluna.com
Exclusive boutique beach
resort and spa. This
upscale cottage and villa
colony has tastefully
decorated accommodations

BELOW: bungalow bedroom, Le Phare Bleu, Grenada.

and genuinely friendly staff.
The perfect romantic
getaway for couples, with
stunning beach and ocean
views. All-inclusive and
European meal plans
available. **$$$**

Mount Cinnamon Grenada
PO Box 3858, St George's,
Grenada, WI
Tel: 473-439 0000
Fax: 473-439 8800
www.mountcinnamongrenada.com
New luxurious boutique
resort on the hillside
overlooking the
spectacular Grand Anse
beach. The Verandah
restaurant serves
delicious seafood. **$$$**

**Le Phare Bleu Resort
and Marina**
Petite Calivigny Bay,
Grenada, WI
Tel: 473-444 2400
www.lepharebleu.com
A new and idyllic beach-
front resort on the south
coast. The mix of dramatic
coastline and lush tropical
landscape makes it
perfect for those who like
both adventure and luxury.
$$$

La Sagesse Nature Centre
PO Box 44, St George's,
Grenada, WI
Tel: 473-444 6458
Fax: 473-444 6458
www.lasagesse.com
Located in St David's,
well away from the tourist
strip, this is a charmingly
informal and small
guesthouse, located on
a spectacular beach.
Good food and a relaxed
atmosphere in its beach-
side restaurant. It is
some distance from
St George's. **$$**

Spice Island Beach Resort
PO Box 6, Grand Anse,
St George's, Grenada, WI
Tel: 473-444 4258
Fax: 473-444 4807
www.spiceislandbeachresort.com
Beautiful beach location;
some rooms with private
pool. All-inclusive terms
available. Ideal for
watersports and swimming,
but not for visitors on a
tight budget. **$$$**

St Ann's Guesthouse
Paddock, St George's,
Grenada, WI
Tel: 473-440 2717
Fax: 473-444 3592
Inexpensive and very
friendly, a no-frills
guesthouse in a pleasant
suburban area. Excellent
food on request, but don't
expect air conditioning or a
pool. **$**

Carriacou

**Carriacou Grand
View Hotel**
Beausejour, Carriacou, WI
Tel/Fax: 473-443 6348
www.carriacougrandview.com
Small and relaxed
apartment hotel
overlooking the picturesque
Hillsborough harbor and
town. Good value for
money. **$**

Hotel Laurena
Middle St, Hillsborough
Carriacou, WI
Tel: 473-443 8759
Fax: 473-443 7356
www.hotellaurena.com
Carriacou's largest and
grandest hotel,
conveniently located just
a few minutes' walk from
the center of town and the
nearest beach. **$$**

GUADELOUPE

Accommodations on
Guadeloupe are varied with
lots of choice, from large
luxury resorts to small
family-run guesthouses and
camp grounds. Hotels are
mainly concentrated around
Gosier, Grand-Terre.

Grande-Terre

Auberge De La Vieille Tour
Montauban, Gosier,

Guadeloupe, FWI
Tel: 590-84 23 23
Fax: 590-84 33 43
www.accor.com
An authentic 18th-century
windmill with 104 de luxe
rooms set in a 7-acre (3-
hectare) tropical park
overlooking the sea. **$$$**

La Cocoteraie
Avenue de l'Europe, Saint François,
Guadeloupe, FWI
Tel: 590-88 79 81

Fax: 590-88 78 33
www.lacocoteraie.com
Pamper yourself in one of
52 suites set around an
immense swimming pool.
With two beaches, tennis
courts, and a golf course
nearby. **$$$**

Les Résidences Yucca
Pointes de la Verdure, Gosier,
Guadeloupe, FWI
Tel: 590-90 46 46
(La Créole Beach)

Fax: 590-90 46 66
www.deshotelsetdesiles.com
Part of a group under the
same management as the
upscale **La Créole Beach**,
this popular complex
features 100 spacious
rooms. Boutiques,
restaurants, nightlife, and
casino are within easy
walking distance. **$$**

Hotel La Toubana
Ste-Anne, Guadeloupe, FWI

Tel: 590-88 07 74
Fax: 590-88 38 90
www.deshotelsetdesiles.com
This hotel offers spectacular vistas of the south coast and offshore island. Surrounded by lush tropical gardens, its 32 intimate cottages feature kitchenettes, terraces, and views. Amenities include a gorgeous pool, a private beach, tennis, and a popular French and creole restaurant. **$$**

Basse-Terre

Domaine de la Pointe Batterie
Chemin de la Batterie, Deshaies
Guadeloupe, FWI
Tel: 590-28 57 03
Fax: 590-28 57 28
www.pointe-batterie.com
Villas and studios situated in a 12-acre (5-hectare) garden overlooking Deshaies Bay. Some villas

ABOVE: sun loungers by the pool at Hotel La Toubana.

have private pools overlooking the sea. **$$**
Le Jardin Malanga
L'Hermitage, Trois-Rivières,
Guadeloupe, FWI
Tel: 590-92 67 57

Fax: 590-92 67 58
www.deshotelsetdesiles.com
This unique, beautifully renovated 1927 estate house and its three spacious guesthouses are

set in lush gardens and have spectacular hill-side views of Les Saintes. A perfect location for exploring the famous Chutes du Carbet. **$$**

MARTINIQUE

Martinique has a wide selection of accommodations to choose from. From vast, upscale resort hotels, to the charming, smaller places which form the Relais Créoles group of hotels, to apartments and guesthouses.

Northern Martinique

Baie du Galion Resort
Presqu'île de la Caravelle Tartane,
97220 Trinité, Martinique, FWI
Tel: 0596-58 65 30
Fax: 0596-58 25 76
www.karibea.com
On Caravelle peninsula near many bays and coves; resort incorporates La Goelette Suites. **$–$$**
Habitation Lagrange
97225 Marigot, Martinique, FWI
Tel: 0596-53 60 60
Fax: 0596-53 50 58
www.habitationlagrange.com
Excellent facilities for all the family. **$$–$$$**
Marouba
Le Coin, 97221 Carbet,
Martinique, FWI
Tel: 0596-78 00 21

Fax: 0596-78 05 65
www.hotel-marouba.net
Situated in a tropical park on the edge of a beautiful volcanic sand beach.
$$–$$$

Central Martinique

Batelière
97233 Schoelcher, Martinique, FWI
Tel: 0596-61 49 49
Fax: 0596-61 70 57
Whether you're on holiday or on a business trip, this hotel offers a fine atmosphere for rest and leisure. **$$**
Frégate Bleue
Frégate Est, 97240 Le François,
Martinique, FWI
Tel: 0596-54 54 66
Fax: 0596-54 78 48
www.fregatebleue.com
Panoramic view of the Atlantic and the islets of Le François. **$$**
Lafayette
5 Rue Liberté, 9700 Fort-de-France, Martinique, FWI
Tel: 0596-73 80 50
Fax: 0596-60 97 75
Renovated, traditional small hotel overlooking La Savane. **$**

Hotel Plein Soleil
Pointe Thalémont, Mansarde
Rancé, 97240 Le François,
Martinique, FWI
Tel: 0596-38 07 77
Fax: 0596-65 58 13
www.pleinsoleil.mq
Small hotel off the beaten track. Excellent cuisine.
$$–$$$

Southern Martinique

Auberge de l'Anse Mitan
36 Rue des Anthuriums, Anse
Mitan, 97229 Les Trois-Ilets,
Martinique, FWI
Tel: 0596-66 01 12
Fax: 0596-66 01 05
www.auberge-ansemitan.com
Small family-run hotel with lovely gardens and views over the bay. **$**
Bakoua Sofitel
La Pointe du Bout, 97229 Les
Trois-Ilets, Martinique, FWI
Tel: 0596-66 02 02
Fax: 0596-66 00 41
www.sofitel.com
Four-star hotel on the beach with fabulous views.
$$$
Diamant les Bains
Bourg du Diamant 97223,

Le Diamant, Martinique, FWI
Tel: 0596-76 40 14
Fax: 0596-76 27 00
Email: diamantlesbains@martinique-hotels.com
Traditional hotel with self-contained bungalows in beach-side grounds. **$**
La Dunette
Bourg, 97227 Ste-Anne,
Martinique, FWI
Tel: 0596-76 73 90
Fax: 0596-76 76 05
www.ladunette.com
Situated not far from the prettiest beach on the island, La Dunette, overlooks the Diamond Rock. **$**
Le Manoir de Beauregard
Route des Salines, 97227
Ste-Anne, Martinique, FWI
Tel: 0596-76 73 40
Fax: 0596-76 93 24
A splendid 18th-century creole house. **$–$$**

PRICE CATEGORIES

Price categories are for a standard double room, for one night:
$ = under US$100
$$ = US$100–200
$$$ = over US$200

MONTSERRAT

A list of bed-and-breakfast accommodations, guesthouses, and self-contained self-catering apartments attached to private homes, as well as some villas with private pools in the north of the island, is available from the Montserrat Tourist Board *(see page 374)*. All hotels add a 7 percent service charge and a 10 percent government tax to the bill.

Erindell Villa Guesthouse
Gros Michel Drive, Woodlands, Montserrat, BWI
Tel: 664-491 3655
Small, friendly guesthouse near Woodlands Bay. Comfortable rooms, meal service, and swimming pool. **$**

Gingerbread Hill
P.O. Box 246
St. Peters, Montserrat, BWI
Tel: 664-491 5812
Family-run guesthouse

situated in tropical forest with stunning views in every direction. A range of accommodations are available, from bunkbeds to the luxurious "Heavenly Suite". Mountain biking and volcano tours can be arranged. **$–$$**

Grand View
PO Box 350, Baker Hill, Cudjoe Head, Montserrat, BWI
Tel: 664-491 2284
Bed and breakfast with lovely views of the north of the island. Eight rooms, and a pleasant restaurant and bar, which hosts the weekly meetings of the Rotary Club. Occasional jazz evenings sponsored by Family Radio in the same building. **$**

Montserrat Moments Inn and The Old Sugar Mill
Manjack Heights, Montserrat, BWI
Tel: 664-491 7707/8707
Fax: 664-491 3599
Email: flogriff@candw.ag

ABOVE: serene scene at Montserrat Moments.

A small inn with simple rooms and lovely location. Air conditioning, private bathroom and shared kitchenette. **$**

Tropical Mansion Suites Hotel
PO Box 404, St John's Main Road,

Sweeney's, Montserrat, BWI
Tel: 664-491 8767
Fax: 664-491 8275
www.tropicalmansion.com
Modern hotel with 18 rooms, a restaurant/bar, and swimming pool. All rooms have verandas. **$$**

ST-BARTHÉLEMY, SABA, AND ST EUSTATIUS

There is a variety of accommodations available on the islands. Large resorts are still quite unusual, but there are villas, apartments, guesthouses, and classy hotels.

As a general rule St-Barths lives up to its reputation as a tropical haven for the wealthy; this is the place for luxurious, intimate hotels. Saba on the other hand has a selection of small comfortable inns, with friendly service and a more personal feel; many offer diving packages to guests. Statia has a more limited choice with small, often family-run lodgings where you will be made to feel most welcome.

St-Barthélemy

Hostellerie des Trois Forces
Vitet 97133, St-Barthélemy, FWI
Tel: 590-27 61 25
Fax: 590-27 81 38
www.3forces.net

Simple cottages with kitchenettes, in a hillside setting. Superb hotel restaurant; pool. **$$**

St-Barths Beach Hotel
Grand Cul de Sac 97133, St-Barthélemy, FWI
Tel: 590-27 60 70
Fax: 590-27 75 57
www.saintbarthbeachhotel.com
A combination of rooms and bungalows near the sea. **$$$**

Hotel Les Mouettes
Lorient Beach, St-Barthélemy, FWI
Tel: 590-27 77 91
Fax: 590-27 68 19
Seven air-conditioned bungalows on Lorient Beach. Unpretentious and good value. **$$**

Le Toiny
Toiny 97133, St-Barthélemy, FWI
Tel: 590-27 88 88
Fax: 590-27 89 30
www.letoiny.com
Small, select plantation-style hotel on a lovely hillside. **$$$**

Le Village St-Jean
St-Jean 97133, St-Barthélemy, FWI
Tel: 590-27 61 39
Fax: 590-27 77 96

www.villagestjeanhotel.com
Good value on popular St Jean beach. **$$–$$$**

Saba

Ecolodge Rendez-Vous
Windwardside, Saba, NA
Tel: 599-416 3888
Get back to nature in one of these simple cottages from where you can enjoy the sounds of tree frogs and birds, without the distractions of phone or TV. **$$**

Queen's Gardens
The Bottom, Saba, NA
Tel: 599-416 3494
www.queensaba.com
A small upscale resort that offers all the facilities and comfort for a wonderful stay. Located on Troy Hill with views of the Caribbean Sea and the mountains. **$$$**

Scout's Place
Windwardside, Saba, NA
Tel: 599-416 2740
Fax: 599-416 2741
www.sabadivers.com
Simple rooms in a typical Saban house in the town

center. Dive packages a specialty. **$–$$**

St Eustatius

Golden Era Hotel
Lower Town, Oranjestad, St Eustatius, NA
Tel: 599-318 2455
Fax: 599-318 2445
Email: goldenerahotel@gmail.com
Slightly delapidated, but well-located on the seafront. Swimming pool and small restaurant. **$–$$**

King's Well
Oranje Bay (between Upper and Lower Town), St Eustatius, NA
Tel/Fax: 599-318 2538
www.kingswellstatia.com
Small and friendly. Simply decorated rooms, some with kitchenettes. Some rooms have a great ocean view. **$–$$**

Old Gin House
Lower Town, Oranjestad, St Eustatius, NA
Tel: 599-318 2319
Attractive seafront hotel built with bricks from an 18th-century cotton gin house. **$$–$$$**

ST KITTS AND NEVIS

Hotels in St Kitts and Nevis are generally small. No hotel is permitted to be more than three floors high, so the gleaming (and impersonal) towers that have sprouted on other islands are unknown here. A number of hotels are converted plantation houses and sugar mills.

Rates vary from the peak in winter (December to April) to the quieter summer season. St Kitts and Nevis also offer a number of apartments, condominiums, and cottages, many for rent at weekly rates. Full details are available from the tourist board and the Hotel and Tourism Association (www.stkittsnevishta.org; *see also page 374*).

St Kitts

Bird Rock Beach Hotel
PO Box 227, St Kitts, WI
Tel: 869-465 8914
Fax: 869-465 1675
www.birdrockbeach.com
Pleasant hotel set in tropical gardens overlooking the beach, with friendly service. **$$**

Frigate Bay Resort
PO Box 137, St Kitts, WI
Tel: 869-465 8935
Fax: 869-465 7050
www.frigatebay.com
Overlooking Frigate Bay and near the golf course. All guests receive free green fees. **$$$**

The Golden Lemon
Dieppe Bay, St Kitts, WI
Tel: 869-465 7260
Fax: 869-465 4019
www.goldenlemon.com
Beautifully restored 17th-century inn and villas, about 15 miles (24 km) from Basseterre. **$$$**

Ocean Terrace Inn
PO Box 65, St Kitts, WI
Tel: 869-465 2754
Fax: 869-465 1057
www.oceanterraceinn.com
Overlooking Basseterre Bay with splendid views of the southeast peninsula and Nevis. Comfortable rooms and water sports are on offer. **$$$**

Ottleys Plantation Inn
PO Box 345, St Kitts, WI
Tel: 869-465 7234
Fax: 869-465 4760
www.ottleys.com
This is a former 18th-century sugar estate, with the Great House and guest cottages in tropical gardens. The views are magnificent. **$$$**

Rawlins Plantation Inn
PO Box 340, St Kitts, WI
Tel: 869-465 6221
Fax: 869-465 4954
www.rawlinsplantation.com
A former plantation Great House which has been converted into an elegant inn with several cottages set in tropical gardens. **$$$**

Royal St Kitts Hotel and Casino
PO Box 406, Frigate Bay, St Kitts, WI
Tel: 869-465 8651
www.royalstkittshotel.com
Formerly known as Jack Tar Village, this hotel has reopened with new Kittitian cultural flair. The hotel's slogan "old times and new Limes" encapsulates the experience. **$$$**

St Kitts Marriott Resort
Frigate Bay, St Kitts, WI
Tel: 869-466 1200
Fax: 869-466 1201
www.stkittsmarriott.com
Luxury resort with a casino and golf course. It has beaches on both the Atlantic and Caribbean sides. **$$$**

Sugar Bay Club
Frigate Bay, St Kitts, WI
Tel: 869-465 8037/6745
www.eliteislandresorts.com
Comfy beach-front property. **$$$**

Timothy Beach Resort
Frigate Bay, St Kitts, WI
Tel: 869-465 8597
Fax: 869-466 7085
www.timothybeach.com
Beach-front rooms and studio accommodations; ideally located for nearby watersports facilities. **$$**

Nevis

Four Seasons Resort
PO Box 565, Nevis, WI
Tel: 869-469 1111
Fax: 869-469 1112
www.fourseasons.com
De luxe resort. Villas and suites with an ocean view or a view of the Robert Trent Jones golf course. **$$$**

Golden Rock Plantation Inn
PO Box 493, Nevis, WI
Tel: 869-469 3346
Fax: 869-469 2113
www.golden-rock.com
Romantic adventure holidays at this atmospheric inn. High in the hills surrounded by cottages. **$$$**

Hermitage Plantation Inn
Fig Tree Parish, St John, Nevis, WI
Tel: 869-469 3477
Fax: 869-469 2481
www.hermitagenevis.com
Historic plantation inn in the oldest wooden building in Nevis. **$$$**

Hurricane Cove Bungalows
Oualie Beach, Nevis, WI
Tel/Fax: 869-469 9462
www.hurricanecove.com
Wooden bungalows perched on a bluff overlooking Oualie Beach, with views of The Narrows and St Kitts. **$$-$$$**

Montpelier Plantation Inn
PO Box 474, St John, Nevis, WI
Tel: 869-469 3462
Fax: 869-469 2932
www.montpeliernevis.com
Charming Great House hotel set high in the mountains on a 60-acre (24-hectare) estate. **$$$**

Mount Nevis Hotel and Beach Club
Shaws Road, New Castle, Nevis, WI
Tel: 869-469 9373/4
www.mountnevishotel.com
From regular rooms to villas, this family-owned establishment has a homey feel. The view of St Kitts from here is sensational. **$$$**

Nisbet Plantation Beach Club
Newcastle, Nevis, WI
Tel: 869-469 9325
Fax: 869-469 9864
www.thereefs.com/nisbet
Lovely rooms and cottages on the site of an 18th-century ocean-side coconut plantation. **$$$**

Oualie Beach Hotel
Oualie Beach, Nevis, WI
Tel: 869-469 9735
www.oualiebeach.com
Gingerbread cottages on the beach. Very quaint and free spirited with a variety of water activities. **$$$**

Pinney's Beach Hotel
PO Box 61, Charlestown, Nevis, WI
Tel: 869-469 5207
Fax: 869-469 1088
E-mail: ntl@caribsurf.com
Comfortable hotel at the south end of the beach. Forty-four air-conditioned rooms. **$-$$**

BELOW: the Great House at Nisbet Plantation Beach Club.

PRICE CATEGORIES

Price categories are for a standard double room, for one night:
$ = under US$100
$$ = US$100–200
$$$ = over US$200

St Lucia

The sky's the limit here. St Lucia has a wide choice of accommodations, from vast all-inclusive resorts and luxury hotels, to intimate inns and guesthouses.

Anse Chastanet
PO Box 700, Soufrière, St Lucia, WI
Tel: 758-459 7000
Fax: 758-459 7700
www.ansechastanet.com
Luxurious hotel in a romantic location that is perfect for a honeymoon, on a picturesque hill side above a palm-fringed beach of dark grey volcanic sand. On the same property, new hotel **Jade Mountain** (www.jademountainstlucia.com) takes luxury to a new level; each "infinity pool sanctuary" in which you stay opens onto a stunning

BELOW: the Royal St Lucian Hotel.

view of the Pitons on one side. Comprehensive diving facilities. **$$$**

Balenbouche Estate
Laborie, St Lucia, WI
Tel: 758-455 1244
www.balenbouche.com
An enchanting and peaceful estate on the rural south coast, sprinkled with artifacts from its sugar producing days. Private cabins or rooms in the historic house, all surrounded by fruit trees. **$–$$**

Bay Gardens
PO Box 1892, Gros Islet, St Lucia, WI
Tel: 758-452 8060
Fax: 758-452 8059
www.baygardenshotel.com
Small award-winning hotel near Reduit Beach. Excellent value for money. **$$**

Discovery at Marigot Bay
At Marigot Bay Spa Resort and Marina Village, PO Box CP 5437, St Lucia, WI
Tel: 758-458 5300
Fax: 758-458 5299
www.discoverystlucia.com
Spacious suites with plunge pools overlooking Marigot Bay. Fine cuisine, spa, and dockside village. **$$–$$$**

Fond Doux Holiday Plantation
P.O. Box 250, Soufriere, St Lucia, WI
Tel: 758-459 7545
Fax: 758-459 7790
www.fonddouxestate.com
Cottages on a 250-year-old cocoa plantation. **$$**

Fox Grove Inn
Mon Repos Post Office, Micoud, St Lucia, WI
Tel/Fax: 758-455 3800
www.foxgroveinn.com
Pretty 12-room hotel on the Atlantic coast, well away from the bustle. Ideal for nature-loving vacationers. **$**

Glencastle Resort
Massade, Gros Islet, St Lucia, WI
Tel: 758-450 0833
Fax: 758-450 0837
www.glencastlehotel.com
Small, attractive resort in the hills above Rodney Bay. **$–$$**

Green Parrot Hotel
Castries, The Morne, St Lucia, WI
Tel: 758-452 3399/3167
Fax: 758-453 2272
Comfortable rooms in a practical hotel located about 3 miles (5 km) outside Castries. **$–$$**

Hummingbird Beach Resort
PO Box 280, Soufrière, St Lucia, WI
Tel: 758-459 7985
Fax: 758-459 7033
www.istlucia.co.uk
Friendly little beach hotel with attractively furnished rooms. **$$–$$$**

Ladera Resort
PO Box 225, Soufrière, St Lucia, WI
Tel: 758-459 7323/5448
Fax: 758-459 5156
www.ladera.com
Considered to be one of the best hotels in the Caribbean, this luxury resort situated between the Pitons, is perched 1,000 ft (305 meters) above Anse de Pitons. The beautiful suites have a plunge pool and an open wall. The property also has a renowned restaurant. **$$$**

Royal, St Lucian Hotel
Reduit Beach, Gros Islet, St Lucia, WI
Tel: 758-452 9999
Fax: 758-452 9639
www.rexresorts.com
Luxury resort with lots of amenities including a spa. **$$$**

The Still Plantation and Beach Resort
PO Box 246, Soufrière, St Lucia, WI
Tel: 758-459 5049/5179
Fax: 758-459 5091
www.thestillresort.com
Generously sized studios on the lovely beach at Soufrière. A resort on two sites: one on the beach and another on a plantation. **$–$$**

St Martin/Sint Maarten

Hotels on St Martin are expensive, especially during the peak winter season (December to April). During the summer season, many of the rates may be substantially discounted, often by 30–50 percent (due to the risk of hurricanes, *see page 324*). Both the French and Dutch sides have small guesthouses, as well as apartments and villas, which can be rented at weekly or monthly rates.

French Side

Hévèa
163 Boulevard de Grand Case
97150, St-Martin, FWI
Tel: 590-875 685
Intimate colonial-style inn with restaurant. **$–$$**

Royale Louisiana
Rue du Général-de-Gaulle, BP 476, Marigot 97055, St-Martin, FWI
Tel: 590-878 651
Fax: 590-879 649
This hotel is conveniently located in the heart of town. **$$**

La Samanna
Baie Longue, PO Box 4077, 97064, St-Martin, FWI
Tel: 590-876 400
Fax: 590-878 786
www.lasamanna.com
An exclusive resort, with excellent facilities. **$$$**

Dutch Side

Divi Little Bay Beach Resort
PO Box 961, Philipsburg, St Maarten, NA
Tel: 590-542 2333

Fax: 590-542 4336
www.divilittlebay.com
Large resort on Little Bay. **$$$**

Oyster Bay Beach Resort
10 Emerald Merit Road, PO Box 239, St Maarten, NA
Tel: 590-543 6040
Fax: 590-543 6695
www.oysterbaybeachresort.com
Expanded and renovated resort on the scenic east coast adjacent to Oyster Pond Marina. **$$–$$$**

Pasanggrahan Royal Inn
19 Front Street, Philipsburg, NA

Tel: 590-542 3588
Fax: 590-542 2885
www.pasanhotel.com
Small atmospheric colonial hotel with pool. The former governor's residence. **$–$$**

Sonesta Maho Beach Hotel
Maho Beach, Rhine Road, St Maarten, NA
Tel: 590-545 2115
Fax: 590-545 3180
www.mahobeach.com
Large resort, casino, restaurants, and shopping. **$$$**

Sunterra Royal Palm Beach Club
Airport Road, Simpson Bay, PO Box 431, St Maarten, NA
Tel: 590-544 3737
www.royalpalmbeachresort.com
Two- and three-bedroom suites on Simpson Bay. **$$**

La Vista Hotel
Billy Folly Road 53, Pelican Key, St Maarten, NA
Tel: 590-544 3005
Fax: 590-544 3010
www.lavistaresort.com
Small, Antillean-style resort on Pelican Point near the beach. **$$–$$$**

Westin St Maarten Dawn Beach
144 Oyster Pond Road, St Maarten, NA
Tel: 590-543 6700
Fax: 590-543 6004
www.westin.com
Large east-coast beach hotel with 317 rooms. It has the largest pool on the island, as well as a casino, nightclub, spa, and dive shop. **$$$**

ST VINCENT AND THE GRENADINES

Apart from St Vincent and Bequia, three islands are given over entirely to upscale vacation resort developments: Young Island, just 200 yds (183 meters) off St Vincent's shore, and Palm Island and Petit St Vincent in the Grenadines.

St Vincent

Beachcombers
PO Box 126, Villa, St Vincent, WI
Tel: 784-458 4283
Fax: 784-458 4385
www.beachcombershotel.com
Individual small cottages pleasantly sited on the beach at Villa. **$–$$**

Cobblestone Inn
PO Box 867, Upper Bay Street, Kingstown, St Vincent, WI
Tel: 784-456 1937
Fax: 784-456 1938
www.thecobblestoneinn.com
Housed in an early 19th-century arrowroot warehouse, this quiet town hotel has two restaurants, including one on the roof. **$$**

Haddon Hotel
McKies Hill, PO Box 144, Kingstown, St Vincent, WI
Tel: 784-456 1897
Fax: 784-456 2027
www.newhaddonhotel.com
Hill-side location on the outskirts of town, 10 minutes' drive from the beach; its air-conditioned rooms have TV and there are tennis courts. **$–$$**

Sunset Shores
PO Box 849, Villa, St Vincent, WI
Tel: 784-458 4411
Fax: 784-457 4800
www.sunsetshores.com

On the beach, with pool and air-conditioned rooms. A 10-minute drive from Kingstown. **$$**

Umbrella Beach Hotel
PO Box 530, Villa, St Vincent, WI
Tel: 784-458 4651
Fax: 784-457 4930
Basic but clean and quaint accommodations on the beach opposite Young Island. **$**

Young Island Resort
PO Box 211, St Vincent, WI
Tel: 784-458 4826,
800-223 1108 (toll-free, US)
Fax: 784-457 4567
www.youngisland.com
Exclusive, luxurious resort on its own small private island. **$$$**

Bequia

Bequia Beach Hotel
Friendship Bay, Bequia, St Vincent and the Grenadines, WI
Tel: 784-458 1600
Fax: 784-458 1700
www.bequiabeachclub.com
Colonial-style rooms, suites, and villas in pleasant surroundings. Private beach, swimming pool, beach bar and restaurant. **$$**

Frangipani
Admiralty Bay, Bequia, St Vincent and the Grenadines, WI
Tel: 784-458 3255
Fax: 784-458 3824
Simple accommodations in a seafaring setting, housed in an old chandlery. The rooms are tastefully decorated and the hotel bar is a popular place to stop for a drink. **$–$$**

Gingerbread Hotel
PO Box 191, Bequia, St Vincent and the Grenadines, WI
Tel: 784-458 3800
Fax: 784-458 3907
www.gingerbreadhotel.com
One-room apartments with kitchen and bathroom. Restaurant, bar, and friendly owners. **$$**

Other Grenadines Islands

Firefly Inn
Mustique, St Vincent and the Grenadines, WI
Tel: 784-488 8414
Fax: 784-488 8514
www.mustiquefirefly.com
Tiny informal, but elegant hotel, in a lovely position on Mustique. Book well in advance. **$$$**

Palm Island Beach Club
Palm Island, St Vincent and the Grenadines, WI
Tel: 784-458 8824
Fax: 784-458 8804
www.palmislandresorts.com
Exclusive, all-inclusive type of resort on a private island surrounded by white sand beach. Watersports, sailing. **$$$**

Petit St Vincent (PSV) Resort
Petit St Vincent, St Vincent and the Grenadines, WI
Tel: 784-458 8801
Fax: 784-458 8428
www.psvresort.com
A delightful resort hideaway where peace and privacy are the order of the day. **$$$**

Tamarind Beach Hotel
Canouan, St Vincent and the Grenadines, WI
Tel: 784-458-8044
Fax: 784-458-8851
www.tamarindbeachhotel.com
Attractive beach-front rooms with balconies in a relaxing setting in Grand Bay. There is an on-site PADI dive center and a restaurant serving Italian and international cuisine. **$$$**

BELOW: interior style at the Firefly Inn, Mustique.

TRINIDAD AND TOBAGO

The two islands can offer a range of accommodations to suit every budget and taste, from international hotel chains and luxury get-away-from-it-all resorts to simple private establishments. For most visitors, Trinidad is the island to party, while Tobago is an ideal place to kick back and relax.

Trinidad

Alicia's House
7 Coblentz Gardens, St Ann's, Port-of-Spain, Trinidad
Tel: 868-623 2802
Fax: 868-623 8560
www.aliciashouse.com
Attractive guesthouse in a residential suburb. $–$$

Asa Wright Nature Centre and Lodge
Blanchisseuse Road, Arima, Trinidad
Tel: 868-667 4655
Fax: 868-667 0493
www.asawright.org
Inn for nature lovers in an isolated location in the Northern Range. Simple rooms and a beautiful tropical garden. Full board only. $$$

La Calypso
46 French Street, Woodbrook, Trinidad
Tel: 868-622 4077
Fax: 868-623 6895
Friendly guesthouse with good service. $

Crowne Plaza Hotel
Wrightson Road, Port-of-Spain, Trinidad
Tel: 868-625 3366
Fax: 868-625 4166
www.ichotelsgroup.com
Modern, comfortable city hotel directly by the harbor, with good views from the restaurant. $$$

Le Grande Almandier
Paria Main Road, Grande Riviere, Trinidad
Tel: 868-670 1013
Fax: 868-670 2294
www.legrandealmandier.com
Friendly, laid-back hotel on the beach at Trinidad's premiere turtle-watching spot. Great restaurant. $–$$

Hilton Trinidad
Lady Young Road, Belmont, Port-of-Spain, Trinidad
Tel: 868-624 3211
Fax: 868-624 4485
www.hiltoncaribbean.com
A good high-end option: central location, plenty of amenities, and live shows in the evening. $$$

Johnson's
16 Buller Street, Woodbrook, Port-of-Spain, Trinidad
Tel: 868-628 7553
Fax: 868-628 7553
Friendly bed-and-breakfast accommodations, central location, and relatively quiet. $–$$

Kapok Hotel
16 Cotton Hill, St Clair, Port-of-Spain, Trinidad

Tel: 868-622 5765
Fax: 868-622 9677
www.kapokhotel.com
Attractive city hotel with two renowned restaurants and great artwork throughout. $$$

Laguna Mar Beach and Nature Hotel
Paria Main Road, Blanchisseuse, Trinidad
Tel: 868-628 3731/669 2963
Fax: 868-628 3737
www.lagunamar.com
Small guesthouse close to the beach and Marianne River. $$

Mount Brasso Estate
Brasso Seco, Paria, Trinidad
Tel: 868-676 7057
Fax: 868-625 8781
www.watervilleestate.com
In the heart of the Northern Range Mountains, this option is perfect for hiking and bird-watching. $–$$

The Normandie Hotel
10 Nook Avenue, St Ann's, Port-of-Spain, Trinidad
Tel: 868-624 1181/2/3/4
Fax: 868-624 0108
www.normandiett.com
Practical, impersonal, and fairly quiet. Swimming pool and Italian restaurant. $$–$$$

Schultzi's
35 Fitt Street, Port-of-Spain, Trinidad
Tel: 868-622 7521
Simple family guesthouse in a central location with a kitchen for self-caterers. $

Tobago

Arnos Vale Hotel
P.O. Box 208, Scarborough, Tobago
Tel: 868-639 2881
Fax: 868-639 4629
www.arnosvalehotel.com
Picturesque, quiet location surrounded by luxuriant vegetation. Small beach. The breakfast buffet is a rendezvous for exotic birds. $$$

Blue Waters Inn
Batteaux Bay, Speyside, Tobago
Tel: 868-660 4341
Fax: 868-660 5195
www.bluewatersinn.com
Comfortable hotel favored by divers in a remote location on the northwest coast. $$$

Coco Reef Hotel
Coconut Bay, Crown Point, Tobago
Tel: 868-639 8571
Fax: 868-639 8574
www.cocoreef.com
Luxury hotel with a small beach and tastefully decorated rooms. Popular with German visitors. $$$

Le Grand Courlan Spa Resort
Stonehaven Bay, Black Rock, Tobago
Tel: 868-639 9667
Fax: 868-639 9292
www.legrandcourlan-resort.com
New, rather impersonal luxury hotel with its own spa and numerous sports facilities. $$$

Kariwak Village
Crown Point, Tobago
Tel: 868-639 8442
Fax: 868-639 8441
www.kariwak.com
Small village of simple, round huts in a lovely tropical garden. A short walk to the beach and live entertainment on the weekend. $$–$$$

Man-O-War Bay Cottages
Man-O-War Bay, Charlotteville, Tobago
Tel: 868-660 4327
www.man-o-warbaycottages.com
Simple but beautifully peaceful cottages with one to three bedrooms, set in colorful gardens. $

Miller's Guesthouse
Bucco, Tobago
Tel: 868-660 8371
www.millers-guesthouse.tripod.com
Simple dormitories and

BELOW: the pool at Rex Turtle Beach Hotel.

beach-side rooms in a great location. **$**

Mount Irvine Bay Hotel and Golf Club0
PO Box 222, Scarborough, Tobago
Tel: 868-639 8871
Fax: 868-639 8800
www.mtirvine.com
Discreet and elegant hotel

with a British air. Golf course surrounded by palm trees on the site of an old sugar mill. **$$$**

Rex Turtle Beach Hotel
Great Courland Bay, Scarborough, Tobago
Tel: 868-639 2851
Fax: 868-639 1495
www.rexcaribbean.com

Pleasant vacation hotel on a beautiful wide beach. Mostly English clientele. **$$**

Richmond Great House
Belle Garden, Tobago
Tel/Fax: 868-660 4444
www.richmondgreathouse.com
Accommodations in an old plantation house on a hill

above Windward Road. Airy, quiet rooms. **$$–$$$**

Vanguard Hotel
Lowlands, Tobago
Tel: 868-660 8500
Fax: 868-660 8503
Formerly the Tobago Hilton, this luxury hotel includes beach-front pool and 18-hole golf course. **$$$**

THE US VIRGIN ISLANDS

ABOVE: the ultimate in luxury at the Ritz Carlton, St Thomas.

Rates for hotels and guest-houses can usually be quoted inclusive or exclusive of meals. Apartments, condominiums, cottages, villas, and camp grounds are also available.

St Thomas

Bolongo Bay Beach Club
7150 Bolongo, St Thomas, USVI 00802
Tel: 800-524 4746
Fax: 340-775 3208
www.bolongobay.com
All-inclusive resort hotel with a range of accommodations, food, and facilities. **$$–$$$**

Elysian Beach Resort
6800 Estate Nazareth, St Thomas, USV 00082
Tel: 800-347 8182
Fax: 340-776 0910
www.elysianbeachresort.net
A superb pool plus excellent water sports and fitness center. **$$$**

Island View Mountain Inn
PO Box 301903, St Thomas, USVI 00803-1903
Tel: 340-774 4270
Fax: 340-774 6167
www.islandviewstthomas.com
Fantastic views from this guesthouse in a beautiful location on Crown Mountain. **$–$$**

Mafolie
7091 Estate Mafolie, St Thomas, USVI 00802
Tel: 340-774 2790
Fax: 340-774 4091
www.mafolie.com
A family-run hotel with splendid harbor view. Free shuttle to Magen's Bay beach, or stay by the pleasant hotel pool. **$–$$**

Ritz Carlton
6900 Great Bay, St Thomas, USVI 00802
Tel: 340-775 3333
Fax: 340-775 4444
www.ritzcarlton.com
A luxury hotel, which was the subject of a US$40m

makeover in 2006, situated in a magnificent setting. Superb restaurant, pool, beach and diving facilities on East Point facing St John. **$$$**

Wyndham Sugar Bay Resort and Spa
6500 Estate Smith Bay, St Thomas, USVI 00802
Tel: 340-777 7100
Fax: 340-777 7200
www.wyndham.com
Excellent facilities for all the family. All-inclusive prices. **$$$**

St Croix

Hotel Caravelle
44a Queen Cross Street, Christiansted, St Croix, USVI 00820
Tel: 340-773 0687
Fax: 340-778 7004
www.hotelcaravelle.com
Traditional hotel with its own jetty at the old harbor in the old town. **$$**

Chenay Bay Beach Resort
5000 Estate Chenay Bay, Route 82, East End Quarter, Christiansted, St Croix, USVI 00824
Tel: 340-773 2918
Fax: 340-773 6665
www.chenaybay.com
Pretty bungalows built into a slope by the sea and set within a vast wildlife park. **$$$**

Pink Fancy
27 Prince Street, Christiansted, St Croix, USVI 00820
Tel: 340-773 8460
Fax: 340-773 6448
www.pinkfancy.com
Old Danish town villa with a fascinating past, originally owned by an ex-showgirl. Decorated with glitzy showbiz memorabilia and interesting antiques. **$$**

Tamarind Reef Hotel and Green Cay Marina
5001 Tamarind Reef, Christiansted,

St Croix, USVI 00820
Tel: 340-773 4455
Fax: 340-773 3989
www.tamarindreefhotel.com
West-Indian-style hotel, fronting the beach. Many of the rooms have kitchenettes. Watersports facilities on offer. **$$–$$$**

St John

Caneel Bay
PO Box 720, St John, USVI 00831-0720
Tel: 340-776 6111
Fax: 340-693 8280
www.caneelbay.com
Resort hotel built in the 1950s by Laurance Rockefeller, and now a Rosewood Resort, located on a peninsula right in the heart of the national park. Very quiet. Seven beaches. **$$$**

Gallows Point Resort
PO Box 58, Cruz Bay, St John, USVI 00831
Tel: 340-776 6434
Fax: 340-776 6520
www.gallowspointresort.com
Neat wooden houses with fully equipped apartments. **$$$**

The Westin St John
PO Box 8310, Great Cruz Bay, St John, USVI 00831
Tel: 340-693 8000
Fax: 340-779 4985
www.westinresortstjohn.com
Resort hotel with huge pool, tennis courts, spa, and extensive grounds. **$$$**

PRICE CATEGORIES

Price categories are for a standard double room, for one night:
$ = under US$100
$$ = US$100–200
$$$ = over US$200

E ATING OUT

RECOMMENDED RESTAURANTS, CAFES, AND BARS

WHAT TO EAT

ABC Islands

Varied and cosmopolitan, on all three islands you will find Indonesian, Chinese, French, Spanish, and Italian restaurants. Aruba's choice tends to cater to the high-end tourism industry with prices to match, whereas Bonaire has more of a local feel and also offers perhaps the best variety. Curaçao also has a good assortment of high-end to budget dining options.

On local menus you will find iguana soup (fish soup made with coconut), goat stew, Dutch-influenced dishes mixing meats with Gouda cheese, spices, and tomato, and a full range of fresh fish dishes. Cornmeal *(funchi)* is often served as a side dish, and snacks like *pastechi* and *krokets* are available at all hours.

Anguilla

As you might expect on a boatbuilding, seafaring island, locally caught seafood is Anguilla's specialty. Conch, spring lobsters, whelks, and tropical fish may be found, prepared in either Continental or the local creole style. Barbecues – of fish, or of the island's ever-popular chicken and goat – are another distinctive aspect of local cuisine.

Barbecues often take place on the beach, and the fishing visitor who charters a boat can often make arrangements to cook the day's catch on the sand by the sea.

Antigua and Barbuda

There are some delicious local dishes worth trying, such as pepperpot, conch, and chicken, and rice and peas. Alternatively, visitors can taste some of Antigua's international cuisine: French, Italian, and Vietnamese cooking are among the options.

Barbados

Barbados has restaurants featuring everything from traditional Bajan cuisine to Chinese, Italian, and American fast food. Most hotels and beach bars serve up flying fish cutters (breaded flying fish in a bun) for lunch. Other specialties are dolphin (dorado), red snapper, hot saltfish cakes, pickled breadfruit and pepperpot, often accompanied by rice and peas, macaroni pie, plantain, sweet potato, or yam. Among the usual fast food chains, look out for the *roti* shop – serving a savory pocket of curried chicken, prawn, beef, or potato.

British Virgin Islands

The cuisine of the BVI includes touches of American and Continental cooking, in addition to such typically Caribbean creations as *funchi* (cornmeal pudding) and *roti* (curry wrapped in a thin chapati). Seafood and tropical fruits and vegetables are fresh and plentiful. Cocktails as starters are very tempting.

Dominica

Apart from the hotels and restaurants listed below, all of which serve creole food using home-grown products, there are many little snack bars all over the island that may (or may not) produce some excellent meals. If you enjoy local Caribbean food, try them. Fresh fruit juices (made with tamarind, guava, sorrel, grapefruit, and so on) are among the delights of Dominican cuisine, along with specialties such as mountain chicken (a large frog endemic to Dominica), crab backs, and *titiri* (fritters made of tiny fish).

Other more "down-home" Dominican dishes include ingredients like saltfish, couscous, ground provisions (*dasheen*, yam, sweet potato), and *calaloo* (young shoots of the *dasheen*) soup. Fruit and vegetables are plentiful: visit the market to see the wonderful range of produce.

Grenada

Grenada's mixed colonial past has endowed the island with an interesting mix of British and French influences. Inevitably, the emphasis tends to be on seafood, but there are many local delicacies worth sampling. Callaloo soup (made from dasheen leaves, rather like spinach) is excellent, as are traditional pepperpot (a stew of almost every possible ingredient), and *lambi* (conch). Exotic game sometimes appears on tourist menus, although some may prefer not to experiment with armadillo, iguana, or manicou. Spices, especially nutmeg, are another favorite, delicious in rum punches.

Guadeloupe

Guadeloupe's cuisine mirrors its many cultures. The local creole specialties combine the finesse of French cuisine, the spice of African cookery, and the exoticism of East Indian and Southeast Asian recipes. Fresh seafood appears on most menus. Other specialties are: shellfish, smoked fish, stuffed land crabs, stewed conch, and a variety of curry dishes.

Guadeloupe is considered one of the true culinary capitals of the Caribbean, with some 200 restaurants recommended by the tourist office, some in hotels and others in lovely settings by the sea.

For a comprehensive listing of Guadeloupe's restaurants see www.antillesresto.com.

Martinique

Martinicans love to eat well and part of Martinique's French feeling is its celebration of good food. Familiar French dishes are given an unfamiliar twist by the use of tropical fruits, vegetables, and seafood. In addition to French-inspired cooking, visitors will also find plenty of spicy Caribbean specialties. Restaurant hours are usually from noon–3pm and 7–10pm. Most restaurants accept major credit cards.

Several beaches have what look like snack bars but which are in fact restaurants serving a delicious set menu of local specialties, such as *accras* (deep-fried fishcakes), direct from a caravan or hut, with awnings over plastic tables and chairs.

Montserrat

Most restaurants and snack bars in the north are small, informal places, many set up by people relocated from the south. Some are only open for breakfast and lunch, others are no more than road-side stands serving excellent rice and peas, fish, chicken, and the like. **Annie Morgan's** in St John's, (open Friday and Saturday), is famous for its goat water (Montserrat's goat stew). The **Emerald Café** at Sweeney's has a more extensive menu than most.

St-Barthélemy, Saba, and St Eustatius

On Saba and St Eustatius, the restaurants tend to offer international food like burgers and pizzas. The food on St-Barths is as cosmopolitan as the jet-setters it attracts; French-creole cuisine predominates but you'll also find everything from pizza to sushi.

St Kitts and Nevis

St Kitts and Nevis have many restaurants specializing in Caribbean, creole, Italian, Indian, and Chinese fare. In addition to the Caribbean's ubiquitous fresh seafood, perhaps the most distinctive feature of St

Kitts and Nevis cuisine is the abundance of fresh vegetables from the islands' volcanic soil.

Tropical produce such as bread-fruit joins items such as eggplant (aubergine), sweet potatoes, and okra on island plates.

St Lucia

St Lucia's cuisine reflects and celebrates its diverse past – from French creole dishes such as *bouillon* (meat or fish cooked in a peppery, broth-like tomato sauce) to more traditional West Indian favorites like saltfish with ground provisions (dasheen, cassava), and even curries and filled Indian *roti* wraps. Other highlights include pumpkin soup, flying fish, pepperpot (a rich and dark meat stew made with cassareep oil), conch, and *tablette* (a sweetmeat made of coconut).

St Vincent and the Grenadines

Spicy Caribbean cuisine predominates with continental and American fare also available. A wide variety of exotic fruits and vegetables, along with an abundance of succulent lobster and other fresh seafood, enrich St Vincent's cooking. Try something unusual – barbecued goat or fresh shark, for example.

St Martin/Sint Maarten

St Martin's restaurants reflect the various cultures which have come together on the island. On both sides, traditional French cooking and spicy Caribbean cuisine are available. Sometimes the two rub off on one another, as when a familiar French recipe is prepared with very un-Gallic tropical fruits. On the Dutch side, dining options include Dutch favorites such as pea soup and sausages. An unexpected dining experience is offered by restaurants serving *rijstaffel*, an Indonesian meal as huge and complex as a Javanese *gamelan*. It comes to St Martin via the Dutch, who previously counted Indonesia among their colonies. There are many notable restaurants in St Martin, particularly in Grand Case.

Trinidad and Tobago

In no other Caribbean country will you find such a colorful mix of origins as on Trinidad and Tobago. The culinary traditions of the African, Indian, Chinese, French, and Latin American settlers have all contributed to the wide variety of cuisine here. It is the

ABOVE: the place for ice-cold cocktails.

home of the Caribbean Indian filled *roti* wrap, the moreish Trinidadian lunch-snack containing curried mango, potato, and pumpkin with your choice of meats or seafood. Other specialties include *pelau* (caramelised meat cooked down with rice in coconut milk); corn, meat, or fish soups; *bake and shark* (succulent fried shark meat served in a sandwich with salads and tamarind sauce); South-American *pasteles*; delicious curried duck; as well as fresh seafood served in a variety of ways.

Eating out here tends to range from budget through to a good range of high-end international options, from Thai to sushi to French and Italian.

US Virgin Islands

The multinational, multiethnic history of the USVI, combined with its tropical location and international reputation as a vacation spot, have contributed to a rich cuisine on the islands. Locally produced fruits and vegetables and fresh seafood provide some of the raw materials for island cooks, who create anything from bullfoot soup (what it sounds like) and *funchi* (cornmeal pudding) to French, Italian, and Chinese food.

Creole Cuisine

A few examples:
Crabes farcis: stuffed crabshell with a spicy crab-based stuffing.
Blaff de poissons ou crustacées (poached fish or shellfish): the ingredients are poached in water containing thyme, parsley, laurel, local chives, and pimento.
Féroce: a mixture made from crushed avocado, codfish, and cassava flour with a touch of hot pepper pimento.
Try a **Ti-Punch** apéritif before a meal and a dark rum afterwards.

ABC ISLANDS

Aruba

Charlie's Bar
Zeppenfeldt Straat 56, San Nicolas
Tel: 297-584 5086
A refreshingly chaotic pub with unique flair and good, unpretentious food. **$$**

Chez Mathilde
Havenstraat 23, Oranjestad
Tel: 297-583 4968
French cuisine in an attractively renovated house dating from the 19th century. **$$$**

Papiamento
Washington 61, Oranjestad
Tel: 297-586 4544
European and local cuisine in an old villa. **$$$**

Que Pasa
Wilhelminastraat 18, Oranjestad
Tel: 297-583 4888
Lively bar and restaurant with an imaginative international menu. **$$**

Bonaire

Bistro de Paris
Kaya Gob. N. Debrot, Kralendijk
Tel: 599-717 7070
Large portions of top-notch French cuisine. French owner and chef. **$$**

Croccantino
Kaya Grandi 48, Kralendijk
Tel: 599-717 5025
Italian dining in an historic town house. **$$$**

Maiky Snack
Kaminda New Amsterdam 30
Tel: 599-567 0078
Local dishes in a rural spot. **$**

The Rose Inn
Kaya Guyaba 4, Rincon
Tel: 599-717 6420
Tree-shaded gourmet creole dining. **$**

Zeezicht
Kaya J.N.E. Craane 12, Kralendijk
Tel: 599-717 8434
Bonaire's oldest restaurant, with a lovely terrace by the harbor. Good fish dishes. **$$**

Curaçao

Belle Terrace
Avila Beach Hotel, Penstraat 130, Willemstad
Tel: 5999-461 4377
Scandinavian and local food in an elegant setting. **$$–$$$**

Bistro Le Clochard
Riffort, Otrabanda
Tel: 5999-462 5666

ABOVE: dining out at the Kura Hulanda Hotel *(see page 325).*

Gourmet cuisine with French-Swiss accents. Delightful location on the Sint Anabaai. **$$$**

Jaanchie's
Westpunt 15
Tel: 5999-864 0126
A congenial garden restaurant famous for its fish soup among other seafood specialties. **$$**

Rijsttafel
Mercuriusstraat 13, Willemstad
Tel: 5999-461 2606
Excellent Javanese cuisine. **$$**

ANGUILLA

Altamer
Shoal Bay West
Tel: 264-498 4040
Parisian chef with 40 years' experience at Maxim's Restaurant. First-class French-based menu. **$$$**

The English Rose
Main Street, The Valley
Tel: 264-497 5353
A restaurant pub that's easy on the wallet and exciting on the palate. Appetizers include fried calamari, buffalo wings, and jerk chicken caesar salad. **$**

Deon's Overlook
Back Street, South Hill
Tel: 264-497 4488
Creative menu in tasteful surroundings. Wonderful views. **$$**

George's at Cap Juluca
Maunday's Bay
Tel: 264-497 6666
An expensive restaurant in an idyllic location, serving Caribbean and Mediterranean dishes. Its executive chef has won competitions in both the Caribbean and the US. Herbs are fresh from the hotel garden. **$$$**

Johnno's
Sandy Ground
Tel: 264-497 2728
Classic Caribbean beach bar with a seafood and barbecue restaurant; this is a popular hangout, with a great atmosphere and live music some evenings and every weekend. **$**

Malliouhana
Meads Bay
Tel: 264-497 6111
Internationally acclaimed for its excellent French-creole cuisine. **$$$**

Mango's Seaside Grill
Barnes Bay
Tel: 264-497 6479
Candlelight, soft music, and dishes include conch chowder, lobster cakes, and grilled snapper. **$$**

Oliver's Seaside Grill
Long Bay
Tel: 264-497 8780
A beach-side restaurant with an Anguillian rock oven used to create a selection of dishes, combining Caribbean and European flavors. **$$$**

Scilly Cay
Scilly Cay, Island Harbour
Tel: 264-497 5123
Lovely setting on its own tiny islet surrounded by coral reefs. Monster-sized grilled lobster and crayfish. **$$–$$$**

Straw Hat
Forest Bay
Tel: 264-497 8300
Anguilla's only restaurant "built in the sea". Great seafood specialties. **$$$**

Tasty's
South Hill
Tel: 264-497 2737
Delicious indigenous cuisine with a European flair. Dishes include marinated conch salad, and trigger fish in island sauce. **$$**

ANTIGUA AND BARBUDA

Antigua

The Admiral's Inn
Nelson's Dockyard, PO Box 713,
St John's
Tel: 268-460 1027
This traditional hotel
restaurant, in English
Harbour, serves great
Caribbean cuisine. The
outdoor terrace is pleasant.
$$
The Beach
Dickenson Bay
Tel: 268-480 6940
An East-meets-West theme
is the order of the day, with
Oriental, Middle Eastern,
and US-style food. Lively
crowd. **$$–$$$**
Chez Pascal
Galley Bay Hill, Galley Bay
Tel: 268-462 3232
Gourmet French food at
this restaurant which

has a lovely view over the
bay. Diners may eat
indoors or on patio.
Accommodations also
available. **$$$**
Harmony Hall
Brown's Bay, near Freetown
Tel: 268-460 4120
A delightful lunch spot
overlooking the old sugar
mill and the bay; Italian
dishes served on the
terrace of a plantation-
style house with an art
gallery and craft shop.
$$–$$$
**Hemingways Caribbean
Café**
St Mary's Street
Tel: 268-462 2763
Popular, balcony café. Fine
Caribbean food and a great
place to watch the world go
by in the center of town.
$–$$

**Mid East Fast Food
and Café**
Redcliffe Quay
Tel: 268-562 3643
Alnother branch on Upper
Newgate Street
Tel: 562 0101
A variety of Middle-Eastern-
influenced foods, sand-
wiches, and snacks. **$**
Natural Nyam
Cross Street
Tel: 268-562 0174
A busy vegan restaurant
with lunch-time specials. **$**
Papa Zouk
Hilda Davis Drive, Gambles,
St John's
Tel: 268-464 6044
Excellent food, mostly fish
and seafood. Casual.
Dinner only. **$–$$**
Pizzas on the Quay
(Big Banana Holding Co.)
Redcliffe Quay

Tel: 268-480 6979
Great pizzas and pasta.
Popular at lunch time.
There is another branch
at the airport. **$**
Roti King
St Mary's Street and Corn Alley
Tel: 268-462 2328
Excellent family-run
restaurant serving tasty
curries and *roti*. **$**

Barbuda

Eda's Joint
Codrington
Tel: 268-460 0412
Traditional food: specialties
include pepperpot, saltfish,
and land crabs, in season. **$**
Palm Tree Restaurant
Codrington
Tel: 268-784 4331
Fresh-baked bread, lobster,
and burgers. **$**

BARBADOS

Bridgetown and
West Coast

Brown Sugar
Aquatic Gap, Bay Street
Tel: 246-426 7684
Bajan and Caribbean
specialties in the
surroundings of a
traditional-style home. This
is a Barbadian favorite.
$$$
The Cliff
St James
Tel: 246-432 1922
Stunning cliff-top setting
matches the quality of the
food cooked by an award-
winning chef. Reservations
recommended. **$$$**
Mango's by the Sea
Speightstown
Tel: 246-422 0704
Overlooking the sea.
Seafood is their specialty,
especially grilled lobster.
$$$
The Mews
2nd Street, Holetown, St James
Tel: 246-432 1122
Superb seafood dishes.
Live jazz on Friday nights. A
good after-dinner
rendezvous spot. **$$$**
Mullins Restaurant
Mullins Beach, St Peter
Tel: 246-422 2044

This casual, relaxed ocean-
side restaurant has daily
specials and a lively atmosphere. Open seven days.
$$
Olive's Bar and Bistro
2nd Street, Holetown
Tel: 246-432 2112
Unpretentious food with a
Caribbean and
Mediterranean flavor. **$$**
Waterfront Café
The Careenage, Bridgetown
Tel: 246-427 0093
Traditional Bajan
specialties and creole
cooking served up to the
sound of live music.
$$–$$$

South Coast

Aqua
Hastings, Christ Church
Tel: 246-420 2995
Stylish waterfront
restaurant with an
innovative menu, with
Bajan and Oriental
specialties. **$$$**
Carib Beach Bar
Sandy Beach, Christ Church
Tel: 246-435 8540
Fish and beach barbecues
are served at this favorite
spot, popular with the
locals. **$$**

**Champers Wine Bar and
Restaurant**
Skeetes Hill, Christ Church
Tel: 246-434 3463
Dine to the sound of the
ocean in this atmospheric
seafront restaurant. On the
Wall art gallery is also on
the complex. **$$$**
David's Place
St Lawrence Main Road, Worthing,
Christ Church
Tel: 246-435 9755
Authentic Barbadian
cuisine. Friendly service.
$$
The Lucky Horseshoe
Worthing, Christ Church
Tel: 246-435 5825
This restaurant has a Tex-
Mex menu with large, tasty
portions served in a
relaxed, friendly
atmosphere. **$$**
La Luna
Enterprise, Christ Church
Tel: 246-420 4689
An elegant open air terrace
restaurant overlooking
beautiful Miami Beach. **$$**
Paradise Pizza
Worthing, Christ Church
Tel: 246-435 9808
Casual pizza parlor serves
delicious pizza, with
takeout and delivery
options. **$$**

Pisces Restaurant
St Lawrence Gap, Christ Church
Tel: 246-435 6564
Local fresh fish and
seafood specialties on the
water's edge. **$$$**

Southeast and
East Coast

The Crane Resort
St Philip
Tel: 246-423 6220
Excellent Bajan buffet lunch
at this elegant hotel on
Sunday. **$$**
New Edgewater
Bathsheba, St Joseph
Tel: 246-433 9900
Noted for its Sunday Bajan
buffets. **$$**
Round House
Bathsheba, St Joseph
Tel: 246-433 9678
Delicious, wholesome
cuisine. A large selection of
rums and live
entertainment. **$$**

PRICE CATEGORIES

Price categories are for
a meal for one person,
excluding drinks:
$ = under US$20
$$ = US$20–40
$$$ = over US$40

THE BRITISH VIRGIN ISLANDS

The *BVI Restaurant Guide* (with map), a free annual publication, is very helpful and it is available at tourist offices and in hotels. It gives details of restaurant addresses, main dishes, opening hours, prices, credit cards, reservations, dress codes, etc. Also check the listing "Dining Out" and the mouth-watering adverts in the *Welcome* magazine.

All hotel restaurants in the BVI are open to non-residents. Dinner reservations are recommended especially during peak season. All Pusser's Restaurants (Waterfront Drive, Road Town; Soper's Hole, West End; Marina Cay and Leverick Bay, Virgin Gorda) serve good salads, huge sandwiches, juicy steaks, and tasty fish.

BELOW: lunch on Deadman's Beach, Peter Island, BVI.

Tortola

Brandywine Bay
East of Road Town, Brandywine Estate
Tel: 284-495 2301
Italian gourmet-style cooking with Caribbean ingredients. There is a magnificent view over the Sir Francis Drake Channel. **$$$**

C & F Restaurant
Purcell Estate, Road Town
Tel: 284-494 4941
A cozy family place in the backyard of Road Town; local cuisine, especially seafood, that is popular with local residents and visitors alike. **$$**

Clem's By The Sea
Carrot Bay
Tel: 284-495 4350
Creole specialties including *funchi* and goat stew, with steelband music on Monday and Saturday nights. **$**

Mrs Scattcliffe's
Carrot Bay
Tel: 284-495 4556
Homey atmosphere. The chef cooks mainly with home-grown vegetables. Specialties include soursop sherbert, coconut bread, and papaya soup *(see page 106)*. Reservations necessary. **$**

The Roti Palace
Russel Hill, Road Town
Tel: 284-494 4196
Good place to go for spicy BVI-size *rotis*. Open for lunch and dinner. **$**

Spaghetti Junction and Bat Cave
Baugher's Bay, Road Town
Tel: 284-494 4880
www.spaghettijunction.net
An Italian restaurant overlooking Road Town's outer harbor. Move on to the Bat Cave after dinner for drinks, music, and dancing. **$**

Virgin Gorda

The Mad Dog
The Baths
Tel: 284-495 5830
Small casual bar serving tasty snacks and sandwiches. **$**

Jost Van Dyke

Foxy's
Great Harbour
Tel: 284-495 9258
This place buzzes with life and exuberance but is especially busy on the weekend because of its famous barbecues on Friday and Saturday, serving great salads, grilled fish, and chicken. During the week the bar offers snack lunches, and mainly seafood or *rotis* are available for dinner. Expect a warm welcome with local songs from Foxy himself playing the guitar *(see page 112)*. **$**

DOMINICA

Big Papa's
Lagon, Portsmouth
Tel: 767-445 6444
Restaurant and sports bar. **$**

Blue Bay
Lagon, Portsmouth
Tel: 767-445 4985
Tasty creole dishes, chicken and seafood specialties. **$$**

Callaloo
King George V Street, Roseau
Tel: 448 3386
Upstairs veranda. **$$**

Guiyave
15 Cork Street, Roseau
Tel: 767-448 2930
Lunches only are served on a pleasant veranda over-looking the street. **$$**

Islet View Restaurant and Bar
Castle Bruce
Tel: 767-446 0378
Creative local menu. Call in advance for dinner. **$**

Mousehole Café
Victoria Street, Roseau
Snack bar serving lunchtime *rotis*, codfish, and bakes and other local specialties. Adjoining La Robe Creole. **$**

Natural Livity
13 King George V St
Tel: 767-265 5912
Rastafarian-run restaurant offering fresh juices and delicious lunches. DJ Friday evenings. **$**

Olive Lander's
Atkinson
Tel: 767-445 7521
Restaurant at **Olive's Guest House**, which has cottage accommodations. On the edge of the Carib Territory and a 15-minute drive from Melville Hall Airport. Order in advance. **$**

Papillote Wilderness Retreat
Trafalgar Falls Road
Tel: 767-448 2287
Lovely restaurant overlooking the valley, near the famous Falls. Reservations are essential. **$$**

Pearl's Cuisine
50 King George V Street, Roseau
Tel: 767-448 8707
Hearty helpings; there is also a takeout service. **$$**

La Robe Creole
3 Victoria Street, Roseau
Tel: 767-448 2896
The capital's smartest restaurant with a delicious variety of dishes. Book ahead. **$$$**

GRENADA

Coconut Beach
Grand Anse
Tel: 473-444 4644
French-creole cooking with occasional live music on the beach. Closed Tuesday. **$$**

Di Vino Italian Wine Bar
Grand Anse
Tel: 473-457 6569
A good selection of wines and light snacks. Live music on Wednesdays. **$$**

Morne Fendue Plantation House
St Patrick
Tel: 473-442 9330
One of Grenada's institutions and a small piece of history. Serves lunch only. It is essential to reserve ahead. **$$**

The Nutmeg
Carenage, St George's
Tel: 473-440 2539
A great place for lunch, overlooking the town's harbor and serving simple food and deservedly famous rum punches. **$$**

Pirate's Cove Terrace Restaurant
Grand View Inn, Morne Rouge
Tel: 473-444 2342
Seafood is a specialty at this eating place, with spectacular views. Often has live music too. **$$$**

Tropicana Inn
Lagoon Road
Tel: 473-440-1586
Popular with local people, this hotel restaurant has a covered terrace and offers large portions of great Chinese as well as Grenadian food. Barbecues on weekends and plenty of loud music.

Carriacou

Callaloo by the Sea
Main Street, Hillsborough
Tel: 473-443 8004
Pleasant seafront veranda dining in popular restaurant with wide choice. **$$**

ABOVE: alfresco, Grenada.

GUADELOUPE

Grande-Terre

Auberge de La Vieille Tour
Gosier
Tel: 590-84 23 23
French and creole specialties and a spectacular view. Open for dinner. **$$$**

Auberge Le Relax
Morne à L'Eau
Tel: 590-24 87 61
Creole cuisine. **$$**

Chez Honoré
Anse à la Gourde, St-François
Tel: 590-88 52 19
Creole specialties and clawless lobster. Open only at lunch times. **$**

Chez Prudence (Folie Plage)
Anse Bertrand
Tel: 590-22 11 17
Creole cuisine. **$-$$**

La Toubana
Durivage, Ste-Anne
Tel: 590-88 25 78
Specialists in huge platters of delicious seafood. **$$-$$$**

Basse-Terre

Couleur Caraibe
Route de la Traversée des Mamelles, Pointe-Noire
Tel: 590-98 89 59
Creole cuisine. **$-$$**

Le Karacoli
Deshaies
Tel: 590-28 41 17
Creole cuisine on the beach. Open lunch times only. **$-$$**

Restaurant du Domaine de Severin
La Boucan, Ste-Rose
Tel: 590-28 34 54
Creole cuisine. **$-$$**

Restaurant du Parc de Valombreuse
Cabout, Petit Bourg
Tel: 590-95 50 50
Creole cuisine. Open for lunch only. **$**

La Belle Chaudière
Chartreux, Le Lamentin
Tel: 590-25 97 46
Excellent creole cuisine served in a rural atmosphere. **$-$$**

MARTINIQUE

La Belle Epoque
97 Route de Didier, Fort-de-France
Tel: 596-64 41 19
Serves French and creole food. Closed Saturday lunch time and Sunday. **$$$**

BELOW: Ti-punch, a potent rum, sugar, and lime cocktail, a specialty of Martinique.

Le Bredas
Prequ'île, Rivière Blanche, St-Joseph
Tel: 596-57 65 52
Chef Bredas has an international reputation for *haute cuisine* with a Caribbean flair. **$$$**

La Cabane des Pêcheurs
Carbet
No phone
Beach restaurant serving a set daily menu. Live music on Friday night and weekends. **$-$$**

Calebasse Café
19 Boulevard Allegre, Marin
Tel: 596-74 69 27
Café, restaurant and jazz bar with a great atmosphere. Popular with locals. **$$**

Cave à Vins
124 Rue Victor Hugo,
Fort-de-France
Tel: 596-70 33 02
Well-established restaurant serving French food. **$$-$$$**

Côte Sud
Trois-Rivières, Ste-Luce
Tel: 596-62 59 63
Seaside seafood restaurant. **$$**

Les Deux Gros
Fond Bellemare, Case Pilote
Tel: 596-61 60 34
French cuisine made with local ingredients. **$$-$$$**

Le Fromager
Route de Fond Denis, St-Pierre
Tel: 596-78 19 07
Serves creole specialties. **$$**

Le Man Soufran
Quartier Cap Chevalier, Ste-Anne
Tel: 596-74 04 48
Beach restaurant with seafood specialties. **$$**

Le Thé à la Menthe
2 Route de Cluny, Fort-de-France
Tel: 596-60 15 60
For a change from French cooking, try the Middle Eastern specialties served here. **$$**

Le Toulou Lou
Pointe Marin, Ste-Anne
Tel: 596-76 73 27
Seafood specialties. **$$**

PRICE CATEGORIES

Price categories are for a meal for one person, excluding drinks:
$ = under US$20
$$ = US$20–40
$$$ = over US$40

MONTSERRAT

Breezes Restaurant
Tropical Mansion Suites, Sweeneys
Tel: 664-491 8767
An international menu as well as Italian food with a Caribbean flavour is offered by this hotel and bar. Buffet lunch on Sundays.

JJ's Cuisine
Sweeney's
Tel: 664-491 9024
Popular restaurant with good-quality lunch (from noon) and dinner (from 7pm); a limited choice of wines. Choose from hearty local specialties or sandwiches and

tasty pastries. Booking advised. **$$**

Oriole Café Bar and Restaurant
Farara Plaza, Brades
Tel: 664-491 7144
Breakfast, lunch, and dinner (reservation only) are served in this handily situated spot next to the tourist office. **$$**

Ponts Beach View
Little Bay
Tel: 664-492 2744
Choose from a wide range of meat, fish, and chicken cooked on an open grill at this rustic restaurant which

commands beautiful views of the sea and cliffs.

Tina's
Brades Main Road, Brades
Tel: 664-491 3538
Very popular with Montserratians. Dine inside or on the veranda. Lunch from noon and dinner from 7pm. This is the place to eat authentic dishes and meet local people. Menu includes curry goat and rice, lasagna, shrimp, and "mountain chicken". **$-$$**

The Windsor Restaurant
Cudjoe Head
Tel: 664-491 2900

Good restaurant with a reasonable wine list. Lunch served from 11.30am and dinner from 6.30pm. Reservations advised. Also a number of apartments available for short-term rent. **$$-$$$**

Ziggy's
Woodlands
Tel: 664-491 8282
One of the island's most popular restaurants. The menu includes marinated lamb, shrimp and daily specials. Open from 7pm only. Reservations essential. **$$$**

ST-BARTHÉLEMY, SABA, AND ST EUSTATIUS

St-Barths

Eddy's
Rue du Centenaire, Gustavia
Tel: 590-27 54 17
French and Caribbean food with a Far-Eastern flavor in an eclectic setting. **$$**

L'Esprit Salines
La Grande Saline
Tel: 590-52 46 10
Casual and leisurely lunch or dinner in the garden dining room, with bar. **$$-$$$**

La Gloriette
Cul de Sac
Tel: 590-27 75 66
Local French-creole cuisine served in a beach-side setting. **$$-$$$**

La Langouste
Hôtel Baie des Anges, Flamands
Tel: 590-27 63 61

Best known for its grilled lobster, French and creole dishes also served. **$$$**

Maya's
Public
Tel: 590-27 75 73
Elegant beach-front dining. Creole dishes and daily specials. **$$-$$$**

Wall House
Gustavia waterfront
Tel: 590-27 71 83
French cuisine, light lunches, gourmet dinners; set menu or à la carte. **$-$$**

Saba

The Gate House
Hell's Gate
Tel: 599-416 2416
Creole dishes and French cuisine. Extensive wine list. **$$-$$$**

My Kitchen
Lambee's Place, Windwardside
Tel: 599-416 2539
Salads, sandwiches, and excellent burgers as well as pastas and main courses. Friendly atmosphere. **$-$$**

Rainforest Restaurant
Ecolodge Rendezvous, Windwardside
Tel: 599-416 5507
On the Crispeen Trail, convenient for hikers. Home-grown fruit and vegetables, often picked once you've ordered; fresh and tasty food. **$-$$**

Scout's Place
Saba Divers and Scout's Place Hotel, Windwardside
Tel: (toll-free) 1-866 656 7222
Run by a German couple, this restaurant offers a diverse menu catering to

European as well as Caribbean palates. **$$**

St Eustatius

Blue Bead Bar and Restaurant
Lower Town, Oranjestad
Tel: 599-318 2873
Good fresh fish and seafood, daily specials, also meat and pizza. **$-$$**

Golden Era Hotel
Oranje Bay, St Eustatius
Tel: 599-318 2455
Serving international, West Indian, and creole food by the ocean or poolside. **$$**

Ocean View Terrace
By Fort Oranje, Oranjestad
Tel: 599-318 2934
Daily specials, mostly fish and seafood; good place for watching the sunset. **$-$$**

ST KITTS AND NEVIS

St Kitts

Ballahoo
The Circus, Basseterre
Tel: 869-465 4197
Caribbean seafood and fruit drinks are served in this popular meeting place with a scenic view from the balcony. Opens 8am. **$$$**

Bobsy's Bar and Grill
Sugar's Complex, Frigate Bay
Tel: 869-466 6133
Seafood specialties, local and international dishes.

Open Monday–Saturday from 11am. **$$-$$$**

Chef Lynn's Island Spice
Sugar's Complex, Frigate Bay
Tel: 869-465 0569
Restaurant serving authentic local cuisine and international dishes. Open Monday–Saturday from 11am. **$$-$$$**

Fisherman's Wharf
Fortlands
Tel: 869-465 2754
Informal dining by the sea, with a menu featuring

grilled seafood. Open 11am–11pm. **$$$**

The Golden Lemon
Dieppe Bay
Tel: 869-465 7260
Celebrating 45 years in 2008, the Golden Lemon is a romantic resort hotel; the excellent restaurant serves continental and Caribbean dishes. Reservations required. **$$$**

Rawlins Plantation Inn
Mount Pleasant
Tel: 869-465 6221

Popular Caribbean buffet lunch and delicious four-course dinners. **$$-$$$**

Royal Palm Restaurant at Ottleys Plantation Inn
Ottleys
Tel: 869-465 7234
Innovative gourmet dining and a popular Sunday brunch in a garden setting. **$$-$$$**

Serendipity
Fort Lands
Tel: 869-465 9999

Delectable dishes served in a dining room overlooking the town of Basseterre and the cruise-ship port. Open for lunch Tuesday–Friday; dinner from 6pm Tuesday–Sunday. **$$–$$$**

Nevis

Cafe des Arts
Charles Town Nevis
Tel: 869-469 7098
Sit in the garden of a gingerbread West Indian house shaded by big evergreen trees and enjoy light lunches, pastries,

croissants, and an array of beverages. **$$**
Golden Rock
Pinney's Beach
Tel: 869-469 3346
Known for its delicious rum punch; located in an early 19th-century stone building. **$$**
The Mill Restaurant
Montpelier
Tel: 869-469 3462
Intimate restaurant in an old sugar mill on the Montpelier Plantation. International dishes with island influences; reservations required. **$**

Miss June's
Jones Bay
Tel: 869-469 5330
Home-cooked Caribbean food in an intimate setting. Reservations are essential because the restaurant opens only on demand. **$$–$$$**
Nisbet Plantation Beach Club
Newcastle
Tel: 869-469 9325
Lunch and Sunday barbecues are served on the beach, while there's formal dining in the Great House. **$$–$$$**

Sunshine's Beach Bar and Grill
Pinney's Beach
Tel: 869-469 5817
Relaxed place right on the beach. Serves grilled lobster, chicken, fish, and shrimp. Open noon–midnight. **$**
Unella's Bar and Restaurant
Charlestown
Tel: 869-469 5574
Unella's has one of the best views in Nevis. Situated on the waterfront, it serves divine seafood. Opens at 8am. **$–$$**

ST LUCIA

ABOVE: lunch in St Lucia.

Caribbean Pirates Restaurant and Bar
La Place Carenage, Castries
Tel: 758-452 2543
Excellent creole cuisine with generous helpings. Open Mon–Sat; Sundays only when a cruise ship is in port. **$–$$**
Castries Central Market
Jeremie Street
Massive selection of local delights at bargain prices, served in crowded, atmospheric passageways at lunch times. **$**
The Charthouse
Rodney Bay
Tel: 758-452 8115
Crayfish and steaks from

the grill, served on the waterfront. **$$–$$$**
The Coal Pot
Vigie Marina, Castries
Tel: 758-452 5566
International and Caribbean specialties from French and local chefs. Castries' best service. **$$**
Dasheene Restaurant and Bar
Ladera Resort, Soufrière
Tel: 758-459 7323
Sophisticated and delicious blend of international and creole cuisine. Dine in an award-winning restaurant with a wonderful mountain-side view of the Pitons. **$$$**

Debbies
Vieux Fort Road, Laborie, Soufrière
Tel: 758-455 1625
Hugely popular and smart local eatery on the south coast serving imaginative Caribbean fare. Try the Sunday-lunch buffet. **$–$$**
Doolittle's
Marigot Beach Club and Dive Resort
Tel: 758-451 4974
A pleasant waterside location combines well with the range of meat, fish and pasta served here; barbecue every Saturday. **$$**
Edge Restaurant
Rodney Bay
Tel: 758-450 3343
Award-winning Caribbean fusion cuisine. Sushi bar. **$$–$$$**
Jacques Waterfront Dining
Vigie Cove, Castries
Tel: 758-458 1900
Fish and seafood restaurant. Excellent sauces. **$$–$$$**
Key Largo
Rodney Bay
Tel: 758-452 0282
Italian pizzeria with authentic pizza baked in a traditional wood-fire oven. Pasta dishes available. **$$**
Ku De Ta
Rodney Bay
Tel: 758-458 4968
Thai cuisine served in an elegant setting. **$$–$$$**
Lifeline Bar and Restaurant
Hummingbird Beach Resort, Soufriere
Tel: 758-459 7985
A mix of creole and French

food features, with the crayfish being particularly noteworthy. **$$**
The Lime
Rodney Bay, near Reduit Beach
Tel: 758-452 0761
A fast-food kitchen with loads of choice and good, reasonably priced St Lucian cuisine. Great *rotis*. Eat in or takeout. **$–$$**
Razmataz
Reduit Beach Road, Rodney Bay
Tel: 758-452 9800
Traditional tandoori cuisine is produced by two Nepalese brothers in this East Indian restaurant, set in a patio garden. Several non-meat options. **$$**
The Shack Bar and Grill
Marigot Bay
Tel: 758-451 4145
Balancing on stilts over the harbor, the Grill's international cooking with a local twist covers seafood, pasta, and T-bone steaks. **$$**
Spinnakers
Reduit Beach, Rodney Bay
Tel: 758-452 8491
This child-friendly place offers a varied menu with plenty of choices to tempt visitors who are wary of too much spice! **$$**

PRICE CATEGORIES

Price categories are for a meal for one person, excluding drinks:
$ = under US$20
$$ = US$20–40
$$$ = over US$40

ST MARTIN/SINT MAARTEN

French Side

Bistrot Nu
Rue de Hollande, Marigot
Tel: 590-87 97 09
Locally popular restaurant serving great seafood, French, and Italian cooking. **$$**

La Brasserie de Marigot
11 Rue du Général de Gaulle, Marigot
Tel: 590-87 94 43
French-Caribbean cooking with a very French ambiance including tables on the sidewalk. Takeout also available. **$$**

Le Cottage
97 Boulevard de Grand Case
Tel: 590-29 03 30
French-creole cuisine prepared by a French chef. Good wine list. Reservations recommended. **$$$**

Le Rainbow
176 Boulevard de Grand Case
Tel: 590-87 55 80
Caribbean-style seafood. **$$**

Le Santal
Nettlé Bay Beach, near Marigot
Tel: 590-87 53 48
Internationally renowned as one of the best restaurants in the Caribbean. Serves excellent French cuisine. **$$$**

La Vie en Rose
Boulevard de France, Marigot
Tel: 590-87 54 42
French-Caribbean flavors on a balcony overlooking the harbor. **$$$**

Dutch Side

The Boathouse
15 Welfare Road, Simpson Bay
Tel: 599-544 5409
Seafood, steaks, and pasta in a pleasantly informal nautical setting. **$$**

Chesterfields
Great Bay Marina, Philipsburg
Tel: 599-542 3484
Seafood and pasta overlooking the water. Popular watering hole for yachties. **$$**

Grand Café Europe
Maho Plaza
Tel: 599-545 4455
Grilled steaks and Dutch seafood, including fresh mussels flown in from Holland. **$$**

Pasanggrahan Royal Inn
19 Front Street, Philipsburg
Tel: 599-542 3588
International cuisine in charming colonial-era beach-front hotel. **$–$$**

La Riviera
16 Front Street, Philipsburg
Tel: 599-525 5725
French and Italian food. **$$**

Saratoga
Simpson Bay Yacht Club
Tel: 599-544 2421
Award-winning restaurant serving eclectic Californian fusion (with French and Japanese influences) cuisine. **$$–$$$**

Wajang Doll
167 Front Street, Philipsburg
Tel: 599-542 2687
Indonesian food on the waterfront. **$$**

ST VINCENT AND THE GRENADINES

St Vincent

Beachcombers Restaurant and Bar
Villa Beach
Tel: 784-458 4283
Lovely casual ambiance with good simple food and open-air dining on the beach. **$–$$**

Bounty
Egmont Street, Kingstown
Tel: 784-456 1776
Snacks and sandwiches at the place where locals go for their lunch. **$**

Cobblestone Inn
Upper Bay Street, Kingstown
Tel: 784-456 1937
Rooftop restaurant serving Caribbean food and hamburgers. **$$**

French Restaurant
Villa Beach
Tel: 784-457 4000
Classic French cuisine with a Caribbean twist. **$$$**

Juliette's
Middle Street, Kingstown
Tel: 784-457 1645
Simple food in the middle of town. **$**

Lime Restaurant and Pub
Villa Harbour, St Vincent
Tel: 784-455 9543
Classic Caribbean dishes in an informal setting. Fresh seafood specialties. **$$**

Ocean Allegro
Villa Harbour
Tel: 784-458 4972
Excellent service, food, and beach view with occasional salsa nights. **$$$**

Bequia

Daphne's
Port Elizabeth
No phone
Creole meals to eat in or takeout at this popular spot. **$**

Whalebones
Port Elizabeth
Tel: 784-458 3233
Caribbean food with an emphasis on seafood, in an atmospheric setting. **$$**

Mustique

Basil's Bar
Britannia Bay
Tel: 784-456 3522
Famous bar built over the water; great for people-watching – this is a popular haunt of the rich and famous. Good seafood dishes. **$$$**

BELOW: crayfish fishermen, Petit St Vincent Island.

TRINIDAD AND TOBAGO

Trinidad

A la Bastille
Corner of Ariapita Avenue and De Verteuil Street, Woodbrook
Tel: 868-622 1789
Parisian-style brasserie serving classic French cuisine. **$$–$$$**

Aspara
13 Queen's Park East, Port-of-Spain
Tel: 868-623 7659
Authentic North Indian cuisine. **$**

Coco's Hot
Laguna Mar Hotel, Blanchisseuse
Tel: 868-628 3731
Superb creole dishes cooked to order. **$$**

Hong Kong City
86A Tragarete Road, Port-of-Spain
Tel: 868-622 3949
Chinese specialties with a creole twist. **$**

Laughing Buddha
86 Frederick Street, Port-of-Spain
Tel: 868-627 0010
Upscale Japanese restaurant with excellent sushi in a suprising downtown location. **$$–$$$**

Tiki Village
Kapok Hotel, Port-of-Spain
Tel: 868-622 5765
Polynesian cuisine, with fish and seafood specialties. **$$**

Veni Mangé
67A Ariapita Avenue, Woodbrook
Tel: 868-624 4597
Best creole cuisine in town. **$$–$$$**

Ylang Ylang
Mount Plasir Hotel, Grande Riviene
Tel: 868-670 8381
Creole, Indian and Italian dishes in a stunning beachside location. Great wine list. **$$–$$$**

Tobago

La Belle Creole
Half Moon Hotel, Bacolet
Tel: 868-639 3551
Top-end creole dining and cocktail list with fine sea views. **$$$**

Black Rock Café
Black Rock
Tel: 868-639 7625
Pretty veranda restaurant with local dishes, steaks, and seafood. **$–$$**

Bonkers
Storebay Local Road, Crown Point
Tel: 868-639 7173
Comfortable restaurant with dependable local dishes and the best cocktails on the island. **$–$$**

Jemma's Seaview Kitchen
Speyside
Tel: 868-660 4066
Top-rate island cuisine served in a cheerful tree house by the sea. **$**

Kariwak Village Restaurant
Store Bay Local Road, Crown Point
Tel: 868-639 8442
Open-air restaurant with imaginative creole dishes. **$$**

Miss Jean
Store Bay Beach Facilities
Tel: 868-639 0211
Simple, inexpensive, and well-seasoned local specialties. **$**

Old Donkey Cart House
Bacolet Street, Scarborough
Tel: 868-639 3551
Wooden house with playfully romantic decor. International and Caribbean cuisine; well-stocked wine cellar. **$$**

Seahorse Inn
Grafton Beach Road
Tel: 868-639 0686
Idyllic situation with sea views. **$**

THE US VIRGIN ISLANDS

St Thomas

Banana Tree Grill
Bluebeard's Castle, Charlotte Amalie
Tel: 340-776 4050
Elegant dining with a beautiful view across the harbor. **$$–$$$**

Coco Joe's
Frenchman's Reef Hotel, Flamboyant Point
Tel: 340-776 8500, ext 6512
Informal dining in beach bar restaurant. **$$**

Craig and Sally's
3525 Honduras, Frenchtown
Tel: 340-777 9949
An eclectic menu with European and Asian influences, which changes daily. Extensive wine list. **$$–$$$**

Hervé's
Kongens Gade, Government Hill, Charlotte Amalie
Tel: 340-777 9703
Restaurant serving excellent French cuisine in a relaxed bistro-style setting. **$$–$$$**

The Inn at Blackbeard's Castle
Blackbeard's Hill
Tel: 340-776 1234
Varied menu of Asian, Caribbean and Mediterranean dishes; good value for money. **$$**

Lulu's
Crown Mountain Road
Tel: 340-774 6800
Reliable Italian fare. Steaks and pizza from 5pm when the bar opens. **$$**

Mafolie Restaurant
Mafolie Hotel, Red Hook
Tel: 340-774 2790
Superb views and seafood, steaks, and salads served at this hotel restaurant. **$$**

Sandra's Terrace
66–7 Smith Bay, Route 38
Tel: 340-775 2699
Generous helpings of good Caribbean food are served in a wonderful setting. **$**

Virgilio's
18 Dronningens Gade, Charlotte Amalie
Tel: 340-776 4920
Superb Italian food in a quaint European-style setting. **$$–$$$**

St Croix

The Buccaneer
Gallows Bay, Christiansted
Tel: 340-712 2100
Four different restaurants under one hotel roof. Classic Mediterranean specialties, often with a tropical twist. **$$–$$$**

Duggans's Reef
Route 82, Teague Bay
Tel: 340-773 9800
Outdoor dining overlooking Buck Island. Pasta, steak and fish with a Caribbean touch. **$$$**

Kendrick's
King Cross Street, Christiansted
Tel: 340-773 9199
A sophisticated, more pricey choice situated in the historical downtown area, this French restaurant is perfect for a special occasion. **$$$**

Tutto Bene
Boardwalk Building, Gallows Bay
Tel: 340-773 5229
Southern Italian cuisine with daily specials. **$$**

St John

Fish Trap
Raintree Court, Cruz Bay
Tel: 340-693 9994
Fresh fish, chicken, and steak are served here in the heart of town. **$$**

The Lime Inn
Cruz Bay, St John
Tel: 340 776 6425
Open since 1984, this local favorite specializes in seafood served in a relaxed open-air atmosphere. An all-you-can-eat shrimp feast is a regular Wednesday occurrence. **$$**

Morgan's Mango
Cruz Bay
Tel: 340-693 8141
Seafood and steak; imaginative dishes with Caribbean recipes; outdoor dining. **$$**

Paradiso
Mongoose Junction
Tel: 340-693 8899
Good food, fair prices, and a casual but classy setting. Seafood and steak with Mediterranean and Oriental flavors. **$–$$**

PRICE CATEGORIES

Price categories are for a meal for one person, excluding drinks:
$ = under US$20
$$ = US$20–40
$$$ = over US$40

A CTIVITIES

THE ARTS, NIGHTLIFE, CARNIVALS, SHOPPING, SPORTS, BEST BEACHES, OUTDOOR ACTIVITIES

THE ARTS

The Caribbean Islands are better known for their musical heritage than the visual arts, but nonetheless there are numerous small art galleries which exhibit and sell work by local artists *(see Shopping, pages 352–4).*

The **Gallery of Caribbean Art** (www.artgallerycaribbean.com) on Barbados exhibits regional art and photography at the Northern Business Center in Speightstown and the Hilton Hotel on Needham's Point.

The **Reichhold Center for the Arts** (www.reichholdcenter.com) is an amphitheater in Brewer's Bay on St Thomas, which hosts performances of every kind, including music and drama. The center, part of the University of the Virgin Islands, attracts local artists and visiting international performers. For further information about what's on and when, call 340-693 1550, or the box office on 340-693 1559. On the eastern side of the island, the **Tillett Gardens Center for the Arts** (www.tillettgardens.com) hosts classical and contemporary concerts, as well as the tri-annual Arts Alive Festival.

On the island of Anguilla, the renowned **Mayoumba Folkloric Theater** perform at La Sirena Hotel in Meads Bay (tel: 264-497 6827) on Thursday evenings. The group keep Anguillan traditions alive through music, dance, and the spoken word.

Two annual film festivals showcase Caribbean cinema – the **Caribbean International Film Festival** (www.caribbeaninternationalfilmfestival.com) on Barbados and the **St-Barth Film Festival** (www.stbarthff.org) on St-Barthélemy.

NIGHTLIFE

Nightlife on the islands ranges from relaxing over a leisurely dinner in a restaurant with a veranda onto the beach to frittering your money away in a casino. In between these options are nightclubs, bars, and live music. The larger hotels provide much of the evening entertainment on the islands, including music and dancing both during and after dinner, flashy floor shows, and "folkloric evenings" composed of elements of the music, dance, and drama native to the Caribbean. Travelers with an interest in the cultural lives of island residents may wish to venture beyond hotel walls in search of steel band, calypso, and reggae music, and of bars and clubs frequented by local people. Nightclubs may be found both in and outside hotels.

The intensity of nightlife varies substantially from island to island.

BELOW: rum punch, anyone?

The more heavily touristed islands may have several special entertainments every night of the week, while the quieter islands may sometimes have little more to offer than dinner to the accompaniment of recorded music, followed by a stroll along the beach. In the latter category, things may pick up a little during the weekends; several establishments have discos that open only on Friday and Saturday nights. On all the islands, the peak tourist season – approximately December through April – is also the peak nightlife season; things are slower during the rest of the year.

ABC Islands

Aruba has upscale restaurants, nightclubs, and bars with live music, and 11 glitzy casinos, while Bonaire is more laid-back, but this island has a few lively places too. Curaçao has sophisticated dining and casinos, open for gambling until the wee hours, and the **Sea Aquarium Beach** has a number of lively bars.
Bongo's Beach Bar, Eden Beach Resort, Kaya Gobernador Nicolaas Debrot, Bonaire, tel: 599-791 1151. Pleasant bar and restaurant just outside Kralendijk.
Garufa Cigar and Cocktail Lounge, Wilhelminastraat 63, Oranjestad, Aruba, tel: 297-82 3677. Cozy bar with a retro interior and live jazz.
Karel's Beach Bar, Kaya J.E. Craane, Kralendijk, Bonaire, tel: 599-717 8434. A lively bar on the waterfront with live music on Friday and Saturday.
Mambo Jambo, Royal Plaza Mall, Oranjestad, Aruba, tel: 297-583 3632. Latin bar serving delicious frozen cocktails. One of Aruba's liveliest nightspots.

Anguilla

Dune Preserve, Rendezvous Bay, tel: 264-772 0637. Funky restaurant and bar owned by local musician Bankie Banx. Home of the annual Moonsplash Music Festival.
Johno's Bar, Sandy Ground, tel: 264-497 2728. Laid-back beach bar with live music at weekends.
Pumphouse Bar, Sandy Ground, tel: 264-497 5154. Bar and restaurant in a converted salt factory.

Antigua and Barbuda

Most resorts provide live entertainment for guests, such as steel pan or reggae bands and limbo dancers. At **Shirley Heights Lookout Restaurant** on the south of the island there is a Sunday evening barbecue and a steel band performing 3–6pm, followed by a reggae band 6–9pm. Start out early, because the road to the Heights becomes pretty congested as locals and visitors head for this popular night out. Casinos include **King's Casino**, Heritage Quay, St John's, tel: 268-462 1727.

Barbados

Barbados is packed with lively places to go at night, especially on the south coast:
The Boatyard, Bay Street, Bridgetown, tel: 246-436 2622. Live bands every evening except Monday and Wednesday.
Harbour Lights, Bay Street, Bridgetown, tel: 246-436 7225. An open-air nightclub on the beach. A dinner show on Monday, and top live bands at weekends.
Jumbie's, St Lawrence Gap, tel: 246-420 7615. Lively, open air-bar opposite the gentle waters of St Lawrence Bay.
McBride's, St Lawrence Gap, Christ Church, tel: 246-435 6352. A lively Irish pub that is busy most nights. It features DJ music and live acts.
Plantation Theatre, St Lawrence Main Road, tel: 246-428 5048. The *Bajan Roots and Rhythms* show is performed here every Wednesday and Friday – a glittering extravaganza dinner show featuring the music and dances of the Caribbean.
The Ship Inn, St Lawrence Gap, tel: 246-420 7447. Top local bands, seven nights a week.
The Waterfront Café, The Careenage, Bridgetown, tel: 246-427 0093. Live music every night with jazz on Thursday, Friday, and Saturday.

British Virgin Islands

Bomba's Surfside Shack, Apple Bay, Tortola, tel: 284-495 4148. A Tortolan institution built from bits of driftwood and other junk, and decorated with a curious collection of objects, including previous customers' underwear.
Foxy's Beach Bar, Jost van Dyke, tel: 284-495 9258. Laid-back bar where owner Foxy Callwood is known to entertain customers with stories and songs.
The Mad Dog, The Baths, Virgin Gorda, tel: 284-495 5830. Casual snack bar that does good cocktails.
Pusser's Co. Store and Pub, Waterfront Drive, Road Town, Tortola, tel: 284-494 3897. British-style pub on the waterfront. Specializes in rum cocktails, including the notorious Pusser's Painkiller.

Dominica

Nightlife in Dominica revolves around hotels and bars, but there are a few other options.
Bambuz, Loubière, tel: 767-448 2899. Pleasant waterside spot with an Asian-influenced menu. People gather to relax, have drinks, or swim. Wednesday is salsa night; DJ on Saturdays.
The Garage, 15 Hanover Street, tel: 767-448 5443. Wonderful blend of modern and traditional in the setting of a stone building. Lively spot for a meal (fish, grilled meats) or a drink. Big-screen TVs for sports; DJ on Fridays.

Grenada

Grenada has many breezy beach bars, especially in the southern part of the island, where most visitors stay. Nightclubs featuring Jamaican dancehall music, Latin music, and soca are also popular.
Club Bananas, True Blue, tel: 473-439 4369. Popular open-air bar and restaurant, with air-conditioned disco.
Karma Night Club, Bar, and Grill, Carenage, St George's, tel: 473-435 2582. Chic nightclub, popular with locals and visitors alike.

Guadeloupe

There are two casinos on the island, in Gosier and St François. Most of the larger hotels provide live evening entertainment, usually on the weekend. For the most upbeat nightlife, head to Gozier, St François, and St Anne.

Martinique

Martinique buzzes with life in the evening, from casinos (at La Batelière and Pointe du Bout) and floor shows to discos and bars. A lot of night-time socializing takes place in and around the Village Creole at Pointe du Bout. For live music and a jazz-club atmosphere, try **Zanzibar** and **Calebasse Café** on the waterfront in Marin.

Montserrat

Montserratians make their own entertainment. Visit Salem, Cudjoe Head, or Festival Village at Little Bay on Friday and Saturday nights for all the bar action. There are some nightclubs: **The Good Life**, at Little Bay, which has DJ music on weekends; **Club Illusion** at St Peters; and **VIP Club** on Baker Hill.
Rum shop tours can be arranged so that visitors can sample the local nightlife and food. Tel: 664-491 5371 for reservations.
Occasional concerts (with local and regional artists) are performed at **Moose's Bitter End Bar** in Little Bay, and there are jazz evenings at **Grand View** on Baker Hill. If you are lucky you will catch one of the performances by the acclaimed folk-

Caribbean Casinos

Visitors will find plenty of opportunities to gamble in the Caribbean. A number of the islands have several casinos, and even some of the region's more relaxed islands have a casino or two.
If you do plan to gamble, be sure to bring along some appropriate clothes. Dress codes in the casinos tend to be a little more formal than those prevailing elsewhere. The legal gambling age is 18 on most islands, but on Guadeloupe and Martinique you must be 21. Photo ID will sometimes be required for admittance, and some casinos charge an admission. All of the following islands have casinos:
● Antigua
● Aruba
● Bonaire
● Curaçao
● Guadeloupe
● Martinique
● St Kitts
● St Martin/Sint Maarten
● Trinidad and Tobago
● US Virgin Islands

Active Nightlife

The following islands are known for having a particularly lively nightlife:
- Aruba
- Barbados
- Curaçao
- Guadeloupe
- Martinique
- St Lucia
- St Martin/Sint Maarten
- Trinidad and Tobago
- US Virgin Islands

singing group The Emerald Community Singers, who sing in season at the **Vue Pointe Hotel** in Old Town.

St-Barthélemy, Saba, and St Eustatius

The main focus of evening entertainment on these islands is on eating out *(see page 344)*, but the **Galaxy Diner** in Windwardside, Saba, has a disco at weekends.

St Kitts and Nevis

There are two casinos on St Kitts – at the St Kitts Marriott and the newly reopened Royal St Kitts Hotel, but the nexus of nightlife is at "**The Strip**", a string of beach bars on Frigate Bay that provide evening entertainment. On weekends the local bands and DJs provide entertainment at clubs.

St Lucia

Friday night is the time to "jump-up" at Gros Islet's regular street party. This event, with its loud music and aromatic food stands, is popular with locals and tourists. The village of Anse la Raye also puts on a Seafood Fiesta every Friday, and on Saturday try the Dennery Fish Night. Most of the hotels provide live entertainment for guests. There are also some nightclubs and bars in Rodney Bay.

St Martin/Sint Maarten

On the Dutch side, nightlife is concentrated around the Las Vegas-style casinos in Philipsburg and the resorts in Simpson Bay and Maho. Nightclubs include: **Bliss** at Caravanserai Resort, near Sunset Beach Bar (Beacon Hill); and **Q Club**, Casino Royale, Maho Beach Hotel.

Casinos include: **Casino Royale**, Maho Beach Hotel; **Pelican Casino**, Pelican Resort; **Mount Fortune Casino**, Sheraton Port de Plaisance;

Golden Casino, Great Bay Beach Hotel; **Coliseum Casino**, Philipsburg; and the Westin St Maarten Dawn Beach Resort casino.

There is live music and dancing in the resorts, such as the Maho Beach Hotel, which has a cabaret in the casino most evenings.

With no casinos on the French side, the focus is on fine restaurants in Grand Case and Marigot *(see page 346)*.

St Vincent and the Grenadines

There are several bar-restaurants in Kingstown which offer a pleasant place to spend the evening.
Basil's Bar and Restaurant, Upper Bay Street, Kingstown, tel: 784-457 2713. Sister restaurant of the famous Basil's Bar Mustique. Serves great seafood.
Cobblestone Inn, Upper Bay Street, Kingstown, tel: 784-456 1937. Rooftop restaurant above Basil's Bar and Restaurant *(see above)*.

Trinidad and Tobago

Trinidad has lots to do in the evening, and it really comes alive during Carnival *(see page 352)* when the island vibrates with steel pan and calypso music and the accompanying parties and wild street parades. Some of the large hotels provide live music and entertainment for guests and there is a selection of bars and nightclubs where visitors can dance the night away. In Tobago, party night is Friday, with the raucous "Sunday School" open-air disco in Buccoo the only other weekly highlight. In particular try:
Mas Camp Pub, French Street, Woodbrook, Port-of-Spain, tel: 868-627 4042. Thirties-upwards crowd; live calypso shows Wednesday and weekends.
Sabor Latino, Shoppes of Maraval, Port-of-Spain. Excellent, friendly, if smallish, club with a mixed crowd and music policy to match. Latin night Thursday.

US Virgin Islands

Duffy's Love Shack, 6500 Red Hook Plaza, Red Hook, St Thomas, tel: 340-779 2080. Down-to-earth bar located in a parking lot. There is another Duffy's Love Shack in Cruz Bay on St John.
Iggie's Beach Bar and Grill, Bolongo Bay Beach, St Thomas, tel: 340-693 2600. Fun beach bar in the Bolongo Bay Beach Club resort with volleyball,

karoake, and good burgers.
Shipwreck Tavern, Al Cohen's Mall, St Thomas, tel: 340-777 1293. Burgers, beer, and sport on the television.

CARNIVAL AND EVENTS

Carnival is celebrated at different times on different islands, with the dates falling roughly into three main groups:
- On Trinidad and Tobago, Dominica, St Thomas, Aruba, Bonaire, Curaçao, St Lucia, Martinique, Guadeloupe, St Martin (French side), and St-Barthélemy, Carnival preserves an association with Easter, being celebrated (on all of these islands except St Thomas) in the period leading up to, and sometimes including, Ash Wednesday. On St Thomas, the celebration occurs after Easter.
- On St Vincent, Anguilla, St John, Barbados, Grenada, the British Virgin Islands, Antigua, Saba, and St Eustatius, Carnival takes place in June, July, or early August. On these islands, Carnival is often held in association with the "August Monday" holiday, which marks the end of the sugar-cane harvest and the emancipation of slaves in the British islands around that time in 1834.
- On St Kitts, Montserrat, and St Croix (in the US Virgin Islands), Carnival takes place in December and early January, in conjunction with the Christmas season.
- On Sint Maarten (Dutch side), Carnival takes place in late April, coinciding with the Dutch Queen's birthday celebrations on April 30.

ABC Islands

February: Carnival (pre-Lent) A lively, month-long event on Curaçao, with Aruba and Bonaire also hosting smaller events.
Easter: Kite Festival (Curaçao).
May: Jazz Festival (Curaçao).
June: Dive Festival (Bonaire); St John's Day (Aruba).
October: Sailing Regatta (Bonaire); Festival de las Americas (Aruba) celebrating the musical styles of the Americas.
November: Catamaran Regatta (Aruba).

Anguilla

January 1: New Year's Day; Boat Race.
February: Moonsplash Music Festival.
March: Anguilla Jazz Festival.

Easter Monday: Boat race.
May: Anguilla Yacht Regatta; Anguilla Day boat race and athletics (May 30).
August: Carnival/Anguilla (first week); Summer Festival.
November: Tranquillity Jazz Festival.

Antigua and Barbuda

January: Men's Tennis Week.
April: Women's Tennis Week; Antigua Sailing Week.
July/August: Carnival – in the week before first Monday in August. Also Mangofest, in celebration of the island's favorite fruit.
October: Jazz Festival; Heritage Day (Oct 21).
November: Independence Week; Half marathon.

Barbados

January: Windsurfing championships; Jazz Festival; the regional cricket series.
February: Holetown Festival.
March: Holders Season.
April: Oistins Fish Festival; Congaline street festival; Caribbean International Film Festival.
May: Gospelfest; Celtic Festival; Mount Gay Regatta.
June: Harris Paints Sailing Regatta.
July: Crop Over festival begins (see box); Sir Garfield Sobers International Schools Cricket Festival.
November: Independence Classic Surfing Championship; NIFCA (National Independence Festival of Creative Arts) cultural events.
December: Run Barbados, the island's marathon; the United Insurance Barbados Golf Open.

British Virgin Islands

March/April: BVI Spring Regatta.
Easter: Virgin Gorda Carnival.
May: BVI Music Festival.
June/July: HIHO International Windsurfing Competition.
July: Fisherman's Day.
August: Emancipation Festival.
September: Jost Van Dyke Festival.
December: Foxy's Old Year Party.

Dominica

Easter: Carnival: Monday and Tuesday preceding Ash Wednesday.
June: Dive Fest: Annual watersports festival (see page 355).
October: World Creole Music Festival: last weekend in month. Three-day vibrant music show.
End Oct/early Nov: Creole Day independence day festivities (national costume is worn).

Grenada

January: Spice Island Fishing Tournament is held at the end of the month. Annual La Source Grenada Sailing Festival.
Mardi Gras: Shakespeare Mas; friendly festival on Carriacou.
Late April: Annual Carriacou Maroon Music Festival.
May/June: Spice Jazz Festival.
June: Fisherman's Birthday in Gouyave at the end of the month.
August: The first weekend is the Carriacou Regatta; the second weekend is Carnival time in Grenada; Rainbow City cultural festival in Grenville.

Guadeloupe

February: Carnival: the biggest festival on the island.
May: International Music Festival on the island of Marie-Galante; Abolition of Slavery (May 27).
July: Gwoka: drum festival in St Anne
August: Tour de la Guadeloupe: international bike race; Chefs' Festival: a parade in traditional dress culminates in a feast of fine food.
November: All Saints and All Souls: the cemeteries come alive as family members clean tombs and picnic with their dead ancestors.
December: Chanté Noël: Christmas carols are sung at parties throughout the month.

Martinique

February: Vaval (Carnival) – four days of jubilation and dancing in the streets. A carnival queen is crowned at the end of the festivities.
March: Foire Exposition, Stade de Dillon at Fort-de-France. Annual exhibit and fair.

Crop Over Festival

The highlight of Barbados's cultural year is the **Crop Over Festival** celebrating the end of the sugar-cane harvest, which starts on the first Saturday of July and continues for five weeks. Top calypso and soca artists compete in the Pic-o-de-Crop contest, and there is a lot of dancing and parading through the streets ending with **Kadooment Day** on the first Monday in August, when everyone dresses up in Carnival costumes and the festivities reach their climax.

Easter: La Pince d'Or Easter Crab Cooking Competition, Grande Rivière.
May: Le Mai de Saint Pierre – festivities in commemoration of the eruption of the Pelée Volcano; Abolition of Slavery festivities; Contemporary Art Market, Marin (international art fair).
June: Crop Over festival, Sainte-Marie. Celebration of the end of the sugar-cane harvest.
July: Fort-de-France Cultural Festival; International Bicycle Race.
August: Yole Race Around Martinique – traditional sailing vessels compete in the island's most popular event.
September: Journée de la Patrimoine – all historical sites are open to the public free of charge.
October: Journee Internationale du Creole; celebration of all things Creole.
November: International Billfish Tournament – one of the biggest sports fishing competitions in the Caribbean; Semi-marathon, Fort-de-France.
December: Rum Festival, Musée du Rhum, St James Distillery; Jazz Festival.

BELOW: a young steelpan-player at a carnival in Trinidad.

Montserrat

December/January: Carnival is the main event: December 15–January 2.

St-Barthélemy, Saba, and St Eustatius

On **St-Barths**, Carnival is held before Lent and the island holds several festivals in August: Fête du Vent in Lorient; Festival of Gustavia; the Feast of St Barthélemy (August 24); the Feast of St Louis (August 25) in Corossol. The St-Barth Film Festival takes place in April.

Saba's Carnival is at the end of July, and **Statia's** the last two weeks of July.

St Kitts and Nevis

Easter Monday: Horse racing, Nevis.
Late June: St Kitts Music Festival.
July–August: Culturama Carnival and arts festival, Nevis.
September: Independence celebrations.
October: Tourism Week.
December/January: National Carnival (mid-December to early January).

St Lucia

April: St Lucia Golf Open.
May: St Lucia Jazz Festival.
June: Dennery Fish Festival.
July: Carnival; storytelling, traditional dancing, and loud soca music characterize the island's biggest event.
August: International Tennis Federation Coca-Cola International (junior tournament); La Rose Flower Festival (songs, dance, and flowers at Micoud).
September: St Lucia Bill Fishing Tournament.
October: Creole Day.
December: Atlantic Rally for Cruisers.

St Martin/Sint Maarten

French Side
Before Lent: Carnival.
Easter: Easter Parade.
July 14: Bastille Day street celebrations and boat races.
July 21: Schoelcher Day street celebrations in Grand Case.
November 11: Discovery Day/Armistice (celebrated by both sides of the island).

Dutch Side
March: Heineken Regatta.
Mid April: Carnival, three-week celebrations at Carnival Village, Philipsburg.

St Vincent and the Grenadines

February: Mustique Blues Festival – the only blues festival in Caribbean.
Easter: Bequia Regatta – boat races and festivities on Bequia; Easterval, a weekend of music, culture, and boat races on Union Island.
July: Carnival: 12 days of calypso and steel pan music culminating in a vibrant, colorful, costumed party.
Late July/early August: Canouan Yacht Races and festivities.
Late November: Petit St Vincent Yacht Races and evening festivities.
December 16–24: Nine Mornings: parades and dances in the days leading up to Christmas.

Trinidad and Tobago

February/March: Hosay, the Shi'ite Muslim festival with processions, music, and dance takes place. Originally held to commemorate the martyrdom of the prophet's grandsons, it has developed into a colorful occasion with parades, music, and dancing.
March: Phagwa – Hindu "Holi" festival, celebrating the arrival of spring with participants covered in pink dye, is celebrated at the time of the March full moon.
Easter: Carnival in Trinidad and Tobago reaches a climax on the Monday and Tuesday before Ash Wednesday, and although not an official public holiday, everything is closed. The lead-up can be almost as frantic, with Panorama, the national steelpan competition, accompanied by nightly calypso performances. On the Tuesday after Easter are the Buccoo goat races, an important social occasion in Tobago.
April: Tobago Jazz Festival.
July: Tobago Heritage Festival, in late July, recalls the cultural legacy of the African slaves. Concerts and displays of traditional dancing are held in many villages.
August: Emancipation Day (August 1), celebrates the end of slavery with a procession through Port-of-Spain.
October/November: Divali, the Hindu Festival of Lights, is held in honor of the goddess Lakshmi. On this day, hundreds of tiny lights are lit by Hindus all over Trinidad and Tobago.
Eid-ul-Fitr, the Islamic New Year festival, also marks the end of Ramadan.

US Virgin Islands

December: St Croix Christmas.
January: Festival (6 Jan).
March 17: St Patrick, St Croix.

Easter: Rolex Regatta.
April: St Thomas Carnival (third week).
July 4: St John's Carnival.
October: St Croix Music and Arts Festival.

SHOPPING

ABC Islands

The ABC Islands have a range of tax-free shopping outlets. While Bonaire shopping is limited, Oranjestad in Aruba is a shoppers' paradise with designer wear, perfume, and local art, but it can be busy when a cruise ship docks. Sometimes stores are open seven days a week here.

Curaçao offers great tax-free purchases, shopping malls, and interesting boutiques, all dotted around Punda in Willemstad.

Anguilla

The most interesting shopping is in the studios of local artists:
L'Atelier Art Studio, North Hill, tel: 264-497 5668. Oil and pastel paintings, and prints.
Devonish Art Gallery, West End Road, The Cove, tel: 264-497 2949. Pottery from local clay deposits.
Estate Hope Art Studio, Crocus Hill, tel: 264-497 8733. Quilts, pillow covers, and wall hangings.
Loblolly Gallery, Crocus Hill Road, tel: 264-497 6006. Paintings and prints, pottery, and jewelry.

Antigua and Barbuda

In St John's, Heritage Quay and Redcliffe Quay attract cruise-ship shoppers with a range of duty-free outlets and a street market. There is an art gallery exhibiting work by Caribbean artists at **Harmony Hall**, Brown's Bay near Freetown (tel: 268-462 27870, www.harmonyhallantigua.com). Try the market in St John's for local produce. Antigua Black pineapple is reputed to be the sweetest in the world.

Barbados

Duty-free shopping is available at many stores throughout the island. To make a duty-free purchase, you must present your immigration slip (given to you when you arrive), or your passport and ticket.

In **Bridgetown** the main shopping area is along Broad Street in Da Costas Mall and Cave Shepherd department store. At **Medford**

ABOVE: batiks and other items for sale on St Martin.

Mahogany Village, Barbarees Hill, you can watch carpenters working with mahogany before you buy.

In **Hastings and Worthing**, the Chattel House Village, in St Lawrence Gap, has a variety of stores selling souvenirs and local crafts. Quayside Center, Hastings Plaza, and Sandy Bank have a wide selection of clothing and souvenirs. On the Wall art gallery (tel: 246-234 9145) at Champers Restaurant in Christ Church displays colorful art.

Holetown has a selection of stores in Sunset Crest shopping plaza, with local crafts, swimwear, and jewelry in the Chattel Village.

British Virgin Islands

An assortment of stores, including duty-free, line Tortola's Main Street in Road Town, including the famous **Pusser's Company Store**, which, apart from its own rum, sells all things nautical, clothes, and antiques and has branches in Soper's Hole Wharf in the west and Leverick Bay in Virgin Gorda. On Wickhams Cay I is a **Crafts Alive Market** selling locally made products. **BVI Apparel** has factory outlets selling clothes and gifts at low prices at Soper's Hole, Baugher's Bay, and Road Town. On Anegada, **Pat's Pottery and Art** features items all made on the island.

Dominica

Look out for quality authentic crafts in the Carib territory, and also in the stores in the center of Roseau.

Grenada

Among the better craft and souvenir stores in St George's is **Yellow Poui Art Gallery** (Young Street, tel: 473-

440 3001). Local specialties include batik and screen-printed items, jewelry, and attractive spice baskets. Spices and oils are available from **Arawak Islands factory** (Frequente Industrial Park, St George, tel: 473-444 3577, www.arawak-islands.com).

Guadeloupe

Shoppers in Guadeloupe searching for quality local arts and crafts, perfume and designer clothing, and all things French will not be disappointed. There are modern shopping facilities at the cruise-ship terminal in Pointe à Pitre with its tropical garden, restaurants, and stores. The largest commercial center with supermarkets is at **Destreland** in Baie Mahault.

The fashionable Rue Frébault in Pointe à Pitre has upscale, fashionable stores. However, most Guadeloupeans go to St Martin/Sint Maarten for serious shopping trips. Authentic purchases from Guadeloupe include music by the group Akiyo, locally made gold jewelry, excellent local coffee, fine embroidery from Vieux Fort, and clothing made from madras. A painting by Michel Rovelas is an excellent investment in contemporary art.

Martinique

There are several modern shopping malls concentrated around the Fort de France area, while the Village Creole at Pointe du Bout has some original boutiques. Martiniquan rum is among the world's finest, and you can buy one of the various makes at distilleries or at local supermarkets. Chocolate made locally by Elot is also worth taking home. Fresh flowers from one of the many tropical

horticultural centers are packaged specially for airline transport.

Local artists whose work is worth acquiring include Claude Cauquil, Louis Laouchez, and Laurent Valère. Manscour, whose atelier is situated in Trinité, specializes in glass sculptures.

Montserrat

There is a small department store in Brades, the **Montserrat Stationery Centre**, which provides much of what islanders and visitors need. Stores selling gifts and souvenirs are found in Brades, Woodlands, and Salem.

St-Barthélemy, Saba, and St Eustatius

On St-Barths, Gustavia and St Jean are best for tax-free luxury goods such as designer wear, perfume, and quality local crafts.

Saba lace, the drawn-thread work, is also known as Spanish work because it originated from Venezuela. It has been made for over 100 years here, and is on sale in stores and from private houses – any taxi driver should be able to take you to an outlet. The Saba Artisan's Foundation sells locally designed and produced clothing and fabric.

St Kitts and Nevis

Situated on 30 acres (12 hectares) of reclaimed land, Port Zante is the shopping center on St Kitts, with duty-free stores, plazas, and restaurants.

Try the **Caribelle Batik** workshop at Romney Manor for imaginative, locally made prints. For paintings, pottery, and printed silk, **Kate Design** has stores at Rawlins Plantation, Basseterre, and Charlestown.

The **Pelican Mall** and **TDC Mall** in Basseterre, and **Fanny's Closet** and the **Four Seasons Resort** in Charlestown, are all worth a stop.

St Lucia

Pointe Seraphine is a modern shopping complex convenient for the cruise-ship crowd. It has a selection of duty-free goods including perfume and designerwear and locally made arts and crafts. **La Place Carenage**, Castries Harbour, has duty-free shopping. Bustling **Castries Market** is worth a look, if only to see the tropical fresh fruit and vegetables and St Lucian handicrafts.

Gablewoods Mall at Sunny Acres, near Choc Bay on the Castries-Gros Islet Highway, has a good supermarket, post office, and a range of other stores. **JQ's Mall** in Rodney Bay Marina has a good selection of souvenirs, budget eateries, and clothing stores.

St Martin/Sint Maarten

For duty-free goods head for Front Street in Philipsburg and Maho Beach and Mullet Bay, or Rue de la République and Marina Porte la Royale in Marigot.

St Vincent and the Grenadines

St Vincent and Bequia are good places to find colorful batiks and lots of locally made art and crafts, such as straw baskets and woodcarvings.

Trinidad and Tobago

In Port-of-Spain, the Normandie Hotel has a well-stocked, if small, mall where visitors can buy locally made batik prints, T-shirts, art and crafts, and a variety of other goods. Other shopping areas of interest for visitors to Trinidad are the malls and shops downtown on Frederick Street, **Grande Bazaar Mall** on the Southern Highway, and **Golf City Mall** at San Fernando in the south of the island. For music, try **Crosby's** at 54 Western Main Road in St James.

On Tobago, craft vendors can be found throughout the island – or try **Cotton House** on Bacolet Street in Scarborough, for clothing, jewelry, and batik art.

US Virgin Islands

The USVI enjoy a duty and sales tax-free status so that most things are 20–50 percent less expensive than on the mainland. Wednesday and Friday are usually the most crowded shopping days, due to the number of visiting cruise ships.

St Thomas has the widest choice of duty-free shopping with a large proportion in Charlotte Amalie; Havensight Mall by the cruise-ship docks and Red Hook on the east coast are modern shopping malls packed with outlets selling jewelry, watches, cameras, liquor, and other duty-free goods. St Thomas also has a selection of handicraft outlets.

St Croix's King's Alley Walk is a new shopping area in Christiansted. In St Croix Leap in the west, there are some excellent woodcarvers.

St John features a variety of local arts and crafts. The most popular shopping areas are Mongoose Junction and Wharfside Village in Cruz Bay.

SPORTS

The climate and geography of the Antilles make the islands perfect for sports enthusiasts, and tourism has helped spark the development of a variety of sports facilities.

Diving

The clear blue waters of the Caribbean are the setting for a marine landscape of breathtaking beauty, a hidden world – accessible only to divers and snorkelers – in which gloriously colored and patterned fish vie for attention with extraordinary coral formations and reefs teeming with life.

All the islands offer equipment and excursion packages, including training packages for those who have never dived before. Addresses of well-reputed dive operators (always check on the reliability of operators and ask to see instructors' certificates) are listed below.

ABC Islands

The tourist offices provide informative brochures listing diving grounds and schools.

The waters around Bonaire are designated as an official marine park; diving in the clear waters off the island is a real experience with its coral reefs and colorful marine life. It is an ideal destination for underwater photographers. Dive operators include:

Aruba: Aruba Pro Dive, Oranjestad, tel: 297-582 5520, fax: 297-587 7722; JADS, Baby Beach, tel: 297-584 6070, www.jadsaruba.com. Operate underwater scooters.

Bonaire: Dive Friends Bonaire, Abraham Boulevard, tel: 599-717 3460, www.dive-friends-bonaire.com; Bruce Bowkers' Carib Inn, J.A. Abraham Boulevard 46, tel: 599-717 8819, www.caribinn.com; Wannadive, Kaya Gobernador Nicolaas Debrot z/n, Kralendijk, tel: 599-717 8884, www.wannadive.com.

Curaçao: Lions Dive Hotel, tel: 5999-434 8888, www.lionsdive.com; Ocean Encounters West, tel: 5999-864 0102, www.oceanencounterswest.com.

Anguilla

Unspoiled, uncrowded diving is on offer on Anguilla, with several wrecks to explore, as well as excellent sites that include Sandy Island, Prickly Pear Cays, and Little Bay. Organize your diving through your hotel or with: **Anguilla Divers**, Mead's Bay, tel: 264-497 4750.

Shoal Bay Scuba, Shoal Bay East, tel: 264-497 4371.

Antigua and Barbuda

Several hotels have their own dive stores. Dive operators include: **Aquanaut Divers**, English Harbour, tel: 268-728 7688, Email: aquanant@candw.ag. **Deep Bay Divers**, St John's, PO Box 2150, tel/fax: 268-7463 8000. **Dive Antigua**, Rex Halcyon Cove, Dickenson Bay, tel: 268-7462 3483, www.diveantigua.com. **Jolly Dive**, Jolly Beach Hotel, Bolans Village, tel: 268-7462 8305.

Barbados

There are several interesting shipwrecks to explore and there is excellent visibility for divers and snorkelers. Several experienced and reputable dive operators offer certification courses for all levels from beginners to advanced instructors: **Underwater Barbados**, Bay Street, St. Michael, tel: 246-426 0655. **West Side Scuba Centre**, Baku Beach, Holetown, St. James, tel: 246-432 2558. **Hightide Watersports**, Coral Reef Club, St James, tel: 246-432 0931. **Dive Barbados**, tel: 246-422 3133. For supplies and repairs contact: **Hazell's Waterworld**, Boatyard Complex, Bay Street, Bridgetown, tel: 246-426 4043.

British Virgin Islands

The wreck of the RMS *Rhone* west of Salt Island is the most popular dive site in the BVI and is also a marine park. Other wrecks include the *Rokus*, located off the southeastern tip of Anegada, and the *Chikuzen*, off the East End, Tortola. Snorkeling and diving is rewarding almost anywhere around the islands. Dive operators in the BVI include: **Dive BVI**, tel: 284-495 5513, www.divebvi.com. Dive shops at the

Scuba Diving

The following islands are renowned for diving:
● Barbados
● Bonaire
● British Virgin Islands
● Curaçao
● Saba
● St Lucia
● Tobago
● US Virgin Islands
Destinations with limited facilities, but wonderful diving include:
● Anguilla
● Dominica
● St Vincent and the Grenadines

Yacht Harbour and Leverick Bay on Virgin Gorda, and on Marina Cay.
Blu Water Divers, Nanny Cay Marine Centre, Tortola, tel: 284-494 2847, www.bluewaterdiversbvi.com.
Kilbride's Sunchaser Scuba, North Sound, Virgin Gorda, tel/fax: 284-495 9638, 800-932 4286 (US).

Dominica

Skin Diver Magazine wrote that Dominica is "...the undisputed diving capital of the Eastern Caribbean as well as one of the most unusual locations." Features include steep 1,000-ft (300-meter) drop-offs, hot springs, pinnacles, and walls. All can be found close to the shore. Dive sites are concentrated along the west coast.

The dive operators offer a variety of packages for both beginners and experienced divers, and also provide accommodations. An annual **Dive Fest** takes place in July, which features diving, kayaking, swimming, fishing, snorkeling, sunset cruises, and other water activities and competitions.

Approved dive operators, who all welcome divers of any level, including beginners and also provide snorkeling equipment, include:
Anchorage Dive Center (at the Anchorage Hotel), PO Box 34, Roseau, tel: 767-448 2638, www.anchoragehotel.dm.
Cabrits Dive Center, Picard Estate, Portsmouth, tel: 767-445 3010, www.cabritsdive.com.
Dive Castaways (at the Castaways Hotel), PO Box 5, Roseau, tel: 767-449 6244, fax: 767-449 6246.
Dive Dominica (at Castle Comfort Lodge), PO Box 2253, Roseau, tel: 767-448 2188, www.divedominica.com.
East Carib Dive, Salisbury, tel: 767-449 6575, www.east-carib-dive.com.
Nature Island Dive, Soufrière, tel: 767-449 8181, www.natureislanddive.com.
Sunset Bay Club and Dive Center, Batalie Beach, Coulibistrie, tel: 767-446 6522, www.sunsetbayclub.com.

Grenada

Grenada and Carriacou offer a good range of diving sites, including the wreck of the *Bianca C*, which sank in 1961 outside St George's, and some spectacular reefs. Grand Anse beach has dive companies, as does Carriacou. Contact:
Aquanauts Grenada, Grand Anse, tel: 473-444 1126, www.aquanautsgrenada.com.
Dive Grenada, Grand Anse, tel: 473-444 1092, www.divegrenada.com.
Carriacou Silver Diving, Hillsborough, tel: 473-443 7882 www.scubamax.com.

ABOVE: snorkeling off the coast of Bonaire.

Guadeloupe

There are excellent dive sites all around Guadeloupe. However, the star attraction, with abundant marine life, is the Réserve Cousteau at Bouillante. Named for Jacques Cousteau, the reserve has dive sites with enticing names like Coral Garden, the Swimming Pool, and the Aquarium. Contact the International Dive Center:
Centre International de Plongée, Plage de Malendure, Pigeon, tel: 590-98 81 72.

Martinique

The most popular dive sites around Martinique include shelf diving off Diamond Rock (Le Rocher du Diamant) and exploring the wrecks in the bay at St Pierre. The wrecks were sunk in 1902 during the eruption of the Mont Pelée volcano. When diving in St Pierre, visit the underwater Maman D'Lo statue that sits at a depth of 33ft (10 meters) just off the southern end of the beach.
Acqua Sud, Le Diamant, tel: 596-76 51 01.

Montserrat

The diving sites of the northwest remain accessible and have benefited from the volcano.
Sea Wolf Diving School (at the Vue Pointe Hotel, Old Towne), tel: 664-496 7807, www.seawolfdivingschool.com. Caters for all levels, from beginner to assistant instructor. Snorkeling equipment is also available.
The Green Monkey Inn and Dive Shop, Little Bay, tel: 664-491 2628, www.divemontserrat.com. Specializes in custom dive trips to suit each individual.

St-Barthélemy, Saba, and St Eustatius

Saba offers superb diving, including breathtaking underwater caves and cliffs inhabited by tropical fish and coral, which are carefully controlled by the Marine Park (tel: 599-416 3295) which encircles the island. From shallow (40-ft/12-meter) patch reefs to deep underwater sea mounts (100ft/30 meters plus), there are dive sites suitable for all levels of experience. Dive sites can only be accessed on trips arranged through local dive shops. There is a hyperbaric recompression chamber on the island.

Dive companies on Saba include:
Saba Deep, Fort Bay, tel: 599-416 3347, www.sabadeep.com.
Saba Divers, Fort Bay, tel: 599-416 3840, www.sabadivers.com.
Sea Saba Dive Center, Windwardside, tel: 599-416 2246, www.seasaba.com.

Statia also offers wonderful diving in clear waters with shipwrecks and relatively few divers. Snorkelers can swim among submerged warehouses and taverns from the old port, and visit shipwrecks – some over 300 years old. Contact:
Dive Statia, tel: 599-318 2435, www.divestatia.com.

St-Barths also has excellent diving, particularly on reefs and islets. Contact: **Plongées Caraïbes**, tel: 590-27 55 94, www.plongee-caraibes.com.

St Kitts and Nevis

With so many shipwrecks around the coast, the waters here are a diver's paradise. However, strong currents make swimming on the Atlantic side of the islands dangerous. Swim safely on the calmer Caribbean side.

On **St Kitts**, the places to try are:
Kenneth's Dive Shop, Newtown Bay Road, Basseterre, tel: 869-465 1950.
Pro-Divers, Turtle Beach, tel: 869-466 3483.
St Kitts Scuba, Bird Rock, tel: 869-465 1189.

On **Nevis**, Oualie Beach is a good snorkeling spot and is also the base for **Scuba Safaris**, tel: 869-469 9518, www.scubanevis.com.

St Lucia
For diving and snorkeling, try:
Anse Chastanet Dive Centre, tel: 758-459 1354.
Marigot Dive Resort, Marigot Bay, tel: 758-451 4974, www.marigotdiveresort.com.

St Martin/Sint Maarten
Diving is mostly from boats onto wrecks. The snorkeling is superb; try Dawn Beach or Little Bay Beach. There are many boats which will take you on snorkeling trips.
Blue Bubbles Watersports and Dive Center, J. Yrausquin Blvd, Great Bay, Philipsburg, tel: 599-554 2502, www.bluebubblessxm.com. Dive centers at Great Bay, Oyster Pond, and Dawn Beach.
Dive Safaris, Bobby's Marina, Philipsburg, tel: 599-542 9001, www.divestmaarten.com. Also has a center at La Palapa Marina, Simpson Bay.

St Vincent and the Grenadines
With abundant coral reefs and excellent visibility, the Grenadines offer first-rate diving conditions. Divers will find a wide range of sponges, corals, fish, exciting marine life, and a number of sunken wrecks.
Dive operators in St Vincent and the Grenadines include:
Dive St Vincent, Young Island Dock, tel: 784-457 4714.
Bequia Dive Adventures, Admiralty Bay, tel: 784-458 3826.
Dive Canouan, Tamarind Beach Hotel, tel: 784-458 8044.
Dive Mustique, Cotton House Hotel, tel: 784-456 4777.
Grenadines Dive, Union Island, tel: 784-458 8138.
Mustique Watersports, Mustique Company, tel: 784-456 3486.

Trinidad and Tobago
The best diving and snorkeling can be found among the exciting reefs around Tobago and its neighboring islands. Dive operators on the island work with beginners and experienced divers. For more details contact:
Manta Dive Centre, Store Bay Road, tel: 868-639 9969, www.mantadive.com.
Scuba Adventure Safari, Pigeon Point Road, Crown Point, tel: 868-660 7767, www.divetobago.com.

US Virgin Islands
Some of the finest diving in the Caribbean is to be found in the USVI. There are many schools and most

hotels offer diving as part of a watersports program.
On **St Thomas**, a particularly lively spot is Coki Beach, good for beginners and children. Diving courses, beach and boat diving, and snorkeling are available. For details contact Coki Beach Dive Club (tel: 340-775 4220, www.cokidive.com). Aqua Action at Secret Harbour Beach Resort (tel: 340-775 6285, www.aadivers.com) on a beautiful bay, prides itself on only dealing with small groups and physically disabled divers. The Chris Sawyer Diving Center, Red Hook, (tel: 340-777 7804, www.sawyerdive.vi) is popular, and has a custom-built dive boat. Branches also at Wyndham Sugar Bay Resort and Caneel Bay, St John. There are day trips to the wreck of the *Rhone*, every Friday. The trip includes gear, two dives, and lunch.
St Croix has a rich marine life, with a fabulous variety of fish, coral, and shipwrecks. Try Dive Experience (tel: 340-773 3307, www.divexp.com), or Cane Bay Dive Shop (tel: 340-773 9913, www.canebayscuba.com).
On **St John**, located in Wharfside Village, Cruz Bay, is Low Key Watersports (tel: 340-693 8999, www.divelowkey.com), a PADI 5-star IDC facility. It has daily diving from beginners to advanced and also kayaking, a popular sport on St John.

Fishing

Fishing is a popular sport throughout the Caribbean. Most fishing boats can be chartered by the day or half day, and can usually accommodate several passengers. Many will quote rates which are all-inclusive of lunch, drinks, snacks, bait, equipment, and any other essential items you might need on your fishing trip.

ABC Islands
Deep-sea fishing off Aruba can be arranged with **Pair-a-Dice Charters**, tel: 297-592 9586. Enthusiastic guides for fly-fishing trips can be arranged through the **Aruba Fly-fishing Club** via their website: www.flyfishingaruba.com.

Anguilla
Fishing from a traditional Anguillan boat can sometimes be arranged, either through a formal charter or through an informal arrangement made with a local fisherman. Ask the fishermen you see launching their boats from the beach. Another possibility is a fishing-boat trip to one of Anguilla's tiny neighboring islands, such as Sombrero Island, which has

a lighthouse open to the public. For sport fishing, contact:
Sandy Island Enterprises, tel: 264-497 5643.

Antigua and Barbuda
The Antigua and Barbuda Annual Sport Fishing Tournament is held in May of each year in Falmouth Harbor. For information on fishing charters, contact the **Antigua and Barbuda Sport Fishing Association**, tel: 268-460-7400, www.antiguabarbudasportfishing.com.

Barbados
Fish for wahoo, dolphin (dorado), barracuda, tuna, and marlin in well-equipped boats with experienced crew. Half-day or full-day charters are available with snacks, lunch, and drinks provided. Some crews will even cook your fish for you, straight out of the sea. Contact:
Fishing Charters Barbados, 50 Ridge Avenue, Durants, tel: 246-429 2326, www.bluemarlinbarbados.com.
Billfisher II, Bridge House Wharf, Bridgetown, tel: 246-431 0741.
Cannon Charters, St James, tel: 246-424 6107.

British Virgin Islands
The following operators offer sport-fishing tours for bonefish and marlin:
Anegada Reef Hotel, tel: 284-495 8002; fax: 284-495 9362.
Pelican Charters, Prospect Reef Harbour, tel: 284-496 7386.

Dominica
Dive Dominica operates half-day and full-day fishing trips.
Dive Dominica (at Castle Comfort Lodge), PO Box 2253, Roseau, tel: 767-448 2188, www.divedominica.com.

Grenada
True Blue Sports Fishing (tel: 473-444 2048) can organize deep-sea fishing expeditions.

Guadeloupe
Deep-sea fishing is centered on the northern Caribbean coast of the island. Companies offer half-day and all-day excursions. Michel, located in Bouillante, tel: 690-55 21 35, is the person to contact for deep-sea fishing in Guadeloupe.

Martinique
The **Centre Pêche Sportive Y. Pelisson**, tel: 596-76 24 20, is the best-known outfit for deep-sea fishing in Martinique. An annual billfish tournament held at the beginning of November attracts serious anglers from as far away as Trinidad and Tobago in the

St Thomas Skyride

For a stunning panoramic view over the beautiful island of St Thomas ride up to Paradise Point on the St Thomas Skyride (tel: 774 9809, www.paradisepointtramway.com). This cable-car ride rises to a height of 700ft (213 meters) in just seven minutes, offering a great lookout from its observation deck. Visitors can spend as long as they like at

the top, where they can also enjoy a choice of light refreshments from the restaurant or café.

Open daily 9am–5pm except on non cruise-ship days; entrance charge, except Wednesday, Friday, and Sunday after 5pm when the ride is free – an ideal time to watch the sunset. Be sure to get there early though.

south to Antigua and Puerto Rico in the north.

Montserrat
For fishing trips, contact **Danny Sweeney**, tel: 664-491 5645.

St-Barthélemy, Saba, and St Eustatius
You can go deep-sea fishing on The Prowler from Sint Maarten on Saba (tel: 599-416 6443/5104).

St Kitts and Nevis
Fishing charters can be arranged through:
Kenneth's Dive Shop, Newtown Bay Road, Basseterre, tel: 869-465 1950.
Nevis Watersports, Oualie Beach, tel: 869-469 9690, www.fishnevis.com.

St Lucia
For deep-sea fishing, contact:
Mystic Man Tours, Soufrière, tel: 758-459 7783.

St Martin/Sint Maarten
For deep-sea fishing charters, contact:
Blue Bubbles Watersports and Dive Center, J. Yrausquin Blvd, Great Bay, Philipsburg, tel: 599-554 2502, www.bluebubblessxm.com.
Rudy's Deep Sea Fishing, Airport Road, Simpson Bay, tel: 599-545 2177, www.rudysdeepseafishing.com.

St Vincent and the Grenadines
For sport-fishing trips contact:
Blue Water Charters, Aquatic Club, Villa, St Vincent, tel: 784-456 1232/458 4205.
Crystal Blue Charters, Indian Bay, St Vincent, tel: 784-457 4532.

Trinidad and Tobago
The colorful sea life and clear waters off Trinidad and Tobago are ideal for fishing. On the north coast of Trinidad anglers can find wahoo and sailfish, and off Tobago it's possible to hook tuna, dolphin (dorado), and even a marlin. There is also the annual Caribbean International Game Fish Tournament. For more information on where to fish and

details of boat charters contact:
Trinidad and Tobago Game Fishing Association, tel: 868-624 5304, www.ttgfa.com.

US Virgin Islands
Deep-sea fishing charters can be arranged from the Yacht Haven Marina in Charlotte Amalia and the American Yacht Harbor at Red Hook.

Golf

Golf is available on Antigua, Aruba, Barbados, British Virgin Islands, Curaçao, Grenada, St Kitts and Nevis, St Lucia, St Martin, the US Virgin Islands, St Vincent and the Grenadines, Guadeloupe, and Martinique. Barbados, Guadeloupe, Martinique, Nevis, and the US Virgin Islands each have at least one 18-hole Robert Trent Jones course. Aruba has one of the oddest courses in the world, with "greens" made of oiled sand.

ABC Islands
There are several well-maintained courses including:
Tierra del Sol, tel: 297-586 0978, an 18-hole golf course in the northwest of Aruba. The **Aruba Golf Club**, tel: 297-583 1644, has an interesting nine-hole course and the **Curaçao Golf Club** in Emmastad is open to members and non-members.

Anguilla
The 18-hole seafront championship course at **Temenos Golf Club** (Merrywing, West End; tel: 264-222 8200, www.temenosanguilla.com), has wonderful views across the sea to St Martin. Designed by Greg Norman, the club is part of a 120-room hotel and private residence St Regis Resort.

Antigua and Barbuda
On Antigua, there are championship golf courses at **Cedar Valley Golf Club** (18-hole), tel: 268-462 0161, and the **Harbour Club**, Jolly Harbour, tel: 268-462 3085.

On Barbuda, guests of the K Club can use the hotel's nine-hole course.

Barbados
Barbados has four beautiful courses, with championship 18-hole courses at Sandy Lane and Royal Westmoreland. However, you can only play at the Royal Westmoreland if you are staying at a hotel which has an access agreement.
Sandy Lane Golf Club, tel: 246-444 2500. Eighteen-hole course.
Royal Westmoreland, tel: 246-422 4653. Eighteen-hole course.
Rockley Resort, tel: 246-435 7873. Nine-hole course.
Almond Beach Village, tel: 246-422 4900. Nine-hole course.
Barbados Golf Club, tel: 246-428 8463. Eighteen-hole course.
Ocean Park, tel: 246-420 7405. Mini golf for all the family,

British Virgin Islands
Apart from a pitch and putt course at the Prospect Reef Resort in Road Town, Tortola, there are no golf courses in the British Virgin Islands.

Dominica
There are no golf courses on Dominica.

Grenada
The Grenada Golf and Country Club is a nine-hole course near Grand Anse, tel: 473-444 4128.

Guadeloupe
For golfing in Guadeloupe, contact **Golf International de St François**, tel: 590-88 41 87. Designed by Robert Trent Jones, the 18-hole championship course is undergoing renovation work but remains open for play. The upgrading project is due for completion by mid-2009.

Martinique
Martinique Golf and Country Club, 97229 Les Trois-Ilets, tel: 596-68 32 81, fax: 596-68 38 97.

Montserrat
Montserrat has no golf courses.

St-Barthélemy, Saba, and St Eustatius
There are no golf facilities on these islands.

St Kitts and Nevis
Golfing enthusiasts are well catered for. **St Kitts** has an 18-hole championship golf course, the Frigate Bay Golf Course, and a nine-hole golf course at Golden Rock (tel: 869-465 8103). **Nevis** has an 18-hole course attached to the Four Seasons Resort (tel: 869-469 1111); non-residents are welcome to play for a fee.

St Lucia

There is a public 18-hole John Ponko designed golf course at the Cap Estate (tel: 758-450 8523) and a private one at the Sandals St Lucia Resort (tel: 758-452 3081).

St Martin/Sint Maarten

Mullet Bay Golf Course, Mullet Bay, tel: 599-545 2850, www.stmaartengolf.com.

St Vincent and the Grenadines

The Trump International Golf Club (owned by billionaire businessman, Donald Trump), on the island of Canouan, is the Grenadines' only golf course. **Trump International Golf Club**, Raffles Resort, Canouan, tel: 784-458 8000, www.trumpgolf.com.

Trinidad and Tobago

The best public course on **Trinidad** is Chaguaramas Golf Course, tel: 868-634 4227, www.chagdev.com. On **Tobago**, Mount Irvine is an 18-hole course which hosts two professional tournaments, tel: 868-639 8871, www.mtirvine.com.

US Virgin Islands

St Thomas has a championship course with beautiful views – Mahogany Run (tel: 340-777 6240). **St Croix** has two 18-hole courses – Carambola (tel: 340-778 5638) and Buccaneer (tel: 340-712 2144).

Tennis

Tennis is played on all islands, to varying degrees. Courts are found primarily within the premises of hotels, but arrangements can be made to use these courts even if you are not a hotel guest. Some islands also have private clubs that are open to visitors, and public courts that operate on a "first come, first served" basis. The more popular islands offer instruction and equipment rental, and many hotels have resident tennis pros to help you improve your game. Barbados even has a tennis resort.

ABC Islands

Aruba offers excellent facilities; contact the **Aruba Tennis Academy**, tel: 297-583 7074, www.arubatennis.com. The **Netherlands Antilles Tennis Federation** (tel: 5999-523 3739, www.natf.an) on Curaçao, can suggest opportunities on the other islands.

Anguilla

Non-residents can play tennis at several hotels, including Cinnamon Reef, Carimar Beach Club, and Rendezvous Bay.

A multimillion-dollar Anguilla Tennis Academy (ATA) is being built with charitable donations to encourage young tennis players. For more information visit www.tennis.ai.

Antigua and Barbuda

Most hotels have private tennis courts. If you require public tennis and squash courts, contact **Temo Sports**, English Harbour, tel: 268-463 6376.

Barbados

Many of the larger hotels have their own tennis courts and will allow non-residents to rent facilities. It is advisable to reserve a court in advance.

British Virgin Islands

The Rosewood Little Dix Bay Hotel offers superb tennis facilites, including seven courts, a tennis clinic, and private lessons.

Dominica

Few hotels or resorts on the island have tennis courts.

Grenada

The larger hotels have tennis courts and allow non-residents to rent facilities. There is a public court at Grand Anse.

Guadeloupe

There are several tennis clubs on Guadeloupe, including:
Ligue de Tennis, Gosier, tel: 590-90 90 97.
Marina Tennis Club, Gosier, tel: 590-90 82 91.
Centre Lamby Lambert, Gosier, tel: 590-90 90 97.

Martinique

Ligue Régionale de Tennis, Petit Manoir, Lamentin, tel: 596-51 50 01.

Montserrat

There are tennis courts at the Vue Point Hotel in Old Towne, tel: 664-491 5210.

St-Barthélemy, Saba, and St Eustatius

Court reservations on St-Barthélemy can be made through **St-Barth Tennis**, which also offers lessons, see www.stbarthtennis.com.

St Kitts and Nevis

Guests at most hotels and resorts can access tennis courts. The Four Seasons Hotel on Nevis is well equipped with four red clay courts and six hard courts.

St Lucia

Anse Chastanet Resort offers tennis courts, otherwise contact the **St Lucia Tennis Association**, Cap Estate, tel: 758-450 0106, www.tennisstlucia.org.

St Martin/Sint Maarten

The **American Tennis Academy** in Cul-de-Sac, on the French part of the island, offers tennis vacations for children and adults.

St Vincent and the Grenadines

The Haddon Hotel (tel: 784-456 1897), on McKies Hill in Kingstown, has tennis courses.

Trinidad and Tobago

The **Trinidad Hilton** in Port-of-Spain and **Mount Irvine Bay Hotel** in Tobago have tennis courts.

US Virgin Islands

Many of the top-end hotels on the US Virgin Islands have good tennis facilities.

Watersports

Waterskiing and windsurfing are available on most islands and all the necessary equipment may be rented. Kitesurfing is also popular. *For information on diving, see pages 354–6.*

A variety of rental options is available for sailing, from mini Sunfish to two-masted yachts and large motorboats. Equipment can be rented, and classes are conducted on almost every island.

If you are interested in chartering a yacht, either crewed or bare boat, for a day or a considerable period of time, *see Getting There, page 318.*

ABC Islands

The ocean off the ABC Islands draws visitors seeking a variety of water activities and sports, from windsurfing and fishing to snorkeling and sailing. The sea is often crystal clear and shallow near the coastline and the coral reefs and a rich fish population can offer hours of fun. Most of the large hotels have watersports or the local tourist office can recommend boat charters.

Carriacou Regatta

The climax of Grenada's yachting year is the Carriacou Regatta, now a huge festival that involves not only local boats and boat-building skills, but parties, parades, and much jollity. It is essential to book accommodations well in advance.

ABOVE: sailing boats in the Grenadines.

Bonaire offers ideal conditions for windsurfing. Lac Bay, on the east side, has become a popular wind- and kitesurfing destination because it has 5 sq. miles (8 sq. km) of reef-protected, shallow water which makes it easy to learn and practice the sport. The world freestyle windsurfing championships are held here every year. Kitesurfing is popular on the west coast south of the salt works. Offshore winds make it imperative to take safety precautions and not kitesurf alone. **Aruba Active Vacations**, Fisherman's Huts, Aruba, tel: 297-586 0989, www.aruba-active-vacations.com.
Kite Surfing Aruba, Bakval 16-L, Aruba, tel: 297-586 5025, www.kitesurfingaruba.com.
Jibe City Windsurfing, Lac Bay, Bonaire, tel: 599-717 5233, www.jibecity.com.
Outdoor Bonaire, tel: 599-791 6272, www.outdoorbonaire.com.

Anguilla
Wooden boat racing is a major interest on Anguilla; in fact it is the national sport, with races taking place on almost every public holiday. The beautiful and distinctive boats are built on the island, and used for fishing as well as racing.
Good snorkeling can be found off many of the beaches; the reefs off Shoal Bay East are very close to the shore, while Scilly Cay (ferry from Island Harbour), Crocus Bay, and Little Bay are also good. Snorkeling can be organized via:
Rollins Ruan, tel: 264-497 3394. A day sail, including lunch, on *Chocolat* is available. Glass-bottomed boats for two can be also be hired.

Antigua and Barbuda
Many of the larger hotels employ at least one member of staff who will arrange fun and games on and in the water. A trip to Green Island for snorkeling and lunch is one recommended trip. For details of this and other ocean-side jaunts ask at your hotel or contact the tourist office (*see page 373*).
Sailing can also be arranged through **Nicholson Yacht Charters**, tel: 268-460 1093, or **Sun Yacht Charters**, St John's, tel: 268-562 2893. If you prefer the rum 'n' sun approach, try a trip on the **Jolly Roger Pirate Ship** from Redcliffe Quay, St John's, tel: 268-462 2064.
For windsurfing lessons and equipment, contact **Patrick's Windsurfing School**, Dutchman's Bay, north of the airport, tel: 268-461 9463.
For a whole variety of watersports, contact **Wadadli Cats**, tel: 268-462 4792; and for deep-sea fishing **Lobster King**, Jolly Beach, tel: 268-462 4363.

Barbados
There is excellent windsurfing to be had at the southernmost point of the island at Silver Sands and Silver Point. Contact:
Club Mistral, Silver Sands Hotel, Silver Sands, Christ Church, tel: 246-428 6001.
Body surfing is good along the southeast coast and you can rent boards on the beach at Crane Beach Hotel. The best surfing around the island is in an area known as the Soup Bowl at Bathsheba on the Atlantic Coast, but beware of the strong currents. For more information contact the **Barbados Surfing Association**, Christ Church, tel: 246-429 6647, www.bsasurf.com.
Mount Gay Regatta in May or June is the highlight of the yachting season. Small sailing boats, such as a Sunfish or Hobie Cat, can be

rented by the hour along the south-coast beaches and the west coast. Sailing trips around the island can include lunch, snorkeling, or a moonlight cruise. The following companies offer private charters:
Tiami Catamaran Sailing Cruises, tel: 246-430 0900.
Heatwave, tel: 246-429 9283.
Cool Runnings, tel: 246-436 0911.

British Virgin Islands
Snorkeling is fun on the rocky edges of many beaches, such as Smuggler's Cove, Tortola, or Deadman's Beach, Peter Island. Norman Island and the rocks nearby called the Indians are also a good choice.
Apple Bay, Cane Garden Bay, and Josiah's Bay are popular windsurfing beaches on Tortola; there are also good conditions in Trellis Bay.
Boardsailing BVI offers lessons for beginners and sailing classes (tel: 284-495 2447). In November, the surfers flock to these bays.
The BVI is one of the best sailing areas in the Caribbean. Some big hotels have small catamarans and Sunfish for their guests, others like Peter Island and Bitter End Yacht Club (with **Nick Trotter's Sailing School**, tel: 284-494 2745) also provide bigger yachts, some with a crew for day sails.
International yacht charterers like **Moorings**, **Stardust**, or **Sun Sail** have branches in Tortola. Check with the tourist board or the *Welcome* magazine for the long list of smaller charter companies. In general, yachts are rented on a weekly basis.

Dominica
Whilst there is limited provision for yacht hire on Dominica, the island is a popular stopping place for yacht charters en route to other Caribbean islands. There are moorings in the scenic Prince Rupert Bay. The Portsmouth Association of Yacht Security can provide assistance with customs clearance, water, and fuel. Whale-watching trips are organized by the dive stores (*see page 355*).

Grenada
Windsurfing and waterskiing facilities are available on Grand Anse beach. The Secret Harbour Hotel rents snorkeling equipment and also organizes windsurfing, yacht charters, and speedboat outings. Grenada has marinas and sheltered harbors. Contact:
Grenada Seafaris, tel: 473-405 7800.
Spice Island Marine Services, tel: 473-444 4257.

Atlantis Adventures

Atlantis Adventures allows visitors a chance to explore the sea without getting their feet wet. The *Atlantis VI* submarine provides a view of the tropical underwater world of the Caribbean, usually only seen by divers. Alternatively, the *SeaWorld Explorer* is a semi-submersible trip that reveals the marine life below the surface, through a glass gallery, while the boat remains above the water. Atlantis Adventures (www.atlantissubmarines.com) has several locations in the Caribbean, including:

ABC Islands: L.G. Smith Boulevard 162, c/o Fatum Building, 2nd Floor, Oranjestad, Aruba, tel: 297-588 6881; Hilton Hotel, John F. Kennedy Blvd, Curaçao, tel: 5999-461 0011.
Barbados: PO Box 394, The Shallow Draught, Bridgetown, tel: 246-436 8929.
St Maarten: 15 Walter Nisbeth Rd, Philipsburg, tel: 599-542 4078.
US Virgin Islands: 9006 Havensight Shopping Center, Suite L, St. Thomas, tel: 340-776 5650.

Spice Kayaking and Eco Tours, tel: 473-439 4942.

A variety of sailing options are available in Grenada. The Grenada Yacht Club in St George's has monthly races for members and visitors. PO Box 117, The Spout, Lagoon Road, St George's, tel: 473-440 6826. www.grenadayachtclub.com.

Guadeloupe

Guadeloupe is a paradise for surfers and yachtsmen and women. There is kitesurfing and windsurfing in and around the lagoon at St François. **Action Kite Caraibes**, St François, tel: 690-868 135, www.guadeloupe-kitesurf.com. Hires equipment and provides lessons.

Surfers head to Moule, which is reputed for the consistency and regularity of its waves. Several surf competitions are held at Moule throughout the year. **Arawak Surf and Body Board**, Le Moule, tel: 590-23 60 68, www.arawak-surf.gp. Offers advice, lessons, and equipment rental.

Guadeloupe has several well-equipped marinas and is a popular yacht-charter destination. With the islands of Les Saintes, Marie-Galante, and Désirade all within easy sailing, the attractions are endless for those who love the sea. The largest marina is **Marina du Bas Du Fort** in Pointe-à-Pitre (tel: 590-90 66 36). There's also the **Marina St François** (tel: 590-88 47 28) and **Marina de Rivière Sens** in Basse Terre (tel: 590-81 77 61).

Martinique

Kitesurfing and windsurfing take place on the Atlantic coast. Popular spots are in Vauclin and Cap Chevalier where the outlying coral reef transforms the entire ocean into a calm lagoon with lots of wind. Anse Trabaud is an out-of-the-way spot where wave riders go to jump Atlantic swells. Even though the spot is less picturesque, the Fort de France Bay has steady, year-round wind and is a favorite place for locals who live and work in the Fort de France area. **Centre Nautique du Vauclin**, Vauclin, tel: 596-74 50 83.

Surfers in Martinique head to Tartane where there are several schools and outlets for equipment hire. The experts head north to the isolated and dangerous spots around Basse Pointe and Grande Riviere. **Comité de Surf de la Martinique**, Trinité, tel: 596-58 02 36. **Ecole de Surf Bliss**, 28, rue du Surf, Anse Bonneville, tel: 596-58 00 96.

Martinique is fast becoming a Caribbean sailing capital. The marina in Marin provides safe, calm mooring with all amenities. The sailing sector benefits from French fiscal incentives and several yacht-charter companies have offices here. There is another smaller marina at Pointe du Bout in Trois Ilets. Martinique is only a day's sailing from the Grenadines and many crews like to start their charter in this French island. Provisioning is excellent as yachtsmen love to stock up with

---

BELOW: windsurfing off St Lucia.

French wines and produce before heading down-island.

Montserrat

Yachts and other small craft can anchor at Little Bay in the north of the island, subject to a small charge levied by the Port Authority.

St-Barthélemy, Saba, and St Eustatius

While Saba does not have a natural harbor or lagoon, the leeward side of the island provides protection from the wind and currents. Yacht moorings are clearly marked with a yellow buoy – all other colored buoys are private. Upon mooring at Saba, yachts are required to register with the Saba Conservation Foundation and the harbour master, both at Fort Bay. Windsurfing is not allowed off the island.

St Kitts and Nevis

The catamarans of St Kitts and Nevis are a great way to relax as you cruise around the coastline. Private and group charters, sunset and moonlight excursions, and snorkeling adventures are available.

St Lucia

For windsurfing and kitesurfing, contact **The Reef**, Anse de Sables Beach, tel: 758-454 3418, www.slucia.com/windsurf.

Choose a yacht or boat charter, crewed or bare boat. Most charter companies are based in Marigot Bay and Rodney Bay. Contact: **St Lucia Yachting Association**, Reduit Beach, Rodney Bay, tel: 758-450 8651, www.stluciayachtclub.com. **Moorings St Lucia**, Marigot Bay Marina, tel: 758-451 4357, www.moorings.com.

St Martin/Sint Maarten

Watersports are a highlight on St Martin, and your hotel will almost certainly be able to organize diving *(see page 356)*, snorkeling, windsurfing, and sailing.

If you fancy crewing aboard an America's Cup 40-ft (12-meter) craft (previous sailing experience not always necessary), then this is the place to do it. There are races between four vessels, sometimes including Dennis Connor's *Stars and Stripes*. Races take place off Philipsburg every Wednesday, lasting about three hours. Contact **Bobby's Marina** (tel: 599-542 2366, VHF 16, www.bobbysmarina.com) for more details.

St Vincent and the Grenadines

To organize bare-boat sailing or a yacht with a crew contact:

Barefoot Yacht Charters, PO Box 39, Blue Lagoon, St Vincent, tel: 784-456 9526, www.barefootyachts.com. **Grenadine Escape**, PO Box 836, Villa, St Vincent, tel: 784-458 6326. **Sunsail**, PO Box 133, Ratho Mill, St Vincent, tel: 784-458 4308.

Trinidad and Tobago

The islands offer good facilties for sailing and windsurfing. Contact the following organizations for more information:
Trinidad and Tobago Yachting Association, Chaguaramas, Trinidad, tel: 868-634 4210, www.ysatt.org.
Windsurfing Association of Trinidad and Tobago, Port-of-Spain, tel: 868-628 8908.
Surfing Association of Trinidad and Tobago, Port-of-Spain, tel: 868-625 6463, www.surfingtt.org.

US Virgin Islands

On **St Thomas**, windsurfing equipment and lessons are widely available (at Sapphire, Magen's, Morningstar beaches, and others) as well as Sunfish sailboats. Snorkeling is good off Sapphire, Hull, and Coki beaches; equipment can be rented.

Sailing is available every day, with most boats leaving around 9.30am, and returning by about 4pm; the cost is roughly US$100. There are many boats available at the marinas or even at your hotel. A couple to note are *Nightwind* at Sapphire Beach Marina (tel: 340-775 4110), and *Winifred*, a classic wooden sailing yacht at Red Hook (tel: 340-775 7898). You can combine onland tours with sailing in the catamaran *Spirit* run by Treasure Isle Cruises (tel: 340-775 9500). For power boats try Nauti Nymph, American Yacht Harbor, Red Hook (East End). This company has a large fleet for self-charter or with a friendly captain (tel: 340-775 5066). If you want to explore beneath the ocean but don't dive, consider a trip on the *Atlantis* Submarine *(see box, page 360)*.

A trip to the snorkeling trail at Buck Island National Monument on **St Croix** is highly recommended. Companies offering half-day excursions (equipment provided) include Llewellyn Charter (tel: 340-773 9027). For other water sports try St Croix Watersports (tel: 773 7060).

On **St John**, there is an underwater snorkeling trail off Trunk Bay; Cinnamon Bay and Salt Pond Bay also offer good snorkeling. Windsurfing equipment can be rented at Cinnamon and Maho. The *Atlantis* Submarine *(see box, page 360)* leaves Cruz Bay once a week. Day sailing trips, including lunch and

snorkeling, can be taken on the catamaran *Adventurer*, sailing daily from Cruz Bay to the idyllic island of Jost Van Dyke (tel: 340-693 7328). Try also Cruz Bay Watersports (tel: 340-776 6234).

BEST BEACHES

ABC Islands

Aruba's bathing options are mainly of the frantic, large resort variety – at Eagle Beach and Palm Beach. The one less-developed beach is Baby Beach at the far eastern end of the island. Bonaire is not known for its sands; nonetheless, Lac Bay Cai in the south of the island has decent bathing.

On Curaçao, the most pretty and low-key option is Grote Knip on the northwestern coast. More touristy and commercial (but still pretty) sands can be found east of town at Sea Aquarium Beach and Jan Thiel Bay.

Anguilla

Highlights among Anguilla's 45 beautiful beaches include: Maunday's Bay, Shoal Bay East and West, Little Bay, Rendezvous Bay, Mead Bay, Crocus Bay, and Sandy Ground.

Antigua and Barbuda

There is one beach for every day of the year on Antigua. Amongst the best are: Half Moon Bay, Long Bay, Galley Bay, and Dark Wood Beach. On Barbuda, the beach on the west side stretches for 17 miles (27km).

Barbados

On the calm, Caribbean west coast, are golden sand beaches with a wide selection of watersports. They include: Heywoods Beach (north of Speightstown), Mullins Beach, with a beach bar, Church Point by the Colony Club Hotel, Paynes Bay, and Fitts Village.

British Virgin Islands

Tortola: Smuggler's Cove, Cane Garden Bay, and Elizabeth Bay.
Virgin Gorda: The Baths, Little Dix Bay, Savannah Bay, and the beach at Bitter End Yacht Club.
Peter Island: Deadman's Bay.
Jost Van Dyke: White Bay.
Anegada: the western half of the south coast.

ABOVE: Maracas Bay, Trinidad.

Dominica

The best black sand beaches along the west coast are Castaways, Picard Beach, Douglas Bay, Batalie, and Toucarie. All are safe for swimming. The few white sand beaches (safe inside the coral reef, although watch out for currents) are along the north coast, at Woodford Hill, Turtle Point, and Pointe Baptiste. The sweeping bays on the Atlantic coast are enticing but dangerous.

Grenada

Some of the best are conveniently close to St George's: Grand Anse, Morne Rouge, and Lance aux Epines. Less popular and wilder (beware of the currents) are Levera and La Sagesse.

Guadeloupe

Pompierre Beach on Terre de Haut, one of the Les Saintes islands, is one of the most beautiful white sand beaches in Guadeloupe. Other stretches of shoreline such as Malendure Beach have black sand and deep-blue sea. The beaches at Gosier and St François are reputed for their turquoise, shallow waters and white sand.

Martinique

The best beaches are on the south and west coasts. In general, Atlantic-coast swimming is dangerous. Look out for the sign: *Baignade Dangereuse* (unsafe for bathing).

Grande Anse at Anse d'Arlet is one of the most popular beaches in Martinique. Situated in a protected bay, the sea is calm and clear, and there are several restaurants on the bay. One of the wildest beaches is Anse Trabaud, a long, isolated stretch of golden sand situated on the Atlantic coast, well worth the long drive. Salines Beach in St Anne is popular with the locals. To protect the environment, cars are not allowed near the beach. The beaches at St Pierre, Carbet, and Prêcheur have black volcanic sand. A trip to the islets at François offers bathing in clear sea on white-sand beaches.

Montserrat

Woodlands Beach is good for diving and for picnics, as is Lime Kiln Beach. Rendezvous Beach is the island's only white-sand beach. Hike there from Little Bay, once a charming black-sand beach, now Montserrat's only sea-access point and the potential site for a new capital.

St-Barthélemy, Saba, and St Eustatius

St-Barths has 14 white sand beaches, of which St Jean is the most popular with restaurants, shops and hotels nearby. More secluded beaches include Marigot and Lorient on the north coast, and Colombier on the northwest peninsula. Grand Cul de Sac is popular with windsurfers.

St Kitts and Nevis

Frigate Bay on St Kitts offers pale sandy beaches and calm waters ideal for swimming. The less-developed, beaches of the southeast peninsula, including Turtle Beach and Sandy Bank Bay, are also good for bathing. The beaches along the north coast are made of black volcanic sand.

On Pinney's Beach on Nevis, golden sand and palm trees stretch for miles. There are quiet, deserted beaches along the north and west coasts and calm seas, including Lover's Beach and Oualie Beach, which is great for families.

St Lucia

The island's most popular tourist beach is Reduit Beach at Rodney Bay. Nonetheless, beautiful and more secluded stretches of sand can be found at Pigeon Point, Anse de Sables (close to Vieux Fort), Anse Chastanet, and Anse de Pitons.

St Martin/Sint Maarten

The beaches are the main attraction on St Martin/Sint Maarten. There are more than 30 dotted along the coast

between the large resort hotels. Some worth trying out are: Dawn Beach, Maho Beach, Mullet Bay, and Cupecoy Beach (nudist beach) on the **Dutch** side; and Baie Nettlé, Anse Marcel, Baie Rouge, Baie Longue, and Baie Orientale (with a section set aside for nude bathing) on the **French** side.

St Vincent and the Grenadines

Throughout the islands of the Grenadines there are a multitude of exceptional white-sand beaches, often tucked away in scenic, secluded bays. Most of the beaches on St Vincent are of the black volcanic sand type, though these can still be very beautiful. There are a number of light-sand beaches in the area of Villa. As with many other Caribbean islands, swimming on the Windward Atlantic coast is not recommended. Wind-whipped waves and craggy rocks make for excellent viewing, but can endanger the swimmer. All of St Vincent's beaches are public. If the route to a beach leads over private land, though, make sure you ask the owner before crossing.

Trinidad and Tobago

On Trinidad, all the best beaches are along the northern coast but beware of the Atlantic currents. Maracas Bay is a stunning strip of sand, popular with locals; Las Cuevas Bay draws a more low-key crowd; and Paria Bay, accessible only on foot, is a beautiful day's hiking trip.

On Tobago, there is no shortage of beautiful sands; try touristy Pigeon Point – or more secluded and stunning Englishman's Bay.

US Virgin Islands

St Thomas: Magen's Bay, Morningstar Beach, Sapphire Bay, Lindberg Bay, Secret Harbor.
St Croix: Buccaneer Bay, Cane Bay, Grapetree Beach, Davis Bay.
St John: Trunk Bay, Caneel Bay, Hawk's Nest Bay, Salt Pond Bay, Maho Bay, Cinnamon Bay.

OUTDOOR ACTIVITIES

Bird-watching

A bird-watching tour to any of the following islands should offer plenty of chances to see some of the region's endemic and migratory birds: Guadeloupe, Martinique,

Volcano Observatory

Flemmings, near St John's on the island of Montserrat, is the scientific hub for volcano monitoring. The scientists welcome visitors from 3.30–4.30pm. Call in advance: 268-491 5647, or visit www.mvo.ms.

Dominica, St Lucia, Grenada, St Vincent, Antigua and Barbuda, and Montserrat.

Trinidad and **Tobago** are noted for their birds. The Caroni Bird Sanctuary (tel: 868-645 1305), south of Port-of-Spain, is home to the national bird, the scarlet ibis, and the Asa Wright Nature Centre (tel: 868-667 4655) has over 100 different species of bird.

The island of **Bonaire** is a favorite with bird-watchers. It is home to 170 species of bird, mainly clustered around Goto Lake, Pekelmeer, Cai, and Dos Pos. Look out for the pink flamingo, Bonaire's national symbol. Bonaire is the site of the Bird Watching Olympics every September.

Male frigate birds, with their distinctive red throats, inflated when attracting females, can be seen on both **Antigua** and **Barbuda**. There is a Frigate Bird Sanctuary on Barbuda, across the mangrove swamps of Codrington Lagoon. **St Lucia** also has thriving colonies of frigate birds at the Maria Islands Nature Reserve. Contact the National Trust on 758-452 5005.

Saba is home to a very healthy population of tropical birds, frigate birds, and other sea birds. The topography provides a wide diversity of vegetation and, as a result, a wide diversity of forest song birds. Contact the trail ranger (sabapark.trails@gmail.com) to arrange a guide or for more information.

In the US, Caribbean bird-watching tours are organized by:
Field Guides Incorporated, 9433 Bee Cave Road, Building 1, Suite 150, Austin TX78733, tel: 512-263 7295, www.fieldguides.com.

Hiking

Rainforests, mountains, waterfalls, and gorgeous views await you. Many of the islands have good-sized national parks with prime hiking opportunities (Dominica, Guadeloupe, Grenada, St Kitts, and St John in the US Virgin Islands, are particularly good), and St Lucia's Pitons offer experienced mountain climbers a chance to test their skills. Guides are often available to lead excursions. Below are details of the islands which offer interesting hikes.

ABOVE: the mighty Pitons of St Lucia.

ABC Islands

Hiking is the best way to study the islands' remarkable flora and fauna, especially through the national parks. Guides are not needed due to clearly marked trails. The exception however is Bonaire; contact **Outdoor Bonaire**, tel: 599-791 6272, www.outdoorbonaire.com.

Barbados

Every Sunday at 6am and 3.30pm, the **Barbados National Trust** guides a walk around different parts of the island – and it's free. Tel: 246-426 2421 for details and meeting points.

British Virgin Islands

There are numerous hiking trails in the Virgin Islands National Park, which lead along beautiful coastline and through mountain forests. Visit www.virgin.islands.national-park.com for more information.

Dominica

Hiking in the rainforest in the interior of Dominica is a magnificent experience. Do not ever go hiking alone – always go with a recommended local tour guide. Established tour operators, with good reputations, include:
Ken's Hinterland Adventure Tours and Taxi Service (Khatts Ltd), tel: 448 4850, www.kenshinterlandtours.com;
Antours, tel: 767-449 3577, www.antours.dm.

Your guesthouse will also recommend reliable guides for either hiking or day tours. Young men from Laudat will offer their services (less expensive than the more established guides) for the arduous hike to the Boiling Lake; take your chances if you feel confident, but many are well-informed. To see the parrots at Syndicate, contact the Forestry

Division based in the **Botanical Gardens**, Roseau, tel: 767-448 2401.

Grenada

One of highlights of Grenada is the Grand Etang National Park in the center of the island. This area of tropical rainforest is home to a huge volcanic crater lake which lies at 1,900ft (840 meters) above sea level. There is a visitors' center with information on local flora and fauna, and well-marked trails which take from 15 minutes to 3 hours to complete.

Guadeloupe

There are over 185 miles (300 km) of marked trails in Guadeloupe. Some are no more than short walks, others are long, strenuous hikes like the climb to the top of the Soufrière volcano and the Carbet waterfall. The national park in Basse Terre (spread over 42,000 acres (17,000 hectares) is the most popular area for hiking. A copy of the guide *28 Trails in Basse Terre* published by the National Parks of Guadeloupe is essential reading for those who love to hike. There are no poisonous snakes in Guadeloupe – the only potential hazard is the heat and humidity that can easily lead to exhaustion and dehydration.
Parc National de la Guadeloupe Habitation Beausoleil, Montéran, tel: 590-80 86 00.

Martinique

Some of the most agreeable walking trails in Martinique are along the southern coastline. The walk from Salines Beach in St Anne along the Atlantic shore to Anse Trabaud is particulary dramatic. Hardy hikers can continue walking all the way to Cap Chevalier. One of the most arduous walks is in the extreme north of the island from Grande Rivière to Prêcheur; the hike takes about 6 hours and is reserved only for the fittest. All trails are marked, and the degree of difficulty is clearly indicated. Information about hiking trails is available from tourist offices, and there are several organizations that specialize in walking tours to some of the most interesting places on the island that are accessible only on foot.
Sentiers de la Caraïbe, tel: 696-94 52 79 or 696-44 04 45.

St-Barthélemy, Saba, and St Eustatius

On **Saba**, you can climb up the 1,064 steps to the top of Mt Scenery; on a clear day you can see for miles. The Saba National Park offers a range of

gentler trails. Some of the most popular include Sandy Cruz (2½ hours one way), Spring Bay (2½ hours one way), and the Ladder (1½ return) – all rated as moderate. The North Coast Trail is rated as extreme and requires a guide to complete this 4-hour trek. The latest information can be obtained at the Trail Shop (tel: 599-416 2630) in Windwardside or by emailing sabapark.trails@gmail.com.

On **Statia**, hikers will find a lush rainforest covering an ancient volcano (The Quill), through which flits a species of iridescent humming-bird that is unique to the island. The tourist office publishes details of trails; some are in poor condition.

St Kitts and Nevis

Hiking is a delightful experience on both islands, with their lush rainforests and mountainous terrain. A particular thrill for the adventurous is the hike down into the crater of an old volcano on Mt Liamuiga in St Kitts. For guided hikes enquire at your hotel or local tourist office. On Nevis, **Eco-Tours Nevis** (tel: 869-469 2091) offer various options, including an Eco-Ramble.

St Lucia

St Lucia **Forestry Department** offers trained hiking guides and maintains the most routes (tel: 758-450 2231, www.slumaffe.org).

For hikes up the Pitons, contact the **Gros Piton Tour Guides Association**, tel: 758-489 0136.

St Martin/Sint Maarten

On the French side of the island, there is a network of trails leading up to the Pic du Paradis, the highest point on the island at 1,400ft (500 meters).

St Vincent and the Grenadines

The Vermont Nature Trails lead through rainforest in the Buccament

Touring Barbados

There are many different ways of touring the island of Barbados, from helicopter to kayak. Tours can be arranged with:
Island Safari, tel: 246-429 5337; fax: 429 8147, www.islandsafari.bb.
Johnson's Tours, tel: 246-426 5181; fax: 429 3528, www.johnson'stours.com.
Adventureland 4x4 Tours, tel: 246-418 3687; fax: 246-436 3687, www.adventurelandbarbados.com.
Bajan Helicopters, tel: 246-431 0069; fax: 246-431 0086, www.bajanhelicopters.com.

Outdoor Hazards

Manchineel trees: these are usually indicated by red stripes painted on them and a warning notice. The apple-like fruit and the resin contain a poisonous substance (the Amerindians used it on their poison arrows) and when it rains they secrete an irritant that burns the skin – so never shelter underneath one. Don't handle the leaves or rub them either.

Sea urchins: when swimming over rocks be careful where you put your feet – stepping on one of these spiny balls is a very painful experience, as a spine may get stuck in your foot.

Sea lice: however tired you may be don't hang on to a buoy or anything else covered in a fine green seaweed because the sea lice living in it can cause a very itchy, painful allergic skin reaction.

Snakes: the only dangerous snakes in the Eastern Caribbean are the fer de lance, found in Trinidad, St Lucia, and Martinique (if it bites it is not usually fatal but hospitalization will be necessary), and the bushmaster and two species of poisonous coral snake only found in Trinidad.

Valley north of Kingstown. There is an information center which can provide route maps.

From the Rabacca Dry River, it is possible to hike up to the crater of La Soufrière, an arduous six-hour round trip that requires an early start, but which is worth the effort for the spectacular views at the top. Trips can be organized through agencies in Kingstown like **HazEco Tours**, tel: 784-457 8634, www.hazecotours.com.

Trinidad and Tobago

Walking is a good way to explore the islands and see the fabulous flora and fauna. Always travel with an experienced guide. For more details contact:
The Forestry Division, Long Circular Road, Port-of-Spain, tel: 868-622 4521, 868-622 7476.
Trinidad and Tobago Field Naturalists' Club, 1 Errol Park Road, St Ann's, tel: 868-687 0514 (evenings and weekends), www.wow.net/ttfnc.
Chaguaramas Development Authority Guided Tours, tel: 868-634 4349, www.chagdev.com.
Pioneer Journeys, Pat Turpin, Man O' War Bay Cottages, Charlotteville, tel: 868-660 4327.

US Virgin Islands

Two-thirds of **St John** is a US National Park so there are many trails to choose from. The national park Visitors' Center in Cruz Bay will give you all the information you need (daily 8am–4.30pm, tel: 340-776 6201).

Reef Bay Trail (tel: 340-776 6201 ext 238) is a lovely downhill hike incorporating a ruined sugar mill, petroglyphs, and a spectacular beach.

Horseback Riding

Horseback is a great way to visit some of the islands, and may even offer you the chance for a canter along a sandy beach. Below are details of the islands where horseback riding is offered.

ABC Islands

On Curaçao, horseback riding is possible in the Christoffel National Park, through **Rancho Alfin**, tel: 5999-864 0535.

Anguilla

Expeditions on horseback, and riding lessons, are offered by: **Cliffside Stables**, tel: 264-497 3667.

Antigua and Barbuda

Riding tours are available at **Spring Hill Riding Club**, Falmouth Harbour, Antigua, tel: 268-460 7787.

Barbados

Caribbean International Riding Centre provides beautiful trail rides with picnics and includes horses suitable for disabled riders (tel: 246-422 7433).
Highland Adventure Centre offers scenic safari hikes and horseback riding in the Scotland district (tel: 246-438 8069, 246-431 8928).

Dominica

For horseback rides for all abilities, contact **High Ride Nature Adventures**, Soufrière, tel: 767-448 6296, www.avirtualdominica.com/highrideadventures.

Grenada

Contact **The Horseman** (tel: 473-440 5368) for lessons or trail riding.

Guadeloupe

There are several stables around Guadeloupe that specialize in beach rides and treks through sugar-cane fields or up the slopes of the Soufrière volcano. Alternatively, you can tour plantations and creole gardens by ox-cart.
Les Attelages du Comté in St Rose, tel: 590-56 61 12 specialize in ox cart tours.

Martinique

Several stables offer horseback treks along beaches and in the countryside.
Ranch Anse Macabou, tel: 696-21 34 22.
Centre Equestre du Diamant, tel: 696-33 31 95.

St-Barthélemy, Saba, and St Eustatius

St-Barth Equitation in Flamands offer rides around St-Barthélemy, tel: 590-629 930.

St Kitts and Nevis

Trinity Stables (tel: 869-465 3226) on St Kitts offers horseback riding with friendly guides.
On Nevis, contact Erica or John Gilbert at: **Nevis Equestrian Centre**, tel: 869-469 8118).

St Lucia

Tour the island on horseback.
East Coast Riding Stables, Fond d'Or Historical Park, tel: 758-453 3242.
Trim's National Riding Academy, Cas-en-Bas, tel: 758-450 8273.

St Martin/Sint Maarten

The Bayside Riding Club offers lessons and two-hour treks along the island's beaches. Contact:
Bayside Riding Club, Rue du Le Galion, tel: 590-873 664.

Trinidad and Tobago

Contact **Horseman Farm and Equestrian Centre**, Valencia, Trinidad, tel: 868-744 4001.

US Virgin Islands

On **St John**, whether you want a horse or donkey, full or half day, sunset or full moon, contact Carolina Corral, Coral Bay (tel: 340-693 5778).
On **St Croix** try Paul and Jill's Equestrian Stables at Sprat Hall Plantation (tel: 340-772 2880).

Cycling

The flat, but rugged terrain of the the ABC Islands is ideal for cycling. It is a good way to discover the land and wildlife, and to reach some of the more secluded beaches. Bonaire is the site of a challenging triathlon in November. It includes a cycle route, a swim, and a run. For details of rentals and tours contact: **Pablito Bike Rental**, Oranjestad, tel: 297-587 8655 or **De Freewheeler Bicycles**, Kralendijk, Kaya Grandi 61, Bonaire, tel: 599-717 8545.

A – Z

A HANDY SUMMARY OF PRACTICAL INFORMATION, ARRANGED ALPHABETICALLY

A ge Restrictions

The legal drinking age throughout the Caribbean is 18. Some car rental agencies only rent cars to drivers over 25, although more usually you have to be 21 or over. As for scuba diving, children as young as eight may participate at some resorts.

B udgeting for Your Trip

Your costs will obviously depend on where you go; the cheapest destinations in the Lesser Antilles are Dominica and Trinidad and Tobago, while resorts in, for example, Bonaire or the US Virgin Islands offer the ultimate in luxury and expense. Self-catering options are clearly more cost effective than the all-inclusive resorts. Getting around by public transport and taxis is a better way of supporting the local community, not to mention more economical, than renting a car.

Business Hours

The siesta, happily, is alive and well in much of the Caribbean, and throughout the region small stores may close for a couple of hours in the early afternoon, when the tropical sun is at its hottest. Stores open early, usually by 8am, certainly by 9am. They begin closing for siesta at noon or a little before, though in some areas, may stay open until 1pm. Business resumes about two hours later – 2pm in most places – with stores remaining open until 6pm. Again, there is some variation; on a few islands, closing time may be as early as 4pm (for example on Dominica). On Saturday, most stores are open in the morning, and many have full afternoon hours as well. Sunday is traditionally a day of rest, for church, and family.

C hildren

The islands are a perfect vacation destination for a family. Many resorts now offer action-packed children's activity programs, and babysitting facilities. Do check with the hotel in advance, however, as during the high season, some hotels do not allow children under 12.

Climate

The principal characteristic of the Caribbean's climate is the relative lack of temperature change from season to season. The islands' proximity to the equator means that seasonal temperature changes are limited to less than 10°F /6°C (*see page 366*, climate chart for Barbados). Year-round, temperatures average around 80°F (27°C) throughout the region. An added bonus is the trade winds, which bring regular, cooling breezes to most of the islands. During the "winter" – which is peak season for tourists in the islands – night-time lows can reach about 60°F (16°C), with daytime highs reaching as much as 90°F (32°C).

Rainfall varies widely, ranging from around 20 inches (50 cm) a year in Curaçao and up to 75 inches (190 cm) a year in Grenada. Rainfall is generally heaviest during October and November, though June is wettest in Trinidad and Tobago. Hurricanes can strike from July to October. The "dry" period, coinciding with the peak tourist season, is from December through April or May.

Hurricanes

Hurricanes are one of the most damaging and dangerous phenomena affecting the Caribbean (*see page 18* for a description of how

CLIMATE CHART

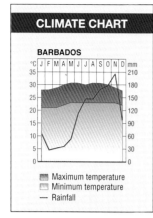

BARBADOS

- Maximum temperature
- Minimum temperature
- — Rainfall

a hurricane forms and develops). Devastating hurricanes in the region have included Ivan in 2004, which caused damage to 90 percent of buildings in Grenada and left more than 30 people dead. The storm also hit Grand Cayman, Jamaica, and St Vincent. In August 2008, Hurricane Gustav wrought devastation in the Greater Antilles, especially in Cuba, Jamaica, and Haiti, but most of the Lesser Antilles was unscathed.

Hurricanes usually occur between July and October, although visitations have been known in June and November, and the official "hurricane season" stretches from the beginning of June to the beginning of November, when some islands celebrate with a Hurricane Deliverance Day. The average lifespan of a hurricane is eight to ten days.

The risk of being hit by a hurricane varies from island to island; the southernmost islands – Aruba, Barbados, Curacao, Bonaire, Grenada, and Trinidad and Tobago – are rarely affected.

For more information, log onto: http://gocaribbean.about.com, and www.nhc.noaa.gov.

Crime and Safety

Crime and safety varies from island to island, with levels to a large extent dependent on such factors as standard of living, population density, and development. The disparity between the income of locals and the wealth of visitors can cause tensions. In some areas, such as Port-of-Spain in Trinidad, going out alone after dusk should be avoided.

The same precautions you take in any large town or city apply here: don't flaunt your wealth, keep your valuables close to you (avoid shoulder bags which can be easily pulled off), don't leave items in parked cars, use the hotel safe where possible, and never leave your possessions unattended anywhere, especially on beaches.

The high media profile given to violent crime against tourists, such as the horrific murder of the honeymoon couple in Antigua in July 2008, does give a skewed impression; the incidence of violent crime against tourists in the Caribbean is actually very low (given its frequency and the number of visitors).

Customs Regulations

Travelers arriving in the Antilles are generally allowed to bring in the following duty-free items:
- personal effects.
- a carton of cigarettes or cigars, or ½ lb (225 grams) of tobacco.
- one bottle (1liter) of an alcoholic drink.
- a "reasonable" amount of perfume.

US Travelers

For US travelers returning to the United States from the USVI, there are a number of importation options. Each individual can bring back up to US$1,200 worth of purchases duty-free. Travelers may also mail home an unlimited number of packages

Hurricane Categories

Hurricanes are categorized from one to five according to the Saffir Simpson Scale, which measures wind speed:
Category 1: 74–95 mph (119–153 kph).
Category 2: 96–110 mph (154–177 kph).
Category 3: 111–130 mph (178–209 kph).
Category 4: 131–155 mph (210–249 kph).
Category 5: over 155 mph (249 kph).

valued at US$50 or less, provided not more than one such package is mailed to any one person in a single day. If you exceed your US$1,200 limit upon returning to the States, the first US$600 worth of merchandise in excess is assessed at a flat duty rate of 10 percent.

Jewelry and Art

US law allows the importation, duty-free, of original works of art. Because of concessions made to developing countries, jewelry made in the Antilles may qualify as original art, and thus be duty-free. If you purchase jewelry, be sure to obtain a certificate from the place of purchase stating that the jewelry was made in the islands. Contact the US Customs Service for further details.

Disabled Travelers

Generally, there are few special facilities such as ramps in public places. However, you will find them in new shopping centers, restaurants, and many modern resorts. Resort hotels may well have a few specially adapted bedrooms or, failing that, first-floor rooms and minimal steps to public rooms.

For more information, visit: www.access-able.com or www.makoa.org.

What to Do if a Hurricane Strikes

- **During the storm** Stay indoors once the hurricane begins buffeting your area. When the eye (the low-pressure area at the center of a hurricane) passes over, there will be a temporary lull in wind and rain for up to half an hour or more. This is not the end of the storm, which will in fact resume (possibly with even greater force) from the opposite direction. Wait for the all-clear from the authorities before starting to venture out of your shelter.

- **If ordered to evacuate** Stay tuned to local radio stations for up-to-date information and instructions. Follow designated routes as quickly as possible. Take with you blankets, a flashlight, extra clothing, and medications. Leave behind pets (which are not permitted inside public shelters).
- **After the storm passes** Drive with caution when ordered to return home. Debris in the roads can be a hazard. Roads near the coast may collapse if soil has been washed

away from beneath them. Steer clear of fallen or dangling utility wires. Stay tuned to radio stations for news of emergency medical, food, housing, and other forms of assistance. If you have been staying in a rented home, re-enter the building with caution and make temporary repairs to correct hazards and minimize further damage. Open windows and doors to air and dry the house. Be particularly careful when dealing with matches or fires in case of gas leaks.

E mbassies and Consulates

ABC Islands

The Netherlands handles consular matters
Canada: Royal Netherlands Embassy, Constitution Square Building, 350 Albert Street, Suite 2020, Ottawa, ON, K1R 1A4, tel: 1-877 388 2443, www.netherlandsembassy.ca.
UK: Embassy of the Netherlands, 38 Hyde Park Gate, London SW7 5DP, tel: 020-7590 3200, www.netherlands-embassy.org.uk.
US: Netherlands Embassy, 4200 Linnean Avenue, Washington DC 20008, tel: 1-877 388 2443, www.netherlands-embassy.org.

Anguilla

The UK handles consular matters.
Canada: British High Commission, 80 Elgin Street, Ottawa, ON, K1P 5K7, tel: 613-237 1530, www.ukincanada.fco.gov.uk.
UK: Foreign and Commonwealth Office, King Charles Street, London SW1A 2AH, tel: 020-7008 1500, www.fco.gov.uk.
US: British Embassy, 3100 Massachusetts Ave NW, Washington DC 20008, tel: 202-588 6500, www.ukinusa.fco.gov.uk.

Antigua and Barbuda

Canada: Embassy of Antigua and Barbuda, 112 Kent Street, Ottawa, ON, K1P 5P2, tel: 613-236 8952, www.oecs.org/ottawa.
UK and Ireland: High Commission for Antigua and Barbuda, 2nd floor, 45 Crawford Place, London W1H 4LP, tel: 020-7258 0070, www.antigua-barbuda.com.
US: Embassy of Antigua and Barbuda, 3216 New Mexico Ave NW, Washington DC 20016, tel: 202-362 5122, email: embantbar@aol.com.

Barbados

Canada: High Commission for Barbados, 55 Metcalfe Street, Suite 470, Ottawa, ON K1P 6L5, tel: 03 236 9517, www.foreign.gov.bb.
UK and Ireland: High Commission of Barbados, 1 Great Russell Street, London WC1B 3ND, tel: 020-7631 4975, www.foreign.gov.bb (email: london@foreign.gov.bb).
US: Embassy of Barbados, 2144 Wyoming Ave NW, Washington DC 20008, tel: 202-939 9200, www.foreign.gov.bb.

British Virgin Islands
(See Anguilla.)

Dominica

UK: Dominican High Commission, 1 Collingham Gardens, London SW5 OHW, tel: 020-7370 5194, www.dominica.embassyhomepage.com.
US: Embassy of Dominica, 3216 New Mexico Ave NW, Washington DC 20016, tel: 202-364 6781, email: embdomdc@aol.com.

Grenada

Canada: Consulate of Grenada, Phoenix House, 439 University Ave, Suite 930, Toronto, ON M5G 1Y8, tel: 416-595 1343, www.grenadaconsulate.com.
UK: Grenada High Commission, The Chapel, Archel Road, London W14 9QH, tel: 020-7385 4415, email: office@grenada-highcommission.co.uk.
US: Embassy of Grenada, 1701 New Hampshire Ave NW, Washinton DC 20009, tel: 202-265 2561, www.grenadaembassyusa.org.

Guadeloupe

France handles consular matters.
Canada: Consulate Général of France, 2 Bloor Street East, Suite 2200, Toronto, ON M4W 1A8, tel: 416-847 1900, www.consulfrance-toronto.org.
UK: Consulate General, 21 Cromwell Road, London SW7 2EN, tel: 020-7073 1200, www.consulfrance-londres.org.
US: Embassy of France, 4101 Reservoir Road NW Washington DC 20007, tel: 202-944 6000, www.ambafrance-us.org.

Martinique
(See Guadeloupe.)

Saba
(See Aruba.)

St-Barths
(See Guadeloupe.)

St Eustatius
(See Aruba.)

St Kitts and Nevis

Canada: Honorary Consulate of St Kitts and Nevis, 133 Richmond Street West, Suite 311, Toronto, ON M5H 2L3, tel: 416-368 7319, www.mofa.gov.kn.
UK: St Kitts and Nevis High Commission, 10 Kensington Court, London W8 5DL, tel: 020-7460 6500, www.mofa.gov.kn.
US: Embassy of St Kitts and Nevis, 3216 New Mexico Ave NW, Washington DC 20016, tel: 202-686 2636, www.embassy.gov.kn.

St Lucia

Canada: Consulate General for St Lucia, 8 King Street East, Suite 700, Toronto, ON M5C 1B5, tel: 416-203 8400, www.stlucia.gov.lc.

Electricity

Different islands run on different electrical currents:
110–120V/60 cycle (US current): US Virgin Islands, British Virgin Islands, Aruba, Sint Maarten (Dutch side), Saba, Trinidad, and Tobago.
110–130V/50 cycle: Anguilla, Bonaire, Barbados, and Curaçao.
220–230V/60 cycle: St Kitts and Nevis, Montserrat, Antigua, and Barbuda.
220–240V/50 cycle: Bonaire, Curaçao, Dominica, Grenada, St-Barthélémy, Saba, St Eustatius, St Martin (French side), Guadeloupe, Martinique, St Lucia, and St Vincent and the Grenadines.

UK: St Lucia High Commission, 1 Collingham Gardens, Earls Court, London SW5 OHW; tel: 020-7370 7123, email: hcslu@btconnect.com.
US: Embassy of St Lucia, 3216 New Mexico Ave NW, Washington DC 20016, tel: 202-364 6792.

St Vincent and the Grenadines

Canada: Consulate of St Vincent and the Grenadines, 333 Wilson Avenue, Suite 601, Toronto, ON, M3H 1T2, tel: 416-398 4277.
UK: St Vincent and the Grenadines High Commission, 10 Kensington Court, London W8 5DL, tel: 020-7565 2874, www.svgtourism.com.
US: Embassy of St Vincent and the Grenadines, 3216 New Mexico Avenue NW, Washington DC 20016, tel: 202-364 6730.

Trinidad and Tobago

Canada: Trinidad and Tobago High Commission, 200 First Avenue, Ottawa, ON K1S 2G6, tel: 613-232 2418, www.ttmissions.com.
UK: Trinidad and Tobago High Commission, 42 Belgrave Square, London SW1X 8NT, tel: 020-7245 9351, www.trinidad.embassy-uk.co.uk.
US: Embassy of Trinidad and Tobago, 1708 Massachusetts Avenue, NW Washington DC 20036, tel: 202-467 6490, www.ttembassy.cjb.net.

US Virgin Islands

Canada: Embassy of the USA, 490 Sussex Drive, Ottawa, ON, K1N 1G8, tel: 613-688 5335, www.ottawa.usembassy.gov.
UK: US Embassy, 24 Grosvenor Square, London W1A 1AE, tel: 020-7499 9000, www.usembassy.org.uk.
US: US Department of State, 2201 C Street NW, Washington DC 20520, tel: 202-647 4000, www.state.gov.

Emergency Numbers

ABC Islands
Aruba: 115
Bonaire: Police 133, Fire 191, Ambulance 114
Curaçao: Police and Fire 911, Ambulance 912, Tourist Safety Service 63 79 11

Anguilla
Emergency 911
Police 911
Dental clinic 497 2343
Hospital 497 2551/2
Pharmacy 497 2366

Antigua and Barbuda
Emergency 999

Barbados
Police 211
Fire 311
Ambulance 511

British Virgin Islands
Police, Fire, Ambulance 999

Dominica
Police, Fire, and Ambulance 999.

Grenada
Police, Fire 911
Coast Guard 399
Ambulance: St George's 434; **St Andrew's** 724; **Carriacou** 774

Guadeloupe
Police 17
Fire and Ambulance 18

Martinique
Police 17
Fire and Ambulance 18

Montserrat
Ambulance 491 2552
Police 491 2555

Saba
Emergency 112

St-Barthélemy
Emergency 18

St Eustatius
Emergency 111

St Kitts and Nevis
Emergency/Ambulance 911
Fire 333
Police 911 **Police info** 707

St Lucia
Emergency 999/911

St Martin/Sint Maarten
Police (French side) 17
(Dutch side) 111
Fire (French side) 18
(Dutch side) 120
Ambulance (French side) 29 04 04
(Dutch side) 130

St Vincent and The Grenadines
Police, Fire, Ambulance 999
Kingstown Hospital 456 1185
Bequia Hospital 458 3294

Trinidad and Tobago
Police 999
Fire and Ambulance 990

US Virgin Islands
St Thomas and **St John**: 911
St Croix: Police and Fire 911, Ambulance 922

Entry Requirements

For travel in and around the islands a valid passport is required, even for US and Canadian citizens (re-entry to the US is impossible without a passport).

Visas are usually required only of visitors from Eastern Europe and Cuba. In addition to proper documents, all travelers must have a return or onward ticket, and adequate funds to support themselves for the duration of their stay.

G ay and Lesbian Travelers

Attitudes toward homosexuality vary from island to island but it's fair to say that the Caribbean is not renowned for its tolerance. Attitudes have improved since the late 1990s when several gay cruise ships were turned away from port, but public signs of affection are not commonplace.

For more information, try: www.gaytravel.com, www.gay.com, or www.iglta.org.

H ealth and Medical Care

Health Hazards

The main (though small) health risk to travelers in the Caribbean is infectious hepatitis or hepatitis A. Although it is not a requirement, an injection of gamma globulin, administered as close as possible before departure, gives good protection against hepatitis A.

The most common illness amongst travellers is diarrhea, caused by a change in diet and unfamiliar bacteria. You can help avoid it by observing scrupulous personal hygiene, eating only washed and peeled fruit, and avoiding contaminated water (drink bottled water if you are unsure).

The Caribbean has the highest incidence of HIV and Aids outside sub-Saharan Africa. Always take precautions.

Sun Protection

The sun in the tropics is much more direct than in temperate regions. Always use high-factor protection, especially on children, and be sure to reapply sunscreen after a dip in the pool or the sea. Bring a brimmed hat, especially if you plan to do any extended hiking, walking, or playing in the midday sun.

Drinking Water

In undeveloped areas away from resorts, it is best to avoid drinking tap water, especially after hurricanes, when water supplies can become contaminated. In these areas, stick to bottled water, and avoid ice in your drinks. Tap water in hotels and restaurants is safe to drink.

Insects

To combat mosquitos, pack a plentiful supply of insect repellent. At night, a mosquito net over the bed provides the best protection, although plug-in repellents are also useful (check the voltage). Mosquitos can carry dengue fever (causing fever, aching bones, and headache). Avoid aspirin if you suspect this disease.

Immunization

No immunizations are required for travelers to the Antilles, unless the traveler is coming from an infected or endemic area. However, it is a good idea to have a tetanus shot if you are not already covered, and possibly gamma globulin. Consult your government's travel health website for details.

Insurance

Comprehensive travel insurance to cover both yourself and your belongings is essential. Make sure you are covered for trip cancellation, baggage or document loss, emergency medical care, repatriation by air ambulance, and accidental death.

I nternet

Most modern hotels in the Caribbean can provide guests with high-speed internet facilities, and there are also an increasing number of independent internet cafés in town centers. Ask your hotel for details.

Languages of the Antilles

The multiplicity of languages in the Antilles reflects the region's checkered colonial past. All of the islands use their own creole language *(see People, page 53)*, as well as a whole array of primary languages, which include:
- **English:** Anguilla, Antigua and Barbuda, British Virgin Islands, Dominica, Grenada, Montserrat, St Kitts and Nevis, St Lucia, St Vincent and the Grenadines, Sint Maarten, Barbados, Trinidad and Tobago, and the US Virgin Islands.
- **French:** Dominica, Guadeloupe, Martinique, St-Barthélemy, St Lucia, and St-Martin.
- **Dutch:** Aruba, Bonaire, and Curaçao.
- **Spanish:** Aruba, Bonaire, and Curaçao.

- **Papiamento** is the local language of Aruba, Bonaire, and Curaçao. It has evolved from a mixture of Spanish, Dutch, Portuguese, and English, as well as African and Caribbean languages.

In addition to the primary languages listed above, Chinese is among the languages spoken on Aruba. English (and, to a lesser extent, other European languages) is spoken in several areas throughout the islands which have a high concentration of foreign travelers, but don't expect everyone to understand you – especially in rural areas and smaller towns. Efforts to communicate with island residents in their own languages are always appreciated.

M oney

A range of currencies is used in the islands. Whatever the official currency, the US dollar is usually readily accepted throughout the islands. The Eastern Caribbean dollar (EC$) is used in the following islands: Anguilla, Antigua and Barbuda, Dominica, Grenada, Montserrat, St Kitts and Nevis, St Lucia, St Vincent and the Grenadines. On French islands, the euro is the preferred currency, although the US dollar is accepted. On the Dutch islands the Antilles florin or guilder is the preferred currency.

In addition, major credit cards and travelers' checks are welcome at the larger hotels, restaurants, and stores.

If you are bringing US dollars it is a good idea to check around before converting your currency, especially if you are on a limited budget. Try to get price quotes in both the local currency and the currency you are carrying. Then check the applicable exchange rate. You may find you can save some money by making purchases in whichever currency gives you greater value.

Banking Hours

Banks are normally open mornings, Monday through Friday from 8am or 8.30am until noon. Many banks also have afternoon opening hours, especially on a Friday. A few banks open on Saturday mornings. You can use your credit and debit cards to withdraw cash from ATMs (cash machines). See under individual islands for specific banking hours.

Tax

Two taxes which you might not expect will be levied on you during your travels in the Lesser Antilles. The first is a government room tax, charged on all hotel rooms, which generally averages 5–10 percent of the total cost. The second is the departure tax. This fee varies from island to island, and is usually payable at the airport upon departure (mostly in local currency). However, it can sometimes be included in the cost of a package holiday.

ABC Islands

The main currency on Aruba is the Aruban florin (Af), while Bonaire and Curaçao use the Netherlands Antilles florin (NAf), also known as the Netherlands Antilles guilder.
Departure Tax: Aruba: US$36.75 for US-bound passengers; US$34 for other international departures. Bonaire: US$32 for international departures; NAf10 for domestic

departures. Curaçao: US$23 for international departures, including to Aruba; US$10 for departures to Bonaire.

Anguilla

The currency is the East Caribbean (EC) dollar. Normal banking hours are Monday–Thursday 8am–3pm, Friday 8am–5pm.
Departure Tax: US$20 is payable at the airport and US$5 at the ferry.

Antigua and Barbuda

The currency is the EC dollar. Banking hours are generally Monday–Thursday 8am–2pm, Friday 8am–4pm. The Bank of Antigua is open Saturday 8am–noon. On St John's, there are ATMs at Woods Shopping Center, Market Street, and High Street. There is a branch of Antigua Commercial Bank in Codrington, Barbuda.
Departure Tax: EC$50 or US$20.

Barbados

The currency is the Barbados (BDS) dollar, which you are not allowed to export. Banks are open Monday–Thursday 8am–2pm, Friday 8am–1pm and 3–5pm.

Value-added tax at 15 percent is added to most goods and services, so check to see whether it's included. The rate is 7.5 percent on hotel accommodations.

Restaurants and hotels usually add a 10 percent service charge, but it is normal to add another 5 percent as a tip. It is also usual to tip porters BDS$1 per item of luggage and room maids BDS$1 per night of your stay.
Departure Tax: BDS$60.

British Virgin Islands

The currency of the BVI is the US$. Banking hours are Monday–Friday 9am–2pm, although some banks are open until 3 or 4pm. There are banks in Road Town (Tortola) and Spanish Town (Virgin Gorda).
Departure Tax: US$20 for travelers

BELOW: unlike many islands, Barbados has its own currency.

leaving by air, US$5 for those leaving by boat.

Dominica
The currency is the EC dollar. Banking hours are usually Monday–Thursday 8am–2pm, Friday 8am–4pm. The National Bank of Dominica, the First Caribbean, the Royal Bank of Canada, and the Bank of Nova Scotia are the main commercial banks, all with branches in Roseau.
Departure Tax: EC$55.

Grenada
The currency is the East Caribbean (EC) dollar. Banks are open Monday–Thursday 8am–3pm, Friday 8am–5pm. They close for lunch 1–2.30pm.
Departure Tax: EC$50 (EC$25 for children between 5 and 12).

Guadeloupe
The local currency is the euro (E), but US dollars (US$) are also accepted at some establishments. Most major credit cards are accepted and you can withdraw cash from ATMs.

Martinique
The local currency on Martinique is the euro (e), but US dollars (US$) are also accepted at some tourist places. Most major credit cards are accepted throughout the island. There are also banks with ATMs.

Montserrat
Montserrat's local currency is the EC (Eastern Caribbean) dollar; US dollars are acceptable in some places. Two banks remain: the Royal Bank of Canada (with an ATM), relocated to Olveston, and the Bank of Montserrat, in the old Hilton bar, above St Peter's.
Departure Tax: US$21 payable in cash when departing the island.

St-Barthélemy, Saba, and St Eustatius
In **St-Barths**, the euro is the official currency, but US dollars are widely accepted. In **Saba** and **Statia**, the florin or Antillean guilder is the official currency, but, again, the dollar is freely used. Credit cards are rarely accepted outside hotels and dive stores. There are several banks in Gustavia, **St-Barths**, some, such as the Crédit Agricole, Rue Jeanne d'Arc, with ATMs.
Departure Tax: **St-Barths**: c4.55; **Saba** and **Statia**: US$5 to Netherlands Antilles, US$20 for international travel, although a number of airlines departing Sint Maarten include the international tax

in the ticket cost. In-transit passengers pay once if flying home via St-Martin/Sint Maarten.

St Kitts and Nevis
The currency on both islands is the EC dollar; US dollars are also widely accepted. Banks are generally open Monday–Thursday 8am–2pm, Friday 8am–4pm. There are ATMs at several banks.
Departure Tax: US$22 from St Kitts and US$20.50 from Nevis (to be paid locally in cash only).

St Lucia
The currency is the EC dollar, although US dollars are also acceptable in most places. There are foreign-exchange facilities in Castries. The National Commercial Bank (NCB) also has a branch at Hewanorra International Airport, open 12.30pm until the last flight leaves.
Departure Tax: EC$68 or US$27, often included in price of air ticket.

St Martin/Sint Maarten
The euro and the florin or Antillean guilder are the official currencies, but US dollars are also universally accepted. Normal banking hours are Monday–Friday 8.30am–3pm. Several banks have ATMs.
Departure Tax: US$30, or US$10 if you are leaving for the Netherlands Antilles islands.

St Vincent and the Grenadines
The currency is the EC dollar. US dollars and major credit cards can be used in most places.
International banks with local branches include Barclays in Kingstown (tel: 784-456 1706), and in Bequia, CIBC in Kingstown (tel: 784-457 1587).
Departure Tax: EC$40.

Trinidad and Tobago
The Trinidad and Tobago dollar (TT$) is the currency on both islands. Most hotels, restaurants, and stores accept major credit cards.
The First Citizens Bank has convenient foreign-exchange booths at Piarco Airport (tel: 868-669 2489) and Crown Point Airport.
Departure Tax: TT$100.

US Virgin Islands
The currency is the US dollar (US$). Normal banking hours are Monday–Thursday 9am–3pm, Friday 9am–5pm. There are ATMs at the airport on St Thomas and in the Banco Popular, Sunny Isles Shopping Center in St Croix, among other places.
Departure Tax: Usually included in the price of your ticket.

ABOVE: devilish fun, Trinidad.

Public Holidays

Easter, May 1 (Labor Day), Christmas, and New Year are public holidays, when nearly all shops and offices are closed, but otherwise holidays vary from island to island.

ABC Islands

January 1	**New Year's Day**
March 18	**Aruba Day**
Easter	**Good Friday, Easter Monday**
April 30	**Rincon Day, Queen's Birthday**
May 1	**Labor Day**
May (variable)	**Ascension Day**
May (variable)	**Whit Monday**
July 2	**Curaçao Flag Day**
September 6	**Bonaire Day**
October 21	**Antillean Day**
December 25	**Christmas Day**
December 26	**Boxing Day**

Anguilla

January 1	**New Year's Day**
March/April	**Good Friday, Easter Monday**
May 1	**Labor Day**
May (variable)	**Whit Monday**
May 30	**Anguilla Day**
June (2nd Sat)	**Queen's Birthday**
August (1st Mon)	**August Monday**
(1st Thur)	**August Thursday**
(1st Fri)	**Constitution Day**
December 19	**Separation Day**
December 25	**Christmas Day**
December 26	**Boxing Day**

Antigua and Barbuda

January 1	**New Year's Day**
March/April	**Good Friday, Easter Monday**
May (1st Mon)	**Labor Day**

May (variable)	**Whit Monday**
July (1st Mon)	**Caricom Day**
August (1st Mon and Tues)	**Carnival**
November 1	**Independence Day**
December 9	**National Heroes Day**
December 25	**Christmas Day**
December 26	**Boxing Day**

Barbados

January 1	**New Year's Day**
January 21	**Errol Barrow Day**
March/April	**Good Friday**
	Easter Monday
April 28	**National Heroes Day**
May 1	**Labor Day**
May (variable)	**Whit Monday**
August (1st Mon)	**Emancipation Day**
(variable)	**Kadooment Day**
November 30	**Independence Day**
December 25	**Christmas Day**
December 26	**Boxing Day**

British Virgin Islands

January 1	**New Year's Day**
March (1st Mon)	**H. Lavity Stoutt's Birthday**
(2nd Mon)	**Commonwealth Day**
March/April	**Good Friday**
	Easter Monday
May (variable)	**Whit Monday**
June 14	**Queen's Birthday**
July 1	**Territory Day**
August (1st Mon Tues, Wed)	**Emancipation Festival**
October 21	**St Ursula's Day**
November 14	**The Prince of Wales's Birthday**
December 25	**Christmas Day**
December 26	**Boxing Day**

Dominica

January 1	**New Year's Day**
March/April	**Good Friday**
	Easter Monday
May 1	**Labor Day**
May (variable)	**Whit Monday**
August (1st Mon)	**August Monday**
November 3	**Independence Day**
November 4	**Community Service Day**
December 25	**Christmas Day**
December 26	**Boxing Day**

Grenada

January 1	**New Year's Day**
February 7	**Independence Day**
March/April	**Good Friday**
	Easter Monday
May 1	**Labor Day**
May 31	**Whit Monday**
June	**Corpus Christi**
August (1st Monday/ Tuesday)	**Emancipation Days**
August	**Carnival**
October 25	**Thanksgiving**
December 25	**Christmas Day**
December 26	**Boxing Day**

Guadeloupe

January 1	**New Year's Day**
February	**Ash Wednesday**
March/April	**Good Friday,**
	Easter Monday
May 1	**Labor Day**
May 8	**VE Day**
May 27	**Abolition Day**
May (variable)	**Ascension Day**
May (variable)	**Whit Monday**
July 14	**Bastille Day**
July 21	**Schoelcher Day (Emancipation)**
August 15	**Assumption Day**
November 1	**All Saints Day**
November 11	**Armistice Day**
December 25	**Christmas Day**

Martinique

January 1	**New Year's Day**
February	**Carnival**
March/April	**Good Friday**
	Easter Monday
May 1	**Labor Day**
May 8	**VE Day**
May (variable)	**Whit Monday**
May 22	**Slavery Abolition Day**
July 14	**Bastille Day**
July 21	**Schoelcher Day**
August 15	**Assumption Day**
November 1	**All Saints Day**
November 11	**Armistice Day**
December 25	**Christmas Day**

Montserrat

January 1	**New Year's Day**
March 17	**St Patrick's Day**
March/April	**Good Friday**
	Easter Monday
May 1	**Labor Day**
May (variable)	**Whit Monday**

BELOW: carnival time in Barbados.

June (2nd Sat)	**Queen's Birthday**
August (1st Mon)	**August Monday**
December 25	**Christmas Day**
December 26	**Boxing Day**
December 31	**Festival Day**

St-Barthélemy, Saba, and St Eustatius

St-Barths: broadly the same as French St-Martin.
Saba and Statia: broadly the same as Dutch Sint Maarten.

November 16	**Statia/America Day**
First Fri in December	**Saba Day**

St Kitts and Nevis

January 1	**New Year's Day**
January 2	**Carnival Last Lap**
March/April	**Good Friday,**
	Easter Monday
May (1st Mon)	**Labor Day**
May (variable)	**Whit Monday**
August (1st Mon)	**Emancipation Day**
(1st Tues)	**Culturama Last Lap**
September 16	**National Heroes Day**
September 19	**Independence Day**
December 25	**Christmas Day**
December 26	**Boxing Day**

St Lucia

January 1–2	**New Year's Celebrations**
February 22	**Independence Day**
March/April	**Easter Good Friday**
May 1	**Labor Day**
August 1	**Emancipation Day**
August 30	**Feast of St Rose de Lima**
October 17	**Feast of La Marguérite**

ABOVE: partying Port-of-Spain, Trinidad.

December 13	**National Day**
December 25	**Christmas Day**
December 26	**Boxing Day**

St Martin/Sint Maarten

Dutch Side

January 1	**New Year's Day**
April 30	**Coronation Day**
May 1	**Labor Day**
May 25	**Ascension Day**
May (variable)	**Whit Monday**
October 21	**Antillean Day**
November 11	**St Maarten Day**
December 15	**Kingdom Day**
December 25	**Christmas Day**
December 26	**Boxing Day**

French Side

January 1	**New Year's Day**
March/April	**Easter Monday**
May 1	**Labor Day**
May 8	**VE Day**
May 25	**Ascension Day**
May (variable)	**Whit Monday**
Late May	**Slavery Abolition Day**
July 14	**Bastille Day**
July 21	**Schoelcher Day**
August 15	**Assumption Day**
November 1	**All Saints Day**
November 11	**St Martin Day**
December 25	**Christmas Day**

St Vincent and The Grenadines

January 1	**New Year's Day**
March/April	**Good Friday**
	Easter Monday
May	**Whit Monday**
July 7	**Caricom Day**
July (early)	**Carnival Tuesday**
August (1st Monday)	**August Monday/ Emancipation Day**
October 27	**Independence Day**
December 25	**Christmas Day**
December 26	**Boxing Day**

Trinidad and Tobago

January 1	**New Year's Day**
March/April	**Good Friday**
March 30	**Spiritual Baptist Liberation Day**
Easter	**Easter Monday**
May 30	**Indian Arrival Day**
June 19	**Labor Day**
June (variable)	**Corpus Christi**
August 1	**Emancipation Day**
August 31	**Independence Day**
September 24	**Republic Day**
October/Nov (variable)	**Divali**
December 25	**Christmas Day**
December 26	**Boxing Day**

US Virgin Islands

January 1	**New Year's Day**
January 6	**Three Kings' Day**
January 16	**Martin Luther King Day**
February (3rd Mon)	**President's Day**
March/April	**Good Friday**
	Easter Monday
May (last Mon)	**Memorial Day**
July 3	**Emancipation Day**
July 4	**Independence Day**
July (4th Mon)	**Supplication Day**
September (1st Mon)	**Labor Day**
October (2nd Mon)	**Columbus Day**
(3rd Mon)	**Thanksgiving (local)**
November 1	**Liberty Day**
November 11	**Veterans' Day**
(last Thurs)	**Thanksgiving (US)**
December 25	**Christmas Day**
December 26	**Boxing Day**

R eligious Services

All the mainstream church denominations can be found on the islands, as well as little-known cults. Attending a local service, perhaps Baptist or Seventh Day Adventist, is a wonderful way to experience an important aspect of Caribbean life, and you will be assured of a warm welcome, as long as you dress smartly and act with decorum and respect. Local tourist offices and free tourist publications should be able to advise you of times of services.

T elecommunications

Phone cards in several denominations are available on the islands. They are useful for avoiding the usually extremely high hotel charges on phone calls. Residents of the US and Canada can use AT&T USA Direct public phones with a charge card. Some public phones allow holders of a European charge card, such as a BT Chargecard, to access the home operator.

If you want to use you cellphone while abroad, check with your network to see if it will work there. If so, the best thing to do is to buy a SIM card locally (from any Cable & Wireless/Digicel outlet).

Area Codes

ABC Islands: Aruba 297; **Bonaire** 599; **Curaçao** 5999.
Anguilla 264. Access codes: AT&T: 800-872 2881; MCI: 800-888 8000.
Antigua and Barbuda 268.
Barbados 246.
British Virgin Islands 284.
Dominica 767.
Grenada 473. Access codes: AT&T: 800-872 2881; MCI: 800-888 8000.
Guadeloupe 590 (must be dialed before dialing the Guadeloupe phone number, which is prefixed with 0590; drop first zero when dialing from abroad).
Martinique 596 (this is the country code, followed by the local number which is prefixed with 0596; drop first zero when dialing from abroad).
Montserrat 664.
St-Barths 590. Access codes: AT&T: 0800-99 0011; MCI: 800-99 0019.
Saba 599.
Statia 5993. Access codes: AT&T: 800-872 2881; MCI: 800-888 8000.
St Kitts and Nevis 869.
St Lucia 758.
St Martin/Sint Maarten The country code for the French side, St Martin, is **590**, and the Dutch side is **599**. The telephone system can be confusing as the French local numbers are already prefixed with 0590, so to call St Martin from abroad you must dial the country code +590 then the local number beginning with 0590 (but drop the first zero) so you have +590 590 and then the following six digits.
St Vincent and the Grenadines 784.
Trinidad and Tobago 868. Access codes: AT&T, 800-872 2881; MCI, 800-888 8000.
US Virgin Islands 340. Access codes: 800-225 5288; MCI, 1-888 757 6655; Sprint: tel: 1-800 877 8000.

Tipping

On most restaurant and hotel bills, you will find that a 10–15 percent service charge has been added by the management. If this is the case, tipping is unnecessary, although a small gratuity given directly to an attentive waitress or bellman is always appreciated. When service is not included, a tip in the 15–20 percent range is appropriate. Taxi drivers should be tipped within this range as well.

Tourist Information Offices

Caribbean Tourism Association
Canada: Taurus House, 512 Duplex Avenue, Toronto M4R 2E3, tel: 416-485 8724, email: ctotoronto@caribtourism.com
UK: 42 Westminster Palace Gardens, Artillery Row, London SW1P 1RR, tel: 020-7222 4335, email: cto@carib-tourism.com; www.caribbean.co.uk
US: 80 Broad Street, 32nd Floor, New York, NY 10004, tel: 212-635 9530, email: ctony@caribtourism.com; www.caribbeantravel.com

ABC Islands

Aruba
Aruba Tourism Authority, 172 L.G. Smith Boulevard, Oranjestad, tel: 297-582 3777, www.aruba.com.
Europe: Aruba Tourism Authority, Schimmelpenninckklaan 1, 2517 JN The Hague, The Netherlands, tel: 70-302 8040, email: ata.europe@aruba.com.
UK: Aruba Tourism Authority, The Saltmarsh Partnership, The Copperfield, 25 Copperfield Street, London SE1 0EN, tel: 020-7928 1600.
US: Aruba Tourism Authority, 100 Plaza Drive, First Floor, Secaucus, NJ 07094, tel: 201-558 1110, 800-TO-ARUBA, email: ata.newjersey@aruba.com.
1 Financial Plaza, Suite 2508, Fort Lauderdale, FL 33394, tel: 954-767 6477, email: ata.florida@aruba.com.
Bonaire
Tourism Corporation Bonaire, Kaya Grandi 2, Kralendijk, tel: 599-717 8322, email: info@tourismbonaire.com, www.infobonaire.com.
Europe: Basis Communicatie B.V.,

Wagenweg 252, PO Box 472, NL-2000 AL Haarlem, The Netherlands, tel: 23-5430 705, email: europe@tourismbonaire.com
US: Adams Unlimited, 80 Broad Street, 32nd Floor, Suite 3202, New York, NY 10004, tel: 212-956 5912, email: usa@tourismbonaire.com.
Curaçao
Curaçao Tourist Board, PO Box 3266, Pietermaai 19, Willemstad, tel: 5999-434 8200, www.curacao-tourism.com, www.curacao.com.
Europe: Curaçao Tourist Bureau Europe, Vasteland 82-84, 3011 BP Rotterdam, Holland, tel: 10-414 2639, www.curacaoinfo.nl.
US: 3361 SW 3rd Avenue, Suite 201, Miami, Florida, 33145, tel: 305-285 0511, email: northamerica@curaçao.com

Anguilla

Anguilla Tourist Board, Coronation Avenue, The Valley, tel: 264-497 2759, 1-800 553 4939 (toll-free), email: atbtour@anguillanet.com, www.anguilla-vacation.com.
Canada: 1875 Old Waterdown Road, Burlington, Canada L7R 3X5, tel: 905-689 7697, email: dpusching@anguillacanada.ca.
UK: 7A Crealock Street, London SW18 2BS, tel: 020-8871 0012, email: anguilla@tiscali.co.uk.
US: 246 Central Avenue, White Plains, NY 10606, tel: 914-287 2400, email: mwturnstyle@aol.com.

Antigua and Barbuda

PO Box 363, Nevis Street, St John's, Antigua, tel: 268-462 0480, www.antigua-barbuda.com, email: deptourism@antigua.gov.ag.

BELOW: old-fashioned phone boxes in Grenada.

Open Monday–Friday 8.30am–4pm, Saturday 8.30am–noon. There is also a small branch at the airport in Arrivals.
Canada: 60 St Claire Avenue East, Suite 304, Toronto, Ontario M4T 1N5, tel: 416-961 3085, email: info@antigua-barbuda-ca.com.
UK: 45 Crawford Place, 2nd Floor, London W1H 4LP, tel: 020-7258 0070, email: tourisminfo@antigua-barbuda.com.
US: 610 5th Avenue, Suite 311, New York, NY 10020, tel: 212-541 4117, email: info@antigua-barbuda.org.

Barbados

The main tourist office is at Harbour Road, Bridgetown (tel: 246-427 2623). There are also offices at the airport (tel: 246-428 7101) and cruise terminal (tel: 246-426 1718). An information kiosk is at **Cave Shepherd** department store, Broad Street, Bridgetown. www.barbados.org.
Canada: 105 Adelaide Street West, Suite 1010, Toronto, Ontario M5H 1P9, tel: 416-214 9880.
UK: 263 Tottenham Court Road, London W1P 9AA, tel: 020-7636 9448.
US: **New York**: 800 2nd Avenue, New York, NY 10017, tel: 212-986 6516/ 800-221 9831 (toll-free in US).
Los Angeles: 3440 Wilshire Boulevard, Suite 1215, Los Angeles, California 90010. tel: 213-380 2198.

British Virgin Islands

Tortola: DeCastro Street, 2nd Floor, AKARA Building, Road Town, tel: 284-494 3134. email: info@bvitourism.com.
Virgin Gorda: Virgin Gorda Yacht Harbour, tel: 284-495 5181, www.bvitourism.com, www.bviwelcome.com.
UK: The BVI Tourist Board, 15 Upper Grosvenor Street, London W1K 7PJ, tel: 020-7355 9585, email: infouk@bvi.org.uk.
US: **New York**: BVI Tourist Board, 1270 Broadway, Suite 705, New York, NY 10001, tel: 800-835 8530 (toll-free in US), 212-696 0400, email: info@bvitourism.com.
Los Angeles: 3450 Wilshire Boulevard, Suite 1202, Los Angeles, California 90010, tel: 213-736 8931, email: info@bvitourism.com.

Dominica

Old Market Square, Roseau (open Monday–Friday 8am–6pm), www.dominica.dm.
UK: Dominica High Commission, 1 Collingham Gardens, London SW5 0HW, tel: 020-7370 5194/5.
US: Dominica Tourist Office, 110–64 Queens Boulevard, PO Box 427, Forest Hills, New York, 11375-6347,

tel: 718-261 9615,
email: dominicany@dominica.dm

Grenada

Grenada Board of Tourism:
Burn's Point, PO Box 293,
St George's, tel: 473-440 2279,
email: gbt@caribsurf.com.
www.grenadagrenadines.com.
Canada: Grenada Tourism Office,
439 University Avenue, Suite 920,
Toronto, Ontario M5G 1Y8, tel: 416-595 1339.
UK: Grenada Tourism Office,
11 Blades Court, 121 Deodar Road,
London SW15 2NU, tel: 020-8877 4516.
US: Grenada Tourism Office, 317
Madison Avenue, Suite 1704, New
York, NY 10017, tel: 212-687 9554.

Guadeloupe

**Office du Tourisme de la
Guadeloupe**, 5 Square de la Banque,
BP 422, 97163 Pointe-à-Pitre,
tel: 590-82 09 30.
Office du Tourisme, Basse-Terre
Tel: 590-81 24 83/0590 81 61 54.
Office Municipal de St-François
Tel: 590-88 48 74.
All towns have local tourism bureaux.
Canada: French Tourist Office
Montréal: 1981 Avenue McGill
College, Suite 490, Montréal H3A
2W9, tel: 514-844 8566.
Toronto: 30 St Patrick Street, Suite
700, Toronto MST 3A3, tel: 416-593 4723.

UK: French Tourist Office (Maison de
la France), 178 Piccadilly, London
W1 0AL, tel: 020-7629 2869.
US: French Tourist Office, 825 Third
Avenue, 29th Floor, New York, NY
10022, tel: 514-288 1904.

Martinique

Office du Tourisme, Aimé Césaire
Airport-Lamentin, tel: 596-42 18 06,
www.martinique.org.
Canada: Comité Martiniquais de
Tourisme, 4000 rue Saint Ambroise,
Bureau 265, Montréal, Québec H4C
2C7, tel: 514-844 8566.
US: Martinique Promotion Bureau,
825 Third Avenue, 29th Floor, New
York, NY 10022, tel: 212-838 7800.

Montserrat

Montserrat Tourist Board, 7 Farara
Plaza, Buildings B and C, PO Box 7,
Brades, tel: 644-491 2230/8730,
www.visitmontserrat.com.
UK: 7 Portland Place, London W1B
1PP, tel: 020-7031 0317, email:
j.panton@montserratgov.co.uk.
US: Cheryl Andrews Marketing Inc.,
2655 Le Jeune Road, Suite 805,
Coral Gables, FL 33134, tel: 305-444 4033, email: montserrat@cheryl
andrewsmarketing.com.

St-Barthélemy, Saba,
and St Eustatius

St-Barths: Quai Général de Gaulle,
Gustavia, tel: 590-27 87 27,
www.st-barths.com.

Saba: Windwardside, tel: 599-416
2231, www.sabatourism.com.
Statia: Fort Oranjestad, tel: 599-318
2433, www.statiatourism.com.

St Kitts and Nevis

St Kitts: Pelican Mall, Bay Road, PO
Box 132, Basseterre, tel: 869-465
4040, www.stkittsnevishta.org.
Nevis: Main Street, Charlestown,
tel: 869-469 7550.
Canada: 133 Richmond St West,
Suite 311, Toronto, Ontario M5H
2L3, tel: 416-368 6707, email:
canada.office@stkittstourism.kn.
UK: 10 Kensington Court, London
W8 5DL, tel: 020-7376 0881,
email: uk-europe.office@stkittstourism.kn.
US: 3216 New Mexico Avenue, NW
Washington DC 2001-2745, tel: 202-364 8123, email: info@stkittstourism.kn.

St Lucia

PO Box 221, Sureline Building, Vide
Bouteille, Castries, tel: 758-452
4094, email: slutour@candw.lc,
www.stlucia.org.
Canada: 8 King Street East, Suite
700, Toronto, Ontario M5C 1BS,
tel: 416-362 4242/1-800 869 0377.
UK: St Lucia Tourist Board, 1
Collingham Gardens, London
SW5 0HW, tel: 020-7341 7000,
email: hslu@btconnect.com.
US: St Lucia Tourist Board, 800
Second Avenue, Suite 400J, 9th
Floor, New York 10017, tel: 212-867
2951, email: stluciatourism@aol.com.

Weddings in the Carribean

There are those who still prefer a traditional wedding at home, followed by a honeymoon away, but others – in increasing numbers – decide to combine the two, and bring family and friends along as well. A Caribbean island makes the perfect destination. Choose a hotel that employs a full-time wedding organizer, or, through your travel agent, choose one of the tour operators who now offer all-in wedding packages. Here are some points to note:

● Rules vary from island to island (contact tourist offices for information), but in most cases it is required that couples be over 18, and for the wedding to be conducted after three working days. Hotels prefer you to be resident there for seven days.
● You will need valid passports, birth certificates, and any relevant divorce or death certificates. Allow approximately half a day to complete administration prior to the ceremony (paperwork can be done

only during government business hours, so check that public holidays don't intervene). On English islands, non-English documents must be translated by an officially recognized translator.
● The marriage may be carried out by a marriage officer or a clergyman. In the latter case, it may be necessary for your home minister to liaise with the island minister; this is always the case for Catholic services.
● The marriage is legally binding.
● The bride and bridegroom can usually choose their own music.
● Wedding outfits (remember the heat and the relaxed setting when planning yours) can usually be pressed before the ceremony; major airlines all have arrangements for transporting them, either boxed or hanging in garment sleeves.
● Wedding photographs and videos can be provided, but the quality may not be the same as in the US and Europe.

● Apart from the cost of staying in the hotel, couples pay an extra fee for the wedding ceremony. Prices vary considerably, depending on the standard of hotel and what extras are offered (these might include anything from a souvenir T-shirt to a sunset cruise). Some of the larger hotels employ a wedding planner.

Weddings in Barbados

To get married in Barbados, apply for a marriage license at the Ministry of Home Affairs in the General Post Office Building, Cheapside, Bridgetown (tel: 246-228 8950). You need to show a valid passport and your original or certified copies of your birth certificate, and proof of divorce (decree absolute) if you have been married before. You also need to show return-air tickets. The license costs BDS$150 plus BDS$25 stamp fee. Many of the larger hotels will plan the formalities and arrange the wedding as part of a package.

ABOVE: after-lunch entertainment, Jolly Beach Resort, Antigua.

St Martin/Sint Maarten

French side: Route de Sandy Ground, Marigot, 97150 Marigot, St-Martin, tel: 590-87 57 21, www.st-martin.org, www.franceguide.com, email: info@st-martin.org.
Dutch side: Sint Maarten Tourist Bureau, Vineyard Office Park, W.G. Buncamper Road, #33 Sint Maarten, tel: 599-542 2337, www.st-maarten.com, email: info@st-maarten.com.
Canada: 1981 Avenue McGill College, Suite 490, Montréal, Québec H3A 2WP, tel: 514-876 9881, email: canada@franceguide.com.
Sint Maarten Tourist Office, 703 Evans Ave, Suite 106, Toronto, Ontario M9C 5E9, tel: 416-622 4300.
France: Office de Tourisme de St-Martin, 30 Rue St-Marc, 75002 Paris, tel: 01-53 29 99 99, email: bureauparis@st-martin.org.
UK: French Government Tourist Office, 178 Piccadilly, London WIJ 9AL, tel: 09068-244123 (60p per minute), email: info-uk@franceguide.com.
US: **St Martin Tourist Bureau**, 675 Third Avenue, Suite 1807, New York, NY 10017, tel: 212-953 2084, 877-956 1234 (toll-free). email: nyoffice@st-martin.org.
Maison de la France USA
New York: 444 Madison Avenue, New York, NY 10022, tel: 212-838 7800, email: info.us@franceguide.com.
Los Angeles: 9454 Wilshire Boulevard, Suite 715, Los Angeles, CA 90212, tel: 310-271 6665, email: info.losangeles@franceguide.com.
Chicago: Consulate General of France, 205 N Michigan Avenue, Suite 3770, 60601 Chicago IL, tel: 410-286 8310, email: info.chicago@franceguide.com
Sint Maarten Tourist Office, 675 Third Avenue, Suite 1806, New York, NY 10017, tel: 212-953 2084, 800-786 2278 (toll-free).

St Vincent and The Grenadines

Ministry of Tourism and Culture, Cruise Ship Terminal, Upper Bay Street, Kingstown, St Vincent, tel: 784-457 1502, www.bequiasweet.com, www.vincy.com, www.svghotels.net, www.svgtourism.com, email: tourism@caribsurf.com.
There are also branches at the E.T. Joshua Airport, tel: 784-458 4379; on Bequia, tel: 784-458 3286 and Union Island, tel: 784-458 8350.
Canada: 333 Wilson Avenue, Suite 601, Toronto, M3H 1T2, tel: 416-630 9292, email: svgtourismtoronto@rogers.com.
UK: 10 Kensington Court, London W8 5DL, tel: 020-7565 2874, email: svgtourismeurope@aol.com.
US: 801 Second Avenue, New York, NY 10017, tel 212-687 4981, 1-800 729 1726, email: svgtory@aol.com.

Trinidad and Tobago

Trinidad
TDC (Tourism Development Company of Trinidad and Tobago), PO Box 222, Maritime Centre, 29 Tenth Avenue. Barataria, tel: 868-675 7034, www.gotrinidadandtobago.com. Information office, Piarco, tel: 868-669 5196.
Tobago
Tobago House of Assembly Division of Tourism, Doretta's Court, 197 Mount Marie, tel: 868-639 2125. Information office, Crown Point Airport, tel: 868-639 0509.
Canada: The RMR Group Inc., Taurus House, 512 Duplex Avenue, Toronto M4R 2E3, tel: 416-485 8724.
UK: Tourism Information Office, Albany House, Albany Crescent, Claygate, Surrey KT10 0PF, tel: 01372-469818, email: trinbago@ihml.com.
US: Tourism Solutions, 2400 East Commercial Boulevard, Suite 412, Fort Lauderdale, Florida, 33308, tel: 954-776 9595.
Travel Trade Hotline, tel: 1-800 748 4224 (toll-free in the US).

US Virgin Islands

St Thomas: there are two visitors' bureaux; one at Tolbod Gade, Charlotte Amalie, tel: 340-774 8784, another at the Welcome Center, Havensight Dock, www.usvi.net, www.usvi-on-line.com, www.usvitourism.vi, www.st-thomas.com.
St Croix: 53A Company Street, Christiansted, tel: 340-773 0495, www.st-croix.com.
St John: the tourism office is next to the post office in Cruz Bay, www.st-john.com.
Canada: 703 Evans Avenue, Suite 106, Toronto, Ontario M9C 5E9, tel: 416-622 7600.
UK: Destination Marketing, Power Road Studios, 114 Power Road, London W4 5PY, tel: 020-8994 0978.
US: **Chicago**: 500 N. Michigan Avenue, Suite 2030, Chicago, IL 60611, tel: 312-670 8784.
Los Angeles: 3460 Wilshire Boulevard, Suite 412, Los Angeles, CA 90010, tel: 213-739 0138.
Miami: 2655 Le Jeune Road, Suite 907, Miami, FL 33134, tel: 305-442 7200.
New York: 1270 Avenue of the Americas, Suite 2108, New York, NY 10020, tel: 212-332 2222.
Washington DC: 444 North Capital Street NW, Suite 298, Washington DC 20001, tel: 202-624 3590.

What to Wear

"Casual" is the word in the Antilles. Cool cotton clothes should make up the majority of your wardrobe. Air conditioning can be set too low and the breezes are cooler at night during the winter, so it's a good idea to bring a light jacket or cotton sweater, just in case. Men should bring a jacket and tie if they plan to visit any casinos – most of them (and some of the fancier restaurants and hotels) require at least a jacket for the evening. A pair of sturdy walking shoes is essential for those planning walks in the mountains and rainforests.

Swimsuits and other beach attire are not appropriate around town. When you venture from beach or poolside into town, cover up – a simple T-shirt and a pair of shorts should do the trick. By following this rule, you will show respect for the standards of many island residents.

Nude or topless (for women) bathing is prohibited everywhere except for Guadeloupe, Martinique, St-Martin, St-Barthélemy, and Bonaire. Guadeloupe, St-Martin, and Bonaire have at least one designated nudist beach.

FURTHER READING

History and Society

Traveller's History of the Caribbean, by James Ferguson. Interlink Books, 2008.
A Short History of the West Indies, by J.H. Parry, Philip Sherlock, and Anthony Maingot. Macmillan Caribbean, 1987.
A Brief History of the Caribbean: From the Arawak and Carib to the Present, by Jan Rogonzinski. Plume, 2000.
The Slave Trade, by Hugh Thomas. Phoenix, 2006.
Last Resorts, The Cost of Tourism in the Caribbean, by Polly Pattullo. Latin American Bureau, 2005.

Natural History

A Field Guide to Reefs of the Caribbean and Florida, by Eugene H. Kaplan. Houghton Mifflin, 1999.
Birds of the West Indies, by Herbert Raffaele et al. Princeton UP, 2003.
Caribbean Wild Plants and Their

Send Us Your Thoughts

We do our best to ensure the information in our books is as accurate and up-to-date as possible. The books are updated on a regular basis using local contacts, who painstakingly add, amend, and correct as required. However, some details (such as telephone numbers and opening times) are liable to change, and we are ultimately reliant on our readers to put us in the picture.

We welcome your feedback, especially your experience of using the book "on the road". Maybe we recommended a hotel that you liked (or another that you didn't), or you came across a great bar or new attraction we missed.

We will acknowledge all contributions, and we'll offer an Insight Guide to the best letters received.

Please write to us at:
  Insight Guides
  PO Box 7910
  London SE1 1WE
Or email us at:
  insight@apaguide.co.uk

Uses, by Penelope N. Honychurch. Macmillan Caribbean, 1986.
The Gardens of Dominica, by Polly Pattullo and Anne Jno Baptiste. Papillote Press, 1998.

Sport

The Complete Diving Guide, Caribbean Volume I, by Colleen Ryan and Brian Savage. World Dive Guide Publications, 1998.
Complete Guide to Diving and Snorkelling Aruba, Bonaire and Curacao, by Jack Jackson. New Holland, 2004.
Caribbean Afoot!: A Walking and Hiking Guide to Twenty Nine of the Caribbean's Best Islands, by M. Timothy O'Keefe. Menasha Ridge Press, 1994.
75 Years of West Indies Cricket, 1928–2003, by Ray Goble and Keith A.P. Sandiford. Hansib Publishing (Caribbean), 2004.
An Illustrated History of Caribbean Football, by James Ferguson. Macmillan Caribbean, 2006.

Fiction

A House for Mr Biswas, by V.S. Naipaul. Picador, 2003. Classic, bittersweet account of a Trinidadian man's search for security.
The Lonely Londoners, by Samuel Selvon. Penguin, 2006. Comic masterpiece of a Trinidadian immigrant's life in 1950s London.
The Wide Sargasso Sea, by Jean Rhys. Penguin 2000. An atmospheric prequel to Charlotte Brontë's classic novel *Jane Eyre*, partly set on the island of Dominica.
The Orchid House, by Phyllis Shand Allfrey. Virago 1991. Acclaimed novel of family tensions and colonial decline in Dominica.
In the Castle of My Skin, by George Lamming. Longman Caribbean, 1979. Growing up in a 1930s Barbadian village during the demise of colonialism. A novel of adolescence and political awakening.
A State of Independence, by Caryl Phillips. Faber and Faber, 1999. A wry study of small-island politics and an exile's return to his homeland.
Omeros, by Derek Walcott. Faber and Faber, 2002. Contemporary working

of homeric epic by St Lucian Nobel Prize-winning poet.
The Dragon Can't Dance, by Earl Lovelace. Faber and Faber, 1998. A story of life in a shanty town on Trinidad which captures all the exuberance of the island's Carnival.
The Penguin Book of Caribbean Verse in English, ed. Paula Burnett. Penguin, 2005. The best available collection of verse from English-speaking Caribbean poets.
Tree of Life, by Maryse Condé. The Women's Press, 1994. A tale of several generations of a Guadeloupean family.

Other Insight Guides

Insight Guides cover nearly 200 destinations, providing information on culture and all the top sights, as well as superb photography. Other Insight Guides to destinations in the Caribbean include: *Barbados, Caribbean Cruises, Cuba, Jamaica,* and *Puerto Rico*.

Insight **Pocket Guides** contain personal recommendations from a local host, a program of carefully timed itineraries and a fold-out map. They are particularly useful for the short-stay visitor intent on making the best use of every moment. Titles covering this region include *Barbados* and *Cuba*.

Insight **Compact Guides** are handy mini-encyclopedias, whose titles include *Antigua and Barbuda* and *St Lucia*.

Insight **FlexiMaps** are designed to complement our guidebooks. They provide full mapping of major destinations, and their easy-to-fold, laminated finish gives them ease of use and durability. The range of titles features the following destinations: *Bahamas, Barbados, Cuba,* and *Jamaica*.

ART & PHOTO CREDITS

INSIGHT GUIDE

CARIBBEAN

Cartographic Editor **Zoë Goodwin**
Production **Linton Donaldson**
Design Consultants **Carlotta Junger, Graham Mitchener**
Picture Research **Celia Stern**

INDEX

Numbers in italics refer to photographs

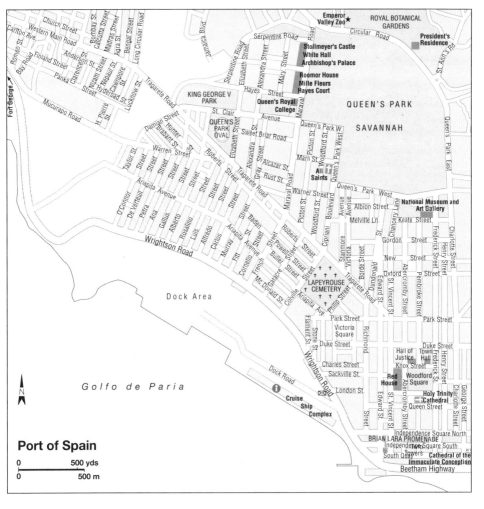

Port of Spain

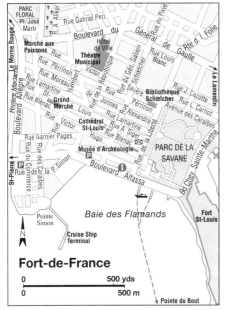

Fort-de-France